Computer Accounting
with
QuickBooks® Pro 2010

Twelfth Edition

Donna Kay, MBA, PhD, CPA, CITP
Maryville University of Saint Louis

QuickBooks Pro 2010
QuickBooks Premier 2010
QuickBooks Premier Accountant 2010

McGraw-Hill
Irwin

The McGraw·Hill Companies

McGraw-Hill
Irwin

COMPUTER ACCOUNTING WITH QUICKBOOKS® PRO 2010, TWELFTH EDITION

ISBN 978-0-07-352715-4
MHID 0-07-352715-7

Vice President & Editor-in-Chief: *Brent Gordon*
VP EDP / Central Publishing Services: *Kimberly Meriwether David*
Editorial Director: *Stewart Mattson*
Publisher: *Tim Vertovec*
Executive Editor: *Richard T. Hercher, Jr.*
Associate Marketing Manager: *Dean Karampelas*
Editorial Coordinator: *Rebecca Mann*
Project Manager: *Robin A. Reed*
Design Coordinator: *Margarite Reynolds*
Cover Designer: *Rick Noel*
Cover Image Credit: *Getty Images*
Production Supervisor: *Nicole Baumgartner*
Media Project Manager: *Balaji Sundararaman*
Compositor: *S4Carlisle Publishing Services*
Typeface: *Optima 11*
Printer: *Worldcolor*

Library of Congress Cataloging-in-Publication Data

Kay [Ulmer], Donna.
  Computer accounting with QuickBooks Pro 2010 / Donna Ulmer. -- 12th ed.
    p. cm.
  Rev. ed. of: Computer accounting with QuickBooks 2006 / Donna Ulmer. 5th ed. c2007.
  "QuickBooks Pro 2010, QuickBooks Premier 2010 QuickBooks Premier 2010: accountant edition."
  ISBN-13: 978-0-07-352715-4 (softcover : alk. paper)
  ISBN-10: 0-07-352715-7 (softcover : alk. paper) 1. QuickBooks. 2. Small business--Accounting--Computer programs. 3. Small business--Finance--Computer programs. I. Ulmer, Donna. Computer accounting with QuickBooks Pro 2006. II. Title.
  HF5679.U45 2011
  657'.8690028553--dc22
                                        2009040827

Why QuickBooks?

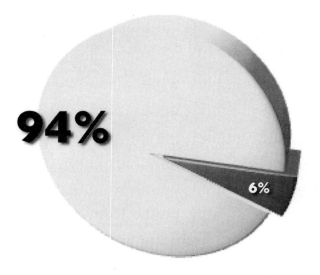

**94+% of Small Business Enterprises
choose QuickBooks Financial Software**

Are You Prepared?

Why

Computer Accounting with

QuickBooks 2010?

- *Computer Accounting with QuickBooks 2010 offers you a complete package to learn the leading small business accounting software*: comprehensive text, QuickBooks software, Student Data CD, Online Learning Center, Student Blog, QuickBooks podcasts, Troubleshooting Guide, LIVE Projects, Electronic Deliverables and more.

- **Student Blog** @ <u>**www.QuickBooksBlog.info**</u> for streamlined learning.

- **QuickBooks Podcasts** target frequently used QuickBooks tasks.

- **Go Green with Electronic Deliverables** and save paper.

- **QuickBooks on your Mac** options for using QuickBooks software with your Mac.

- **Troubleshooting QuickBooks** to navigate software issues. Troubleshooting tips in an appendix and on the QuickBooks Blog.

- **Quick Guide** for **JIT (Just-in-Time) Learning** provides quick and easy, step-by-step explanations covering frequently used tasks.

- **Reflection: A Wish and A Star** at the end of each chapter highlights learning and reflection for each chapter.

- **Time-saving Workflow** approach to using QuickBooks software either at home or on campus. Never before has a QuickBooks text offered this versatility.

- **LIVE Project: QuickBooks in Action** makes using QuickBooks software for live businesses easier than ever.

DEAR STUDENT-

Computer Accounting with QuickBooks makes learning QuickBooks software easy. What distinguishes this book from others is simple. This text focuses on you—the learner—and the most effective way for you to learn QuickBooks.

I hope you find value in this edition's features that include:

- *Student Blog.* QuickBooks Student Blog @ www.QuickBooksBlog.info with podcasts, electronic templates, and much more.
- *Going Green.* Consistent with the sustainability initiatives on many college campuses, this edition offers three options for saving paper and sending electronic deliverables to your professor.
- *QuickBooks for Your Mac.* If you are using a Mac, this edition offers you solutions for running QuickBooks on your Mac.
- *Live Project: QuickBooks in Action.* Chapter 13 guides you through the development of an authentic QuickBooks application that can be used as a capstone project or as a service learning project for a not-for-profit. By integrating and synthesizing skills learned in the course, the QuickBooks in Action project provides you with an effective mastery opportunity and bolsters your resume with professional experience.

Using a hands-on approach, this text integrates understanding accounting with mastery of QuickBooks software. Furthermore, proven instructional techniques based on action research are incorporated throughout the text to make your mastery of QuickBooks as effortless as possible. Designed for maximum flexibility to meet your needs, *Computer Accounting with QuickBooks* can be used either in a QuickBooks course or independently at your own pace.

The text uses a highly effective three-step approach that aids you in constructing your own customized learning based on what you already know:

1. *Chapter Tutorials.* Providing numerous screen shots and detailed instructions, chapters in *Computer Accounting with QuickBooks* are designed as tutorials for you to initially learn the accounting software features. All chapters are based on realistic, virtual company cases to enhance your understanding of the business environment in which QuickBooks is used. Podcasts @ www.QuickBooksBlog.info reinforce chapter tutorials.

2. *Learning Activities.* To improve long-term retention of your software skills and mastery of QuickBooks, learning activities are included at the end of the chapters. Designed with fewer instructions to test your understanding and, when needed, to develop your skills at quickly seeking out additional information to complete tasks, the activities consist of exercises, projects and web quests. JIT Learning, the ability to seek out information as needed, is an increasingly important skill in a rapidly changing business environment. *Computer Accounting with QuickBooks* is designed to seamlessly facilitate your development of this crucial skill. In addition, the virtual cases challenge you to apply and develop both software and problem-solving skills.

3. *Reflection.* Reflection improves learning and retention. A reflection exercise, "A Wish and A Star," appears at the end of each chapter to highlight what you have learned.

You have made a great choice to learn QuickBooks.

Best wishes for your continued success,

Donna Kay

ABOUT THE AUTHOR

Donna Kay is Assistant Professor of Accounting and Accounting Information Systems at Maryville University in Saint Louis, Missouri, where she teaches both undergraduate and graduate accounting. Dr. Kay earned B.S. and MBA degrees from Southern Illinois University at Edwardsville before receiving a Ph.D. from Saint Louis University, where she conducted action research on the perceived effectiveness of instructional techniques in the computer classroom. Named to Who's Who Among American Women, Dr. Kay holds certifications as both a Certified Public Accountant (CPA) and Certified Informational Technology Professional (CITP) and is an active member of the American Institute of Certified Public Accountants, the Missouri Society of CPAs (MSCPA), the American Accounting Association, Teachers of Accounting at Two-Year Colleges, the National Business Education Association, and the Missouri Association of Accounting Educators. Dr. Kay serves on the Information Technology Committee of the MSCPA.

Donna always enjoys hearing from QuickBooks educators and can be reached through the *Computer Accounting with QuickBooks* Online Learning Center or through her QuickBooks Blog @ www.QuickBooksBlog.info.

ACKNOWLEDGMENTS

Special thanks to:

- *The McGraw-Hill team whose efforts continue to make this text a best seller: Stewart Mattson, Tim Vertovec, Dick Hercher, Rebecca Mann, and Dean Karampelas.*

- *An amazing QuickBooks team: Kim Temme of Maryville University of Saint Louis for her meticulous accuracy checking and editing, Anna Boulware of Saint Charles Community College for her verification of all solutions; Sandy Roman for her coordination of the instructor supplements to accompany the text; Beth Williams for her careful quality control; Ali Olia for his heroic IT assistance; and Intuit's Trae Harris for his work to package the QuickBooks software with this text.*

- *My Maryville University accounting colleagues, Kim, Karen, and Mark; our remarkable Dean Pam; and Marilyn and Mary Ellen of our Center for Teaching and Learning for their inspiration for the reflection activity, A Wish and A Star.*

- *All the QuickBooks educators who share ideas, comments, suggestions, and encouragement.*

CONTENTS

CONTENTS DETAIL

SECTION 1 EXPLORING QUICKBOOKS WITH ROCK CASTLE CONSTRUCTION

SECTION 2 QUICKBOOKS ACCOUNTING FOR ENTREPRENEURS

SECTION 3   QUICK GUIDE

SECTION 4   QUICKBOOKS EXTRAS

CONTENTS OVERVIEW

Designed as hands-on tutorials for initially learning QuickBooks, *Computer Accounting with QuickBooks* chapters provide numerous screen captures and detailed instructions. To improve long-term retention of your software skills, end-of-chapter learning activities are designed with fewer instructions to test your understanding and, when needed, to develop your skills to quickly seek out additional information to complete the task. The ability to find information as needed, or JIT Learning, is an increasingly important skill in a rapidly changing business environment. The design of *Computer Accounting with QuickBooks* seamlessly facilitates your development of this crucial skill. Each chapter concludes with *Reflection: A Wish and A Star* to further reinforce and improve your retention of chapter material. Additionally, a virtual company case runs throughout the text, enabling you to better understand how various transactions and activities are interrelated in the business environment.

Designed in four sections, this text offers:

SECTION 1 EXPLORING QUICKBOOKS WITH ROCK CASTLE CONSTRUCTION focuses on learning the basics of entering transactions and generating reports using the sample company, Rock Castle Construction.

SECTION 2 QUICKBOOKS ACCOUNTING FOR ENTREPRENEURS builds upon Section 1, covering the entire accounting cycle, including new company setup as well as QuickBooks advanced features for accountants. The Paint Palette, a case that runs throughout the second section, starts out as a sole proprietor service business, then expands to become a merchandising corporation. Using a progressive approach, the text gradually introduces advanced features while maintaining continuity and interest.

SECTION 3 QUICK GUIDE provides step-by-step instructions for frequently used customer, vendor, and employee tasks in a convenient, user-friendly resource.

SECTION 4 QUICKBOOKS EXTRAS are appendices including Install & Register QuickBooks Software, Back Up and Restore QuickBooks Files, Troubleshooting QuickBooks, Electronic Deliverables, and more.

Section 1 Exploring QuickBooks with Rock Castle Construction includes:

Chapter 1 Quick Tour of QuickBooks 2010. This chapter provides a guided tour of the software using QuickBooks Navigation tools and introducing the QuickBooks sample company, Rock Castle Construction. Other topics include the *Workflow* and *Restart & Restore* approaches for backup files.

Chapter 2 Customizing QuickBooks and the Chart of Accounts. This chapter introduces how to customize QuickBooks and the chart of accounts to meet specific business needs. Other topics include customizing QuickBooks security.

Chapter 3 Banking. This chapter focuses on the checking account and check register for a small business. Topics include making deposits, writing checks, and reconciling a bank statement.

Chapter 4 Customers and Sales. Chapter 4 demonstrates how to record customer transactions. Topics include how to create invoices, record sales, record customer payments, and print customer reports.

Chapter 5 Vendors, Purchases, and Inventory. This chapter focuses on recording vendor transactions, including creating purchase orders, paying bills, and printing vendor reports.

Chapter 6 Employees and Payroll. Chapter 6 covers time-tracking, billing tracked time, and processing payroll using QuickBooks payroll service. Manual payroll preparation is covered in Chapter 11.

Chapter 7 Reports and Graphs. In this chapter, you complete the accounting cycle by creating a trial balance and entering adjusting entries. In addition, you learn how to create a variety of reports and graphs using QuickBooks, including exporting reports to Microsoft® Excel® software.

SECTION 2 QUICKBOOKS ACCOUNTING FOR ENTREPRENEURS INCLUDES:

CHAPTER 8 NEW COMPANY SETUP. Chapter 8 covers how to use the EasyStep Interview feature to set up a new company in QuickBooks. You also learn how to create customer, vendor, and item lists.

CHAPTER 9 ACCOUNTING FOR A SERVICE COMPANY. Chapter 9 records transactions for an entire year using the company created in Chapter 8. Expanded end-of-chapter learning activities include a short exercise setting up a new company and entering transactions. Project 9.1 provides an opportunity to integrate all the QuickBooks skills covered thus far in a comprehensive virtual case.

CHAPTER 10 MERCHANDISING CORPORATION: SALES, PURCHASES & INVENTORY. After learning how to set up a merchandising corporation with inventory, you record transactions for the first month of operations. Project 10.1 is a comprehensive virtual case for a merchandising corporation.

CHAPTER 11 MERCHANDISING CORPORATION: PAYROLL. Chapter 11 covers how to set up and record payroll using QuickBooks manual payroll approach. Project 11.1 continues and builds upon Project 10.1.

CHAPTER 12 ADVANCED QUICKBOOKS FEATURES FOR ACCOUNTANTS. This chapter covers the advanced features of QuickBooks software including budgets, estimates, progress billing, credit card sales, accounting for bad debts, memorized reports, the audit trail, and accountant's copy. Using the advanced features of QuickBooks, Project 12.1. is a continuation of Project 9.1.

CHAPTER 13 LIVE PROJECT: QUICKBOOKS IN ACTION. This chapter outlines the project management milestones for development of a QuickBooks accounting system. Providing you with an opportunity to apply QuickBooks software to a live project, QuickBooks in Action gives you hands-on professional experience for your resume.

Section 3 Quick Guide includes:

QuickBooks Software. Instructions and resources for installing and updating your QuickBooks software.

Company Commands. Find step-by-step instructions for frequently used company commands including new company setup, back up and restore, and customizing QuickBooks.

Chart of Accounts. Step-by-step instructions are listed for entering and updating the chart of accounts.

Transactions. Instructions for customer, vendor, employee, and banking transactions are conveniently summarized for you in the Quick Guide.

Entries. In one resource, you can learn about various journal entries used with QuickBooks including adjusting and correcting entries.

Reports. Quickly locate instructions for creating QuickBooks reports.

Section 4 QuickBooks Extras includes:

Appendix A Install & Register QuickBooks Software. This appendix provides step-by-step instructions for installing and registering your QuickBooks software.

Appendix B Back Up & Restore QuickBooks Files. Save time using the streamlined *Workflow* and *Restart & Restore* approaches for saving QuickBooks files. Detailed instructions for backing up and restoring your QuickBooks files are included.

Appendix C Troubleshooting QuickBooks. This appendix provides you with valuable tips and frequently asked questions to troubleshoot QuickBooks issues.

Appendix D Electronic Deliverables. Consistent with sustainability and going green initiatives on many college campuses today, *Computer Accounting with QuickBooks* offers you three easy ways to create electronic deliverables instead of paper printouts to send your professor. Check out this appendix to learn more.

Appendix E QuickBooks for Mac. Consistent with today's trend toward Macs on college campuses and in the business environment, this appendix directs you to resources for running QuickBooks on your Mac.

Appendix F QuickBooks Blog. A student blog www.QuickBooksBlog.info is offered with *Computer Accounting with QuickBooks 2010.* View podcasts, download electronic deliverable templates, and much more.

ROADMAP TO VIRTUAL CASES

Virtual company cases throughout the text better prepare you to use QuickBooks accounting software in a business environment. Use of virtual cases provide a realistic context to enhance your understanding of how various QuickBooks tasks relate to business operations.

Your roadmap to related learning activities for each virtual case follows.

ROCK CASTLE CONSTRUCTION VIRTUAL CASE:

Related Learning Activities
Chapter 1 & Exercises
Chapter 2 & Exercises
Chapter 3 & Exercises
Chapter 4 & Exercises
Chapter 5 & Exercises
Chapter 6 & Exercises
Chapter 7 & Exercises

PAINT PALETTE VIRTUAL CASE:

Related Learning Activities
Chapter 8
Exercise 8.1
Chapter 9
Exercise 9.1
Exercise 9.2
Exercise 9.3
Exercise 9.4
Exercise 9.5
Chapter 12

VILLA FLOOR & CARPET VIRTUAL CASE:

Related Learning Activities
Exercise 8.2
Exercise 9.6

THE PAINT PALETTE STORE VIRTUAL CASE:

Related Learning Activities
Chapter 10
Chapter 11

MUJERES YARNS VIRTUAL CASE:

Related Learning Activities
Exercise 10.1
Exercise 11.1

TUSCANY LANDSCAPES VIRTUAL CASE:

Related Learning Activities
Project 9.1
Project 12.1

TOMASO'S MOWERS & MORE VIRTUAL CASE:

Related Learning Activities
Project 10.1
Project 11.1

SECTION 1
EXPLORING QUICKBOOKS WITH ROCK CASTLE CONSTRUCTION

CHAPTER 1
QUICK TOUR OF QUICKBOOKS 2010

CHAPTER 2
CUSTOMIZING QUICKBOOKS AND THE CHART OF ACCOUNTS

CHAPTER 3
BANKING

CHAPTER 4
CUSTOMERS AND SALES

CHAPTER 5
VENDORS, PURCHASES, AND INVENTORY

CHAPTER 6
EMPLOYEES AND PAYROLL

CHAPTER 7
REPORTS AND GRAPHS

CHAPTER 1
QUICK TOUR OF QUICKBOOKS 2010

SCENARIO

Mr. Rock Castle, owner of Rock Castle Construction, called to hire you as his accountant. His former accountant unexpectedly accepted a job offer in Hawaii, and Rock Castle Construction needs someone immediately to maintain its accounting records. Mr. Castle indicates they use QuickBooks to maintain the company's accounting records. When you tell him that you are not familiar with QuickBooks software, Mr. Castle reassures you, *"No problem! QuickBooks is easy to learn. Stop by my office this afternoon."*

When you arrive at Rock Castle Construction, Mr. Castle leads you to a cubicle as he rapidly explains Rock Castle's accounting.

"Rock Castle needs to keep records of transactions with customers, vendors, and employees. We must keep a record of our customers and the sales and services we provide to those customers. Also, it is crucial for the company to be able to bill customers promptly and keep a record of cash collected from them. If we don't know who owes Rock Castle money, we can't collect it.

"Rock Castle also needs to keep track of the supplies, materials, and inventory we purchase from vendors. We need to track all purchase orders, the items received, the invoices or bills received from vendors, and the payments made to vendors. If we don't track bills, we can't pay our vendors on time. And if Rock

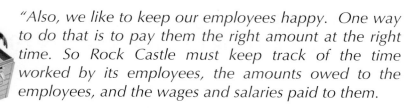

Castle doesn't pay its bills on time, the vendors don't like to sell to us.

"Also, we like to keep our employees happy. One way to do that is to pay them the right amount at the right time. So Rock Castle must keep track of the time worked by its employees, the amounts owed to the employees, and the wages and salaries paid to them.

"QuickBooks permits Rock Castle to keep a record of all of these transactions. Also, we need records so we can prepare tax returns, financial reports for bank loans, and reports to evaluate the company's performance and make business decisions.

"Your first assignment is to learn more about QuickBooks." Mr. Castle tosses you a QuickBooks training manual as he rushes off to answer a phone call.

Slightly overwhelmed by Mr. Castle's rapid-fire delivery, you sink into a chair. As you look around your cubicle, you notice for the first time the leaning tower of papers stacked beside the computer, waiting to be processed. No wonder Mr. Castle wanted you to start right way. Opening the QuickBooks training manual, you see the following page.

CHAPTER 1
LEARNING OBJECTIVES

In Chapter 1, you will learn about the following QuickBooks features:

ACCOUNTING INFORMATION SYSTEMS

> Accounting is the language of business. Learning accounting is similar to learning a foreign language. As you use this text, you will learn terms and definitions that are unique to accounting.

QuickBooks is accounting software that provides an easy and efficient way to collect and summarize accounting information. In addition, QuickBooks creates many different reports that are useful when managing a business.

The objective of an accounting system is to collect, summarize, and communicate information to decision makers. Accounting information is used to:

- Prepare tax returns to federal and state tax agencies.

- Prepare financial statements for banks and investors.

- Prepare reports for managers and owners to use when making decisions. Such decisions include: Are our customers paying their bills on time? Which of our products are the most profitable? Will we have enough cash to pay our bills next month?

TRANSACTIONS

An accounting system collects information about *transactions*. As a company conducts business, it enters into transactions (or exchanges) with other parties such as customers, vendors, and employees. For example, when a business sells a product to a customer, there are two parts to the transaction:

1. The business *gives* a product or service to the customer.
2. In exchange, the business *receives* cash (or a promise to pay later) from the customer.

Business

Cash Product

Customer

DOUBLE-ENTRY ACCOUNTING

Double-entry accounting has been used for over 500 years. In Italy in the year 1494, Luca Pacioli, a Franciscan monk, wrote a mathematics book that described double-entry accounting. At that time, the double-entry system was used by the merchants of Venice to record what was given and received when trading.

Double-entry accounting is used to record what is exchanged in a transaction:

1. The amount *received*, such as equipment purchased, is recorded with a *debit*.

2. The amount *given*, such as cash or a promise to pay later, is recorded with a *credit*.

For a debit and credit refresher, see Chapter 3.

Each entry must balance; debits must equal credits. In a manual accounting system, accountants make debit and credit entries in a Journal using paper and pencil. When using QuickBooks for your accounting system, you can enter accounting information in two different ways: (1) onscreen Journal, and (2) onscreen forms.

1. **Onscreen Journal.** You can make debit and credit entries in an onscreen Journal shown below. Notice the similarities between the onscreen Journal and a manual Journal.

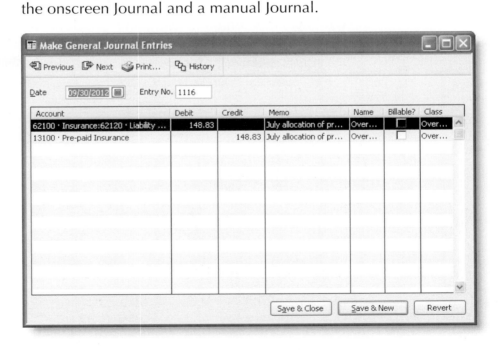

Instead of using the onscreen Journal, you can use onscreen forms to enter information in QuickBooks.

2. **Onscreen forms.** You can enter information about transactions using *onscreen forms* such as the onscreen check and the onscreen invoice shown below.

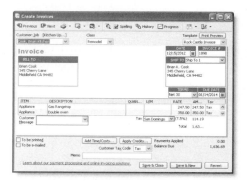

When preparing a customer's bill, record the information in an onscreen invoice.

When writing a check, QuickBooks uses an onscreen check to record the check information.

QuickBooks automatically converts information entered in onscreen forms into double-entry accounting entries with debits and credits. QuickBooks maintains a list of journal entries for all the transactions entered—whether entered using the onscreen Journal or onscreen forms.

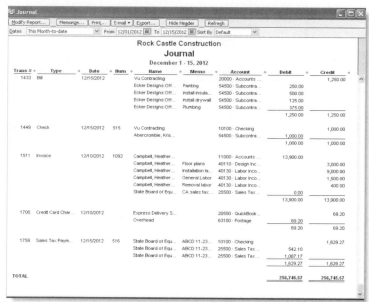

QUICKBOOKS ACCOUNTING SYSTEM

Steps to create an accounting system using QuickBooks are:

Step 1: **Set up a new company data file.** QuickBooks uses an EasyStep Interview that asks you questions about your business. QuickBooks then automatically creates a company data file for your business. In Section 1 of this text, Exploring QuickBooks with Rock Castle Construction, you will use a sample company data file that has already been created for you. In Section 2, you will set up a new company using the EasyStep Interview. To learn how to set up a company file, see Chapter 8.

Step 2: **Create a Chart of Accounts.** A Chart of Accounts is a list of all the accounts for a company. Accounts are used to sort and track accounting information. For example, a business needs one account for Cash, another account to track amounts customers owe (Accounts Receivable), and yet another account to track inventory. QuickBooks automatically creates a Chart of Accounts in the EasyStep Interview. QuickBooks permits you to modify the Chart of Accounts later, after completing the EasyStep Interview.

Step 3: **Create lists.** QuickBooks uses lists to record and organize information about:

- **Customers**.
- **Vendors**.
- **Items** (items purchased and items sold, such as inventory).
- **Employees**.
- **Other** (such as owners).

Step 4: **Enter transactions.** Enter transaction information into QuickBooks using the onscreen Journal or onscreen forms (such as onscreen invoices and onscreen checks).

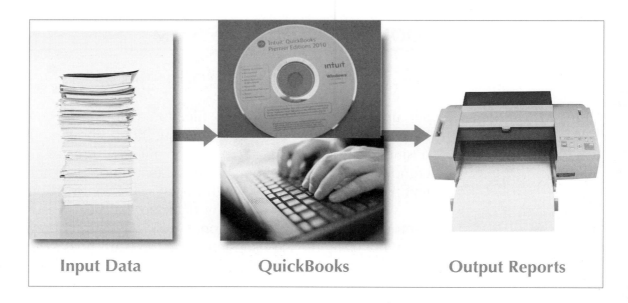

Input Data   **QuickBooks**   **Output Reports**

Step 5: **Prepare reports.** Reports summarize and communicate information about a company's financial position and business operations. Financial statements are standardized financial reports that summarize information about past transactions. Financial statements are provided to external users, such as bankers and investors. In addition, financial statements may be used by internal users, such as managers. The primary financial statements for a business are:

- **Balance Sheet**: summarizes what a company owns and owes on a particular date.

- **Profit and Loss Statement** (or **Income Statement**): summarizes what a company has earned and the expenses incurred to earn the income.

- **Statement of Cash Flows**: summarizes cash inflows and cash outflows for operating, investing, and financing activities of a business.

Other financial reports are created specifically for internal users (managers) to assist in making decisions. An example of such a report is a cash budget that projects amounts of cash that will be collected and spent in the future.

In Section 1: Exploring QuickBooks, you will learn about Step 2: creating a Chart of Accounts; Step 3: creating lists; Step 4: entering transactions; and Step 5: preparing reports. In Section 2: Small Business Accounting, you will learn how to set up a new company in QuickBooks as well as review Steps 2 through 5.

INSTALL QUICKBOOKS

If you are using the trial version of QuickBooks software that is packaged with your text, see *Appendix A: Install & Register QuickBooks Software* for instructions to install and register the software.

After installing the software, **you must register the software** with Intuit or you will be locked out of the software. If registered, you will be able to use the QuickBooks software for 140 days.

Register your QuickBooks software! Failure to register your QuickBooks trial version software will result in the software no longer functioning.

START QUICKBOOKS

To start QuickBooks software, click the **QuickBooks** icon on your desktop. If a QuickBooks icon does not appear on your desktop, in Microsoft® Windows®, click **Start > Programs > QuickBooks > QuickBooks Pro 2010** (or QuickBooks Premier 2010).

OPEN COMPANY

After starting QuickBooks software, the following *Welcome to QuickBooks Pro 2010* window appears. From this screen you can:

1. View a QuickBooks tutorial.

2. Explore QuickBooks using sample companies.

3. Create a new company using the EasyStep Interview.

4. Open an existing QuickBooks company file.

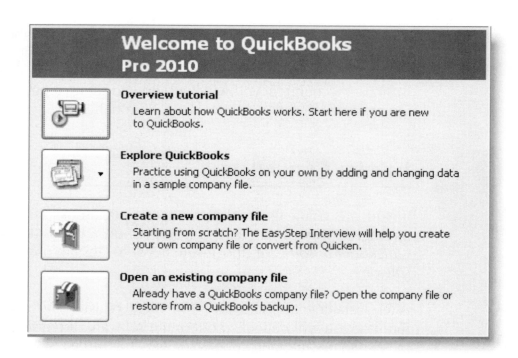

If QuickBooks software has been used before, the following window will appear instead:

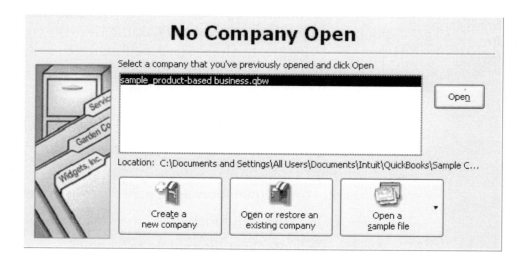

Three different types of QuickBooks files are:

1. **.QBW file.** This is the regular company file that has a .QBW extension. It is a QuickBooks <u>w</u>orking file that is usually saved to the hard drive (C:) of your computer.

2. **.QBB file.** This is a QuickBooks <u>b</u>ackup file. You can save a backup file to the hard drive or to other media such as a USB drive or memory stick, a CD drive or a network drive. Backup files are compressed files and used only if the working (.QBW) file fails.

3. **.QBM file.** This is a QuickBooks <u>m</u>ovable file, also called a portable file. These files are compressed and are used to e-mail or move a company file to another computer.

The .QBW file is the only QuickBooks file in which you can enter data and transactions. The .QBB and .QBM files are compressed and must be converted to .QBW files before they can be used to enter data and transactions.

For your convenience, QuickBooks backup (*.QBB) data files accompany *Computer Accounting for QuickBooks Pro 2010*. You will find the data files on the CD packaged with your text or you can download the data files.

Before using the data files on the CD, you must copy the files to your desktop or removable media. Or go to the Online Learning Center at www.mhhe.com/kay2010 for instructions on downloading data files.

To open the QuickBooks data file for Chapter 1:

Step 1: Copy the Chapter 1 data file (.QBB) from the data files CD to the desktop for faster processing.

If you prefer, you can download the data file for Chapter 1 from the Online Learning Center (OLC). Follow the onscreen instructions on the OLC to download the QuickBooks backup company data files (.QBB).

Step 2: From the QuickBooks Menu bar, click **File > Open or Restore Company**.

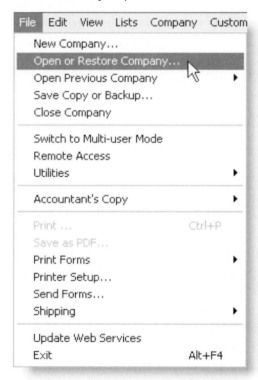

Step 3: Select **Restore a backup copy (.QBB)**. Click **Next**.

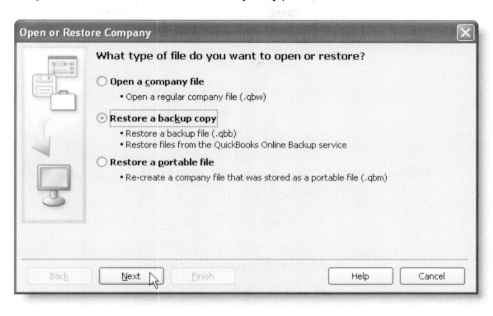

Step 4: When the following *Open or Restore Company* window appears, select **Local backup**. Click **Next**.

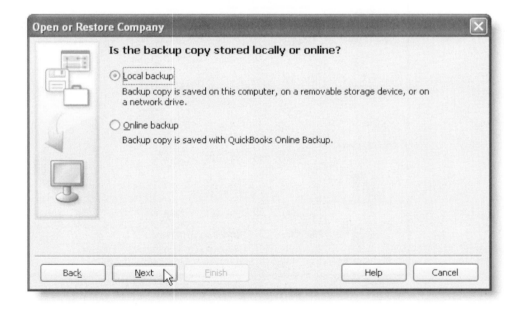

Step 5: Identify the location and file name of the backup company file for Chapter 1.

- If you copied the Chapter 1 backup file to your desktop, use the *Look in* field to find the location of the backup file on the desktop. If you downloaded or copied the Chapter 1 backup file to a USB flash drive, for example, use the *Look in* field to find the backup file on the USB drive.

  In the following example, the data file was copied to a USB flash drive (E:) so first you would select Look in E:, the USB drive.

- Select the file: **Chapter 1 Data.**

- The *Files of type* field should automatically display: **QBW Backup (*.QBB)**.

- Click **Open**.

Step 6: When the following window appears, click **Next**.

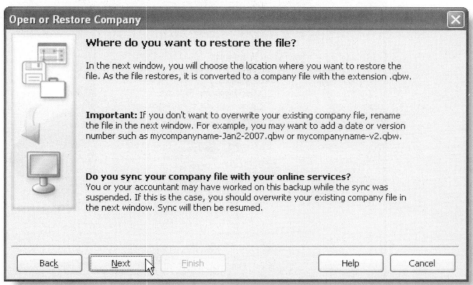

Step 7: Identify the file name and location of the new company file (.QBW) file. You can save the .QBW (working file) on your desktop, your USB drive, or hard drive (C:).

QBW files can be saved to the Desktop or to your storage device if there is adequate storage space.

- Select the location to save the .QBW file. If saving to the C: drive, select Save in: **C:\Document and Settings \Users\(Shared) Documents\Intuit\QuickBooks\ Company Files**.

- File name: **[your name] Chapter 1**. Insert your name in the file name so that you can identify your files.

- The *Save as type* field should automatically appear as **QuickBooks Files (*.QBW)**. The .QBW extension indicates that this is a QuickBooks working file.

- Click **Save** to save the QuickBooks working file.

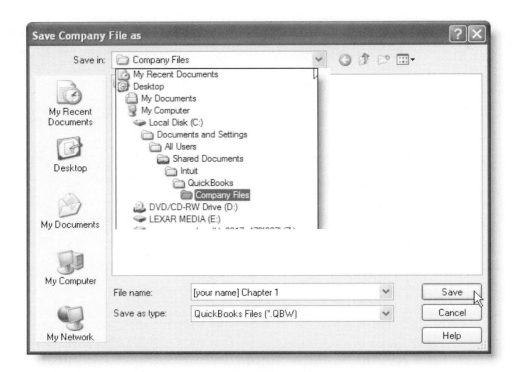

Step 8: Click **OK** when the following window appears.

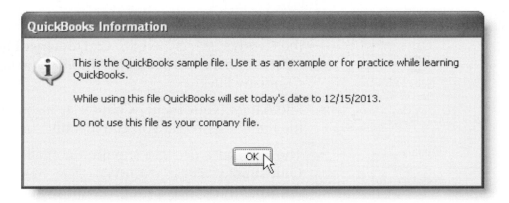

Step 9: Click **OK**.

QUICKBOOKS LEARNING CENTER

The *QuickBooks Learning Center* window may appear on your screen. The Learning Center is a useful tool to review QuickBooks features. It consists of tutorials divided into the following sections:

- Overview & Setup
- Customers & Sales
- Vendors & Expenses
- Inventory
- Payroll
- Process Payments
- What's New

If you want to return to the Learning Center at a later time, click **Help > Learning Center Tutorials**.

To proceed with using QuickBooks software, click the **Go to QuickBooks** button in the lower right corner of the window.

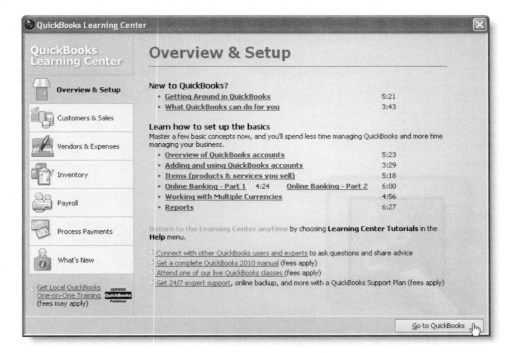

CHANGE COMPANY NAME

In order to identify your printouts, add your name to the company name and Checking account. When you create reports and checks, your name will then appear on the printouts.

To change a company name in QuickBooks, complete the following:

Step 1: From the Menu bar, select **Company > Company Information**.

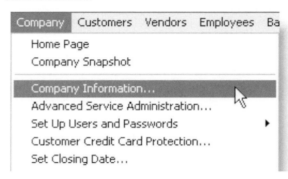

Step 2: When the following *Company Information* window appears, enter **[your name] Chapter 1** in the *Company Name* field before Rock Castle Construction.

The company name that appears in the Title bar of the QuickBooks window and on reports can differ from the backup company file name.

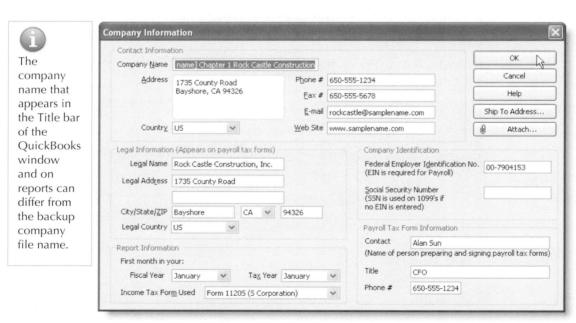

Step 3: Click **OK** to close the *Company Information* window.

To add your name to the company Checking account, complete the following:

Step 1: Click the **Chart of Accounts** icon in the *Company* section of the Home page.

Step 2: When the following *Chart of Accounts* window appears, select **Checking**.

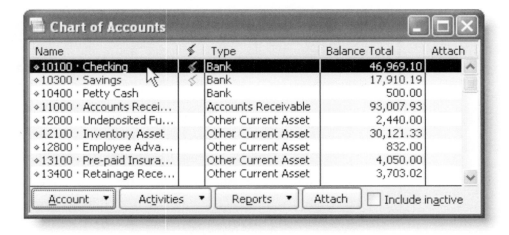

Step 3: **Right-click** the mouse to display the following pop-up menu, then select **Edit Account**.

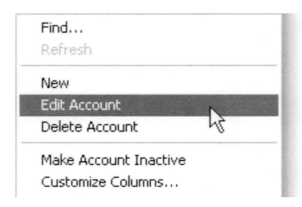

Step 4: When the following *Edit Account* window appears, enter **[your name]** in the *Account Name* field before the word Checking.

Step 5: Click **Save & Close** to save the changes and close the *Edit Account* window.

Step 6: **Close** the *Chart of Accounts* window by clicking the ⊠ in the upper right corner of the *Chart of Accounts* window.

QUICKBOOKS NAVIGATION

QuickBooks offers four different ways to navigate in QuickBooks 2010 software:

- Home page
- Icon bar
- Menu bar

Menu bar: Click on the Menu bar to reveal a drop-down menu for each area.

Icon bar: Click on icons to display customer, vendor, and employee centers and frequently used windows, such as customer invoices.

Home page: Click the Home icon to reveal flowcharts of frequently used tasks.

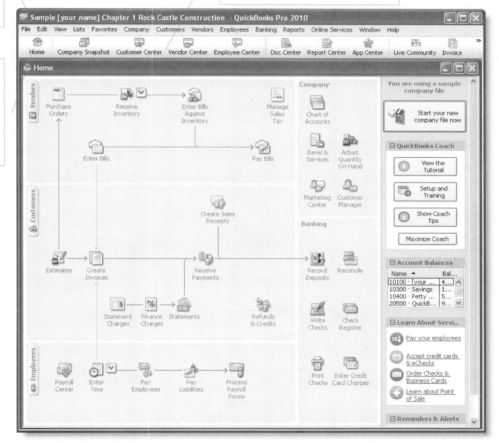

HOME PAGE

Another convenient feature is the Open Window List. To view all open windows, select **View > Open Window List**.

To view the QuickBooks Home page, click the **Home** icon. The Home page contains the main categories of transactions and tasks:

1. *Customer* or sales transactions
2. *Vendor* or purchase transactions
3. *Employee* or payroll transactions
4. *Banking* transactions
5. *Company* tasks

QUICKBOOKS COACH

QuickBooks Coach permits you to explore the workflows shown on the Home page using a Coach.

To turn on the Coach Tips:

Step 1: From the right side of the Home page, click **Show Coach Tips**.

Step 2: To spotlight the workflow, click a Coach icon . For example, to spotlight the workflow for customer transactions, click the **Coach** icon beside **Create Invoices**. The numbered steps in recording credit sales workflow are shown below.

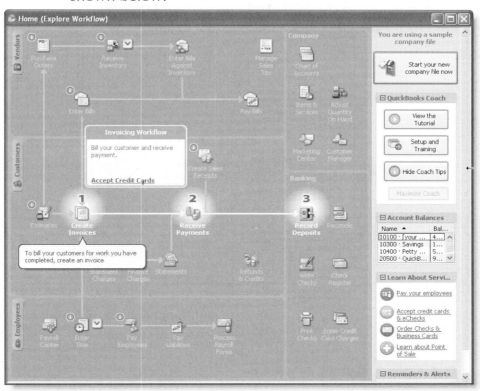

Step 3: Although you can leave the Coach Tips displayed while using QuickBooks, if you prefer to hide the Coach Tips, click **Hide Coach Tips** in the *QuickBooks Coach* window.

CUSTOMERS

The *Customers* section is a flowchart of the main activities associated with sales and customers. You can:

- Create estimates.

- Create invoices to bill customers.

- Record refunds and credits for merchandise returned by customers.

- Record payments received from customers (cash, check, and credit card payments).

Flowchart of sales and **customer** transactions.

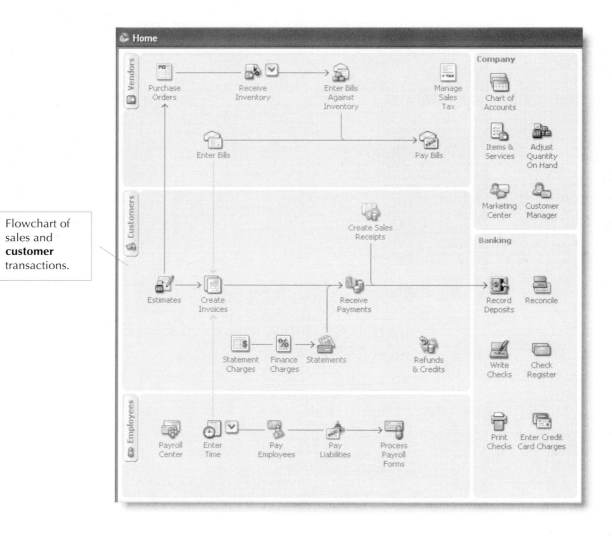

VENDORS

From the *Vendors* flowchart, you can record:

- Purchase orders (orders placed to purchase items).
- Inventory received.
- Bills received.
- Bills paid.
- Sales tax paid.

Flowchart of **vendor** and purchase transactions.

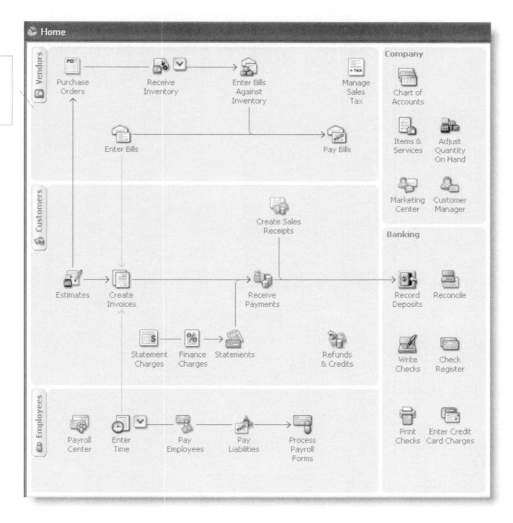

EMPLOYEES

From the *Employees* flowchart, you can:

- Enter time worked.
- Pay employees.
- Pay payroll tax liabilities.
- Process payroll forms.

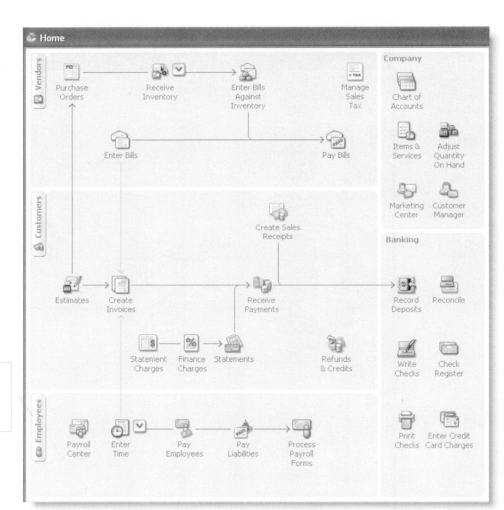

Flowchart of **employee** and payroll transactions.

BANKING

From the *Banking* flowchart, you can:

- Record deposits.
- Write checks.
- Reconcile your bank statement.
- Open your check register.
- Enter credit card charges.

Access the Chart of Accounts from the **Company** section.

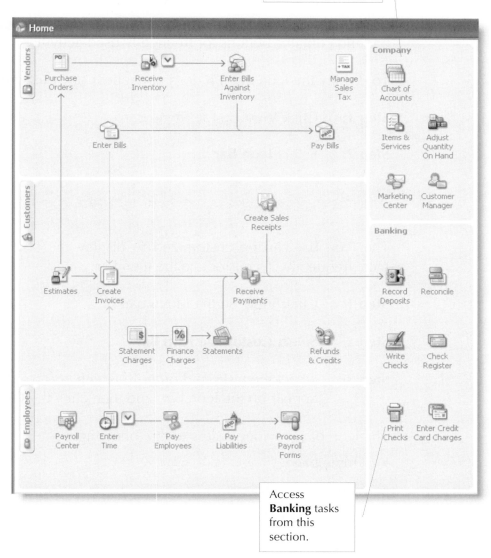

Access **Banking** tasks from this section.

COMPANY

From the *Company* section, you can access:

- Chart of Accounts. A list of accounts a company uses to track accounting information.
- Items & Services. A list of items and services that a company buys and/or sells.

QUICKBOOKS ICON BAR

The QuickBooks Icon bar is a toolbar that appears beneath the Menu bar and contains buttons for frequently used activities.

To display the Icon bar if it does not appear on your screen:

Step 1: Click **View** on the Menu bar.

Step 2: Select **Icon Bar**.

The Icon bar can be customized to display the tasks that you use most frequently. To customize the Icon bar:

Step 1: Click **View** on the Menu bar.

Step 2: Select **Customize Icon Bar**.

Step 3: Select the tasks and order in which you would like them to appear on the Icon bar, and then click the **OK** button.

The Icon bar provides access to the following:

- Home page
- Company Snapshot
- Customer Center
- Vendor Center

- Employee Center
- Document Center
- Report Center

The Doc Center is not active in the sample company. It is covered in Chapter 12.

Step 1:   To view the Home page, click the **Home** icon on the Icon bar.

The Home page flowchart shows the *Customers*, *Vendors*, *Employees*, *Banking*, and *Company* sections.

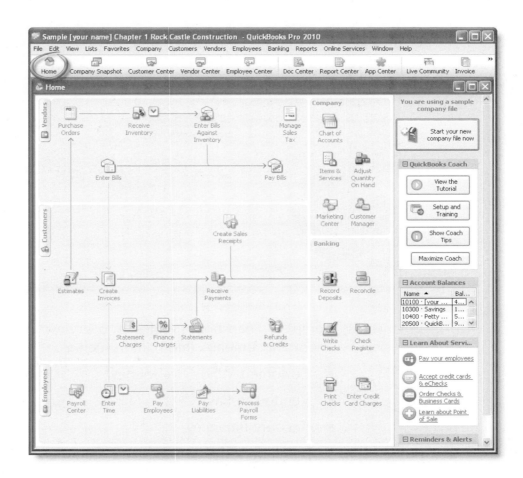

Step 2: Click the **Company Snapshot** icon to view this feature in QuickBooks Pro 2010.

Company Snapshot provides an overview by summarizing important company information such as:

- Customers Who Owe Money

- Vendors to Pay

- Account Balances

- Reminders of Due Dates and Amounts

Step 3: Click the **Customer Center** icon on the Icon bar to display the following Customer Center.

You can also access the Customer Center by clicking on the **Customers** button in the *Customers* section of the Home page.

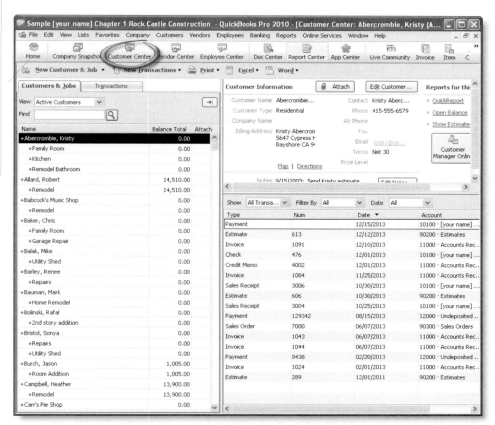

The Customer Center summarizes information about customers, jobs, and customer transactions. The information can be printed or exported to Excel or Word.

Step 4: Click the **Vendor Center** icon on the Icon bar to display the following Vendor Center.

You can also access the Vendor Center by clicking on the **Vendors** button in the *Vendors* section of the Home page.

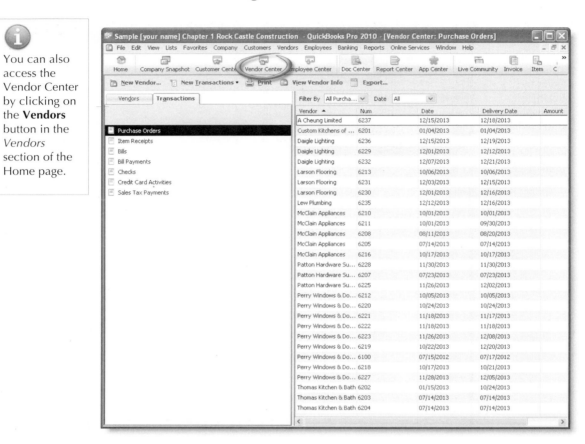

The Vendor Center summarizes information about vendors and vendor transactions. The information can be printed or exported to Excel.

Step 5:   Click the **Employee Center** icon on the Icon bar to display the following Employee Center.

You can also access the Employee Center by clicking on the **Employees** button in the *Employees* section of the Home page.

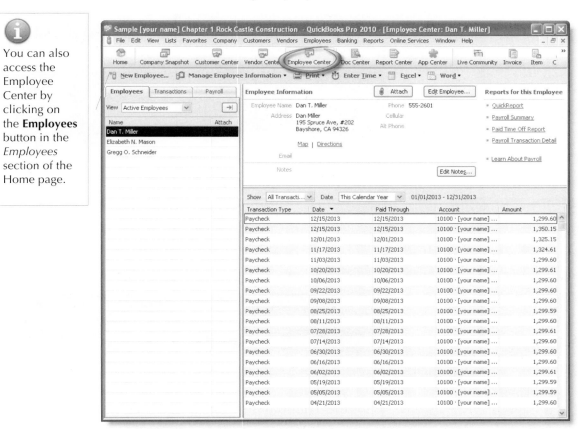

Step 6:   Click the **Report Center** icon on the Icon bar to view the Report Center.

To prepare a report:

- Select the type of report from the report categories on the left of the window.

- Select the desired report from the choices on the right side of the window.

- Select the date range.

- Select Print to print out the report.

- Select Export to send the report to Microsoft Excel.

 If you are taking an online course and need an electronic report, click the **Export** button to export the report to Excel. See Appendix D for more information about electronic deliverables.

To print the Trial Balance for Rock Castle Construction:

- Select **Accountant & Taxes** from the report categories on the left of the window.

- Select **Carousel View**.

- Select **Trial Balance** report.

- Select the date range: **11/01/2013** To **11/30/2013**.

- Select **Display Report** icon.

 Total Debits equal $1,061,566.46.

- ▣ Select **Print** to print out the report.

- Click the ☒ in the upper right corner of the *Trial Balance* window to close the report window. If asked if you would like to memorize the report, click **No**.

QuickBooks Menus

You can also access tasks using the Menu bar across the top of the *QuickBooks* window.

Step 1: Click **File** on the Menu bar and the following drop-down menu will appear.

From the File drop-down menu, you can perform tasks including the following:

- Create a new company file.

- Open or restore an existing company file.

- Open a previous company file.

- Save a copy or back up a company file.

- Close a company file.

- Switch to multi-user mode when QuickBooks is used on a network.

- Use utilities such as importing and exporting files.
- Create a copy of your QuickBooks company file for your accountant.

Print tasks include:

- Printing to a printer.
- Saving as a PDF file.
- Print Forms permits you to print forms such as invoices, sales receipts, and tax forms.
- Printer Setup permits you to select a printer as well as fonts and margins.
- Send Forms permits you to e-mail various QuickBooks forms, such as sending invoices to customers.

To remove the File drop-down menu from the screen, click anywhere outside the drop-down menu or press the **Esc** (Escape) key.

Step 2: Click **Edit** on the Menu bar and the following drop-down menu appears:

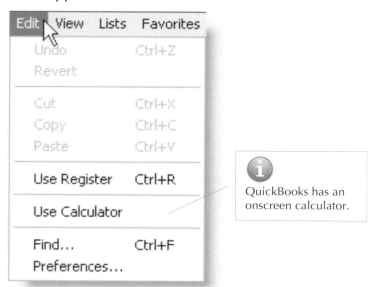

From the Edit drop-down menu, you can undo, cut, copy, paste, and edit information entered in QuickBooks.

The Edit menu changes based upon which windows are open. For example:

- Click the **Home** icon to display the Home page, then click the **Purchase Orders** icon in the *Vendors* section to display the Purchase order form.

- Click **Edit** menu. Now the Edit menu will appear as follows:

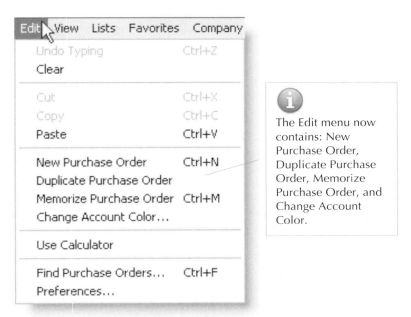

The Edit menu now contains: New Purchase Order, Duplicate Purchase Order, Memorize Purchase Order, and Change Account Color.

Step 3:   Click **View** on the Menu bar to display the following drop-down menu. Select **Open Window List**.

Select **Home** in *Open Windows*. Notice that the *Create Purchase Orders* window also appears. Any open windows appear here, permitting you to easily move between open windows.

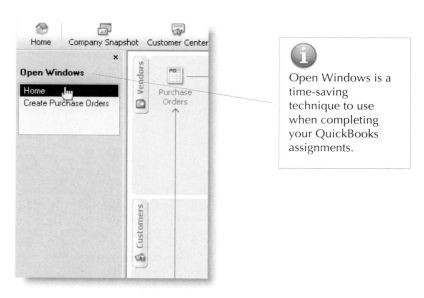

Open Windows is a time-saving technique to use when completing your QuickBooks assignments.

Step 4:   Click **Lists** on the Menu bar to display the following drop-down menu.

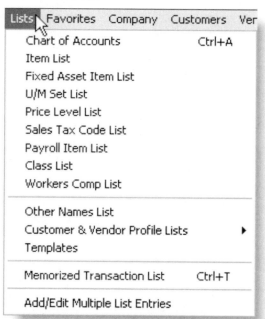

From the Lists drop-down menu, you can access various lists of information.

- **Chart of Accounts**. A list of accounts used to record transactions.

- **Item List**. A list of inventory items that you buy and sell or a list of services provided to customers.

- **Payroll Item List**. A list of items related to payroll checks and company payroll expense such as salary, hourly wages, federal and state withholding, unemployment taxes, Medicare, and Social Security.

- **Templates**. A list of templates for business forms, such as invoices and purchase orders.

- **Memorized Transaction List**. A list of recurring transactions that are memorized or saved. For example, if your company pays $900 in rent each month, then the rent payment transaction can be memorized to eliminate the need to reenter it each month.

Step 5: Click **Company** on the Menu bar to display the drop-down menu.

From the Company menu, you can:

- Access company information and, for example, change the company name.

- Set up users and restrict access to certain parts of QuickBooks.

- Change your password.

- Set up budgets and use planning decision tools.

- Create a To Do List and Reminders.

- Access the Chart of Accounts and onscreen Journal.

- Implement document management.

Step 6: The next four items on the Menu bar display drop-down menus listing various activities related to the four major types of transactions for a company:

- Customer

- Vendor

- Employee

- Banking

File Edit View Lists Favorites Company Customers Vendors Employees Banking Reports Online Services Window Help

QuickBooks Accountant Premier version includes an Accountant menu between Favorites and Company on the Menu bar.

Some of the frequently used activities on these drop-down menus can also be accessed from the Home page.

Step 7: Click **Reports** on the Menu bar to display the list of reports that QuickBooks can create for your company. These reports can also be accessed from the Report Center in the Icon bar.

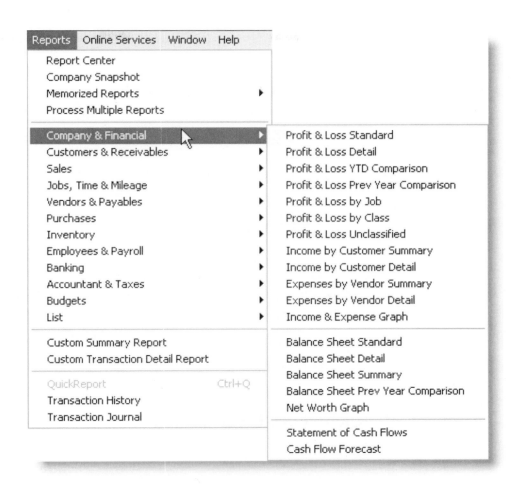

Step 8: Click **Online Services** on the Menu bar to display the drop-down menu. From this menu you can access your online services, marketing, website, and incorporation services.

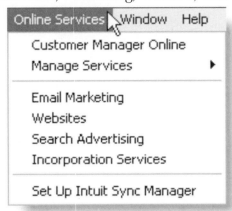

Step 9: Click **Window** on the Menu bar to display the drop-down menu. From this menu you can switch between windows to display onscreen.

- If not already selected, select **Create Purchase Orders** from the drop-down menu.

- **Close** the *Purchase Order* window by clicking the ⊠ at the right side of the Menu bar.

QuickBooks Help Menu

QuickBooks has several Help features to assist you in using QuickBooks software.

Click **Help** on the Menu bar to display the drop-down menu of Help features.

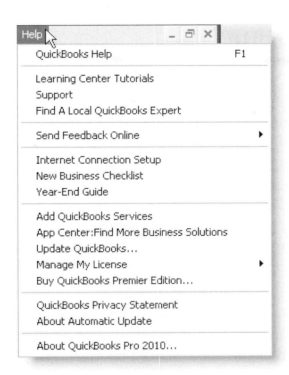

See **Appendix C Troubleshooting QuickBooks: Correcting Errors** for more information about fixing mistakes.

Help features that QuickBooks provides include:

- **QuickBooks Help** (search, relevant topics, and online forum)

- **Learning Center Tutorials** (tutorials to learn QuickBooks)

- **Support** (online QuickBooks support and resource centers)

- **New Business Checklist** (assistance in setting up a new business)

- **Year-End Guide** (assistance in closing the accounting period)

- **App Center: Find More Business Solutions** (a website containing small business software applications)

QUICKBOOKS HELP

After selecting *QuickBooks Help* from the Help menu, the *Have a Question?* window appears. This window contains two tabs:

- **Live Community** tab: this acclaimed QuickBooks online forum lets you ask a question, give advice, and discover what the small business community is talking about now.

- **Help** tab: select **Relevant Topics** for instructions about windows currently displayed onscreen, or **Search** the QuickBooks database for answers to your questions.

Next, you will use QuickBooks Search to search for information about contact management. QuickBooks has a contact synchronization feature that permits you to transfer information from your contact management software, such as Microsoft Outlook, to update your customer and vendor lists in QuickBooks 2010. This feature permits you to enter the contact information only once.

To learn more about using contact management with QuickBooks:

Step 1:   Click **QuickBooks Help** from the Help menu, and the following *Have a Question?* window will appear.

Step 2:   Click the **Search** tab.

Step 3:   In the *Search* field, type: **synchronize contacts**. Click the **arrow**.

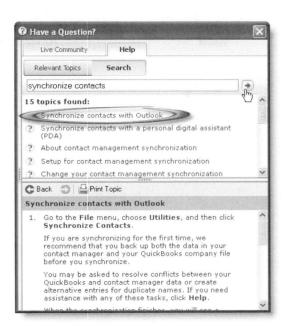

Step 4: Select **Synchronize contacts with Outlook**. If you receive an error message regarding your browser, click Yes and continue.

Step 5: Read about synchronizing contacts with Outlook. To print the Help information, click the ▣ **Print Topic** icon, then select your printer and click **Print**.

The Relevant Topics Help feature provides information about the window displayed on your screen. To use the Relevant Topics feature for the *Write Checks* window:

Step 1: Click the **Write Checks** icon in the *Banking* section of the Home page.

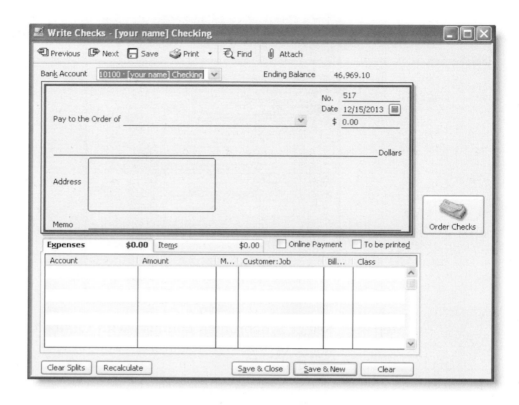

Step 2: Click **QuickBooks Help** from the Help menu. Then click the **Relevant Topics** tab in the following *Have a Question?* Window. Select **Edit information on a check**.

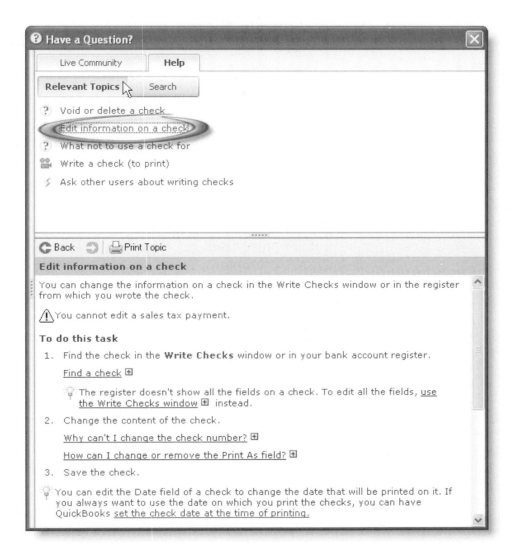

Step 3: Read about editing information on a check. To print the Help information, click the ▤ **Print Topic** icon, then select your printer and click **Print**.

Step 4: **Close** the *QuickBooks Help* window by clicking the ⊠ in the upper right corner of the *Help* window.

Step 5: **Close** the *Write Checks* window.

SAVE COMPANY FILES

As mentioned earlier, three types of QuickBooks files are:

1. **.QBW file.** The QuickBooks working file that is saved to the hard drive (C:) of your computer.

2. **.QBB file.** The QuickBooks backup file used only if the working file (.QBW) fails. You can save a backup file to the hard drive, a network drive, or other storage devices, such as a USB flash drive.

3. **.QBM file.** The QuickBooks movable file, also called a portable file, used to e-mail or move a company file to another computer.

The .QBW file is the only QuickBooks file in which you can enter data and transactions. When you enter transactions into a .QBW file, it is automatically saved. The typical workflow for a business is to use the .QBW (QuickBooks Working) file to record transactions and periodically back up to a .QBB (QuickBooks Backup) file.

A sound disaster recovery plan includes a backup system. For example, a good backup system is to have a different backup for each business day: Monday backup, Tuesday backup, Wednesday backup, and so on. Then if it is necessary to use the backup file and the Wednesday backup, for example, fails, the company has a Tuesday backup to use. Furthermore, it is recommended that a business store at least one backup at a remote location.

You can schedule a backup at regular intervals or every time you close a QuickBooks company file.

The backup file is used only if the company's working file (.QBW) fails. If the company's working file (.QBW) fails, the backup file (.QBB) can be restored and used. Therefore, it is important that the backup copy is as up to date as possible in case it must be used to replace lost company data. The backup file (.QBB) is compressed and must be converted to a working file (.QBW) before you can use it to enter data or transactions.

You can back up a company file by selecting File menu > Save Copy or Back Up. Then identify the file name and location for the backup file.

Note that you cannot open a backup file (.QBB). First, the backup file must be restored or unzipped before it can be opened and used. To restore a company file, select File menu > Open or Restore Company > Restore a Backup Copy (.QBB). Then follow the onscreen instructions. The backup file is restored to the hard drive of the computer as a working file (.QBW).

In this text, you will save a .QBB file at the end of each chapter, exercise assignment, or project.

When using *Computer Accounting with QuickBooks*, you can approach saving your company files in one of two ways:
1. Workflow Approach
2. Restart & Restore Approach

WORKFLOW APPROACH

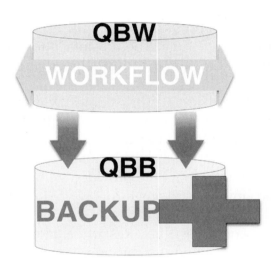

Use the Workflow approach if you will be using the same computer and the same .QBW file. Just as in a business workflow, since you are using the same computer, you can continue to use the same .QBW file. You will make backups at the end of each chapter and exercise; however, you will not need to use the backup unless your .QBW file fails.

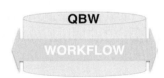

Look for the Workflow icon for instructions for this approach.

RESTART & RESTORE APPROACH

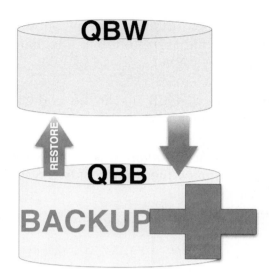

Use the Restart & Restore approach if you will be moving between campus and home computers. When you finish your QuickBooks work session, you will back up to a .QBB file in order to move the QuickBooks file to another computer.

When you restart your work session on another computer, you will restore the backup (.QBB) file.

There are two ways you can do this:

A. Restore your own .QBB file. The advantage to using you own file is that your name is already included in the company name.

B. Restore the .QBB data file that comes with the *Computer Accounting with QuickBooks* text (available on CD or download from the Online Learning Center). There is a .QBB data file for each chapter except chapters 8, 10, and 13. The advantage to using the data file provided with your text is that you avoid carrying forward any errors in your company file.

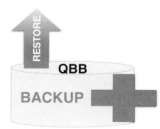

Look for the Restart & Restore icon for instructions for this approach.

Important: Check with your instructor to find out which approach (Workflow or Restart & Restore) you should use.

QuickBooks Backup (.QBB) Files

Instructions for backing up QuickBooks files are also contained in *Appendix B: Back Up & Restore QuickBooks Files.*

To save a backup (.QBB) file:

Step 1: With the QuickBooks working file (*.QBW) open, click **File > Save Copy or Backup**.

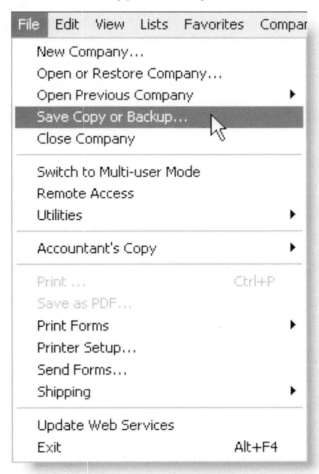

Step 2: Select **Backup copy** when the following window appears. Click **Next**.

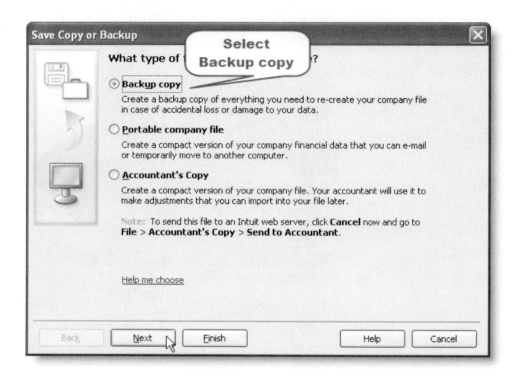

Step 3: Backup files can be saved over the Internet using QuickBooks Online Backup service or to a local backup, such as a USB flash drive, network folder, or hard drive.

You will be using a local backup, so when the following window appears, select **Local backup.**

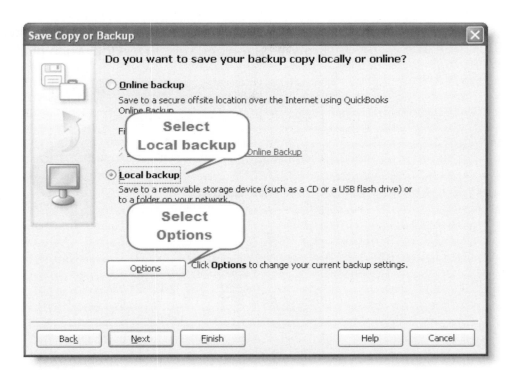

Step 4: Select **Options** to specify where you will be storing your backups.

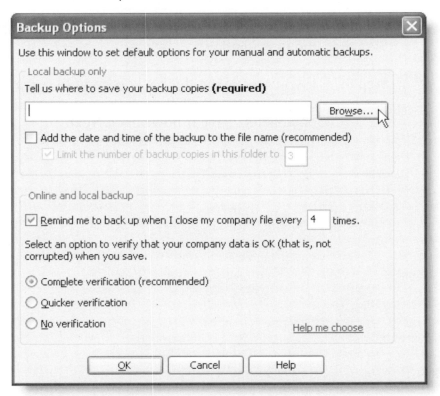

To make it easier to find your backup files, click the **Browse** button and select **Desktop**. Then click **OK**.

Click **OK** to close the **Backup Options** window. Select **Use this Location** if a *QuickBooks* warning window appears.

Click **Next** to finalize Local backup selection and move to the next window.

Step 5: If you are saving the backup copy to a removable storage device such as a USB flash drive, insert the storage device now. Select **Save it now**. Click **Next**.

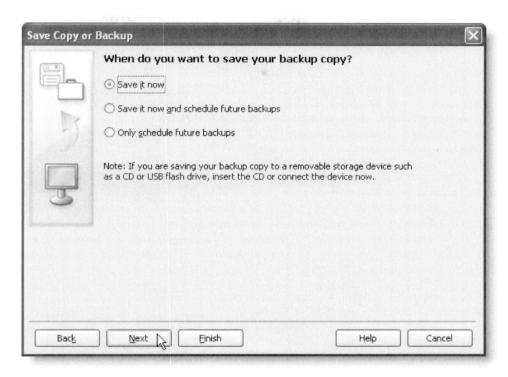

Step 6: Designate where you would like your backup copies stored. You can save the backup to the desktop and then copy to a removable storage device later or you can save directly to the removable storage device.

Ask your instructor where you should save your backup files.

When the following *Save Backup Copy* window appears:

- Change the *Save in* field to the location your instructor specifies. For example, if saving to removable storage media, select the USB flash drive. If saving to the computer's hard disk, save to the Desktop to make it easier to locate the files later.

- Change the *File name* field to **[your name] Chapter 1 Backup** as shown. Depending on your operating system settings, the file extension .QBB may appear automatically. If the .QBB extension does not appear, *do not type it.*

- The *Save as type* field should automatically appear as **QBW Backup (*.QBB).**

- Click **Save**.

Step 7: If a warning message appears, click **Use this Location**. Click **OK** when the following message appears.

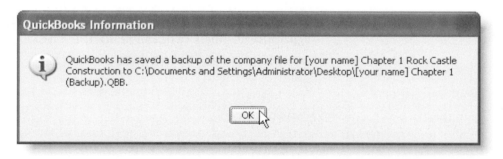

If you are using the workflow approach, leave your .QBW file open and proceed directly to Exercise 1.1.

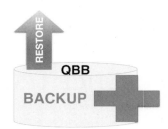

If you are using the Restart & Restore approach and are ending your computer session now, use the following directions to close the company file and exit QuickBooks.

When you restart, you will restore your backup file to complete Exercise 1.1.

CLOSE COMPANY

To close a QuickBooks company file:

Step 1: From the Menu bar, select **File**.

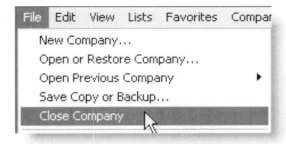

Step 2: Click **Close Company**.

If the company file is left open when you exit QuickBooks, the next time anyone uses the QuickBooks software, the company file might still be open, permitting access to your company accounting records.

EXIT QUICKBOOKS

To exit QuickBooks, click the ⊠ in the upper right corner of the *QuickBooks* window, *or* click **File** menu > **Exit**.

PODCASTS

Watch the Chapter 1 **Podcast** at www.QuickBooksBlog.info. Review the chapter, see the backup and restore features demonstrated, and more. Bookmark www.QuickBooksBlog.info for your future use.

MULTIPLE-CHOICE PRACTICE TEST

A **Multiple-Choice Practice Test** for Chapter 1 is on the *Computer Accounting for QuickBooks Pro* Online Learning Center at www.mhhe.com/kay2010. Try the Practice Test and see how many questions you answer correctly.

EXTRAS!

Section 3: Quick Guide contains quick, easy step-by-step directions for frequently used QuickBooks tasks, including correcting errors. You can find *Quick Guide* at the back of your text or online at www.mhhe.com/kay2010. *Check it out!*

Deliverables Checklist is a list of the reports and documents that you are to deliver to your instructor for grading. You can find the Chapter 1 Deliverables Checklist at the end of the chapter or online at www.mhhe.com/kay2010. Staying organized saves time. Use the checklist to organize your reports, checking off the reports as completed. Then include the checklist with your reports for grading.

Appendix D: Electronic Deliverables shows you how to save your QuickBooks reports electronically. Download the Electronic Deliverables Excel templates at www.QuickBooksBlog.info. Check with your instructor to see if you should deliver your reports electronically.

Join the QuickBooks Student Community to connect to other QuickBooks accounting students @ www.QuickBooksBlog.info.

LEARNING ACTIVITIES

Important: Ask your instructor whether you should complete the following assignments by printing requested reports or creating electronic deliverables (see Appendix D: Electronic Deliverables).

EXERCISE 1.1: PRINT FINANCIAL STATEMENTS

SCENARIO

While working at your computer, you notice Mr. Castle heading toward you. Adding another stack of papers to your overflowing inbox, he says, *"I need a profit and loss statement and a balance sheet for November as soon as possible. I haven't seen any financial statements since our former accountant left."*

As he walks away, Mr. Castle calls over his shoulder, *"From now on I'd like a P&L and balance sheet on my desk by the first of each month."*

TASK 1: OPEN COMPANY FILE

WORKFLOW

If you will be using the same computer and the same Chapter 1.QBW file, you can use the Workflow approach.

If your Chapter 1.QBW file is not already open, open it by selecting **File > Open Previous Company**. Select your **Chapter 1 .QBW file.**

Change the company name to **[your name] Exercise 1.1** by selecting **Company** menu > **Company Information.**

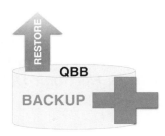

RESTART & RESTORE

If you are not using the same computer as you used in Chapter 1, you must use the Restart and Restore approach.

Restore your **Chapter 1 Backup.QBB** file using the directions in *Appendix B: Back Up & Restore QuickBooks Files*.

The company name appears on reports and can differ from the file name. See **Quick Guide** for additional instructions for changing the company name.

After restoring the file, change the company name to **[your name] Exercise 1.1** by selecting **Company** menu > **Company Information.**

If a QuickBooks Information window appears with a message about the sample company file, click **OK**.

TASK 2: PRINT PROFIT & LOSS STATEMENT

The Profit & Loss Statement (also called the Income Statement) lists income earned and expenses incurred to generate income. Summarizing the amount of profit or loss a company has earned, the Profit & Loss Statement is one of the primary financial statements given to bankers and investors.

See Section 3: **Quick Guide** for step-by-step directions.

Print the Profit & Loss Statement for Rock Castle Construction by completing the following steps:

Step 1:   Click the **Report Center** icon in the Icon bar.

Step 2:   Select type of report: **Company & Financial**.

Step 3:   Select report: **Profit & Loss Standard**.

Step 4:   Select the date range: **Last Month**. The *Dates* field will now be: **11/01/2013** to **11/30/2013**. Select the **Display Report** icon. Your screen should now appear as the following profit & loss statement.

| Modify Report... | Memorize... | Print... | E-mail ▼ | Export... | Hide Header | Collapse | Refresh |

| Dates | Last Month | ▼ | 11/01/2013 🔲 | To | 11/30/2013 🔲 | Columns | Total only | ▼ | Sort By | Default | ▼ |

[your name] Exercise 1.1 Rock Castle Construction
Profit & Loss
November 2013

Accrual Basis

	Nov 13
Ordinary Income/Expense	
Income	
40100 · Construction Income	
40130 · Labor Income	▶ 13,384.50 ◀
40140 · Materials Income	21,256.00
40150 · Subcontracted Labor Income	32,910.00
Total 40100 · Construction Income	67,550.50
40500 · Reimbursement Income	
40520 · Permit Reimbursement Income	225.00
Total 40500 · Reimbursement Income	225.00
Total Income	67,775.50
Cost of Goods Sold	
50100 · Cost of Goods Sold	2,127.16
54000 · Job Expenses	
54200 · Equipment Rental	300.00
54300 · Job Materials	9,578.79
54400 · Permits and Licenses	225.00
54500 · Subcontractors	26,990.00
54599 · Less Discounts Taken	-106.40
Total 54000 · Job Expenses	36,987.39
Total COGS	39,114.55
Gross Profit	28,660.95
Expense	
60100 · Automobile	
60110 · Fuel	111.80
60130 · Repairs and Maintenance	218.00
Total 60100 · Automobile	329.80
60600 · Bank Service Charges	12.50
62100 · Insurance	
62110 · Disability Insurance	82.06
62120 · Liability Insurance	748.83
62130 · Work Comp	1,255.83
Total 62100 · Insurance	2,086.72
62400 · Interest Expense	
62420 · Loan Interest	101.14
Total 62400 · Interest Expense	101.14
62700 · Payroll Expenses	
62710 · Gross Wages	8,456.33
62720 · Payroll Taxes	646.89
62730 · FUTA Expense	0.00
62740 · SUTA Expense	0.00
Total 62700 · Payroll Expenses	9,103.22
64200 · Repairs	
64220 · Computer Repairs	0.00
Total 64200 · Repairs	0.00
64800 · Tools and Machinery	350.00
65100 · Utilities	
65110 · Gas and Electric	97.53
65120 · Telephone	91.94
65130 · Water	24.00
Total 65100 · Utilities	213.47
Total Expense	12,196.85
Net Ordinary Income	16,464.10
Other Income/Expense	
Other Income	
70100 · Other Income	43.89
Total Other Income	43.89
Net Other Income	43.89
Net Income	**16,507.99**

Step 5: Click the **Print** button at the top of the *Profit and Loss* window.

- Select the appropriate printer.

- Select **Portrait** orientation.

- Select **Fit report to 1 page(s) wide**.

- ▣ Click **Print** to print the Profit & Loss Statement for November.

If your instructor has requested electronic deliverables, see *Appendix D: Electronic Deliverables* for instructions.

Step 6: Click the ☒ in the upper right corner of the *Profit & Loss* window to close the window.

> ☑ *Net income is $16,507.99.*

Step 7: ✐ **Circle** the single largest income item appearing on the Profit & Loss Statement for the month of November.

Step 8: ✐ **Circle** the single largest expense item appearing on the Profit & Loss Statement for the month of November.

TASK 3: PRINT BALANCE SHEET

The Balance Sheet is the financial statement that summarizes the financial position of a business. Listing assets, liabilities, and equity, the Balance Sheet reveals what a company owns and what it owes.

To print the Balance Sheet for Rock Castle Construction at November 30, 2013, complete the following steps:

Step 1: From the *Report Center* window, select type of report: **Company & Financial**.

Step 2: Select report: **Balance Sheet Standard**.

Step 3: Select date range: **Last Month** with *Dates* field from **11/01/2013** to **11/30/2013**. Select the **Display Report** icon.

Step 4: 🖨 **Print** the Balance Sheet.

Step 5: Click the ☒ in the upper right corner of the *Balance Sheet* window to close the window.

     Total Assets equal $652,098.45.

Step 6: ✏ **Circle** the single largest asset listed on Rock Castle Construction's November 2013 Balance Sheet.

Task 4: Save Exercise 1.1 File

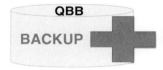

Save a backup of your Exercise 1.1 file. Use the file name: **[your name] Exercise 1.1 Backup.QBB**. See *Appendix B: Back Up & Restore QuickBooks Files* for instructions.

Leave your QuickBooks .QBW file open if you are completing Exercise 1.2 now.

Workflow

If you are proceeding to Chapter 2 and using the same computer, you can leave your .QBW file open and use it for Chapter 2.

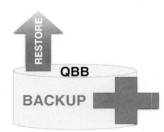

Restart & Restore

If you are stopping your QuickBooks work session and changing computers, you will need to restore your .QBB file when you restart.

EXERCISE 1.2: QUICKBOOKS HELP

In this exercise, you will use QuickBooks Help to obtain additional information about using QuickBooks.

TASK 1: BACKUP FILES AND PORTABLE FILES

Use QuickBooks Help to search for information about QuickBooks Backup files and QuickBooks Portable files.

Step 1:   🖨 **Print** the information you find.

Step 2:   ✐ **Circle** or highlight the information on the printout about differences between backup files and portable files.

TASK 2: YOUR CHOICE

Use QuickBooks Help to learn more about a QuickBooks feature of your choice.

Step 1:   🖨 **Print** the information.

Step 2:   ✐ **Circle** or highlight the information on the printout that you find the most useful.

EXERCISE 1.3: WEB QUEST

QuickBooks also offers QuickBooks Premier Accountant Edition software that is used by accounting professionals.

The websites used in the Web Quests are subject to change due to Web page updates.

Step 1:   Go to the www.quickbooks.com Web page.

Step 2:   🖳 On the QuickBooks website, locate and **print** information about QuickBooks Premier Accountant Edition software.

Step 3:   🖊 On your printout, **circle** the additional features the Accountant Edition provides that you find the most beneficial.

DELIVERABLES CHECKLIST CHAPTER 1
NAME:

INSTRUCTIONS:
1. CHECK OFF THE DELIVERABLES YOU COMPLETED.
2. ATTACH THIS PAGE TO YOUR DELIVERABLES.

CHAPTER 1
☐ Trial Balance
☐ Contact Management Printout
☐ Edit Information on a Check Printout

EXERCISE 1.1
☐ Task 2: Profit & Loss Statement
☐ Task 3: Balance Sheet

EXERCISE 1.2
☐ Task 1: Help Topic Printout
☐ Task 2: Your Choice Help Topic Printout

EXERCISE 1.3
☐ QuickBooks Product Comparison

This **Deliverables Checklist** is also available online at www.mhhe.com/kay2010.

Appendix D: Electronic Deliverables contains instructions for saving your QuickBooks reports electronically. Download **Electronic Deliverables Excel Templates** at www.QuickBooksBlog.info.

Check with your instructor to see if you should deliver your reports electronically or in hard copy.

REFLECTION: A WISH AND A STAR ★

Reflection improves learning and retention. Reflect on what you have learned after completing Chapter 1 that you did not know before you started the chapter.

A Star:

What did you like best that you learned about QuickBooks in Chapter 1?

A Wish:

If you could pick one thing, what do you wish you knew more about when using QuickBooks?

NOTES:

CHAPTER 2
CUSTOMIZING QUICKBOOKS
AND THE CHART OF ACCOUNTS

SCENARIO

The next morning when you arrive at work, Mr. Castle is waiting for you, pacing in the aisle outside your cubicle.

He looks at you over the top of his glasses, his voice tense when he asks, *"Do you have the P&L and balance sheet ready?"*

"Yes sir!" you reply, handing him the financial statements.

The creases in his brow disappear as his eyes run down the statements, murmuring to himself as he walks away, *"The banker waiting in my office should like this…."*

As he rounds the corner, he calls back to you, *"See your inbox for account changes we need to make. And password protect that QuickBooks file so every Tom, Dick, and Harry can't get into our accounting records!"*

Chapter 2
Learning Objectives

In Chapter 2, you will learn about the following QuickBooks features:

INTRODUCTION

In Chapter 2, you will learn about customizing QuickBooks to meet entrepreneurs' specific accounting needs. You will also learn about a company's Chart of Accounts, a list of all the accounts used by a company to collect accounting information. QuickBooks software automatically creates a Chart of Accounts when a new company file is created. In this chapter, you will learn how to customize QuickBooks and the Chart of Accounts by adding, editing, and deleting accounts. In addition, in Chapter 2, you will learn how to restrict access to your QuickBooks accounting records using passwords to improve security and controls. Finally, you can customize the digital snapshot of your company using the QuickBooks feature, Company Snapshot.

Failure to register your QuickBooks trial version software will result in the software no longer functioning.

Start QuickBooks by clicking on the **QuickBooks desktop icon** or click **Start > Programs > QuickBooks > QuickBooks Pro 2010**.

WORKFLOW APPROACH

Use the Workflow approach if you are using the same computer and the same .QBW file from the prior chapter. Just as in a business, since you are using the same computer, you can continue to use the same .QBW file. You will make backups at the end of Chapter 2; however, you will not need to use the backup unless your .QBW file fails.

Step 1: If your .QBW file is not already open, open it by selecting **File > Open Previous Company**. Select your most recent **.QBW file.**

Step 2: Change the company name to **[your name] Chapter 2** by selecting **Company** menu **> Company Information.**

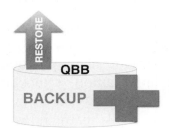

RESTART & RESTORE APPROACH

Use the Restart & Restore approach if you are restarting your work session and moving your QuickBooks files between campus and home computers. When you restart your work session, first you will restore the backup (.QBB) file.

Step 1: Restore the **Backup.QBB** file using the directions in *Appendix B: Back Up & Restore QuickBooks Files*.

You can restore:

A. Your .QBB file from the last exercise completed in the previous chapter. For example, in this case you would restore the backup file: [your name] Exercise 1.1 Backup.QBB. The advantage to using your own file is that your name is already included in the company name.

B. The Chapter 2.QBB data file that comes with the *Computer Accounting with QuickBooks* text (available on CD or download from the Online Learning Center). The advantage to using the data file provided with your text is that you avoid carrying forward any errors in your company file.

Step 2: After restoring the file, change the company name to **[your name] Chapter 2** by selecting **Company** menu > **Company Information.**

CUSTOMIZE QUICKBOOKS

QuickBooks is an accounting system that permits a company to conveniently collect accounting information and store it in a single file. QuickBooks has streamlined the way that many entrepreneurs maintain accounting records. Furthermore, QuickBooks offers four main ways to customize QuickBooks to meet entrepreneurs' specific accounting needs.

1. Choose an industry-specific version of QuickBooks Premier

2. Customize QuickBooks using Preferences

3. Customize QuickBooks Favorites

4. Customize the QuickBooks Chart of Accounts

CUSTOMIZE WITH QUICKBOOKS PREMIER

In addition to QuickBooks Pro, Intuit offers two types of QuickBooks Premier:

1. *QuickBooks Industry Edition* offers more advanced features than QuickBooks Pro and permits you to customize QuickBooks by selecting a version with industry-specific features. QuickBooks Premier Industry Edition has six industry versions from which you can choose.

> General Business
> Contractor
> Manufacturing & Wholesale
> Nonprofit
> Professional Services
> Retail

2. *QuickBooks Premier Accountant Edition* is designed for accounting firms that provide QuickBooks services to multiple clients.

CUSTOMIZE QUICKBOOKS USING PREFERENCES

QuickBooks Pro and QuickBooks Premier can be further customized using QuickBooks preferences.

To customize QuickBooks preferences:

Step 1: Select **Edit** menu > **Preferences**.

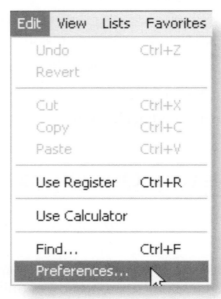

Step 2: From the *Preferences* window, you can select the area of QuickBooks you would like to customize. The left scrollbar lists the different types of preferences. In this case, select **Desktop View** to customize your Home page.

There are two tabs: My Preferences and Company Preferences. Select **My Preferences**.

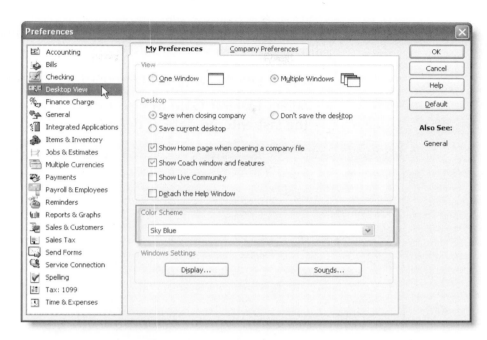

Step 3:   Select the **Color Scheme** that you would like to use for your QuickBooks Desktop.

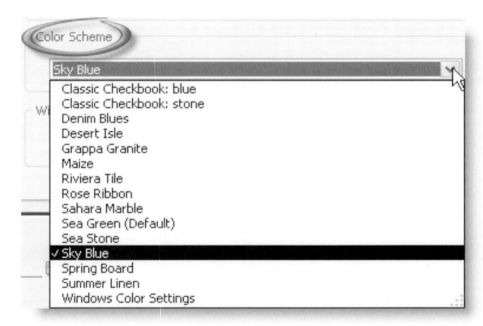

Step 4: Next, customize the default date for new transactions as follows:

- Select **General** in the *Preferences* scrollbar window.

- Select Default Date to Use for New Transactions: **Use the last entered date as default**.

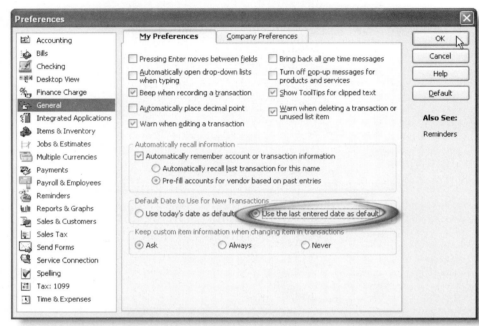

Step 5: Click **OK** to close the *Preferences* window and save your changes.

As you can see from the *Preferences* window, there are many areas of QuickBooks that you can customize to meet the specific needs of your particular company. QuickBooks now offers the ability to use multiple currencies as seen in the preceding *Preferences* scrollbar.

CUSTOMIZE QUICKBOOKS FAVORITES

QuickBooks 2010 offers a Favorites menu that you can customize with up to 30 of your favorite QuickBooks menu items.

To customize the Favorites menu:

Step 1:   Select **Favorites** menu > **Customize Favorites**.

Step 2:   To add an item to the Favorites menu, select the item in the *Customize Your Menus* window. In this case, select **Chart of Accounts**, then click **Add**.

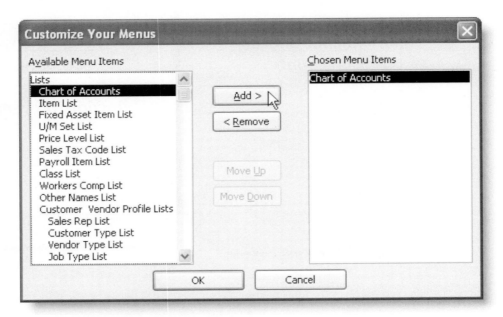

Step 3:   Click **OK** to close the *Customize Your Menus* window.

Next, you will learn how to customize the QuickBooks Chart of Accounts.

CHART OF ACCOUNTS

The Chart of Accounts is a list of accounts and account numbers. A company uses accounts to record transactions in the accounting system. Accounts (such as the Cash account or Inventory account) permit you to sort and track information.

QuickBooks will automatically create a Chart of Accounts when you set up a new company. Then you may customize the Chart of Accounts, adding and deleting accounts as necessary to suit your company's specific needs. QuickBooks also permits you to use subaccounts.

Accounts can be categorized into the following groups:

Balance Sheet Accounts

Assets

Liabilities

Equity

Profit & Loss Accounts

Income (Revenue)

Expenses

Non-Posting Accounts
Purchase Orders

Estimates

BALANCE SHEET ACCOUNTS

The Balance Sheet is a financial statement that summarizes what a company owns and what it owes. Balance Sheet accounts are accounts that appear on the company's Balance Sheet.

Review the Balance Sheet you printed in Exercise 1.1 for Rock Castle Construction. Three types of accounts appear on the Balance Sheet:
1. Assets
2. Liabilities
3. Owners' (or Stockholders') Equity

> ASSETS = LIABILITIES + OWNERS' EQUITY

1. **Assets** are resources that a company owns. These resources are expected to have *future benefit*.

   Asset accounts include:

   - Cash.

   - Accounts receivable (amounts to be *received* from customers in the future).

   - Inventory.

   - Other current assets (assets likely to be converted to cash or consumed within one year).

   - Fixed assets (property used in the operations of the business, such as equipment, buildings, and land).

   - Intangible assets (such as copyrights, patents, trademarks, and franchises).

2. **Liabilities** are amounts a company owes to others. Liabilities are *obligations*. For example, if a company borrows $10,000 from the bank, the company has an obligation to repay the $10,000 to the bank. Thus, the $10,000 obligation is shown as a liability on the company's Balance Sheet.

   Liability accounts include:

   - Accounts payable (amounts that are owed and will be *paid* to suppliers in the future).

   - Sales taxes payable (sales tax owed and to be *paid* in the future).

If you are unsure whether an account is an asset account, ask the question: *Does this item have future benefit?* If the answer is yes, the item is probably an asset.

If you are unsure whether an account is a liability account, ask the question: *Is the company obligated to do something, such as pay a bill or provide a service?* If the answer is yes, the item is probably a liability.

The difference between a note payable and a mortgage payable is that a mortgage payable has real estate as collateral.

- Interest payable (interest owed and to be *paid* in the future).

- Other current liabilities (liabilities due within one year).

- Loan payable (also called notes payable).

- Mortgage payable.

- Other long-term liabilities (liabilities due after one year).

3. **Owners' equity** accounts (stockholders' equity for a corporation) represent the net worth of a business. Equity is calculated as assets (resources owned) minus liabilities (amounts owed).

Different types of business ownership include:

- Sole proprietorship (an unincorporated business with one owner).

- Partnership (an unincorporated business with more than one owner).

- Corporation (an incorporated business with one or more owners).

Owners' equity is increased by:

- Investments by owners. For a corporation, owners invest by buying stock.

- Net profits retained in the business rather than distributed to owners.

Owners' equity is decreased by:

OWNERS' EQUITY = ASSETS - SIABILITIES

- Amounts paid to owners as a return for their investment. For a sole proprietorship or partnership, these are called withdrawals. For a corporation, they are called dividends.

- Losses incurred by the business.

The following QuickBooks Learning Center graphic shows the relationship of assets, liabilities, and owners' equity accounts.

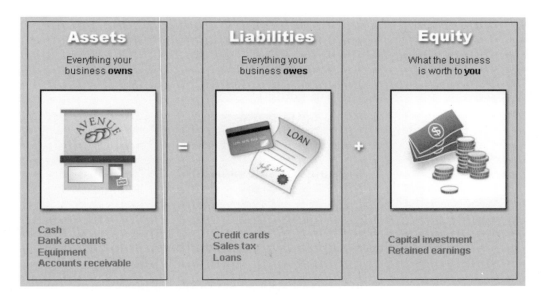

Balance Sheet accounts are referred to as *permanent accounts*. Balances in permanent accounts are carried forward from year to year. Thus, for a Balance Sheet account, such as Cash, the balance at December 31 is carried forward and becomes the opening balance on January 1 of the next year.

INCOME STATEMENT (PROFIT & LOSS) ACCOUNTS

The Income Statement (also called the Profit and Loss Statement or P&L Statement) reports the results of a company's operations, listing income and expenses for a period of time. Income Statement accounts are accounts that appear on a company's Income Statement.

Review the Income Statement you printed in Exercise 1.1 for Rock Castle Construction. QuickBooks uses two different Income Statement accounts:

1. Income accounts
2. Expense accounts

1. **Income** accounts record sales to customers and other revenues earned by the company.   Revenues are the prices charged customers for goods and services provided.

    Examples of Income accounts include:

    - Sales or revenues.

    - Fees earned.

    - Interest income.

    - Rental income.

    - Gains on sale of assets.

2. **Expense** accounts record costs that have expired or been consumed in the process of generating income. Expenses are the costs of providing goods and services to customers.

    Examples of Expense accounts include:

    - Cost of goods sold expense.

    - Salaries expense.

    - Insurance expense.

    - Rent expense.

    - Interest expense.

> **INCOME (OR REVENUE)**
> - **EXPENSES**
> = **NET INCOME**

Net income is calculated as income (or revenue) less cost of goods sold and other expenses.   Net income is an attempt to match or measure efforts (expenses) against accomplishments (revenues).

Income Statement accounts are called *temporary* accounts because they are used for only one year. At the end of each year, temporary accounts are closed (the balance reduced to zero).

For example, if an Income Statement account, such as Advertising Expense, had a $5,000 balance at December 31, the $5,000 balance would be closed or transferred to owners' equity at year-end. The opening balance on January 1 for the Advertising Expense account would be $0.00.

The following QuickBooks Learning Center graphic summarizes the five types of accounts in the Chart of Accounts.

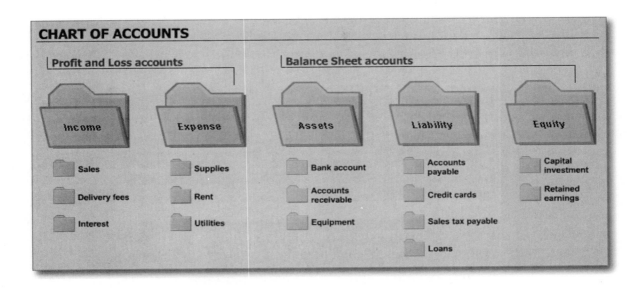

NON-POSTING ACCOUNTS

Non-posting accounts are accounts that do not appear on the Balance Sheet or Income Statement. However, these accounts are needed to track information necessary for the accounting system.

Examples of non-posting accounts include:

- Purchase orders: documents that track items that have been ordered from suppliers.
- Estimates: bids or proposals submitted to customers.

LISTS

QuickBooks uses lists to provide additional supporting detail for selected accounts.

QuickBooks lists include:

1. **Customer List.** Provides information about customers, such as customer name, customer number, address, and contact information.

2. **Vendor List.** Provides information about vendors, such as vendor name, vendor number, and contact information.

3. **Employee List.** Provides information about employees for payroll purposes including name, Social Security number, and address.

4. **Item List.** Provides information about the items or services sold to customers, such as hours worked and types of items.

5. **Payroll Item List.** Tracks detailed information about payroll, such as payroll taxes and payroll deductions. The Payroll Item List permits the use of a single or limited number of payroll accounts while more detailed information is tracked using the Item List for payroll.

6. **Class List.** Permits income to be tracked according to the specific source (class) of income. An example of a class might be a department, store location, business segment, or product line.

Lists are used so that information can be entered once in a list and then reused as needed. For example, information about a customer, such as address, can be entered in the Customer List. This customer information then automatically appears on the customer invoice.

CUSTOMIZE CHART OF ACCOUNTS

Obtain a copy of the tax form for your business at www.irs.gov. Then modify your Chart of Accounts to track the information needed for your tax return.

When you set up a new company, QuickBooks automatically creates a Chart of Accounts. Then you can customize the Chart of Accounts to suit your specific needs by adding, deleting, and editing accounts.

DISPLAY CHART OF ACCOUNTS

You can display the Chart of Accounts in three different ways:
1. From the Company menu
2. From the *Company Snapshot* window
3. From the *Company* section of the Home page

To view the Chart of Accounts for Rock Castle Construction from the Home page, complete the following steps:

Step 1:   To display the *Chart of Accounts* window, click the **Chart of Accounts** icon in the *Company* section of the Home page.

For each account, the account name, type of account, and the balance of the account are listed.

The Account button at the bottom of the window displays a drop-down menu for adding, editing, and deleting accounts. Or you can right-click to display a pop-up menu to add and edit accounts.

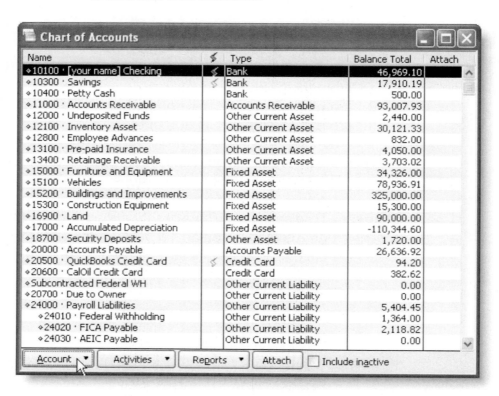

DISPLAY ACCOUNT NUMBERS

Account numbers are used to uniquely identify accounts. Usually account numbers are used as a coding system to also identify the account type. For example, a typical numbering system for accounts might be as follows.

Account type determines whether the account appears on the Balance Sheet or Income Statement.

Account Type	Account No.
Asset accounts	1000 – 1999
Liability accounts	2000 – 2999
Equity accounts	3000 – 3999
Revenue (income) accounts	4000 – 4999
Expense accounts	5000 – 5999

QuickBooks preferences will determine whether the account number is displayed in the Chart of Accounts. If account numbers are not displayed in Rock Castle Construction's chart of account, select the QuickBooks preference to view account numbers as follows.

To display account numbers:

Step 1:   Select **Edit** menu > **Preferences**.

Step 2:   When the following *Preferences* window appears:

- Click the **Accounting** icon in the left scrollbar.

- Then select the **Company Preferences** tab.

- Select **Use account numbers** to display the account numbers in the Chart of Accounts.

- Then click **OK**.

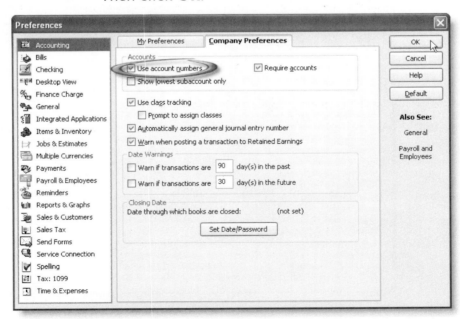

Step 3:   If the Chart of Accounts does not appear on your screen, , click **Window** menu > **Chart of Accounts**.

The Chart of Accounts should now list account numbers preceding the account name.

ADD NEW ACCOUNTS

You can customize the Chart of Accounts by adding, deleting, and editing accounts as needed to meet your company's specific and changing needs.

Rock Castle Construction has decided to begin advertising and would like to add an Advertising Expense account to the Chart of Accounts.

To add a new account to the Chart of Accounts:

Step 1:   Click the **Account** button at the bottom of the *Chart of Accounts* window to display a drop-down menu, then click **New**.

Step 2:   Select Account Type: **Expense**. Click **Continue**.

Step 3:   In the *Add New Account* window:

- Verify the Account Type: **Expense**.

- Enter the new Account Number: **60400**.

- Enter the Account Name: **Advertising Expense**.

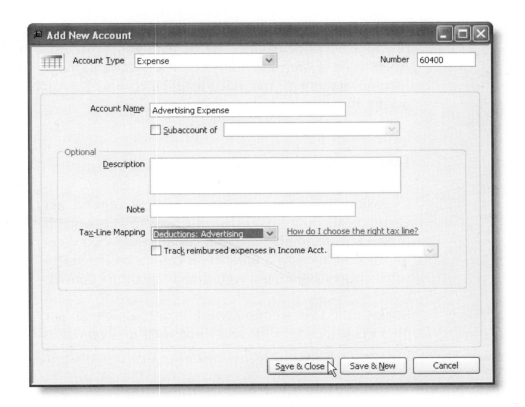

Selecting the appropriate Tax Line ensures that QuickBooks provides the information needed to complete your tax return.

- Leave Subaccount unchecked. Subaccounts are subcategories of an account. For example, Rock Castle Construction has an Automobile Expense account (Account No. 60100) and three Automobile Expense subaccounts: Fuel (Account No. 60110), Insurance (Account No. 60120) and Repairs and Maintenance (Account No. 60130).

- Select Tax-Line Mapping: **Deductions: Advertising**. This indicates the Advertising Expense account balance will appear as a deduction on Rock Castle Construction's tax return.

Step 4:   Click **Save & Close** to save the changes and close the *New Account* window.

Notice that Account 60400 Advertising Expense now appears on the Chart of Accounts.

If the new account had been a Balance Sheet account (an asset, liability, or equity account), QuickBooks would ask you for the opening account balance as of your QuickBooks start date. Since Advertising Expense is an Expense account that appears on the Income Statement and not the Balance Sheet, QuickBooks did not ask for the opening balance.

DELETE ACCOUNTS

Occasionally you may want to delete unused accounts from the Chart of Accounts. You can only delete accounts that are not being used. For example, if an account has been used to record a transaction and has a balance, it cannot be deleted. If an account has subaccounts associated with it, that account cannot be deleted.

Rock Castle Construction would like to delete an account it does not plan to use, the Printing and Reproduction Expense account.

To delete an account:

Select **View** menu > **Open Window List** to display all open windows. From the Open Window List, select the *Chart of Accounts* window.

Step 1:   Display the *Chart of Accounts* window.

Step 2:   Select the account to delete. In this case, click **63300: Printing and Reproduction**.

Step 3:   Click the **Account** button at the bottom of *the Chart of Accounts* window.

Step 4:   Click **Delete Account**.

Step 5:   Click **OK** to confirm that you want to delete the account.

EDIT ACCOUNTS

Next, you will edit an account. Rock Castle Construction would like to change the name of the Advertising Expense account to Advertising & Promotion.

To change the name of the Advertising Expense account to Advertising & Promotion:

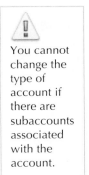

Select **View** menu > **Open Window List** to display all open windows. From the Open Window List, select the *Chart of Accounts* window.

⚠

You cannot change the type of account if there are subaccounts associated with the account.

Step 1: If necessary, display the *Chart of Accounts* window.

Step 2: Select the account to edit: **60400 Advertising Expense**.

Step 3: Click the **Account** button in the lower left corner of the *Chart of Accounts* window or **right-click** the mouse to display the pop-up menu.

Step 4: Click **Edit Account** to open the *Edit Account* window.

Step 5: Make changes to the account information. In this case, change Account Name to: **Advertising & Promotion**.

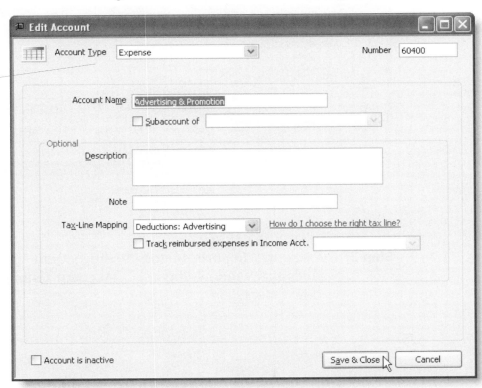

Step 6: Click **Save & Close** to save the changes. Advertising Expense should now appear as Advertising & Promotion in the *Chart of Accounts* window.

PRINT CHART OF ACCOUNTS

QuickBooks provides an Account Listing report that lists the Chart of Accounts plus the account balances.

To print the Account Listing report:

Step 1: Display the *Chart of Accounts* window.

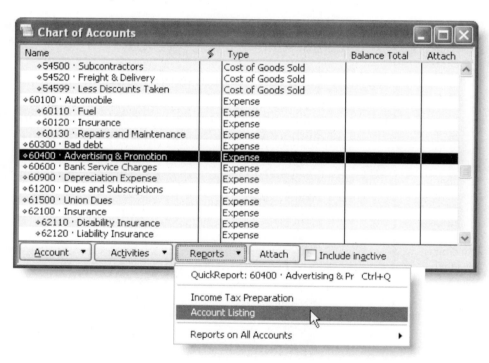

Step 2: Click the **Reports** button at the bottom of the *Chart of Accounts* window, then click **Account Listing** on the dropdown menu.

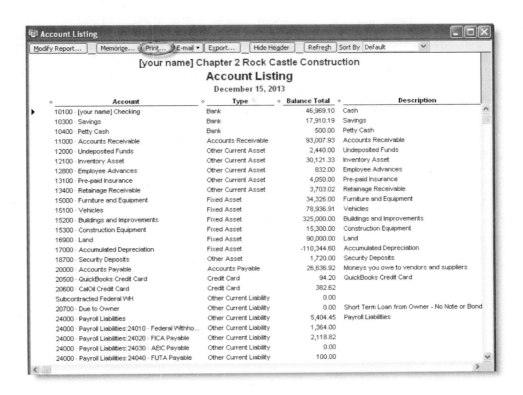

Go Green. See Appendix D for information about using electronic deliverables.

Step 3: 📇 **Print** the Account Listing report as follows:

- Click the **Print** button at the top of the *Account Listing* window.

- Select orientation: **Portrait**.

- Select **Fit report to 1 page(s) wide** that appears in the lower left of the window.

- Click **Print**.

Step 4: **Close** the *Account Listing* window and the *Chart of Accounts* window.

CUSTOMIZE QUICKBOOKS SECURITY

QuickBooks permits a company to conveniently collect accounting information and store it in a single file. Much of the accounting information stored in QuickBooks is confidential, however, and a company often wants to limit employee access.

Password protection can be used to customize and limit access to company data and improve security and control.

Two ways to restrict access to accounting information stored in a QuickBooks company data file are:

1. Password protect the company file so that individuals must enter a user ID and password to open the company file.

2. Limit access to selected areas of the company's accounting data. For example, a user may access accounts receivable to view customer balances but not be able to access payroll or check writing.

Only the QuickBooks Administrator can add users with passwords and grant user access to selected areas of QuickBooks. The QuickBooks Administrator is an individual who has access to all areas of QuickBooks.

To add a new user and password protection to a company file:

Step 1:   Click **Company > Set Up Users and Passwords > Set Up Users**.

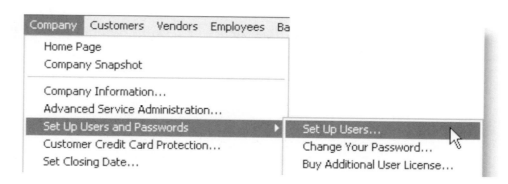

If Admin does not appear in the *User List* window, select **Add User**, then add Admin.

Step 2: First, set up a QuickBooks Administrator who has access to all areas of QuickBooks. The Administrator can then add new users. To add the Administrator password:

- From the *User List* window, select **Admin > Edit User**.

- Enter and then confirm a **password** of your choice. *Write the password on the inside cover of your text.*

- Select a **challenge question** and enter your answer.

- Click **Next**.

Step 3: Only the QuickBooks Administrator can add new users. To add another user, click **Add User**.

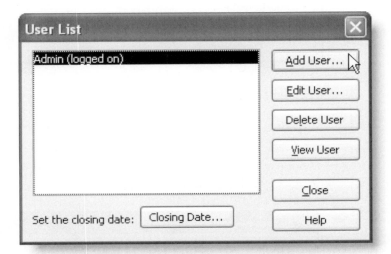

Step 4: In the following *Set up user password and access* window:

- Enter **[Your Name]** in the *User Name* field.

- At this point, if you were adding another employee as a user, you would ask the employee to enter and confirm his or her password. In this instance, simply enter and confirm a **password** of your choice. *Write the password on the inside cover of your text.*

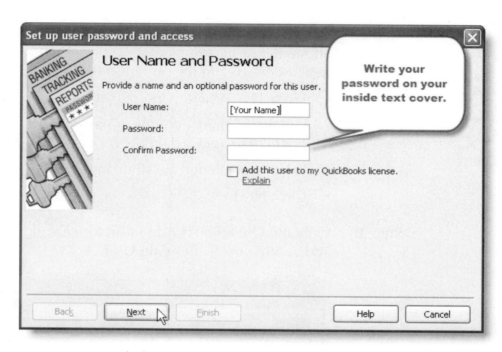

- Click **Next**.

Step 5: In the following window, you can restrict user access to selected areas of QuickBooks or give the user access to all areas of QuickBooks. Select: **All areas of QuickBooks**, then click **Next**.

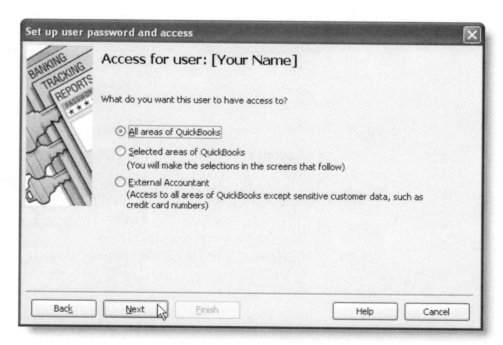

Step 6: Select **Yes** to confirm that you want to give access to all areas of QuickBooks.

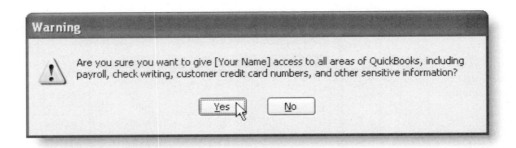

Step 7: The next window summarizes the user's access for each QuickBooks area, indicating access to create documents, print, and view reports. Click **Finish**.

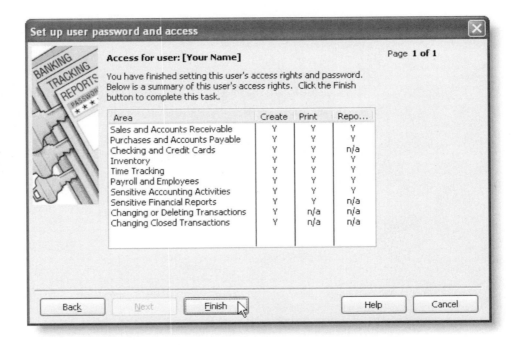

Step 8:   Two names (Administrator and Your Name) should appear on the User List. Click **Close** to close the *User List* window.

Write your password on the inside of your text cover.
You will not be able to access your company file without your password.

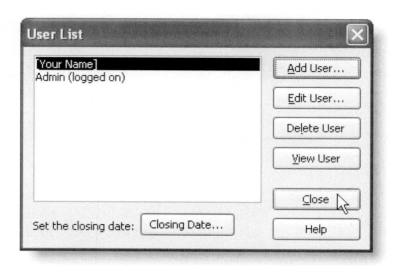

Now whenever you open the company file for Rock Castle Construction, you will be asked to enter your user name and password.

CUSTOMIZE QUICKBOOKS COMPANY SNAPSHOT

The QuickBooks Company Snapshot provides a digital dashboard for your company. The Company Snapshot gives you an overview of key information for your company and lets you perform key tasks.

Customize QuickBooks by using Company Snapshot to:

- Choose which accounts to view
- Receive payments
- Pay bills
- Select which reminders to see

A vital aspect of maintaining an accounting system is tracking due dates for tax and vendor payments. In addition, billing and collections of customer payments must be scheduled in a timely manner to ensure adequate cash flows to operate the business. QuickBooks has three different features to assist in tracking tasks:

1. **Reminders.** Shows only those tasks that are currently due, including tasks from the To Do List.
2. **To Do List.** Tracks all tasks to be completed. You can add items to the To Do List, mark items complete, and print the list.
3. **Alerts Manager.** Lists tasks and due dates related to taxes and regulations. These alerts will appear as Reminders as they become due.

Reminders appear in the Company Snapshot to keep you apprised of what task is due next. If you are responsible for maintaining an accounting system, you can view Reminders each day to see what accounting tasks require your attention.

Next, you will learn how to customize the Company Snapshot to assist you in tracking tasks.

Step 1: To open the Company Snapshot, click the **Company Snapshot** icon.

The Company Snapshot summarizes:

- Account Balances
- Customers Who Owe Money
- Vendors to Pay
- Reminders

Step 2: To customize the Company Snapshot:

- Select **Add Content**.
- Select **Vendors to Pay**.
- Select **Reminders**.

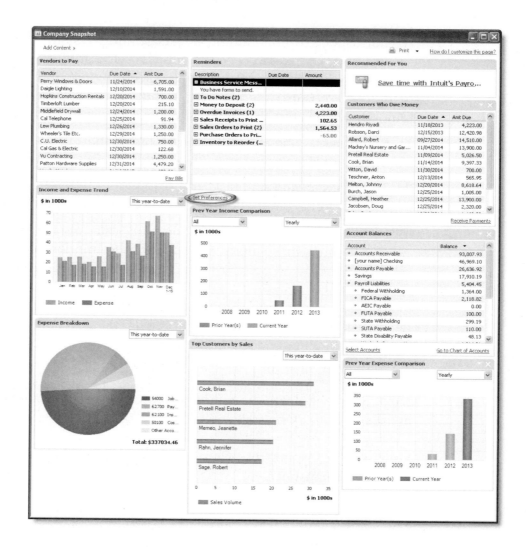

Step 3:   To customize Reminders on the Snapshot, click the **Set Preferences** button below *Reminders*. Notice that the following *Preferences* window that appears is the same *Preferences* window you used earlier to customize your Desktop View and Default Date.

Step 4:   Select Show List: **Overdue Invoices** and **Bills to Pay**. The Reminders on the Snapshot will now show the list for overdue invoices and bills to pay. This will enable you to maintain better control over these important accounting functions. Click **OK** to close the *Preferences* window.

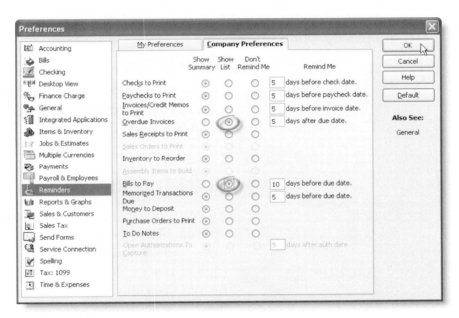

Step 5:   Close and then reopen the Company Snapshot to update. Notice that now the Reminders window lists specific customers' overdue invoices to track.

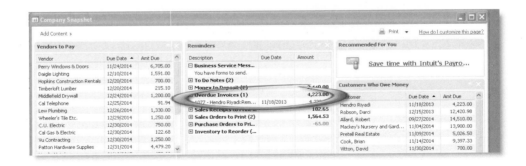

In Chapter 2 you learned a few ways to customize QuickBooks to meet the specific needs of enterprises. QuickBooks can be customized further using additional Preferences features.

SAVE CHAPTER 2

 Save a backup of your Chapter 2 file using the file name: **[your name] Chapter 2 Backup.QBB**. See *Appendix B: Back Up & Restore QuickBooks Files* for instructions.

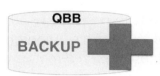

WORKFLOW

If you are using the workflow approach, leave your .QBW file open and proceed directly to Exercise 2.1.

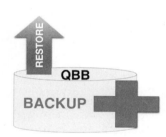

RESTART & RESTORE

If you are using the Restart & Restore approach and ending your computer session now, close your .QBW file and exit QuickBooks. When you restart, you will restore your backup file to complete Exercise 2.1.

PODCASTS

Watch the Chapter 2 **Podcast** at www.QuickBooksBlog.info. Review the chapter, see how to customize QuickBooks, and more. Bookmark www.QuickBooksBlog.info for your future use.

MULTIPLE-CHOICE PRACTICE TEST

A **Multiple-Choice Practice Test** for Chapter 2 is on the *Computer Accounting for QuickBooks Pro* Online Learning Center at www.mhhe.com/kay2010. Try the Practice Test and see how many questions you answer correctly.

EXTRAS!

Section 3: Quick Guide contains quick, easy step-by-step directions for frequently used QuickBooks tasks, including correcting errors. You can find *Quick Guide* at the back of your text or online at www.mhhe.com/kay2010. *Check it out!*

Deliverables Checklist is a list of the reports and documents that you are to deliver to your instructor for grading. You can find the Chapter 2 Deliverables Checklist at the end of the chapter or online at www.mhhe.com/kay2010. Staying organized saves time. Use the checklist to organize your reports, checking off the reports as completed. Then include the checklist with your reports for grading.

Appendix D: Electronic Deliverables shows you how to save your QuickBooks reports electronically. Also, watch the Electronic Deliverables Podcast at www.QuickBooksBlog.info. Check with your instructor to see if you should deliver your reports electronically.

Join the QuickBooks Student Community to connect to other QuickBooks accounting students @ www.QuickBooksBlog.info.

LEARNING ACTIVITIES

Important: Ask your instructor whether you should complete the following assignments by printing requested reports or creating electronic deliverables (see Appendix D: Electronic Deliverables).

EXERCISE 2.1: TO DO LIST

SCENARIO

When you return to your cubicle after lunch, you find the following note stuck to your computer screen.

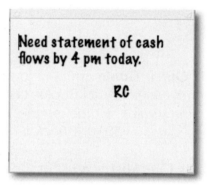

In addition to printing out the Statement of Cash Flows, you decide to add a task to your QuickBooks To Do List to remind you to print out the financial statements for Rock Castle each month.

TASK 1: OPEN COMPANY FILE

WORKFLOW

If you are using the Workflow approach, you will use the same .QBW file.

If your QBW file is not already open, open it by selecting **File > Open Previous Company**. Select your **.QBW file.**

Change the company name to **[your name] Exercise 2.1** by selecting **Company** menu > **Company Information.**

RESTART & RESTORE

If you are not using the same computer, you must use the Restart and Restore approach.

Restore your **Chapter 2 Backup.QBB** file using the directions in *Appendix B: Back Up & Restore QuickBooks Files.*

After restoring the file, change the company name to **[your name] Exercise 2.1** by selecting **Company** menu > **Company Information.**

If a QuickBooks Information window appears with a message about the sample company file, click **OK**.

TASK 2: ADD A TASK TO THE TO DO LIST

To help you keep track of the financial statements that Mr. Castle would like prepared each month, add a task to your To Do List that will then automatically appear in your Company Snapshot Reminders when due. You will add the task for December and January.

To add a task to the To Do List, complete the following steps:

Step 1:   From the menu bar, select **Company > To Do List**.

Step 2:   Click the **To Do** button in the lower left corner of the *To Do List* window.

Step 3: Click **New**.

Step 4: Enter the December task: **Print financial statements for Mr. Castle**. Remind me on: **12/12/2013**.

Step 5: Click the **Next** button to add another task.

Step 6: Enter the January task: **Print financial statements for Mr. Castle**. Remind me on: **01/01/2014**.

Step 7: Click **OK** to save the task and close the window.

Step 8: Close the *To Do List* window.

TASK 3: PRINT STATEMENT OF CASH FLOWS

The Statement of Cash Flows summarizes a company's cash inflows and cash outflows. The cash flows are grouped by activity:

- Cash flows from operating activities. Cash flows related to the operations of the business—providing goods and services to customers.

- Cash flows from investing activities. Cash flows that result from investing (buying and selling) long-term assets, such as investments and property.

- Cash flows from financing activities. Cash flows that result from borrowing or repaying principal on debt or from transactions with owners.

Print the Statement of Cash Flows for Rock Castle Construction by completing the following steps:

Step 1:   Click the **Report Center** icon in the Icon bar.

Step 2:   Select type of report: **Company & Financial**.

Step 3:   Select report: **Statement of Cash Flows**.

Step 4:   Select the date range: **Last Month**. The *From* field should now be: **11/01/2013**. The *To* field should be: **11/30/2013**.

Step 5:   ▣ **Print** the Statement of Cash Flows as follows:

- Click the **Display Report** icon.

- Click the **Print** button at the top of the *Statement of Cash Flows* window.

- Select the appropriate printer.

- Select **Portrait** orientation.

- Select **Fit to 1 page(s) wide**.

- Click **Print** to print the Statement of Cash Flows.

Step 6:   **Close** the *Statement of Cash Flows* window.

Step 7:   Then **close** the *Report Center* window.

> ☑   ***Net cash provided by operating activities is $25,016.93.***

Step 8:   ✐ **Circle** the net change in cash for the period on the Statement of Cash Flows printout.

TASK 4: MARK TASK COMPLETE

Mark the task to print November financial statements as completed.

To mark a task complete:

Step 1:   Open the *To Do List* window.

Step 2:   Select the To Do task: **12/12/2013 Print financial statements for Mr. Castle**.

Step 3:   With the mouse pointer on the selected task, right-click. When the onscreen menu appears, select **Mark as Done**. A ✓ should now appear in front of the task, and the task drops to the bottom of the To Do List.

Step 4:   ⎙ **Print** the To Do List as follows:

- Click the **Reports** button at the bottom of the *To Do List* window.

- Click **Detail List**.

- Click **Print**. Select Print to: **Printer**. Click **Print**.

- **Close** the *To Do List* window.

TASK 5: SAVE EXERCISE 2.1

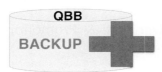

Save a backup of your Exercise 2.1 file using the file name: **[your name] Exercise 2.1 Backup.QBB**. See *Appendix B: Back Up & Restore QuickBooks Files* for instructions.

WORKFLOW

If you are proceeding to Exercise 2.2 and using the same computer, you can leave your .QBW file open and use it for Exercise 2.2.

RESTART & RESTORE

If you are stopping your QuickBooks work session and changing computers, you will need to restore your .QBB file when you restart.

EXERCISE 2.2: EDIT CHART OF ACCOUNTS

SCENARIO

When you return to your cubicle after your afternoon break, another note is stuck to your computer screen.

Beginning January 1, I want a report listing advertising costs and promotion costs separately so we can track effectiveness.

RC

In order to track advertising costs separately from promotion costs, you decide to make the following changes to the Chart of Accounts.

1. Rename Account 60400 Advertising & Promotion account to: Selling Expense.

2. Add two subaccounts: 60410 Advertising Expense and 60420 Promotion Expense.

After these changes, the Chart of Accounts should list the following accounts:

▪ Account 60400: Selling Expense
▪ Subaccount 60410: Advertising Expense
▪ Subaccount 60420: Promotion Expense

TASK 1: OPEN COMPANY FILE

WORKFLOW

If you are using the Workflow approach, you will use the same .QBW file.

If your QBW file is not already open, open it by selecting **File > Open Previous Company**. Select your **.QBW file.**

Change the company name to **[your name] Exercise 2.2** by selecting **Company** menu **> Company Information.**

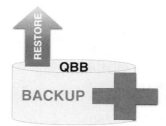

RESTART & RESTORE

If you are using the Restart and Restore approach, restore your backup file using the directions in *Appendix B: Back Up & Restore QuickBooks Files.*

After restoring the file, change the company name to **[your name] Exercise 2.2** by selecting **Company** menu **> Company Information.**

If a QuickBooks Information window appears with a message about the sample company file, click **OK**.

TASK 2: EDIT ACCOUNT

Edit the Chart of Accounts to change the name of Account 60400 from Advertising & Promotion to Selling Expense.

Step 1: Open the *Chart of Accounts* window by clicking the **Chart of Accounts** icon in the *Company* section of the Home page.

Step 2: Select account: **60400 Advertising & Promotion**.

Step 3: Click the **Account** button at the bottom of the *Chart of Accounts* window, then select **Edit Account** from the drop-down menu.

Step 4: Change the account name from Advertising & Promotion to: **Selling Expense**.

Step 5: Click **Save & Close** to save the changes.

TASK 3: ADD SUBACCOUNTS

Add two subaccounts to the Selling Expense account:
1. Advertising Expense
2. Promotion Expense

Step 1: Click the **Account** button at the bottom of the *Chart of Accounts* window, then select **New** to open the *Add New Account* window.

Step 2: Select Account Type: **Expense**. Click **Continue**.

Step 3: Enter Account Number: **60410**

Step 4: Enter Account Name: **Advertising Expense**.

Step 5:   ✓ **Check** the box in front of the *Subaccount of* field.

Step 6:   From the drop-down list, select subaccount of: **60400 Selling Expense**.

Step 7:   From the drop-down list for Tax-Line Mapping, select **Deductions: Advertising**.

Step 8:   Click **Save & New**.

Step 9:   Using the preceding instructions, add the next subaccount: **60420 Promotion Expense**. Click **Save & Close**.

Step 10:   🖨 **Print** the revised Chart of Accounts. (Hint: From the *Chart of Accounts* window, click the **Reports** button, then click **Account Listing**.

▪ Remember to use **Portrait** orientation and **Fit to 1 page(s) wide**.

▪ ✏ **Circle** the subaccounts that you added.

TASK 4: SAVE EXERCISE 2.2

Save a backup of your Exercise 2.2 file using the file name: **[your name] Exercise 2.2 Backup.QBB**. See *Appendix B: Back Up & Restore QuickBooks Files* for instructions.

WORKFLOW

If you are using the Workflow approach, you can leave your .QBW file open and use it for the next chapter.

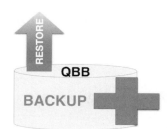

RESTART & RESTORE

If you are stopping your QuickBooks work session and changing computers, you will need to restore your .QBB file when you restart.

EXERCISE 2.3: WEB QUEST

When setting up a Chart of Accounts for a business, it is often helpful to review the tax form that the business will use. Then a company's Chart of Accounts can be customized to track information needed for the tax form. The tax form used by the type of organization is listed below.

Type of Organization	Tax Form
Sole Proprietorship	Schedule C (Form 1040)
Partnership	Form 1065 & Schedule K-1
Corporation	Form 1120
S Corporation	Form 1120S

In this exercise, you will download a tax form from the Internal Revenue Service website.

Step 1: Go to the Internal Revenue Service website:
www.irs.gov

Step 2: As shown in the preceding table, a sole proprietorship files tax form Schedule C that is attached to the individual's Form 1040 tax form.

- **Print** the tax form Schedule C: Profit or Loss From Business (Sole Proprietorship).

- **Circle** Advertising Expense on the Schedule C.

Step 3: An S Corporation files Form 1120S.

- **Print** Form 1120S (S Corporation).

- **Circle** Advertising Expense on Form 1120S.

DELIVERABLES CHECKLIST CHAPTER 2
NAME:

INSTRUCTIONS:
1. CHECK OFF THE DELIVERABLES YOU COMPLETED.
2. ATTACH THIS PAGE TO YOUR DELIVERABLES.

CHAPTER 2
☐ Chart of Accounts (Account Listing)

EXERCISE 2.1
☐ Task 3: Statement of Cash Flows
☐ Task 4: To Do List

EXERCISE 2.2
☐ Task 3: Revised Chart of Accounts (Account Listing)

EXERCISE 2.3
☐ Schedule C Tax Form
☐ 1120S Tax Form

This **Deliverables Checklist** is also available online at www.mhhe.com/kay2010.

Appendix D: Electronic Deliverables contains instructions for saving your QuickBooks reports electronically. Download **Electronic Deliverables Excel Templates** at www.QuickBooksBlog.info.

Check with your instructor to see if you should deliver your reports electronically or in hard copy.

REFLECTION: A WISH AND A STAR ☆

Reflection improves learning and retention. Reflect on what you have learned after completing Chapter 2 that you did not know before you started the chapter.

A Star:

What did you like best that you learned about QuickBooks in Chapter 2?

A Wish:

If you could pick one thing, what do you wish you knew more about when using QuickBooks?

NOTES:

CHAPTER 3
BANKING

SCENARIO

The next morning as you pass the open door of Mr. Castle's office, you notice he is looking at the financial statements you prepared. You try to slip past his door unnoticed, but you take only a few steps when you hear him curtly call your name.

You turn to see Mr. Castle charging toward you with documents in hand.

"I need you to keep an eye on the bank accounts. Cash is the lifeblood of a business. A business can't survive if it doesn't have enough cash flowing through its veins to pay its bills. So it's very important that someone keep an eye on the cash in our bank accounts—the cash inflows into the accounts and the cash outflows from the accounts. That is your job now."

Handing you more documents, Mr. Castle continues, *"We fell behind on our bank reconciliations. Here is last month's bank statement that needs to be reconciled."*

CHAPTER 3
LEARNING OBJECTIVES

In Chapter 3, you will learn about the following QuickBooks features:

INTRODUCTION

In Chapter 3, you will learn about using QuickBooks to perform banking tasks, such as making deposits, writing checks, reconciling bank statements, and online banking.

Start QuickBooks by clicking on the **QuickBooks desktop icon** or click **Start > Programs > QuickBooks > QuickBooks Pro 2010**.

WORKFLOW

Use the Workflow approach if you are using the same computer and the same .QBW file from the prior chapter. Just as in a business, since you are using the same computer, you can continue to use the same .QBW file. Although you will make backups, you will not need to use the backup files unless your .QBW file fails.

Step 1: If your .QBW file is not already open, open it by selecting **File > Open Previous Company**. Select your **.QBW file.**

Step 2: Change the company name to **[your name] Chapter 3** by selecting **Company** menu > **Company Information.**

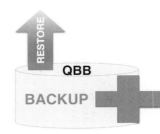

RESTART & RESTORE

Use the Restart & Restore approach if you are restarting your work session and moving your QuickBooks files between campus and home computers, for example. When you restart your work session, first you will restore the backup (.QBB) file.

Step 1: Restore the **Backup.QBB** file using the directions in *Appendix B: Back Up & Restore QuickBooks Files*.

You can restore:

A. Your .QBB file from the previous chapter. The advantage to using you own file is that your name is already included in the company name.

B. The Chapter 3 Backup.QBB data file that comes with the *Computer Accounting with QuickBooks* text (available on CD or download from the Online Learning Center). The advantage to using the data file provided with your text is that you avoid carrying forward any errors in your company file.

If the *QuickBooks Login* window appears with the User Name **Admin**:

- Leave the *User Name* field as **Admin**.
- Leave the *Password* field **blank**.
- Click **OK**.

Step 2: After restoring the file, change the company name to **[your name] Chapter 3** by selecting **Company** menu **> Company Information.**

BANKING NAVIGATION

If necessary, click the **Home** icon in the Icon bar to display the Home page.

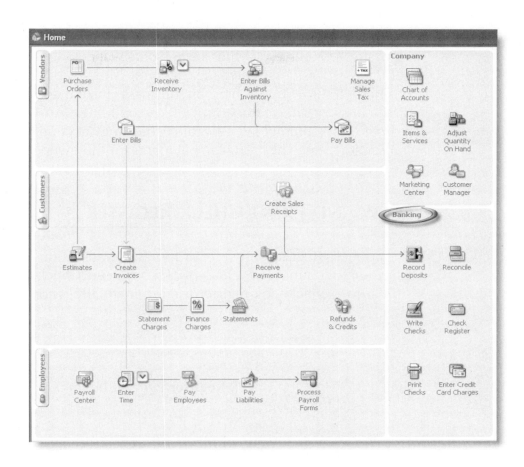

From the *Banking* section of the Home page, you can:

- Record deposits (cash flowing into the Checking account).
- Write checks (cash going out of the Checking account).
- Print checks.
- Reconcile bank statements.
- View Check Register.
- Enter credit card charges.

A business should establish a **business** checking account completely separate from the owner's **personal** checking account. The company's business checking account should be used *only* for business transactions, such as business insurance and mortgage payments for the company's office building. An owner should maintain a completely separate checking account for personal transactions, such as mortgage payments for the owner's home.

VIEW AND PRINT CHECK REGISTER

The Check Register is a record of all transactions affecting the Checking account. The QuickBooks onscreen Check Register looks similar to a checkbook register used to manually record deposits and checks.

To view the QuickBooks Check Register:

Step 1: Click the **Check Register** icon in the *Banking* section of the Home page.

Step 2: The following window will appear asking you to specify a bank account. Select **10100 [your name] Checking**, then click **OK**.

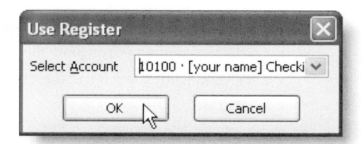

Step 3:   The following *Check Register* window should appear on your screen. Notice there are separate columns for:

- Payments (checks)
- Deposits
- Balance

If necessary, scroll up or down to locate the Sergeant Insurance entry or use the Go To feature.

Split indicates that a payment is split between two or more accounts.

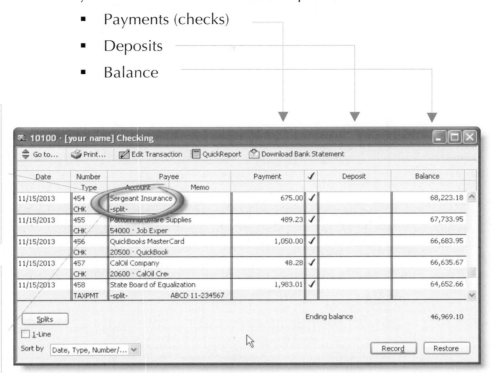

Small enterprises that have strictly cash-based operations sometimes simply use the Check Register to record all transactions. Such enterprises record payments and deposits directly into the Check Register using the Record button. However, most business enterprises require the more advanced features of the QuickBooks accounting software that are covered in the following chapters.

Step 4:   QuickBooks drill-down feature permits you to double-click some items to drill-down and view the supporting documents.

To view the check for the Sergeant Insurance transaction, double-click the **Sergeant Insurance** entry on **11/15/2013** in the Check Register.

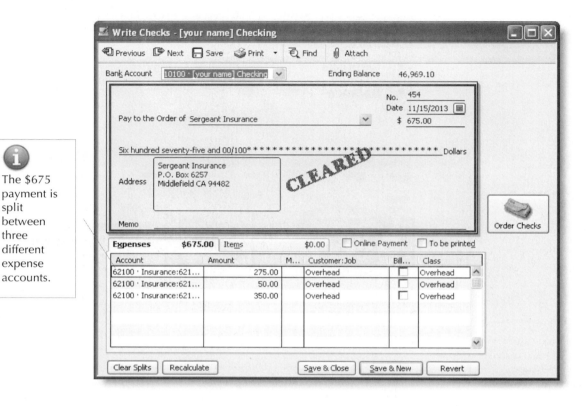

The $675 payment is split between three different expense accounts.

Step 5: The check is stamped *Cleared*, indicating it has already cleared the bank with funds paid to Sergeant Insurance.

Close the *Write Checks* window by clicking on the ⊠ in the upper right corner of the window.

If you wanted to double check to make certain the Sergeant Insurance bill had not been erroneously paid twice, you can use the QuickReport feature of the Check Register to view all payments to Sergeant Insurance.

Step 1: Display the Check Register. In the register, click on the **11/15/2013 Sergeant Insurance** payment for $675 to select it.

Step 2: Select the **QuickReport** button at the top of the *Check Register* window.

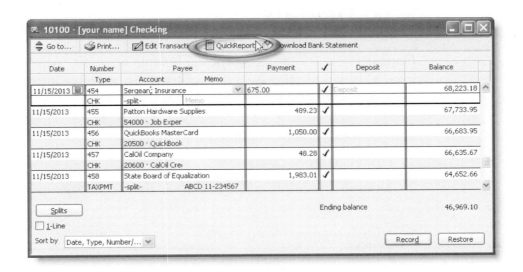

Step 3: When the *Register QuickReport* window appears:

- Enter Dates: **This Fiscal Year**.

- Select the appropriate print options, then click **Print**.

☑ ***This fiscal year's total for Sergeant Insurance is $-17,062.74.***

Step 4: ✏ **Circle** Check No. 454 to Sergeant Insurance dated 11/15/2013 on the printout.

Step 5: **Close** the *QuickReport* window and then the *Check Register* window by clicking the ⊠ in the upper right corner of each window.

You can record deposits and checks directly in the Check Register or use the *Make Deposits* window and the *Write Checks* window.

MAKE DEPOSITS

Deposits are additions to the Checking account. Any cash coming into a business should be recorded as a deposit to one of the company's accounts.

QuickBooks classifies deposits into two types:

1. Payments from customers.

2. Nonsales receipts (deposits other than customer payments) such as:

   - Cash received from loans.

   - Investments from owners.

   - Interest earned.

   - Other income, such as rental income.

Payments from customers are entered using the *Customer*s section of the Home page. For more information about recording payments from customers, see Chapter 4: Customers and Sales.

Deposits other than customer payments are recorded using the *Banking* section of the Home page.

Mr. Castle wants to invest an additional $72,000 in the business by depositing his $72,000 check in Rock Castle Construction's Checking account.

To record nonsales receipts (a deposit other than a customer payment):

Step 1: From the *Banking* section of the Home page, click the **Record Deposits** icon. The following *Payments to Deposit* window will appear.

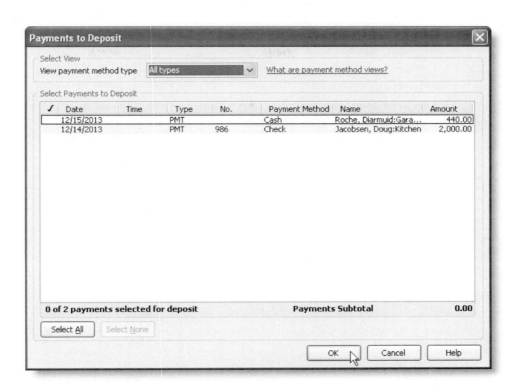

Step 2:   QuickBooks uses a two-step process to record payments received:

1. Record the payment received but not yet deposited (undeposited funds).

2. Record the deposit.

The payments listed in the *Payments to Deposit* window are undeposited funds that have been recorded as received but not yet deposited in the bank. Since these amounts will be deposited at a later time, confirm that none of the payments have been selected for deposit, then click **OK**.

Step 3:   When the following *Make Deposits* window appears, record Mr. Castle's $72,000 deposit as follows:

- Select Deposit To: **10100 [your name] Checking.**

- Select Date: **12/15/2013**.

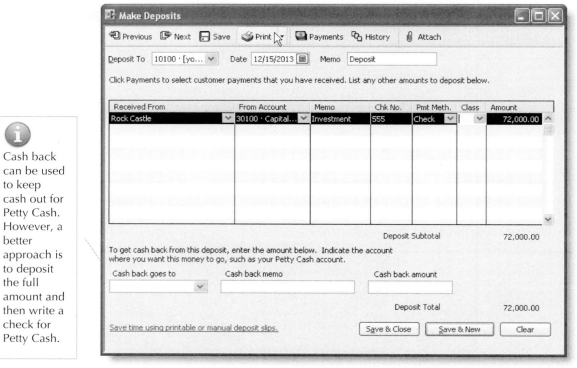

Cash back can be used to keep cash out for Petty Cash. However, a better approach is to deposit the full amount and then write a check for Petty Cash.

- Click in the *Received From* column and type: **Rock Castle**. Press the **Tab** key. When prompted, select **Quick Add** to add the name to the Name List.

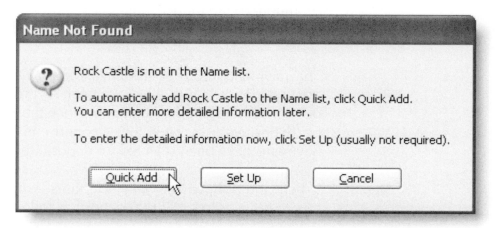

- Select Name Type: **Other**, then click **OK**.

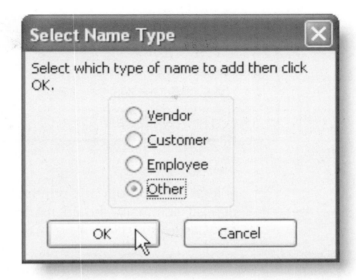

Select the account from the drop-down list or type **30100** and QuickBooks automatically completes the account title.

- Click in the *From Account* column. From the drop-down list of accounts, select **30100 Capital Stock**. Press **Tab**.

- Enter Memo: **Investment**.

- Enter Check No.: **555** (the number of Mr. Castle's check).

- From the Payment Method drop-down list, select **Check**.

- Enter Amount: **72000**. (QuickBooks will automatically enter the comma in the amount.)

Step 4:   QuickBooks permits you to print a deposit slip using a QuickBooks preprinted form and a deposit summary. Next, you will print a deposit summary.

To print a summary of the deposit you just recorded:

- Click the **Print** button at the top of the *Make Deposits* window.

- Select **Deposit summary only**. Then click **OK**.

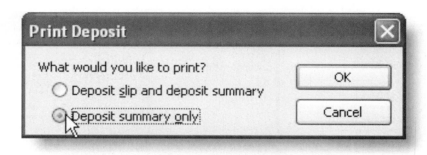

- Select the appropriate printer, then click **Print**. The deposit summary should list the $72,000 check from Mr. Castle.

  Mr. Castle's $72,000 investment in the company has now been recorded as a deposit in Rock Castle Construction's Checking account.

Step 5: Close the *Make Deposits* window by clicking the **Save & Close** button.

WRITE CHECKS

A business needs to track all cash paid out of the company's checking account. Examples of payments include purchases of inventory, office supplies, employee salaries, rent payments, and insurance payments.

Supporting documents (source documents) for payments include canceled checks, receipts, and paid invoices. These source documents provide proof that the transaction occurred; therefore, source documents should be kept on file for tax purposes.

QuickBooks provides two ways to pay bills:

One-step approach to bill paying:

❶ Record and pay the bill at the same time. When using this approach, the bill is paid when it is received.

Two-step approach to bill paying:

❶ Record the bill when it is received.

❷ Pay the bill later when it is due.

Covered in Chapter 3: Banking.

ONE-STEP APPROACH TO BILL PAYING

❶ Pay Bills When Received: Record bill and print check to pay bill.

QuickBooks:
1. Reduces the Checking account (credit).
2. Records an expense (debit).

Covered in Chapter 5: Vendors, Purchases, and Inventory.

TWO-STEP APPROACH TO BILL PAYING

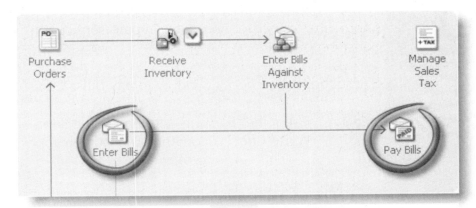

❶ Enter Bills: Record bills for services, such as utilities.

QuickBooks:
1. Records an expense (debit).
2. Records an obligation (liability) to pay later (credit).

❷ Pay Bills: Select bills to pay, then print checks.

When the bill is paid and the obligation fulfilled, QuickBooks:
1. Reduces the liability (debit).
2. Reduces the Checking account (credit).

The *Write Checks* window (One-Step Approach) should **not** be used to pay:

1. Paychecks to employees for wages and salaries. Instead, from the *Employees* section of the Home page, use the *Pay Employees* window.

2. Payroll taxes and liabilities. From the *Employees* section, use the *Pay Liabilities* window.

3. Sales taxes. From the *Vendors* section, use the *Pay Sales Taxes* window.

4. Bills already entered in the *Enter Bills* window. From the *Vendors* section, use the *Pay Bills* window.

The *Write Checks* window (One-Step Approach) can be used to pay:

1. Expenses, such as rent, utilities, and insurance.

2. Non-inventory items, such as office supplies.

3. Services, such as accounting or legal services.

In this chapter, you will use the *Write Checks* window (One-Step Approach) to pay a computer repair service bill for Rock Castle Construction.

To use the *Write Checks* window to pay bills:

> You can also open the *Write Checks* window by clicking the **Check** icon on the Icon bar.

Step 1: From the *Banking* section of the Home page, click the **Write Checks** icon and an onscreen check will appear.

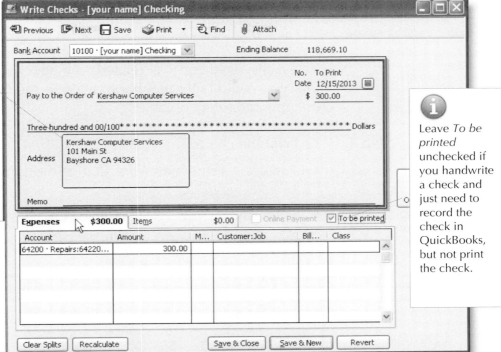

QuickBooks automatically completes the address using address information from the Vendor List.

If you use handwritten *and* computer-printed checks, to keep check numbers in sequence, set up 2 subaccounts for the Checking account:
1. Computer-printed checks subaccount.
2. Handwritten checks subaccount.

If you use more than one Checking account, change the Checking account color:
1. Edit menu.
2. Change Account Color.

Leave *To be printed* unchecked if you handwrite a check and just need to record the check in QuickBooks, but not print the check.

Step 2:   Enter the check information as follows:

- Select Bank Account: **[your name] Checking**.

- Select Date: **12/15/2013**.

- For the *Pay to the Order of* field, select: **Kershaw Computer Services**. (Select Kershaw from the drop-down list or type the first few letters of the name.)

- Enter the check amount: **300**.

- Click the checkbox preceding **To be printed** so that a check mark appears. This tells QuickBooks to both record and print the check. The *Check No.* field will now display: To Print.

Step 3:   Next, if necessary, record the payment in the correct account using the lower portion of the *Write Checks* window:

- Click the **Expenses** tab.

- Select Account: **64220 Repairs: Computer Repairs**. The $300 should automatically appear in the expense *Amount* column.

FYI: If the payment was related to a specific customer or job, you could enter that information in the *Customer: Job* column and select Billable.

Step 4:   🖨 **Print** the check:

- Click the **Print** button located at the top of the *Write Checks* window.

- Enter Check No.: **517**, then click **OK**.

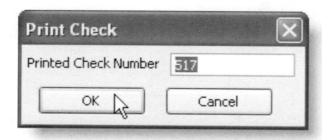

> ℹ️
>
> Instead of printing one check at a time, you can record all your checks and then print them all at once:
> 1. **File** menu
> 2. **Print Forms**
> 3. **Checks**

- If you are using the preprinted check forms, insert check forms in the printer now.

- Select Check Style: **Standard**.

- Select: **Print company name and address**.

- Select the appropriate printer.

- Click **Print**.

- Click **OK** if your check printed correctly. If you need to reprint any, select the appropriate checks, then click OK.

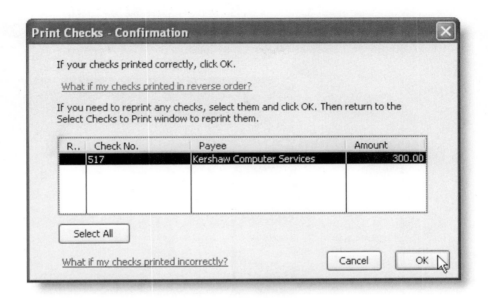

Step 5:   Click **Save & Close** to close the *Write Checks* window. QuickBooks automatically records the check in the Check Register.

PRINT JOURNAL

QuickBooks uses two different ways to enter information:

1. Onscreen forms, such as the onscreen check you just completed.

2. An onscreen Journal using debits and credits.

When you enter information into an onscreen form, QuickBooks automatically converts that information into a journal entry with debits and credits. If you will not be using the Journal, you may skip this section.

To view the journal entry for the check that you just recorded:

Step 1:   Click the **Report Center** icon in the Icon bar to open the *Report Center* window.

Step 2:   Select: **Accountant & Taxes**.

Step 3:   Select: **Journal**.

Step 4:   Set Dates: **Today** From: **12/15/2013** To: **12/15/2013**.

Step 5:   Select the **Display report** icon.

Step 6:   Your *Journal* window should appear as follows.

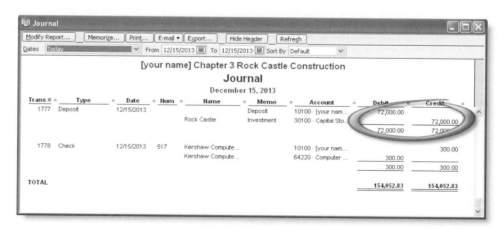

Step 7: The journal entry to record the deposit of Mr. Castle's $72,000 check includes a debit to the Checking account and a credit to Account 30100 Capital Stock.

The five different types of accounts are listed below along with the effects that debits and credits have on them.

Account Type	Debit/Credit	Effect on Balance
Asset	Debit	Increase
Liability	Credit	Increase
Owners' Equity	Credit	Increase
Revenues (Income)	Credit	Increase
Expenses	Debit	Increase

For example, the following summarizes information about debits and credits and their effects on account balances to record the deposit of an owner's investment in capital stock.

Account	Account Type	Debit/Credit	Effect on Balance
Checking	Asset	Debit	Increase
Capital Stock	Equity	Credit	Increase

Step 8: Notice the entry on 12/15/2013 to record the check written to Kershaw Computers for computer repair services. This entry debits (increases) the balance of the expense account, Computer Repairs, and credits (decreases) the Checking account balance.

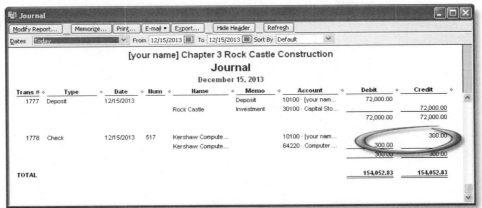

Step 9: Double-click on a journal entry, to *drill down* to the related source document. If you double-click on the journal entry that records the computer repair, the *Write Checks* window appears, displaying the onscreen check that you just prepared. **Close** the *Write Checks* window.

Step 10: Next, you will create a filter as follows:

- Click **Modify Report**.
- Click the **Filters** tab.
- Choose Filter: **Name**.
- From the drop-down Name List, select: **Kershaw Computer Services**.
- Click **OK** to close the *Modify Report: Journal* window.

Step 11: 🖨 **Print** the Journal report. Use **Landscape** orientation and check **Fit report to 1 page wide**.

Step 12: **Close** the *Journal* window and the *Report Center* window.

RECONCILE BANK STATEMENTS

Typically once a month, the bank sends a Checking account bank statement to you. The bank statement lists each deposit, check, and withdrawal from the account during the month.

A bank reconciliation is the process of comparing, or reconciling, the bank statement with your accounting records for the Checking account. The bank reconciliation has two objectives: (1) to detect errors and (2) to update your accounting records for unrecorded items listed on the bank statement (such as service charges).

Differences between the balance the bank reports on the bank statement and the balance the company shows in its accounting records usually arise for two reasons:

1. **Errors** (either the bank's errors or the company's errors).

2. **Timing differences.** This occurs when the company records an amount before the bank does or the bank records an amount before the company does. For example, the company may record a deposit in its accounting records, but the bank does not record the deposit before the company's bank statement is prepared and mailed.

    Timing differences include:

Items the bank has not recorded yet, such as:

- **Deposits in transit:** deposits the company has recorded but the bank has not.

- **Outstanding checks:** checks the company has written and recorded but the bank has not recorded yet.

Items the company has not recorded yet, such as:

- **Unrecorded charges:** charges that the bank has recorded on the bank statement but the company has not recorded in its accounting records yet. Unrecorded charges include service charges, loan payments, automatic withdrawals, and ATM withdrawals.

- **Interest earned on the account:** interest the bank has recorded as earned but the company has not recorded yet.

The following bank statement lists the deposits and checks for Rock Castle Construction according to the bank's records as of November 20, 2013.

BANK STATEMENT

Rock Castle Construction
1735 County Road
Bayshore, CA 94326

11-20-2013
Checking

Previous Balance	10-20-2013	$71,452.58
+ Deposits	0	0.00
- Checks	4	4,161.56
- Service Charge		10.00
+ Interest Paid		0.00
Ending Balance	11-20-2013	$67,281.02

Deposits

Date	Amount
	0.00

Checks Paid

Date	No.	Amount
10-31-2013	433	712.56
10-31-2013	436	24.00
11-14-2013	451	3,200.00
11-19-2013	460	225.00

Thank you for banking with us!

To reconcile this bank statement with Rock Castle's QuickBooks records, complete the following steps:

Step 1: From the *Banking* section of the Home page, click the **Reconcile** icon to display the *Begin Reconciliation* window shown below.

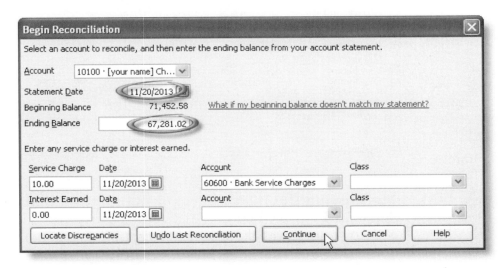

Step 2: Select Account to Reconcile: **[your name] Checking**.

Step 3: Enter date shown on the bank statement: **11/20/2013**.

Step 4: Compare the amount shown in the *Beginning Balance* field with the beginning (previous) balance of **$71,452.58** on the bank statement.

Step 5: In the *Ending Balance* field, enter the ending balance shown on the bank statement: **$67,281.02**.

Step 6: In the *Service Charge* field, enter the bank's service charge: **$10.00**. Then change the date to **11/20/2013** and select the Account: **Bank Service Charges**.

Step 7: Click **Continue**.

Click on deposits and checks that have cleared the bank and are listed on the bank statement.

If you use Online Banking, click the **Matched** button to reconcile online transactions and mark online transactions as cleared.

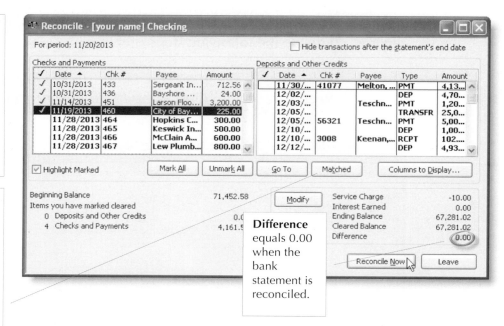

Step 8: To mark deposits that have been recorded by the bank, simply click on the deposit in the *Deposits and Other Credits* section of the *Reconcile* window.

Step 9: To mark checks and payments that have cleared the bank, simply click on the check in the *Checks and Payments* section of the *Reconcile* window.

Step 10: After marking all deposits and checks that appear on the bank statement, compare the Ending Balance and the Cleared Balance at the bottom of the *Reconcile* window.

 The Difference amount in the lower right corner of the Reconcile window should equal $0.00.

If the difference is $0.00, click **Reconcile Now**. (NOTE: If you are not finished and plan to return to this bank reconciliation later, click **Leave.)**

If there is a difference between the Ending Balance and the Cleared Balance, then try to locate the error or use QuickBooks Locate Discrepancies feature.

Step 11: When the *Select Reconciliation Report* window appears, select type of Reconciliation Report: **Detail**. Click **Display**. Then select **Print** or **Export** to generate the report.

Step 12: Circle the items on the bank reconciliation report that you marked as cleared for the November bank reconciliation.

You have now completed the November bank reconciliation for Rock Castle Construction.

ONLINE BANKING

QuickBooks offers an Online Banking feature so that you can conduct banking transactions online using the Internet.

To learn more about online banking:

Step 1: Display the **Check Register** for **[your name] Checking**.

Step 2: Click the **Download Bank Statement** button.

Step 3: Click **Continue** to use the Side-by-Side Mode and display the following *Online Banking Center* window.

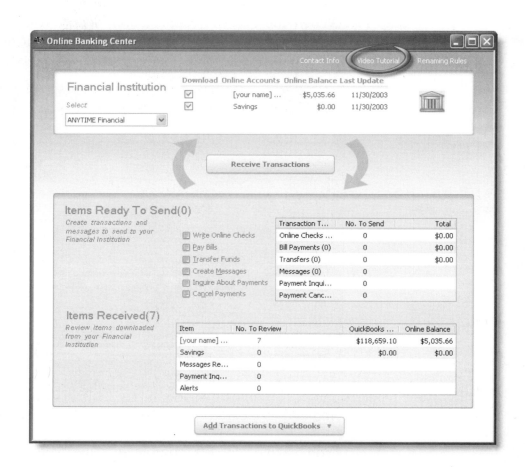

Step 4: Select **Video Tutorial** at the top of the *Online Banking Center* window.

Step 5: Play the online banking video tutorial, completing the onscreen tasks as required.

Step 6: When finished, close the online banking tutorial. Close the Online Banking Center and the Check Register.

SAVE CHAPTER 3

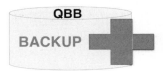

Save a backup of your Chapter 3 file using the file name: **[your name] Chapter 3 Backup.QBB**. See *Appendix B: Back Up & Restore QuickBooks Files* for instructions.

WORKFLOW

If you are using the workflow approach, leave your .QBW file open and proceed directly to Exercise 3.1.

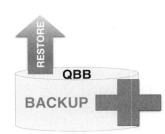

RESTART & RESTORE

If you are using the Restart & Restore approach and are ending your computer session now, close your .QBW file and exit QuickBooks. When you restart, you will restore your backup file to complete Exercise 3.1.

PODCASTS

Watch the Chapter 3 **Podcast** at www.QuickBooksBlog.info to view a screencast of QuickBooks banking features.

MULTIPLE-CHOICE PRACTICE TEST

A **Multiple-Choice Practice Test** for Chapter 3 is on the *Computer Accounting for QuickBooks Pro* Online Learning Center at www.mhhe.com/kay2010. Try the Practice Test and see how many questions you answer correctly.

EXTRAS!

Section 3: Quick Guide contains quick, easy step-by-step directions for frequently used QuickBooks tasks, including correcting errors. You can find *Quick Guide* at the back of your text or online at www.mhhe.com/kay2010. *Check it out!*

Deliverables Checklist is a list of the reports and documents that you are to deliver to your instructor for grading. You can find the Chapter 3 Deliverables Checklist at the end of the chapter or online at www.mhhe.com/kay2010. Staying organized saves time. Use the checklist to organize your reports, checking off the reports as completed. Then include the checklist with your reports for grading.

Appendix D: Electronic Deliverables shows you how to save your QuickBooks reports electronically. Also, watch the Electronic Deliverables Podcast at www.QuickBooksBlog.info. Check with your instructor to see if you should deliver your reports electronically.

Join the QuickBooks Student Community to connect to other QuickBooks accounting students @ www.QuickBooksBlog.info.

LEARNING ACTIVITIES

Important: Ask your instructor whether you should complete the following assignments by printing requested reports or creating electronic deliverables (see Appendix D: Electronic Deliverables).

EXERCISE 3.1:
MAKE DEPOSIT, VOID CHECK, AND WRITE CHECK

SCENARIO

As you glance up from your work, you notice Mr. Castle charging past your cubicle with more documents in hand. He tosses a hefty stack of papers into your creaking inbox. *"Here is another deposit to record. Also, Washuta called to say they did not receive the check we sent them. You will need to void that check—I believe it was check no. 470. I have already called the bank and stopped payment. Also, here are more bills to pay."*

TASK 1: OPEN COMPANY FILE

WORKFLOW

If you are using the Workflow approach, you will use the same .QBW file.

If your QBW file is not already open, open it by selecting **File > Open Previous Company**. Select your **.QBW file.**

Change the company name to **[your name] Exercise 3.1** by selecting **Company** menu > **Company Information.**

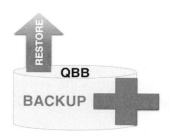

RESTART & RESTORE

If you are not using the same computer, you must use the Restart and Restore approach.

Restore your **Chapter 3 Backup.QBB** file using the directions in *Appendix B: Back Up & Restore QuickBooks Files*.

After restoring the file, change the company name to **[your name] Exercise 3.1** by selecting **Company** menu > **Company Information.**

TASK 2: MAKE DEPOSIT

Step 1: Record the deposit for Mr. Castle's $1,000 check (No. 556). Record the deposit in Account 30100 Capital Stock with a deposit date of 12/15/2013.

Step 2: 🖶 **Print** the deposit summary.

TASK 3: FIND CHECK

Find Check No. 470 made out to Washuta & Son in the QuickBooks Check Register by completing the following steps.

Step 1: View the Check Register. (Click **Check Register** icon in the *Banking* section of the Home page.)

Step 2: Next, search the Check Register for Check No. 470 using the Go To feature. Click the **Go to** button in the upper left corner of the *Check Register* window.

Step 3: In the *Go To* window:

- Select Which Field: **Number/Ref.**

- Enter Search For: **470**.

Step 4: Click the **Next** button. If asked if you want to search from the beginning, click **Yes**.

Step 5: Check No. 470 on 11/28/2013 to Washuta & Son Painting should appear in the *Check Register* window.

Step 6: **Close** the *Go To* window.

Step 7: To view Check No. 470, double-click on the Check Register entry for Washuta & Son Painting to drill down to the check. After viewing the check, **close** the *Check* window.

TASK 4: VOID CHECK

The next task is to void Check No. 470. There are two ways to remove a check amount from the Check Register:

1. Delete the check: This removes all record of the transaction.

2. Void the check: QuickBooks changes the amount deducted in the Check Register to zero, but the voided check still appears in the Check Register, thus leaving a record of the transaction. Should questions arise later about the transaction, a voided check provides a better record than a deleted check.

For Check No. 470, you want to maintain a record of the transaction; therefore, you want to void the check rather than delete it.

Void Check No. 470 by completing the following steps:

Step 1: Select **Check No. 470** in the Check Register, then click **Edit *on the Menu bar***. (***Note:*** There is an Edit Transaction button in the *Checking* window and an Edit button on the Menu bar. Use the *Edit button on the Menu bar*.)

Step 2: Select **Void Bill Pmt - Check**. VOID should now appear next to Check No. 470 in the Check Register.

Step 3: Click the **Record** button in the lower right corner of the *Check Register* window.

Step 4: When asked if you are sure you want to record the voided check, click **Yes**.

Step 5: 🖨 **Print** the Check Register for 11/28/2013.

Step 6: ✏ **Circle** Check No. 470 on the Check Register printout and verify that Check No. 470 is void, showing a check amount of $0.00.

Step 7: **Close** the *Check Register* window.

TASK 5: WRITE CHECK

Step 1: Write checks to pay the following bills and save.

Check No.	Select: To be printed
Date	12/15/2013
Vendor	Express Delivery Service
Amount	$45.00
Expense Account	54520 Freight & Delivery

Check No.	Select: To be printed
Date	12/15/2013
Vendor	Davis Business Associates
Amount	$200.00
Expense Account	60410 Advertising Expense

Step 2: 🖨 **Print** checks in a batch as follows:

- Click the down arrow by the **Print** button in the *Write Checks* window. Select **Print Batch**.

- When the *Select Checks to Print* window appears, **select only the preceding two checks that you entered**. Your total for checks to print should be $245.00

- First Check Number is **518**.

- Click **OK**.

- Select **Standard** check style.

- Select **Print company name and address**.
- Click **Print**.

TASK 6: SAVE EXERCISE 3.1

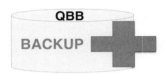

Save a backup of your Exercise 3.1 file using the file name: **[your name] Exercise 3.1 Backup.QBB** . See *Appendix B: Back Up & Restore QuickBooks Files* for instructions.

WORKFLOW

If you are proceeding to Exercise 3.2 and using the same computer, you can leave your .QBW file open and use it for Exercise 3.2.

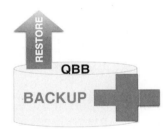

RESTART & RESTORE

If you are stopping your QuickBooks work session and changing computers, you will need to restore your .QBB file when you restart.

EXERCISE 3.2: BANK RECONCILIATION

SCENARIO

When you arrive at work the next morning, Rock Castle Construction's December bank statement is on your desk with the following note from Mr. Castle attached.

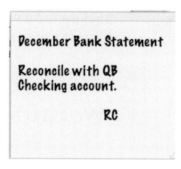

December Bank Statement

Reconcile with QB
Checking account.

RC

TASK 1: OPEN COMPANY FILE

WORKFLOW

If you are using the Workflow approach, you will use the same .QBW file.

If your QBW file is not already open, open it by selecting **File > Open Previous Company**. Select your **.QBW file.**

Change the company name to **[your name] Exercise 3.2** by selecting **Company** menu **> Company Information.**

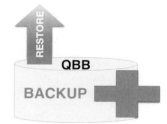

RESTART & RESTORE

If you are using the Restart and Restore approach, restore your backup file using the directions in *Appendix B: Back Up & Restore QuickBooks Files*.

After restoring the file, change the company name to **[your name] Exercise 3.2** by selecting **Company** menu **> Company Information.**

TASK 2: PRINT PREVIOUS BANK STATEMENT

If the difference between the Ending Balance and the Cleared Balance is not zero, and you want to return to the bank reconciliation later, do NOT click *Reconcile Now*. Instead, click **Leave**.

⊞ **Print** the previous bank reconciliation as follows:

Step 1:   Click **Report Center > Banking > Previous Reconciliation**. Select **Display report** icon.

Step 2:   Select Type of Report: **Summary**.

Step 3:   Select: **Transactions cleared at the time of reconciliation**.

Step 4:   Click **Display**.

Step 5:   ⊞ **Print** the Reconciliation Summary report.

TASK 3: RECONCILE BANK STATEMENT

After you click **Reconcile Now**, you can return to this Bank Reconciliation by selecting **Reports** menu > **Banking > Previous Reconciliation**.

Another way to change the status of a cleared item:
1. Display the Check Register.
2. Click the Cleared Status column until the appropriate status (cleared or uncleared) appears.

Reconcile Rock Castle's December bank statement that appears on the following page. If necessary, change the Statement Date and Service Charge Date to **12/20/2013**.

In the Reconcile window (lower left corner) "Items you have marked cleared" should agree with the December bank statement:

10 Deposits and Other Credits	**$58,413.56**
12 Checks and Payments	**$15,996.28**
Ending Balance	**$109,688.30**
Cleared Balance	**$109,688.30**
Difference	**$ 0.00**

TASK 4: PRINT BANK RECONCILIATION REPORT

⊞ **Print** a Summary Reconciliation report.

BANK STATEMENT		
Rock Castle Construction	12-20-2013	Checking Account
Previous Balance	11-20-2013	$67,281.02
+ Deposits	10	58,413.56
- Checks	12	15,996.28
- Service Charge	1	10.00
+ Interest Paid		0.00
Current Balance	12-20-2013	$109,688.30

Deposits	
Date	**Amount**
11-30-2013	4,135.50
12-02-2013	4,706.01
12-03-2013	1,200.00
12-05-2013	5,000.00
12-05-2013	25,000.00
12-10-2013	102.65
12-10-2013	1,000.00
12-12-2013	4,936.12
12-14-2013	4,700.00
12-15-2013	7,633.28

Checks Paid		
Date	**No.**	**Amount**
11-28-2013	464	300.00
11-28-2013	465	500.00
11-28-2013	466	600.00
11-28-2013	467	800.00
11-28-2013	468	6,790.00
11-28-2013	469	2,000.00
11-30-2013	471	24.00
11-30-2013	472	656.23
11-30-2013	473	686.00
11-30-2013	474	218.00
11-30-2013	475	2,710.90
12-01-2013	476	711.15

Thank you for banking with us!

TASK 5: SAVE EXERCISE 3.2

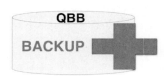

Save a backup of your Exercise 3.2 file using the file name: **[your name] Exercise 3.2 Backup.QBB**. See *Appendix B: Back Up & Restore QuickBooks Files* for instructions.

WORKFLOW

If you are using the Workflow approach, you can leave your .QBW file open and use it for the next chapter.

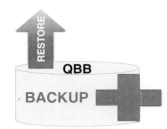

RESTART & RESTORE

If you are stopping your QuickBooks work session and changing computers, you will need to restore your .QBB file when you restart.

EXERCISE 3.3: WEB QUEST

Various preprinted check forms and deposit slips are available from Intuit. These preprinted forms can be used with your printer to create checks and deposit slips.

THE WEB INFORMATION LISTED IS SUBJECT TO CHANGE.

Step 1: Go to www.quickbooks.com.

Step 2: Locate and 🖨 **print** information about preprinted checks and deposits slips.

Step 3: ✍ Using word processing software or e-mail software, prepare and 🖨 **print** a short e-mail to Mr. Castle recommending which check forms and deposit slips Rock Castle Construction should purchase for use with QuickBooks.

DELIVERABLES CHECKLIST CHAPTER 3
NAME:

INSTRUCTIONS:
1. CHECK OFF THE DELIVERABLES YOU HAVE COMPLETED.
2. TURN IN THIS PAGE WITH YOUR DELIVERABLES.

CHAPTER 3

- ☐ Check Register
- ☐ Deposit Summary
- ☐ Check
- ☐ Journal
- ☐ Bank Reconciliation Report

EXERCISE 3.1

- ☐ Task 2: Deposit Summary
- ☐ Task 4: Check Register
- ☐ Task 5: Checks

EXERCISE 3.2

- ☐ Task 2: Previous Bank Statement Report
- ☐ Task 4: Bank Reconciliation Report

EXERCISE 3.3

- ☐ QuickBooks Preprinted Forms

This **Deliverables Checklist** is also available online at www.mhhe.com/kay2010.

Appendix D: Electronic Deliverables contains instructions for saving your QuickBooks reports electronically. Download **Electronic Deliverables Excel Templates** at www.QuickBooksBlog.info.

Check with your instructor to see if you should deliver your reports electronically or in hard copy.

REFLECTION: A WISH AND A STAR ✭

Reflection improves learning and retention. Reflect on what you have learned after completing Chapter 3 that you did not know before you started the chapter.

A Star:

What did you like best that you learned about QuickBooks in Chapter 3?

A Wish:

If you could pick one thing, what do you wish you knew more about when using QuickBooks?

NOTES:

CHAPTER 4
CUSTOMERS AND SALES

SCENARIO

Just as you are finishing the last bank reconciliation, Mr. Castle reappears. He always seems to know just when you are about to finish a task.

"While cash flow is crucial to our survival," he says, *"we also need to keep an eye on profits. We are in the business of selling products and services to our customers. We have to be certain that we charge customers enough to cover our costs and make a profit."*

Mr. Castle pulls out a pen and begins scribbling on a sheet of paper on your desk:

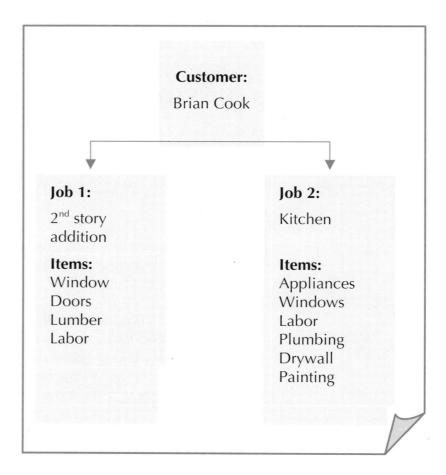

"We track the costs of each job we work on. A job is a project for a specific customer. For example, we are working on two jobs for Brian Cook: Job 1 is a second story addition and Job 2 is a kitchen remodeling job.

"In QuickBooks we use items to track the products and services we use on each project. On the 2nd story addition job we used four different items."

Pushing a stack of papers toward you, Mr. Castle says, "Here are some customer transactions that need to be recorded in QuickBooks."

CHAPTER 4
LEARNING OBJECTIVES

In Chapter 4, you will learn about the following QuickBooks features:

INTRODUCTION

In Chapter 4, you will learn how to use QuickBooks software to record customer transactions, including sales to customers and collection of customer payments. Furthermore, you will learn about financial reports that will help you manage your sales.

Start QuickBooks by clicking on the **QuickBooks desktop icon** or click **Start > Programs > QuickBooks > QuickBooks Pro 2010**.

WORKFLOW

Use the Workflow approach if you are using the same computer and the same .QBW file from Exercise 3.2 of the prior chapter.

Step 1: If your .QBW file is not already open, open it by selecting **File > Open Previous Company**. Select your **.QBW file.**

Step 2: Change the company name to **[your name] Chapter 4** by selecting **Company** menu > **Company Information.**

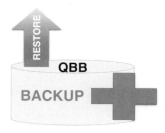

RESTART & RESTORE

Use the Restart & Restore approach if you are restarting your work session.

Step 1: Restore the **Backup.QBB** file using the directions in *Appendix B: Back Up & Restore QuickBooks Files*.

You can restore your .QBB file from the previous chapter or the Chapter 4 Backup.QBB data file that comes with the *Computer Accounting with QuickBooks* text (available on CD or download from the Online Learning Center).

If the *QuickBooks Login* window appears with the User Name **Admin**:

- Leave the *User Name* field as **Admin**.
- Leave the *Password* field **blank**.
- Click **OK**.

Step 2: After restoring the file, change the company name to **[your name] Chapter 4** by selecting **Company** menu > **Company Information**.

CUSTOMER NAVIGATION

If necessary, click the **Home** icon in the Icon bar to display the Home page.

❶ Customer pays with cash, check, or credit card at time of sale.

❷ Customer buys on credit and then pays later.

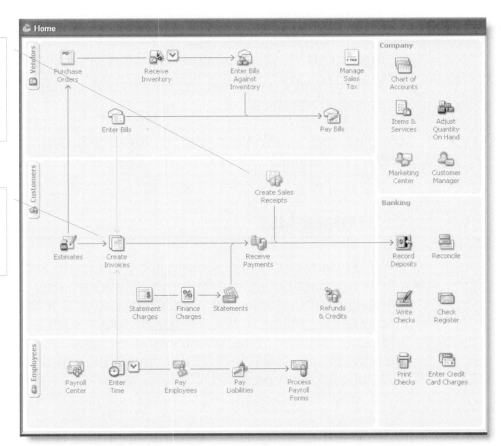

The *Customers* section of the Home page is a flowchart of customer transactions. As the flowchart indicates, Rock Castle Construction can record a customer sale in two different ways:

❶ **Create Sales Receipts.** The customer pays when Rock Castle Construction provides the good or service to the customer. The customer pays with cash, check, or credit card at the time of sale. The sale is recorded on a sales receipt.

❷ **Create Invoice/Receive Payment.** The sale is recorded on an invoice when the good or service is provided to the customer. The customer promises to pay later. These customer promises are called *accounts receivable* — amounts that Rock Castle Construction expects to *receive* in the future. The customer may pay its account with cash, check, credit card, or online payment.

Other QuickBooks features available from the *Customers* section include:

- **Finance Charges**. Add finance charges to customer bills whenever bills are not paid by the due date.

- **Statements**. Prepare billing statements to send to customers.

- **Refunds and Credits**. Record refunds and credits for returned or damaged merchandise.

The first step in working with customer transactions is to enter customer information in the Customer List.

CUSTOMER LIST

The Customer List contains customer information such as address, telephone number, and credit terms. Once customer information is entered in the Customer List, QuickBooks automatically transfers the customer information to the appropriate forms, such as sales invoices and sales returns. This feature enables you to enter customer information only once instead of entering the customer information each time a form is prepared.

The Customer List in QuickBooks also tracks projects (jobs) for each customer. For example, Rock Castle Construction is working on two projects for Brian Cook:

Job 1: 2nd Story Addition

Job 2: Kitchen

VIEW CUSTOMER LIST

To view the Customer List for Rock Castle Construction:

Step 1:   Click the **Customer Center** icon in the Icon bar.

Step 2:   The following *Customer Center* appears, listing customers and jobs. Notice the two jobs listed for Brian Cook: (1) 2nd story addition and (2) Kitchen.

The Customers & Jobs List displays:

- The customer name.

- The job name.

- The balance for each job.

To view additional information about a customer, click the customer or job name. The *Customer/Job Information* section displays:

- Customer address and contact information.

- Transaction information for the customer.

- Estimate information (if an estimate for the job was prepared).

- Notes about the job.

ADD NEW CUSTOMER

Rock Castle Construction needs to add a new customer, Tom Whalen, to the Customer List.

To add a new customer to the Customer List:

Step 1: Click the **New Customer & Job** button at the top of the Customer Center.

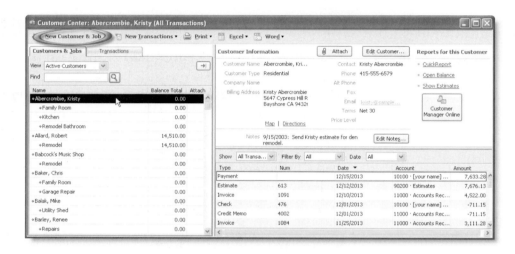

Step 2: Click **New Customer** on the drop-down menu.

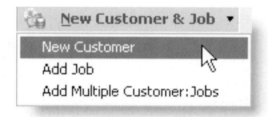

Step 3: The follow *New Feature* window may appear describing how you can add and edit multiple list entries using Excel and QuickBooks. This feature permits you to paste from Excel into QuickBooks software to speed up adding and editing list entries. Select **Do not display this message in the future**. Click **OK**.

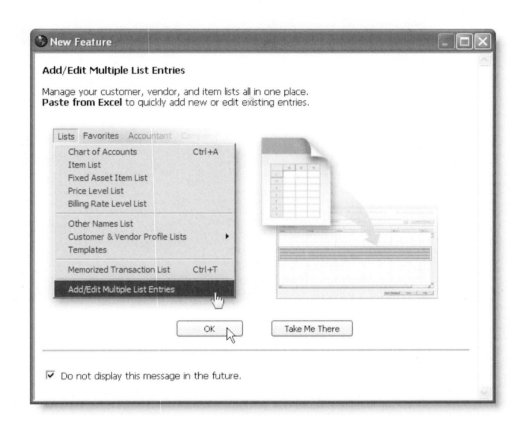

Step 4: A blank *New Customer* window should appear. Enter the information shown below in the *New Customer | Address Info* window.

Customer	Whalen, Tom
Mr./Ms./...	Mr.
First Name	Tom
M.I.	M
Last Name	Whalen
Contact	Tom Whalen
Phone	415-555-1234
Alt. Ph.	415-555-5678
Addresses **Bill To**	100 Sunset Drive Bayshore, CA 94326

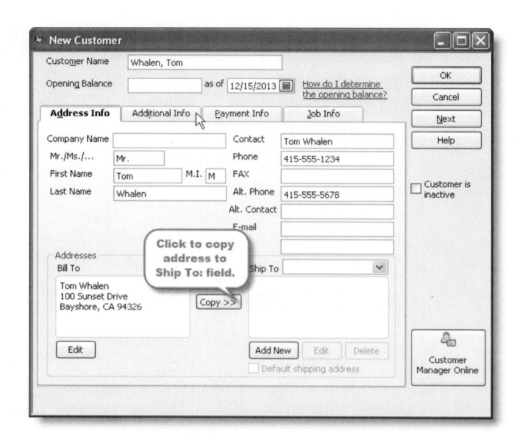

Step 5:   Click the **Additional Info** tab to display another customer information window. Enter the following information into the *Additional Info* fields.

Type	Residential
Terms	Net 30
Tax Item	San Tomas
Tax Code	Tax

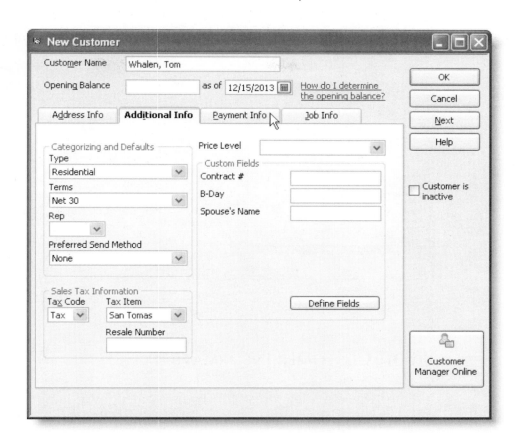

Step 6: To enter payment information for the customer, click the **Payment Info** tab.

Step 7: Enter the following information in the *Payment Info* fields:

Account	7890
Credit Limit	50,000
Preferred Payment	Check

Step 8: Click **OK** to add the new customer to Rock Castle Construction's Customer List.

Step 9:   Click the **Name bar** to alphabetize the Customer List.

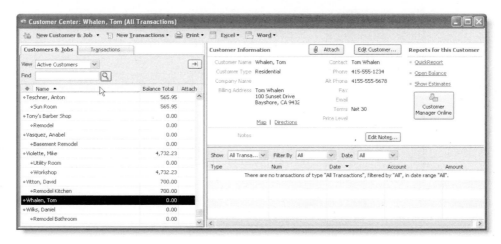

EDIT CUSTOMER INFORMATION

Enter the e-mail address for Tom Whalen by editing the customer information as follows:

Step 1:   Select **Tom Whalen** in the *Customers & Jobs* window.

Or **Right-click > Edit Customer: Job.**

Step 2:   Click   the   **Edit   Customer**   button   in   the   *Customer Information* window.

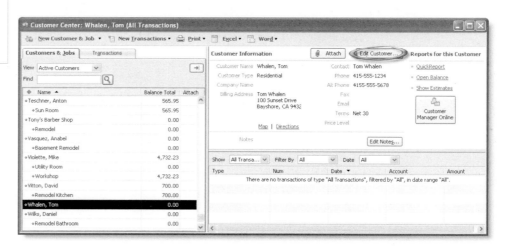

Step 3:   When the *Edit Customer* window appears, enter or revise the customer or job information as needed. In this instance, click the **Address Info** tab. Then enter the e-mail address: **twhalen@www.com**.

Step 4:   Click **OK** to record the new information and close the *Edit Customer* window.

ADD A JOB

To add the Screen Porch job for Tom Whalen, complete the following steps:

Step 1:   Click on the customer, **Tom Whalen**, in the *Customers & Jobs* window.

Or **Right-click > Add Job.**

Step 2:   Click the **New Customer & Job** button at the top of the *Customer Center* window. Select **Add Job** from the drop-down menu.

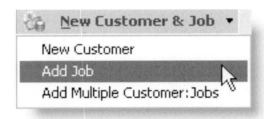

Step 3:   In the *New Job* window, enter the Job Name: **Screen Porch**. Then enter the Opening Balance: **0.00**.

Step 4:   Click the **Job Info** tab.

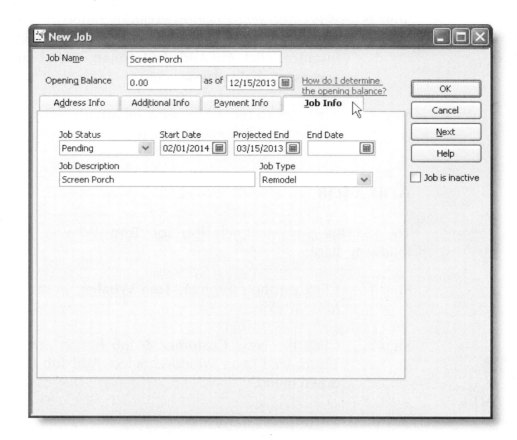

Step 5: Enter the following information in the *Job Info* fields:

Job Status	Pending
Start Date	02/01/2014
Projected End	03/15/2014
Job Description	Screen Porch
Job Type	Remodel

Tom Whalen tells Rock Castle Construction that he will hire them to do the screen porch job on one condition—he needs Rock Castle Construction as soon as possible to replace a damaged exterior door that will not close. Rock Castle sends a workman out to begin work on replacing the door right away.

To add the Exterior Door job:

Step 1: From the *Screen Porch Job* window, click **Next** to add another job.

Step 2: In the *Job Name* field at the top of the *New Job* window, enter: **Exterior Door**. Enter Opening Balance: **0.00**.

Step 3: Click the **Job Info** tab, then enter the following information.

Job Status	Awarded
Start Date	12/15/2013
Projected End	12/18/2013
Job Description	Replace Exterior Door
Job Type	Repairs

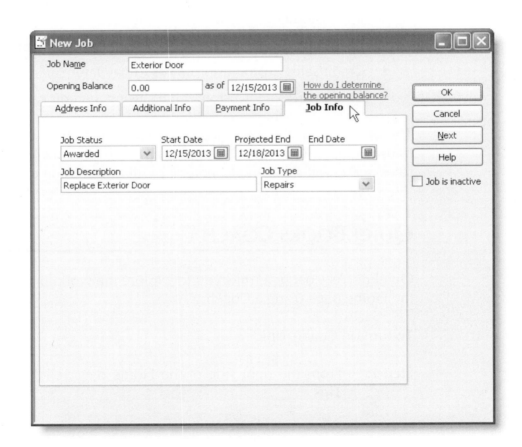

Step 4: Click **OK** to record the new job and close the *New Job* window.

Step 5: As shown below, Rock Castle Construction's Customer List should now list two jobs for Tom Whalen: Exterior Door and Screen Porch. **Close** the *Customer Center* window.

◇Whalen, Tom	0.00
◇Exterior Door	0.00
◇Screen Porch	0.00

RECORDING SALES IN QUICKBOOKS

How you record a sale in QuickBooks depends upon how the customer pays for the goods or services. There are three possible ways for a customer to pay for goods and services:

- Cash sale: Customer pays cash (or check) at the time of sale.

- Credit sale: Customer promises to pay later.

- Credit card sale: Customer pays using a credit card.

The diagrams on the following pages summarize how to record sales transactions in QuickBooks. This chapter covers how to record cash sales and credit sales and Chapter 12 will cover credit card sales.

QUICKBOOKS COACH

QuickBooks Coach permits you to explore the workflows shown on the Home page using a Coach.

To turn on Coach Tips:

Step 1: From the right side of the Home page, click **Show Coach Tips**.

Step 2: To spotlight the workflow, click a Coach icon. To see a Coach tip about a form, position your mouse (pointer) over any spotlighted form.

For example, to spotlight the workflow for cash sales, click the **Coach** icon  beside **Create Sales Receipts**.

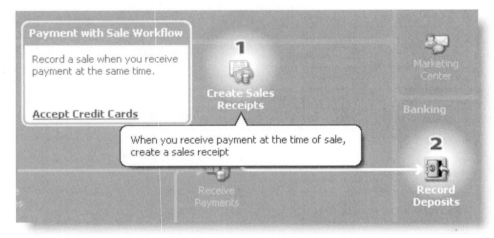

> ⓘ Use the Sales Receipt form to record a daily or weekly sales summary. For more information about using sales summaries, use QuickBooks Help.

Step 3: To spotlight the workflow for credit sales that are invoiced, click the **Coach** icon beside **Create Invoices**.

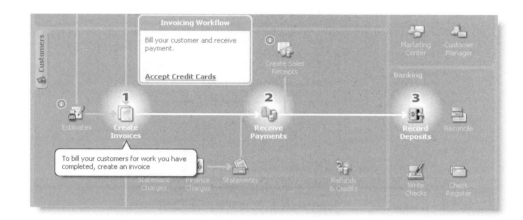

Step 4: Although you can leave the Explore Workflow and Coach Tips displayed while using QuickBooks, if you prefer to hide the Coach Tips, click **Hide Coach Tips** in the *QuickBooks Coach* window.

CASH SALES

When a customer pays for goods or services at the time the good or service is provided, it is typically called a cash sale.

Recording a cash sale in QuickBooks requires two steps:

> **1. Create Sales Receipts.** Create a sales receipt to record the cash sale.

> **2. Record Deposits.** Record the bank deposit.

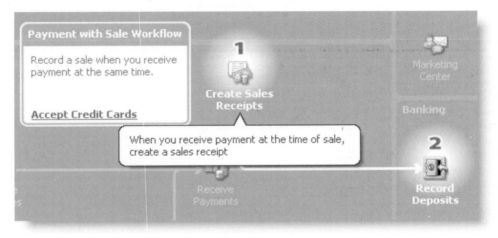

One of Rock Castle Construction's customers, Ernesto Natiello, wants to purchase an extra set of cabinet pulls that match the cabinets that Rock Castle Construction installed. Ernesto pays $10 in cash for the extra cabinet pulls.

To record the cash sale in QuickBooks:

Step 1: From the *Customers* section of the Home page, click **Create Sales Receipts** to display the *Enter Sales Receipts* window. Close the *Customize Your QuickBooks Forms* window if it opens. If asked if you would like to complete the Payment Interview, select **No**.

Step 2: Enter the following information in the *Enter Sales Receipts* window:

- Enter Customer: **Natiello, Ernesto**.
- Select Date: **12/15/2013**.

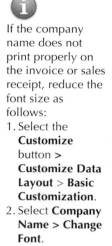

If the company name does not print properly on the invoice or sales receipt, reduce the font size as follows:
1. Select the **Customize** button > **Customize Data Layout** > **Basic Customization**.
2. Select **Company Name** > **Change Font**.
3. Select font size **8** or **10**.

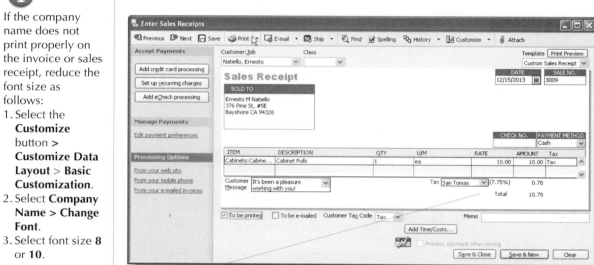

Since type of customer (an individual) and item are subject to tax, QuickBooks automatically calculates and adds the sales tax.

- Select Payment Method: **Cash**.
- Select Item: **Cabinet Pulls**.
- Select Quantity: **1**.
- Enter Rate: **10.00**.
- Select Customer Message: **It's been a pleasure working with you!**
- Select **To be printed** checkbox.

Step 3: 🖶 **Print** the sales receipt:

- Click the **Print** button at top of the *Sales Receipts* window.
- Select Print on: **Blank paper**.

- If necessary, uncheck: **Do not print lines around each field**.
- Click **Print**.

Step 4: Click **Save & Close** to record the cash sale and close the *Enter Sales Receipts* window.

QuickBooks will record the $10.78 as undeposited funds. Later, you will record this as a bank deposit to Rock Castle's Checking account.

CREDIT SALES

Credit sales occur when Rock Castle Construction provides goods and services to customers and in exchange receives a promise that the customers will pay later. This promise to pay is called an account receivable because Rock Castle expects to *receive* the account balance in the future.

Recording a credit sale in QuickBooks requires three steps:

1. **Create Invoices.** Create an invoice to bill the customer for the product or service provided. QuickBooks records accounts receivable and the sales amount.

2. **Receive Payments.** Receive payment from the customer. QuickBooks reduces accounts receivable and increases undeposited funds.

3. **Record Deposits.** Deposit the customer's payment in the bank.

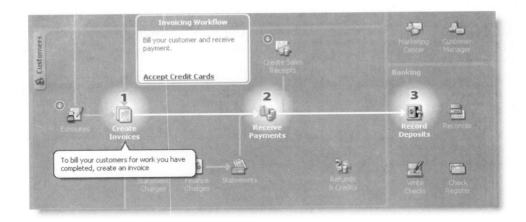

CREDIT SALES: CREATE INVOICES

An invoice is used to record sales on credit when the customer will pay later. An invoice is a bill that contains detailed information about the items (products and services) provided to a customer.

For more information about time tracking, see Chapter 6.

If QuickBooks' time-tracking feature (tracking time worked on each job) is *not* used, then time worked on a job is entered directly on the invoice. In this chapter, assume that time tracking is not used and that time worked on a job is entered on the invoice form.

Next, you will create an invoice for Rock Castle Construction. Rock Castle sent a workman to the Whalen residence immediately after receiving the phone call from Tom Whalen requesting an exterior door replacement as soon as possible. The workman spent one hour at the site the first day.

Click the **Estimates** icon to create a customer estimate using QuickBooks.

In this instance, Rock Castle Construction was not asked to provide an estimate before starting the work. Charges for products and labor used on the Whalen door replacement job will be recorded on an invoice.

To create an invoice to record charges:

Add new customers from the *Invoices* window: Select **Add New** from the Customer drop-down list.

Step 1: In the *Customers* section of the Home page, click the **Create Invoices** icon to display the *Create Invoices* window.

Step 2: Select the Template: **Rock Castle Invoice**.

Step 3: Enter the Customer:Job by selecting **Whalen, Tom: Exterior Door** from the drop-down Customer & Job List. Make certain to select the customer name and the correct job: Exterior Door.

To record customer charges as work is performed but before final billing, mark the sales invoice as pending.

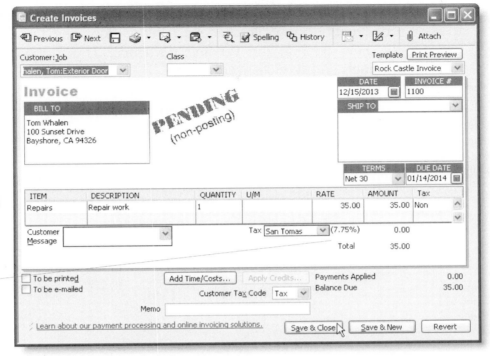

No sales tax on labor.

Step 4: Enter charges for the service provided the customer:

- Select Item: **Repairs.** Press **Tab.**

- Description should automatically display: Repair work.

- Enter Quantity: **1** (hour).

- The Rate should automatically display $35.00.

- The Amount should automatically display $35.00.

- From the drop-down list, select Tax: **Non-Taxable Sales**.

Step 5: You will wait until the job is complete to print the invoice. In the meantime, you will mark the invoice as pending:

- **Right-click** to display the pop-up menu.

- Select: **Mark Invoice As Pending**.

Step 6: If you wanted to enter another invoice, you would click **Save & New**. Instead, click **Save & Close** to close the *Create Invoices* window.

A **Progress Invoice** is used if the customer is billed as the work progresses rather than when the work is fully completed.

See **Correcting Errors** in the **Quick Guide** if you would like assistance correcting mistakes.

To print envelopes for invoices and shipping labels, click the down arrow by the Print icon.

Later in the day on December 15, 2013, one of the Rock Castle Construction crews located an exterior door and finished installing the new door at the Whalen residence. The following additional products and services were used:

Exterior wood door	1 @ $120	Taxable Sales
Repair work	4 hours	Non-Taxable Sales

Step 1: To display the invoice for the Exterior Door Repair job again:

- Click the **Create Invoices** icon.
- When the *Create Invoices* window appears, click **Edit** menu > **Find Invoices**.
- Enter Invoice No.: **1100**.
- Click **Find**.

Step 2: Enter the exterior door and additional repair labor as new line items on Invoice No. 1100 for the Whalen Exterior Door job.

Step 3: Mark the invoice as final as follows:

- **Right-click** to display the pop-up menu.
- Select: **Mark Invoice as Final.**

Step 4: With Invoice No. 1100 displayed, print the invoice as follows:

- Select the **Print** icon. If asked if you want to record your changes, select **Yes**.
- Select Print on: **Blank paper**.
- If necessary, uncheck: **Do not print lines around each field**.
- Click **Print**.

Step 5: Click **Save & Close** to close the *Create Invoices* window. If asked if you want to record your changes, select **Yes**.

QuickBooks will record the sale and record an account receivable for the amount to be received from the customer in the future.

If the company name does not print properly on the invoice or sales receipt, reduce the font size as follows:

5. Select the **Customize** button > **Customize Data Layout** > **Basic Customization**.
6. Select **Company Name** > **Change Font**.
7. Select font size **8** or **10**.

> ☑ *The Invoice Total is $304.30. Notice that the Exterior Door is a taxable item and QuickBooks automatically calculates and adds sales tax of $9.30 for the door.*

ONLINE BILLING

QuickBooks has the capability to e-mail invoices to customers. Customer e-mail addresses are filled in automatically from the Customer List information. You can e-mail single invoices or send a batch of invoices.

Although you cannot e-mail invoices from the sample company files, to demonstrate how to e-mail invoices:

Step 1: Open Invoice No. 1100 on your screen. (Click the **Create Invoices** icon, then click **Previous** until the invoice appears or click the **Find** button and enter Invoice No. **1100**.)

Step 2: Click the **arrow** beside the **Send** icon at the top of the *Create Invoices* window.

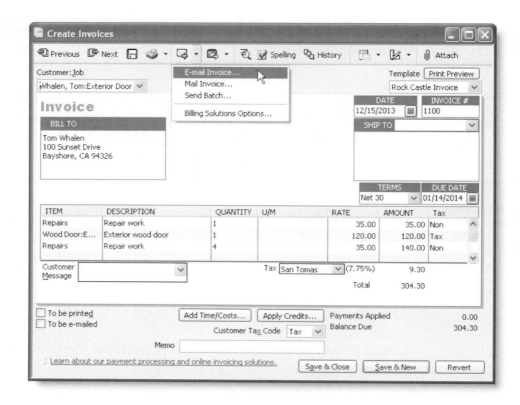

Step 3:   To e-mail the invoice, you would select E-mail Invoice. Since this is a sample company file, you will not be able to e-mail the invoice and this is for demonstration purposes only.

Select **Mail through QuickBooks** from the *Send Invoices* window to learn about QuickBooks invoice mailing service.

Step 4:   If you were e-mailing the invoice, the following *Send Invoice* window would appear. Notice that both Rock Castle Construction's e-mail address and the customer's e-mail address are automatically completed from the e-mail information contained in the Customer List. Also notice that if a title, such as Mr., is not entered in the Customer List information, then the e-mail may have to be revised accordingly.

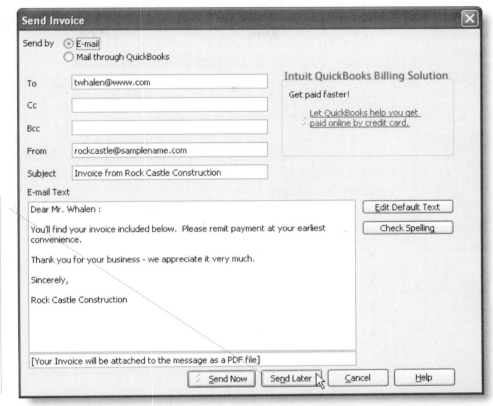

Click **Send Now** to e-mail the individual invoice or click **Send Later** to send the invoice in a batch with other invoices later.

Step 5:   If additional invoices are prepared, a batch of invoices can be sent at the same time using e-mail by clicking **Send Batch** from the drop-down menu (or click Send Forms from the File menu). If you were e-mailing the invoices, you would select the invoices to send and then click Send Now. Since this is a sample company, you will not be able to e-mail the invoices so click **Send Later** if that is enabled on your version.

Step 6:   If necessary, close the *QuickBooks Send Forms* window.

Step 7:   To close the *Create Invoices* window, click **Save & Close**.

If your company signs up for Online Bill Paying services, after receiving your e-mail invoices, customers can pay you online.

CREDIT SALES: CREATE REMINDER STATEMENTS

Reminder statements are sent to remind customers to pay their bills. A reminder statement summarizes invoice charges and provides an account history for the customer. It does not provide the detailed information that an invoice provides.

If a company wants to provide a customer with detailed information about charges, a copy of the invoice should be sent instead of a reminder statement.

Reminder statements summarize:

- The customer's previous account balance.
- Charges for sales during the period.
- Payments received from the customer.
- The customer's ending account balance.

To print a QuickBooks reminder statement for the Whalen Exterior Door job:

Step 1: Click the **Statements** icon in the *Customers* section of the Home page to display the *Create Statements* window.

Step 2: Select Template: **Intuit Standard Statement**.

Step 3: Select Statement Date: **12/16/2013**.

Step 4: Select Statement Period From: **11/17/2013** To: **12/16/2013**.

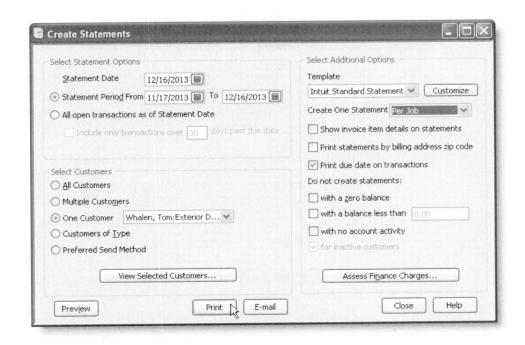

Step 5: In the *Select Customers* section, select **One Customer**. From the drop-down list, select **Whalen, Tom: Exterior Door**.

Step 6: Select Create One Statement: **Per Job**.

Step 7: Check **Print due date on transactions**.

Step 8: 🖶 Click **Print** to print the reminder statement, then click **Close**.

CREDIT SALES: RECORD CUSTOMER PAYMENTS

Recall that when recording credit sales in QuickBooks, you first create an invoice and then record the customer's payment. When a credit sale is recorded on an invoice, QuickBooks records (debits) an Account Receivable—an amount to be received from the customer in the future. When the customer's payment is received, the Account Receivable account is reduced (credited).

Customers may pay in the following ways:

1. **Credit card**, such as Visa, MasterCard, American Express, or Diners Club over the phone, in person, or by mail. Using QuickBooks' Merchant Account Service, you can obtain online authorization and then download payments directly into QuickBooks.

2. **Online** by credit card or bank account transfer.

3. **Customer check** delivered either in person or by mail.

To record the customer's payment by check for the Exterior Door job, complete the following steps:

Step 1: Click the **Receive Payments** icon in the *Customers* section of the Home page to display the *Receive Payments* window.

Step 2: Select Date: **12/17/2013**.

Step 3: Select Received From: **Whalen, Tom: Exterior Door**.

Invoice No. 1100 for $304.30 should appear as an outstanding invoice.

Step 4: Select Invoice Number **1100** when it appears.

QuickBooks will automatically enter the selected invoice amount of $304.30 into the Amount field. If the full amount of the invoice is not received from the customer, then the amount received can be entered into the Amount field.

Step 5: Select: Pmt. Method: **Check**. Enter Check No. **1005**.

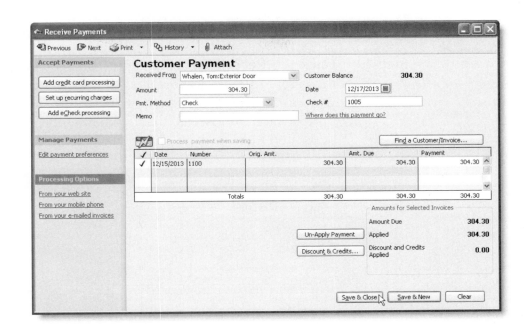

Step 6:   Click **Save & Close** to record the payment and close the *Receive Payments* window.

QuickBooks will increase (debit) cash and decrease (credit) the customer's account receivable.

RECORD BANK DEPOSITS

After recording a customer's payment in the *Receive Payments* window, the next step is to indicate which payments to deposit in which bank accounts.

To select customer payments to deposit:

Step 1: Click the **Record Deposits** icon in the *Banking* section of the Home page to display the *Payments to Deposit* window. The *Payments to Deposit* window lists undeposited funds that have been received but not yet deposited in the bank.

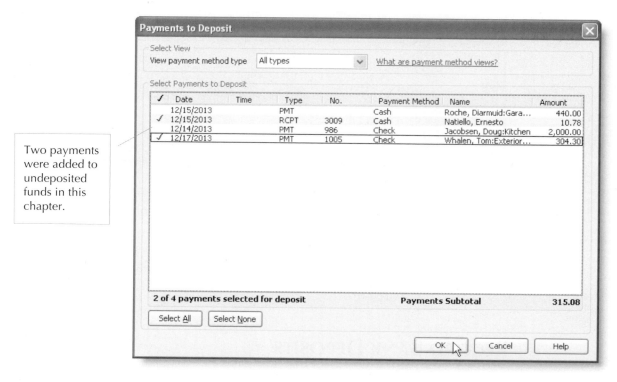

Two payments were added to undeposited funds in this chapter.

Step 2: **Select** the above two payments that were added to undeposited funds in this chapter.

- $10.78 cash receipt from Ernesto Natiello on 12/15/2013

- $304.30 cash payment from Tom Whalen on 12/17/2013

Step 3: Click **OK** to display the following *Make Deposits* window.

Step 4:   Select Deposit To: **[your name] Checking**. Select Date: **12/17/2013**.

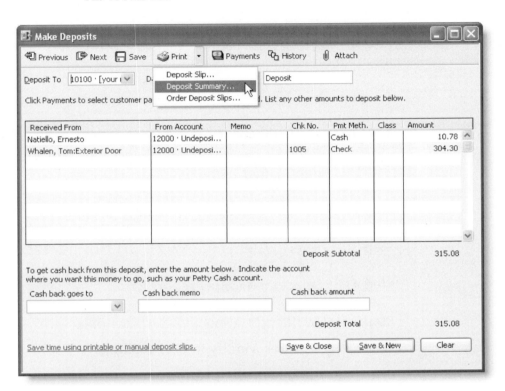

Step 5:   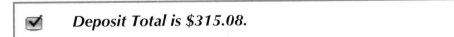 Click the **arrow** on the **Print** button. Select: **Deposit Summary**. Select printer settings, then click **Print**.

Step 6:   Click **Save & Close** to record the deposit and close the *Make Deposits* window.

☑   *Deposit Total is $315.08.*

PRINT JOURNAL ENTRIES

As you entered transaction information into QuickBooks' onscreen forms, QuickBooks automatically converted the transaction information into journal entries.

To print the journal entries for the transactions you entered:

Step 1: Click **Report Center** icon in the Icon bar to display the *Report Center* window. Select the **Grid View** in the upper right corner of the window.

Step 2: Select: **Accountant & Taxes > Journal**.

Step 3: Select Dates From: **12/15/2013** To: **12/17/2013**.

Step 4: Select the **Display report** icon.

Step 5: To filter for a specific customer only:

- Click **Modify Report > Filters**.
- Select Filter: **Name**.
- Select: **Whalen, Tom**, then click **OK**.

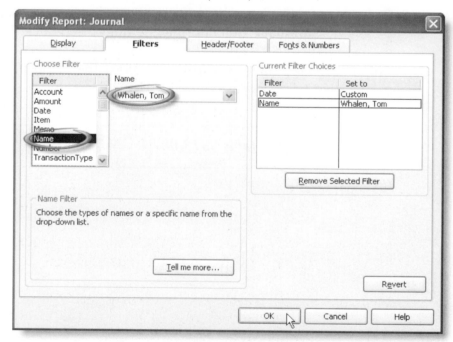

Step 6: 🖨 **Print** the Journal using **Portrait** orientation.

Step 7: 🖉 **Circle** the journal entry that corresponds to Invoice No. 1100. Notice that the journal entry records an increase (debit) to Accounts Receivable for $304.30, the net amount of the invoice.

CUSTOMER REPORTS

There are many different customer reports that a business may find useful. QuickBooks creates reports to answer the following questions:

- Which customers owe us money?
- Which customers have overdue balances?
- Which customers are profitable?
- Which jobs are profitable?

Customer reports can be accessed in QuickBooks in several different ways:

1. **Report Center.** Permits you to locate reports by type of report (Click Report Center icon, then click Customers & Receivables.)

2. **Reports Menu.** Reports on the Reports menu accessed from the Menu bar are grouped by type of report. (From the Reports menu, click Customers & Receivables.)

3. **Memorized Customer Reports.** Selected customer reports are memorized for convenience. (From the Reports menu, select Memorized Reports, Customers.)

In this chapter, you will use the Report Center to access customer reports.

Step 1: To display the Report Center, click the **Report Center** icon on the Icon bar. Select the **List View** icon.

Step 2: Select: **Customers & Receivables** to display customer reports that can be accessed in QuickBooks.

Step 3: Notice that the customer reports are divided into three categories:

- Accounts Receivable Aging reports.

- Customer Balance reports.

- Customer List reports.

ACCOUNTS RECEIVABLE REPORTS: WHICH CUSTOMERS OWE US MONEY?

Accounts Receivable reports provide information about which customers owe your business money. When Rock Castle Construction makes a credit sale, the company provides goods and services to a customer in exchange for a promise that the customer will pay later. Sometimes the customer breaks the promise and does not pay. Therefore, a business should have a credit policy to ensure that credit is extended only to customers who are likely to keep their promise and pay their bills.

After credit has been extended, a business needs to track accounts receivable to determine if accounts are being collected in a timely manner. The following reports provide information useful in tracking accounts receivable.

1. Accounts Receivable Aging Summary (the age of amounts due you by customers).

2. Accounts Receivable Aging Detail.

3. Customers with Open Invoices (invoices that have not yet been paid).

4. Collections Report (which customer accounts are overdue with their contact information).

ACCOUNTS RECEIVABLE AGING SUMMARY REPORT

The Accounts Receivable Aging Summary report provides information about the age of customer accounts. This report lists the age of accounts receivable balances. In general, the older an account, the less likely the customer will pay the bill. Therefore, it is important to monitor the age of accounts receivable and take action to collect old accounts.

To print the Accounts Receivable Aging Summary:

Step 1: From the Report Center, select **Customers & Receivables > A/R Aging Summary**.

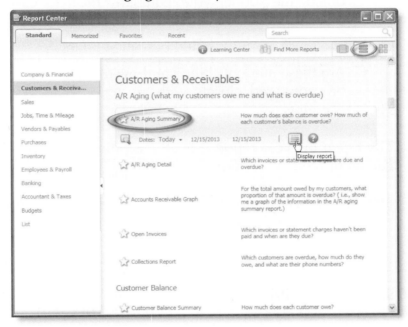

Step 2: Select Date: **Today**. Click **Display report** icon.

Step 3: If necessary, adjust the column widths by clicking and dragging.

Step 4: **Export** the report to Excel. (Click the **Export** button **> a new Excel workbook > Export**.)

Step 5: **Highlight** all overdue customer accounts.

Step 6: **Print** the report from Excel.

Step 7: **Save** the Excel report. (Click the Excel **Office** button, click **Save As**, specify the Excel file name: **Aging Report**.) **Close** Excel.

Step 8: **Close** the *A/R Aging Summary* window.

CUSTOMERS WITH OPEN INVOICES REPORT

Customers with open invoices are those who have an unbilled or unpaid balance. It is important to track the status of open accounts to determine:

- Are these amounts unbilled? The sooner the balances are billed, the sooner your company receives cash to pay your bills.

- Are these amounts billed but not yet due?

- Are these amounts billed and overdue? These accounts should be monitored closely with an action plan for collecting the accounts.

The Open Invoices report lists all customers with open balances and can be printed as follows:

Step 1:   From the *Customers & Receivables* section of the Report Center, click **Open Invoices**.

Step 2:   Select Date: **Today**. Select **Display report** icon.

Step 3:   📧 **Print** the Open Invoices report using **Portrait** orientation.

Step 4:   Notice the *Aging* column in the report. This column indicates the age of overdue accounts.

Step 5:   **Close** the *Open Invoices* window.

COLLECTIONS REPORT: CUSTOMERS WITH OVERDUE BALANCES

When reviewing the age of accounts receivable, a business should monitor overdue accounts closely and maintain ongoing collection efforts to collect its overdue accounts.

The Collections Report lists customers with overdue account balances. In addition, the Collections Report includes a contact phone number for convenience in contacting the customer.

To print the Collections Report summarizing information for all customers with overdue balances:

Step 1:   From the *Customers & Receivables* section of the Report Center, select: **Collections Report**.

Step 2:   Select: **Today**. Click the **Display report** icon.

Step 3:   One customer has an overdue balance. To obtain more information about the specific invoice, simply double-click on the invoice.

Step 4:   ▣ **Print** the Collections Report using **Portrait** orientation.

Step 5:   **Close** the *Collections Report* window.

The Collections Report provides the information necessary to monitor and contact overdue accounts and should be prepared and reviewed on a regular basis.

PROFIT AND LOSS REPORTS: WHICH CUSTOMERS AND JOBS ARE PROFITABLE?

To improve profitability in the future, a business should evaluate which customers and jobs have been profitable in the past. This information permits a business to improve profitability by:

- Increasing business in profitable areas.
- Improving performance in unprofitable areas.
- Discontinuing unprofitable areas.

The following QuickBooks reports provide information about customer and job profitability:

1. Income by Customer Summary.
2. Income by Customer Detail.
3. Job Profitability Summary.
4. Job Profitability Detail.

INCOME BY CUSTOMER SUMMARY REPORT

To determine which customers are generating the most profit for your business, it is necessary to look at both the sales for the customer and the associated costs. To print the Income by Customer Summary Report:

Step 1: From the Report Center, click **Company & Financial > Income by Customer Summary**.

Step 2: Select: **This Fiscal Year-to-date**. Click the **Display report** icon.

Step 3: ⌨ **Print** the report.

Step 4: ✏ **Circle** Rock Castle Construction's most profitable customer.

Step 5: **Close** the *Income by Customer Summary* window.

JOB PROFITABILITY SUMMARY REPORT

To print the Job Profitability Summary Report:

Step 1: From the Report Center, click **Jobs, Time & Mileage > Job Profitability Summary.**

Step 2: Select Date: **This Fiscal Year**. Click the **Display report** icon.

Step 3: ⌨ **Print** the report using **Portrait** orientation.

Step 4: ✏ **Circle** the job that generated the most profit for Rock Castle Construction.

Step 5: **Close** the *Job Profitability Summary* window.

QuickBooks offers other additional reports about customers that provide information useful to a business. These reports can be accessed from the Report Center.

SAVE CHAPTER 4

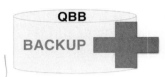

Save a backup of your Chapter 4 file using the file name: **[your name] Chapter 4 Backup.QBB**. See *Appendix B: Back Up & Restore QuickBooks Files* for instructions.

WORKFLOW

If you are using the workflow approach, leave your .QBW file open and proceed directly to Exercise 4.1.

RESTART & RESTORE

If you are using the Restart & Restore approach and are ending your computer session now, close your .QBW file and exit QuickBooks. When you restart, you will restore your backup file to complete Exercise 4.1.

PODCASTS

Watch the Chapter 4 **Podcast** at www.QuickBooksBlog.info. Review the chapter and see how to invoice customers and receive payments using QuickBooks. Bookmark www.QuickBooksBlog.info for your future use.

MULTIPLE-CHOICE PRACTICE TEST

A **Multiple-Choice Practice Test** for Chapter 4 is on the *Computer Accounting for QuickBooks Pro* Online Learning Center at www.mhhe.com/kay2010. Try the Practice Test and see how many questions you answer correctly.

EXTRAS!

Section 3: Quick Guide contains quick, easy step-by-step directions for frequently used QuickBooks tasks, including correcting errors. You can find *Quick Guide* at the back of your text or online at www.mhhe.com/kay2010. *Check it out!*

Deliverables Checklist is a list of the reports and documents that you are to deliver to your instructor for grading. You can find the Chapter 4 Deliverables Checklist at the end of the chapter or online at www.mhhe.com/kay2010. Staying organized saves time. Use the checklist to organize your reports, checking off the reports as completed. Then include the checklist with your reports for grading.

Appendix D: Electronic Deliverables shows you how to save your QuickBooks reports electronically. Also, watch the Electronic Deliverables Podcast at www.QuickBooksBlog.info. Check with your instructor to see if you should deliver your reports electronically.

Join the QuickBooks Student Community to ask questions and share tips @ www.QuickBooksBlog.info.

LEARNING ACTIVITIES

Important: Ask your instructor whether you should complete the following assignments by printing requested reports or creating electronic deliverables (see Appendix D: Electronic Deliverables).

EXERCISE 4.1: BILL CUSTOMER

SCENARIO

"I just finished the Beneficio job, Mr. Castle." A workman tosses a job ticket over your cubicle wall into your inbox as he walks past. *"Mrs. Beneficio's pet dog, Wrecks, really did a number on that door. No wonder she wanted it replaced before her party tonight. Looks better than ever now!"*

You hear Mr. Castle reply, *"We want to keep Mrs. Beneficio happy. She will be a good customer."*

TASK 1: OPEN COMPANY FILE

WORKFLOW

If you are using the Workflow approach, you will use the same .QBW file.

If your QBW file is not already open, open it by selecting **File > Open Previous Company**. Select your **.QBW file.**

Change the company name to [**your name**] **Exercise 4.1** by selecting **Company** menu > **Company Information.**

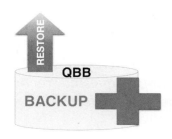

RESTART & RESTORE

If you are not using the same computer, you must use the Restart and Restore approach.

Restore your **Chapter 4 Backup.QBB** file using the directions in *Appendix B: Back Up & Restore QuickBooks Files*.

After restoring the file, change the company name to **[your name] Exercise 4.1** by selecting **Company** menu > **Company Information**.

TASK 2: ADD NEW CUSTOMER& JOB

Step 1:   Add Mrs. Beneficio as a new customer.

Add a new customer from the *Customer Center* or from the *Create Invoices* window.

Address Info:	
Customer	Beneficio, Katrina
Mr./Ms./…	Mrs.
First Name	Katrina
M.I.	L
Last Name	Beneficio
Contact	Katrina
Phone	415-555-1818
Alt. Ph.	415-555-3636
Addresses: **Bill To**	10 Pico Blvd Bayshore, CA 94326

Additional Info:	
Type	Residential
Terms	Net 30
Tax Code	Tax
Tax Item	San Tomas

Payment Info:	
Account No.	12736
Credit Limit	10,000
Preferred Payment Method	VISA

Step 2: **Close** the *New Customer* window.

Step 3: Add a new job for Katrina Beneficio.

Job Name: Door Replacement	
Job Status	Closed
Start Date	12/17/2013
Projected End	12/17/2013
End Date	12/17/2013
Job Description	Interior Door Replacement
Job Type	Repairs

TASK 3: CREATE INVOICE

Step 1: Create an invoice for an interior door replacement using the following information:

Customer: Job	Beneficio, Katrina: Door Replacement
Customer Template	Rock Castle Invoice
Date	12/17/2013
Invoice No.	1101
Items	1 Wood Door: Interior @ $72.00 1 Hardware: Standard Doorknob @ 30.00 Installation Labor: 3 hours

Step 2: ▣ **Print** the invoice.

 The Invoice Total is $214.91.

TASK 4: SAVE EXERCISE 4.1

Save a backup of your Exercise 4.1 file using the file name: **[your name] Exercise 4.1 Backup.QBB**. See *Appendix B: Back Up & Restore QuickBooks Files* for instructions.

WORKFLOW

If you are proceeding to Exercise 4.2 and using the same computer, you can leave your .QBW file open and use it for Exercise 4.2.

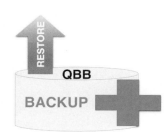

RESTART & RESTORE

If you are stopping your QuickBooks work session and changing computers, you will need to restore your .QBB file when you restart.

EXERCISE 4.2: RECORD CUSTOMER PAYMENT AND CUSTOMER CREDIT

SCENARIO

"It's time you learned how to record a credit to a customer's account." Mr. Castle groans, then rubbing his temples, he continues, *"Mrs. Beneficio called earlier today to tell us she was very pleased with her new bathroom door. However, she ordered locking hardware for the door, and standard hardware with no lock was installed instead. Although she appreciates our prompt service, she would like a lock on her bathroom door. We sent a workman over to her house, and when the hardware was replaced, she paid the bill.*

"We need to record a credit to her account for the standard hardware and then record a charge for the locking hardware set. And we won't charge her for the labor to change the hardware."

TASK 1: OPEN COMPANY FILE

WORKFLOW

If you are using the Workflow approach, you will use the same .QBW file.

If your QBW file is not already open, open it by selecting **File > Open Previous Company**. Select your **.QBW file.**

Change the company name to **[your name] Exercise 4.2** by selecting **Company** menu > **Company Information.**

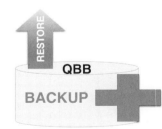

RESTART & RESTORE

If you are using the Restart and Restore approach, restore your backup file using the directions in *Appendix B: Back Up & Restore QuickBooks Files.*

After restoring the file, change the company name to **[your name] Exercise 4.2** by selecting **Company** menu > **Company Information.**

TASK 2: RECORD CUSTOMER CREDIT

Record a credit to Mrs. Beneficio's account for the $30.00 she was previously charged for standard door hardware by completing the following steps:

Step 1:   Click the **Refunds and Credits** icon in the *Customers* section of the Home page.

Step 2:   Select Customer and Job: **Beneficio, Katrina: Door Replacement.**

Step 3:   Select Template: **Custom Credit Memo**. Credit No. 1102 should automatically appear.

Step 4:   Select Date: **12/20/2013**.

Step 5:   Select Item: **Hardware Standard Doorknobs**.

Step 6:   Enter Quantity: **1**.

Step 7:   🖶 **Print** the Credit Memo.

Step 8:   **Save** the Credit Memo.

Step 9:   When the following Available Credit window appears, select **Apply to an invoice**.

Step 10: When the following *Apply Credit to Invoices* window appears, select **Invoice No. 1101**. Click **Done**.

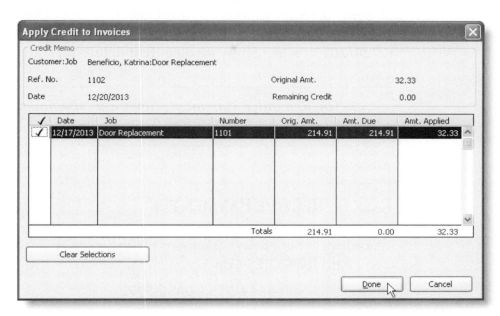

Step 11: If necessary, click **Save & Close** to close the *Create Credit Memos/Refunds* window.

 The Credit Memo No. 1102 totals $-32.33 ($30.00 plus $2.33 tax).

TASK 3: CREATE INVOICE

Step 1: Create a new invoice (Invoice No. 1103) for Katrina Beneficio: Door Replacement on 12/20/2013 to record the charges for the interior door locking hardware.

Step 2: **Print** the invoice.

Invoice No. 1103 totals $40.95.

TASK 4: PRINT REMINDER STATEMENT

Print a reminder statement for the Beneficio Door Replacement Job for 12/20/2013. Use Statement Period From: **12/02/2013** To: **12/20/2013**. Select **Show invoice item details on statements**.

 The Reminder Statement shows a total amount due of $223.53.

TASK 5: RECEIVE PAYMENT

Record Mrs. Beneficio's payment for the door replacement by VISA credit card for $223.53 on 12/20/2013.

- Card No.: **4444-5555-6666-7777**
- Exp. Date: **07/2014**
- Click **Save & Close** to close the *Receive Payments* window.

TASK 6: RECORD BANK DEPOSIT

Step 1: Record the deposit for $223.53 on 12/20/2013.

Step 2: **Print** a deposit summary using **Portrait** orientation.

TASK 7: SAVE EXERCISE 4.2

Save a backup of your Exercise 4.2 file using the file name: **[your name] Exercise 4.2 Backup.QBB**. See *Appendix B: Back Up & Restore QuickBooks Files* for instructions.

WORKFLOW

If you are using the Workflow approach, you can leave your .QBW file open and use it for the next chapter.

RESTART & RESTORE

If you are stopping your QuickBooks work session and changing computers, you will need to restore your .QBB file when you restart.

EXERCISE 4.3:
CUSTOMER REPORTS & COLLECTION LETTERS

In this exercise, you will create additional customer reports that a business might find useful.

TASK 1: OPEN COMPANY FILE

WORKFLOW

If you are using the Workflow approach, you will use the same .QBW file.

If your QBW file is not already open, open it by selecting **File > Open Previous Company**. Select your **.QBW file.**

Change the company name to **[your name] Exercise 4.3** by selecting **Company** menu > **Company Information.**

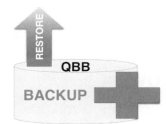

RESTART & RESTORE

If you are using the Restart and Restore approach, restore your backup file using the directions in *Appendix B: Back Up & Restore QuickBooks Files.*

After restoring the file, change the company name to **[your name] Exercise 4.3** by selecting **Company** menu > **Company Information.**

TASK 2: EDIT CUSTOMER LIST

Edit Ecker Designs' e-mail address in the Customer List.

Step 1:   Open the Customer Center.

Step 2:   Select customer: **Ecker Designs**.

Step 3:   Click **Edit Customer:Job** to display the *Edit Customer* window for Ecker Designs.

Step 4:   Edit the e-mail address for Ecker Designs: **decker@www.com**.

Step 5:   Click **OK** to save the customer information and close the *Edit Customer* window.

TASK 3: PRINT CUSTOMER REPORT

📠 **Print** the transactions for Ecker Designs as follows.

Step 1:   From the Customer List, select **Ecker Designs.**

Step 2:   In the *Customer Information* section, transactions for Ecker Designs should appear. With your cursor over the *Customer Transaction* section of the *Customer Center* window, **right-click** to display the following pop-up menu. Select **View as a Report**.

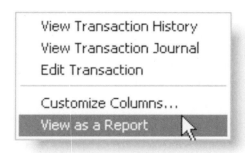

Step 3:   Select Dates From: **11/01/2013** To: **12/31/2013**.

Step 4:   **Print** the report for Ecker Designs.

> ⓘ *The last amount charged to Ecker Design's account was Invoice No. 1086 for $1,468.30 on November 30, 2013.*

Step 5:   **Close** the *Report* window and the *Customer Center* window.

TASK 4: ACCOUNTS RECEIVABLE AGING DETAIL REPORT

 Print the Accounts Receivable Aging Detail report for Rock Castle Construction as follows.

Step 1:   From the Report Center, select **Customers & Receivables**.

Step 2:   Select **A/R Aging Detail** report.

Step 3:   Select Date: **12/15/2013**.

Step 4:   **Print** the A/R Aging Detail report.

Step 5: ✏ **Circle** the account(s) that are overdue.

TASK 5: COLLECTION LETTER

Next, prepare a collection letter to the customer with an overdue account.

Step 1: From the Customer Center, select the customer(s) with overdue accounts.

Step 2: Click on the **Word** icon at the top of the Customer Center.

Step 3: Select: **Prepare Collection Letters**.

Step 4: If prompted, select **Copy** to copy the letter templates. When the following window appears, make the selections as shown. Click **Next**.

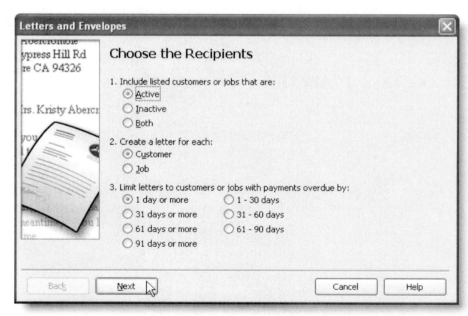

Step 5:   Select **Hendro Riyadi**. Click **Next**.

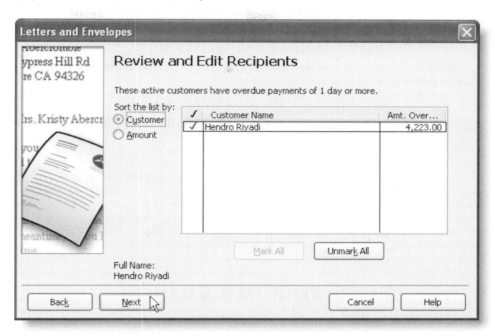

Step 6:   Select **Formal collection > Next**.

Step 7:   Enter Name: **Rock Castle**. Enter Title: **President**. Click
Next.

Step 8: If a missing information message appears, click **OK**. Click **Retry** if necessary.

Step 9: QuickBooks will automatically open Word and prepare the collection letter. ▣ **Print** the letter from Word.

Step 10: Save the Word document by clicking the **Office** button > **Save As**. Name the document: **[your name] Exercise 4.3 Collection Letter**.

Step 11: Click **Cancel** when asked if you would like to print envelopes.

Step 12: **Close** the Customer Center.

TASK 6: PRINT TRIAL BALANCE

In this task, you will print a Trial Balance to double check that your accounting system is in balance and your account balances are correct.

▣ **Print** the Trial Balance as follows.

Step 1: From the Report Center, select **Accountant and Taxes > Trial Balance**.

Step 2: Select Dates From: **12/20/2013** To: **12/20/2013**.

Step 3: ▣ **Print** the Trial Balance.

Step 4: Compare your printout totals and account balances to the following printout. Correct any errors you find.

Modify Report...	Memorize...	Print...	E-mail ▾	Export...	Hide Header	Collapse	Refresh

Dates Custom ▾ From 12/20/2013 🔲 To 12/20/2013 🔲 Sort By Default ▾

[your name] Exercise 4.3 Rock Castle Construction
Trial Balance

Accrual Basis   As of December 20, 2013

	Dec 20, 13	
	Debit	Credit
10100 · [your name] Checking	120,442.71	
10300 · Savings	17,910.19	
10400 · Petty Cash	500.00	
11000 · Accounts Receivable	93,007.93	
12000 · Undeposited Funds	2,440.00	
12100 · Inventory Asset	29,740.22	
12800 · Employee Advances	832.00	
13100 · Pre-paid Insurance	4,050.00	
13400 · Retainage Receivable	3,703.02	
15000 · Furniture and Equipment	34,326.00	
15100 · Vehicles	78,936.91	
15200 · Buildings and Improvements	325,000.00	
15300 · Construction Equipment	15,300.00	
16900 · Land	90,000.00	
17000 · Accumulated Depreciation		110,344.60
18700 · Security Deposits	1,720.00	
20000 · Accounts Payable		27,136.92
20500 · QuickBooks Credit Card		94.20
20600 · CalOil Credit Card		382.62
24000 · Payroll Liabilities:24010 · Federal Withholding		1,364.00
24000 · Payroll Liabilities:24020 · FICA Payable		2,118.82
24000 · Payroll Liabilities:24030 · AEIC Payable	0.00	
24000 · Payroll Liabilities:24040 · FUTA Payable		100.00
24000 · Payroll Liabilities:24050 · State Withholding		299.19
24000 · Payroll Liabilities:24060 · SUTA Payable		110.00
24000 · Payroll Liabilities:24070 · State Disability Payable		48.13
24000 · Payroll Liabilities:24080 · Worker's Compensation		1,214.31
24000 · Payroll Liabilities:24100 · Emp. Health Ins Payable		150.00
25500 · Sales Tax Payable		976.24
23000 · Loan - Vehicles (Van)		10,501.47
23100 · Loan - Vehicles (Utility Truck)		19,936.91
23200 · Loan - Vehicles (Pickup Truck)		22,641.00
28100 · Loan - Construction Equipment		13,911.32
28200 · Loan - Furniture/Office Equip		21,000.00
28700 · Note Payable - Bank of Anycity		2,693.21
28900 · Mortgage - Office Building		296,283.00
30000 · Opening Bal Equity		38,773.75
30100 · Capital Stock		73,500.00
32000 · Retained Earnings		61,756.76
40100 · Construction Income	0.00	
40100 · Construction Income:40110 · Design Income		36,729.25
40100 · Construction Income:40130 · Labor Income		208,505.42
40100 · Construction Income:40140 · Materials Income		120,160.67
40100 · Construction Income:40150 · Subcontracted Lab...		82,710.35
40100 · Construction Income:40199 · Less Discounts giv...	48.35	
40500 · Reimbursement Income:40520 · Permit Reimbur...		1,223.75
40500 · Reimbursement Income:40530 · Reimbursed Fre...		896.05
50100 · Cost of Goods Sold	15,709.35	
54000 · Job Expenses:54200 · Equipment Rental	1,850.00	
54000 · Job Expenses:54300 · Job Materials	98,935.90	
54000 · Job Expenses:54400 · Permits and Licenses	700.00	
54000 · Job Expenses:54500 · Subcontractors	63,217.95	
54000 · Job Expenses:54520 · Freight & Delivery	842.10	
54000 · Job Expenses:54599 · Less Discounts Taken		201.81
60100 · Automobile:60110 · Fuel	1,588.70	
60100 · Automobile:60120 · Insurance	2,850.24	
60100 · Automobile:60130 · Repairs and Maintenance	2,406.00	
60400 · Selling Expense:60410 · Advertising Expense	200.00	
60600 · Bank Service Charges	145.00	
62100 · Insurance:62110 · Disability Insurance	582.06	
62100 · Insurance:62120 · Liability Insurance	5,885.96	
62100 · Insurance:62130 · Work Comp	13,657.07	
62400 · Interest Expense:62420 · Loan Interest	1,995.65	
62700 · Payroll Expenses:62710 · Gross Wages	110,400.10	
62700 · Payroll Expenses:62720 · Payroll Taxes	8,445.61	
62700 · Payroll Expenses:62730 · FUTA Expense	268.00	
62700 · Payroll Expenses:62740 · SUTA Expense	1,233.50	
63100 · Postage	104.20	
63600 · Professional Fees:63610 · Accounting	250.00	
64200 · Repairs:64210 · Building Repairs	175.00	
64200 · Repairs:64220 · Computer Repairs	300.00	
64200 · Repairs:64230 · Equipment Repairs	1,350.00	
64800 · Tools and Machinery	2,820.68	
65100 · Utilities:65110 · Gas and Electric	1,164.16	
65100 · Utilities:65120 · Telephone	841.15	
65100 · Utilities:65130 · Water	264.00	
70100 · Other Income		146.80
70200 · Interest Income		229.16
TOTAL	**1,156,139.71**	**1,156,139.71**

TASK 7: PRINT JOURNAL

🖨 **Print** the Journal as follows.

Step 1:   From the Report Center, select **Accountant and Taxes > Journal**.

Step 2:   Select Dates From: **12/17/2013** To: **12/20/2013**.

Step 3:   🖨 **Print** the Journal.

TASK 8: SAVE EXERCISE 4.3

Save a backup of your Exercise 4.3 file using the file name: **[your name] Exercise 4.3 Backup.QBB**. See *Appendix B: Back Up & Restore QuickBooks Files* for instructions.

WORKFLOW

If you are using the Workflow approach, you can leave your .QBW file open and use it for the next chapter.

RESTART & RESTORE

If you are stopping your QuickBooks work session and changing computers, you will need to restore your .QBB file when you restart.

EXERCISE 4.4: WEB QUEST

Rock Castle has heard that QuickBooks now offers a Point of Sale product to go with QuickBooks. He wants to know more about the product and whether it is a good choice for Rock Castle Construction.

Step 1: Using an Internet search engine, such as Google, research QuickBooks Point of Sale products.

Step 2: 📧 Prepare an e-mail to Rock Castle summarizing the main features of the Point of Sale product. Include your recommendation whether this is a worthwhile product for Rock Castle Construction to use.

DELIVERABLES CHECKLIST CHAPTER 4
NAME:

INSTRUCTIONS:
1. **CHECK OFF THE DELIVERABLES YOU HAVE COMPLETED.**
2. **TURN IN THIS PAGE WITH YOUR DELIVERABLES.**

CHAPTER 4
- ☐ Cash Sales Receipt
- ☐ Invoice No. 1100
- ☐ Reminder Statement
- ☐ Deposit Summary
- ☐ Journal
- ☐ Accounts Receivable Aging Summary Report
- ☐ Open Invoices Report
- ☐ Collections Report
- ☐ Income by Customer Summary Report
- ☐ Job Profitability Summary Report

EXERCISE 4.1
- ☐ Task 3: Invoice No. 1101

EXERCISE 4.2
- ☐ Task 2: Credit Memo No. 1102
- ☐ Task 3: Invoice No. 1103
- ☐ Task 4: Statement
- ☐ Task 6: Deposit Summary

EXERCISE 4.3
- ☐ Task 3: Customer Report
- ☐ Task 4: Accounts Receivable Aging Detail Report
- ☐ Task 5: Customer Collection Letter
- ☐ Task 6: Trial Balance
- ☐ Task 7: Journal

EXERCISE 4.4

☐ QuickBooks Point of Sale

REFLECTION: A WISH AND A STAR ☆

Reflection improves learning and retention. Reflect on what you have learned after completing Chapter 4 that you did not know before you started the chapter.

A Star:

What did you like best that you learned about QuickBooks in Chapter 4?

A Wish:

If you could pick one thing, what do you wish you knew more about when using QuickBooks?

NOTES:

CHAPTER 5
VENDORS, PURCHASES, AND INVENTORY

SCENARIO

As you work your way through stacks of paper in your inbox, you hear Mr. Castle's rapid footsteps coming in your direction. He whips around the corner of your cubicle with another stack of papers in hand.

In his usual rapid-fire delivery, Mr. Castle begins, *"This is the way we do business."* He quickly sketches the following:

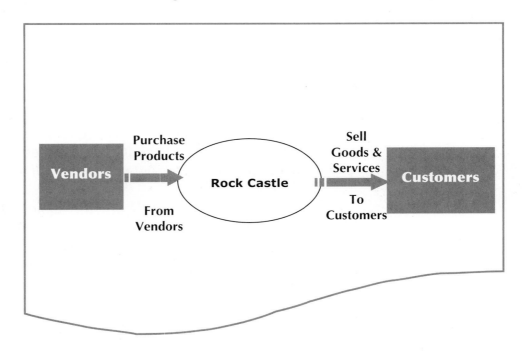

"We purchase products from our vendors and suppliers, and then we sell those products and provide services to our customers. We use QuickBooks to track the quantity and cost of items we purchase and sell."

Mr. Castle tosses the papers into your inbox. *"Here are vendor and purchase transactions that need to be recorded."*

A few minutes later, Mr. Castle races past your cubicle engaged in an intense conversation on his mobile phone. He tosses a sticky note over your cubicle wall, the note landing on your computer screen.

JIT Learning

Clueless as to the meaning of Mr. Castle's latest note, you wait for him to circle back and explain. Within minutes, he circles past your cubicle and barks out, *"Check out the Quick Guide at the back of your book—it's the only way I managed until you arrived.*

"I call it JIT Learning—learn the QuickBooks feature you need—just in time to use it—"

Before you can reply, Mr. Castle is gone. You turn to the Quick Guide to find another one of Mr. Castle's sticky notes marking the page.

CHAPTER 5
LEARNING OBJECTIVES

In Chapter 5, you will learn about the following QuickBooks features:

INTRODUCTION

In Chapter 5 you will focus on using QuickBooks to record vendor transactions, including placing orders, receiving goods, and paying bills.

QuickBooks considers a vendor to be any individual or organization that provides products or services to your company.

QuickBooks considers all of the following to be vendors:

- Suppliers from whom you buy inventory or supplies.

- Service companies that provide services to your company, such as cleaning services or landscaping services.

- Financial institutions, such as banks, that provide financial services including checking accounts and loans.

- Tax agencies such as the IRS. The IRS is considered a vendor because you pay taxes to the IRS.

- Utility and telephone companies.

If your company is a merchandising business that buys and resells goods, then you must maintain inventory records to account for the items you purchase from vendors and resell to customers.

The following diagram summarizes vendor and customer transactions.

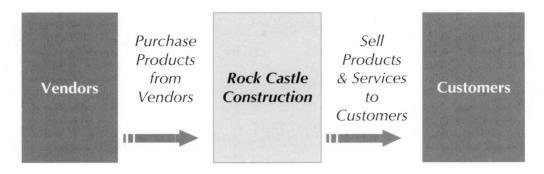

Vendor Transactions	Customer Transactions
1. Enter vendor information	7. Enter customer information
2. Set up inventory	8. Sell goods and bill customers
3. Order goods	9. Receive customer payments
4. Receive goods	10. Deposit customer payments
5. Receive bill	
6. Pay for goods	

The following table summarizes how to record Rock Castle Construction's business operations using QuickBooks.

	Activity	Record Using...
1.	Record vendor information.	*Vendor List*
2.	Record inventory information: Set up inventory records to track the quantity and cost of items purchased.	*Items List*
3.	Order goods: Use purchase orders (PO's) to order goods from vendors.	*Purchase Orders*
4.	Receive goods: Record goods received as inventory.	*Receive Items*
5.	Receive bill: Record an obligation to pay a bill later (Accounts Payable).	*Enter Bills*
6.	Pay for goods: Pay bills for the goods received.	*Pay Bills*
7.	Record customer information.	*Customer List*
8.	Sell goods and bill customers: Record customer's promise to pay later (Account Receivable).	*Invoice*
9.	Receive customer payment: Record cash collected and reduce customer's Account Receivable.	*Receive Payments*
10.	Deposit customers' payments in bank account.	*Deposit*

Vendor Transactions (rows 1–6)

Customer Transactions (rows 7–10)

Start QuickBooks by clicking on the **QuickBooks desktop icon** or click **Start > Programs > QuickBooks > QuickBooks Pro 2010**.

WORKFLOW

Use the Workflow approach if you are using the same computer and the same .QBW file from the prior chapter.

Step 1: If your .QBW file is not already open, open it by selecting **File > Open Previous Company**. Select your **.QBW file.**

Step 2: Change the company name to **[your name] Chapter 5** by selecting **Company** menu **> Company Information.**

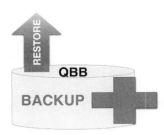

RESTART & RESTORE

Use the Restart & Restore approach if you are restarting your work session.

Step 1: Restore the **Backup.QBB** file using the directions in *Appendix B: Back Up & Restore QuickBooks Files.*

You can restore your .QBB file from the previous chapter (Exercise 4.3) or the Chapter 5 Backup.QBB data file that comes with the *Computer Accounting with QuickBooks* text (available on CD or download from the Online Learning Center).

If the *QuickBooks Login* window appears with the User Name **Admin**:

- Leave the *User Name* field as **Admin**.

- Leave the *Password* field **blank**.

- Click **OK**.

Step 2: After restoring the file, change the company name to **[your name] Chapter 5** by selecting **Company** menu **> Company Information.**

VENDOR NAVIGATION

After opening the company file for Rock Castle Construction, click the **Home** page icon in the Icon bar.

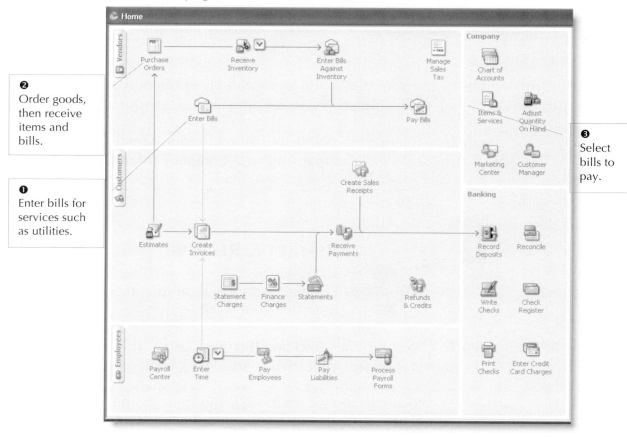

❷ Order goods, then receive items and bills.

❶ Enter bills for services such as utilities.

❸ Select bills to pay.

The *Vendors* section of the Home page is a flowchart of vendor transactions. As the flowchart indicates, Rock Castle Construction can record bills in QuickBooks as follows.

❶ Record services received. Use the *Enter Bills* window to record bills for services received. Examples include rent, utilities expense, insurance expense, and accounting and professional services. QuickBooks will record an obligation (Accounts Payable liability) to pay the bill later.

❷ Record goods purchased. Use the *Purchase Orders* window to record an order to purchase goods. Use the *Receive Items* window to record goods received. When the bill is received, use the *Enter Bills* window to record the bill. Again, when the bill is entered, QuickBooks records Accounts Payable to reflect the obligation to pay the bill later.

❸ **Select bills to pay.** Use the *Pay Bills* window to select the bills that are due and you are ready to pay.

Another QuickBooks feature available from the *Vendors* section of the Home page includes:

Manage Sales Tax: Sales taxes are charged on retail sales to customers. The sales tax collected from customers must be paid to the appropriate state agency.

VENDOR LIST

The first step in working with vendor transactions is to enter vendor information in the Vendor List.

The Vendor List contains information for each vendor, such as address, telephone number, and credit terms. Vendor information is entered in the Vendor List and then QuickBooks automatically transfers the vendor information to the appropriate forms, such as purchase orders and checks. This feature enables you to enter vendor information only once in QuickBooks instead of entering the vendor information each time a form is prepared.

VIEW VENDOR LIST

To view the Vendor List for Rock Castle Construction:

Step 1: Click the **Vendor Center** icon in the Icon bar.

Step 2: Click the **Vendors** tab. The following Vendor List appears listing vendors with whom Rock Castle Construction does business. The Vendor List also displays the balance currently owed each vendor.

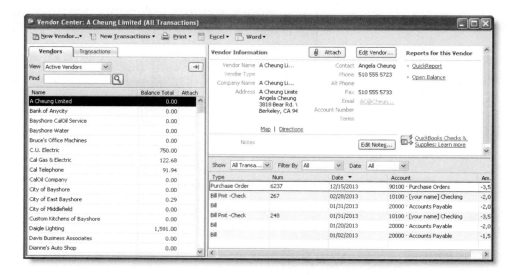

Step 3:   To view additional information about a vendor, click the vendor's name, and Vendor Information will appear on the right side of the Vendor Center.

ADD NEW VENDOR

Rock Castle Construction needs to add a new vendor, Kolbe Window & Door, to the Vendor List.

To add a new vendor to the Vendor List:

Step 1:   Click the **New Vendor** button at the top of the Vendor Center.

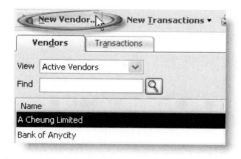

Step 2: A blank *New Vendor* window should appear. Enter the information shown below into the *New Vendor | Address Info* window.

Vendor	Kolbe Window & Door
Company Name	Kolbe Window & Door
Address	58 Chartres Bayshore, CA 94326
Contact	John Kolbe
Phone	415-555-1958
Alt. Contact	Joseph
E-mail	Kolbe@windowdoor.com
Print on check as	Kolbe Window & Door

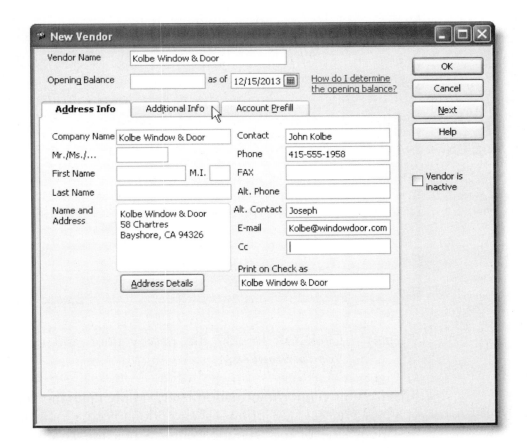

Step 3: Click the **Additional Info** tab and enter the following information.

Account	58101
Type	Materials
Terms	Net 30
Vendor eligible for 1099	Yes
Tax ID	37-1958101

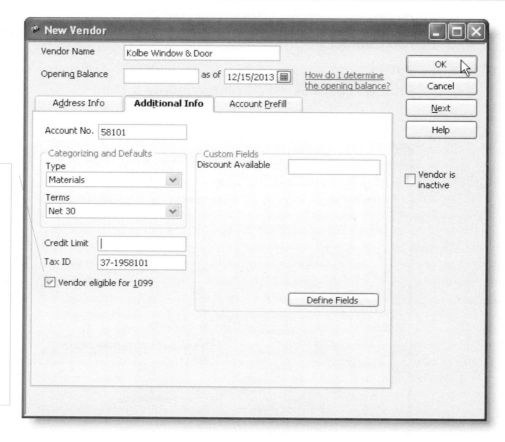

IRS Form 1099 must be completed for sole proprietorships and partnerships to which you paid $600 or more in a year. The vendor's Tax ID No. is required to complete the 1099.

Step 4: Click **OK** to add the new vendor and close the *New Vendor* window.

FYI: To edit vendor information later, simply click the vendor's name in the *Vendor List* window. The vendor information will appear on the right side of the Vendor Center. Click the Edit Vendor button, make the necessary changes in the *Edit Vendor* window that appears, and then click OK to close the *Edit Vendor* window.

PRINT VENDOR LIST

🖨 **Print** the Vendor List as follows:

Step 1: Click the **Print** button at the top of the Vendor Center.

Step 2: Select **Vendor List** from the drop-down menu.

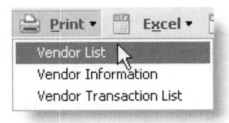

Step 3: When the *Print Reports* window appears, select **Portrait** and **Fit report to 1 page wide**.

Step 4: Click **Print**.

Step 5: **Close** the Vendor Center.

The Items and Services List, discussed next, is used to record information about goods and services purchased from vendors.

ITEMS: INVENTORY ITEMS, NON-INVENTORY ITEMS, AND SERVICES

Items provide supporting detail for accounts.

QuickBooks defines an item as anything that your company buys, sells, or resells including products, shipping charges, and sales taxes. QuickBooks classifies goods and services purchased and sold into three different categories of items:

1. **Service Items:** Service items can be services that are purchased *or* sold. For example, service items include:

   ▪ Services you *buy* from vendors, such as cleaning services.

   ▪ Services you *sell* to customers, such as installation labor.

QuickBooks tracks inventory costs using the weighted-average method. QuickBooks does not use FIFO (First-in, First-out) or LIFO (Last-in, First-out) inventory costing. The average cost of an inventory item is displayed in the *Edit Item* window.

QuickBooks does *not* track the **quantity** of non-inventory items. If it is important for your business to know the quantity of an item on hand, record the item as an inventory item.

2. **Inventory Items:** Inventory items are goods that a business purchases, holds as inventory, and then resells to customers. QuickBooks traces the quantity and cost of inventory items in stock.

   For consistency, the *same* inventory item is used when recording *sales* and *purchases*. QuickBooks has the capability to track both the cost and the sales price for inventory items. For example, in Chapter 4, you recorded the *sale* of an inventory item, an interior door. When the interior door was recorded on a sales invoice, QuickBooks automatically updated your inventory records by reducing the quantity of doors on hand. If you *purchased* an interior door, then you would record the door on the purchase order using the same inventory item number that you used on the invoice, except the purchase order uses the door cost while the invoice uses the door selling price.

3. **Non-Inventory Items:** QuickBooks does not track the quantity on hand for non-inventory items. Non-inventory items include:

   - Items purchased for a specific customer job, such as a custom countertop.

   - Items purchased and used by your company instead of resold to customers, such as office supplies or carpentry tools.

   - Items purchased and resold (if the quantity on hand does not need to be tracked).

ITEMS AND SERVICES LIST

The Items and Services List (Item List) summarizes information about items (inventory items, non-inventory items, and service items) that a company purchases or sells.

To view the Item List in QuickBooks:

Step 1:   Click the **Items & Services** icon in the *Company* section of the Home page.

Step 2: The following *Item List* window will appear.

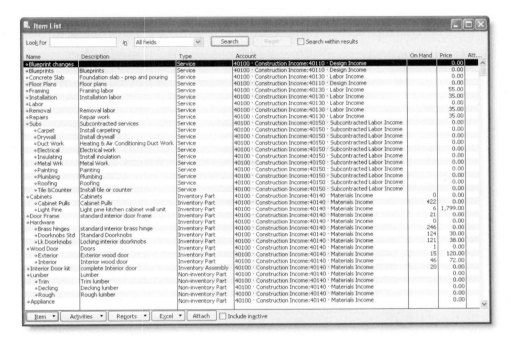

Notice the Item List contains the following information:

- Item name.

- Item description.

- Item type (service, inventory, non-inventory, other charge, discount, sales tax item).

- Account used.

- Quantity on hand.

- Price of the item.

Scroll down through the list to view the inventory and non-inventory items for Rock Castle Construction.

ADD NEW ITEM

Rock Castle Construction needs to add two new items to the Item List: bifold doors and bifold door hardware. Because Rock Castle Construction wants to track the quantity of each item, both will be inventory items.

To add an inventory item to the Item List:

Step 1: From the *Item List* window, **right-click** to display the following pop-up menu. Select **New**.

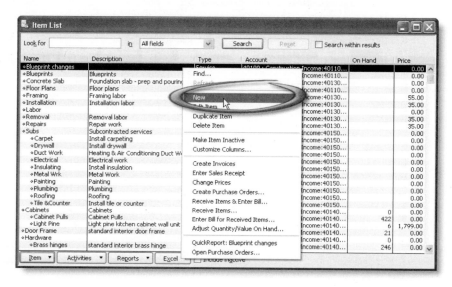

Step 2: In the *New Item* window that appears, you will enter information about the bifold door inventory item. From the Type drop-down list, select **Inventory Part**.

Use **Group** if the items are bought or sold as a package.

Step 3: Enter the following information in the *New Item* window.

Item Name/Number	Bifold Doors
Subitem of	Wood Door
Manufacturer's Part Number	BD42
Description on Purchase Transactions	Bifold interior door
Description on Sales Transactions	Bifold interior door
Cost	45.00
COGS Account	50100 – Cost of Goods Sold
Preferred Vendor	Kolbe Window & Door
Sales Price	70.00
Tax Code	Tax
Income Account	40140 Materials Income
Asset Account	12100 – Inventory Asset
Reorder Point	2
Qty on Hand	0
Total Value	0.00
As of	12/15/2013

If spell checker starts, click **Add** to add Bifold to dictionary.

Step 4: Click **Next** to record this inventory item and clear the fields to record another inventory item.

Step 5: Enter bifold door knobs as an inventory item in the Item List using the following information:

Item Name/Number	Bifold Knobs
Subitem of	Hardware
Manufacturer's Part Number	BK36
Description on Purchase Transactions	Bifold door hardware
Description on Sales Transactions	Bifold door hardware
Cost	6.00
Sales Price	10.00
Tax Code	Tax
COGS Account	50100 – Cost of Goods Sold
Preferred Vendor	Patton Hardware Supplies
Income Account	40140 Materials Income
Asset Account	12100 – Inventory Asset
Reorder Point	2
Qty on Hand	0
Total Value	0.00
As of	12/15/2013

Step 6: Click **OK** to record the item and close the *New Item* window.

PRINT ITEM LIST

⊟ **Print** the Item List as follows:

Step 1:   Click the **Reports** button in the lower left corner of the *Item List* window.

Step 2:   Select **Item Listing**.

Step 3:   Click the **Print** button.

Step 4:   Select the **Landscape** print setting, then click **Print**.

Step 5:   **Close** the *Item List* window.

VENDOR TRANSACTIONS

After creating a Vendor List and an Item List, you are ready to enter vendor transactions.

There are two basic ways to enter vendor transactions using QuickBooks.

1. **Enter Bills.** This is used to record services, such as utilities or accounting services. After the bill is entered, it is paid when it is due.

2. **Enter Purchase Order, Receive Inventory, Enter Bill.** This is used to record the purchase of inventory items where it is necessary to keep a record of the order placed. The purchase order provides this record.

Next, we will use QuickBooks Coach to view the workflow for vendor transactions.

QuickBooks Coach

QuickBooks Coach permits you to explore the workflow for vendor transactions on the Home page.

To turn on the *Explore* mode and show Coach Tips:

Step 1: From the right side of the Home page, click **Show Coach Tips**.

Step 2: To spotlight the workflow for enter bills, click the **Coach** icon beside **Enter Bills**.

The workflow that appears pertains to entering bills for services and non-inventory items is shown below.

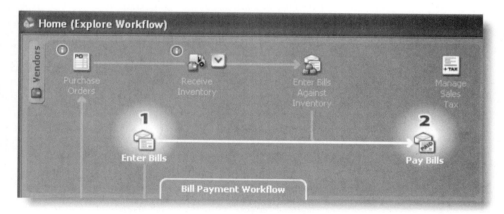

Step 3: To spotlight the workflow for purchasing inventory items, click the **Coach** icon 🛈 beside **Purchase Orders**.

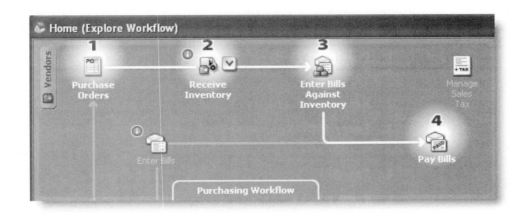

Step 4: Although you can leave the Explore Workflow and Coach Tips displayed while using QuickBooks, if you prefer to hide the Coach Tips, click **Hide Coach Tips** in the *QuickBooks Coach* window.

PURCHASE INVENTORY

Display the Home page to view the flowchart of vendor transactions. Recording the purchase of inventory using QuickBooks involves the following steps:

1. **Purchase Orders.** Create a purchase order to order items from vendors.

2. **Receive Inventory.** Record inventory items received.

3. **Enter Bills Against Inventory.** Record bill received and the obligation to pay the vendor later (accounts payable).

4. **Pay Bills.** Select bills to pay.

5. **Print Checks.** Print checks to vendors. Since the obligation is fulfilled, accounts payable is reduced.

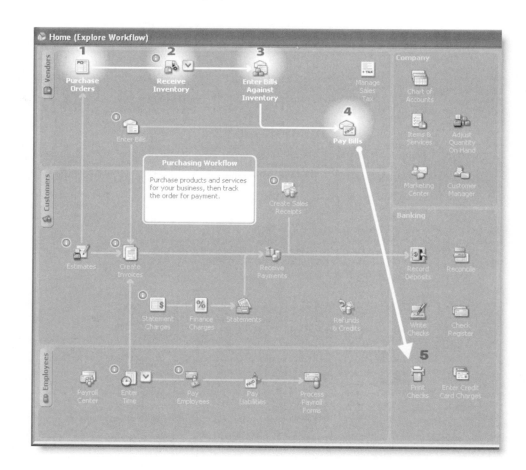

CREATE PURCHASE ORDERS

A purchase order is a record of an order to purchase inventory from a vendor.

Rock Castle Construction wants to order 6 bifold interior doors and 6 sets of bifold door hardware to stock in inventory.

To create a purchase order:

Step 1: Click the **Purchase Orders** icon in the *Vendors* section of the Home page.

Step 2: From the drop-down Vendor List, select the vendor name: **Kolbe Window & Door**.

Step 3: Select Template: **Custom Purchase Order**.

Step 4: Enter the Purchase Order Date: **12/20/2013**.

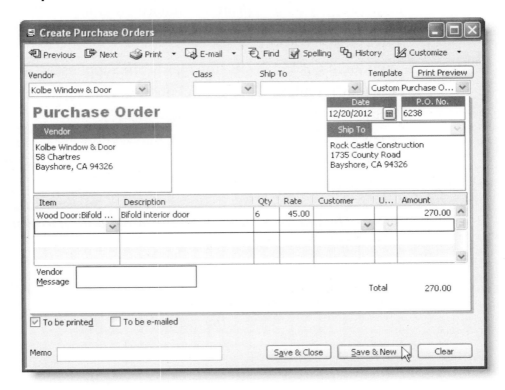

Step 5: Select item ordered: **Wood Doors: Bifold Doors**. ($45.00 now appears in the *Rate* column.)

Step 6: Enter Quantity: **6**. ($270.00 should now appear in the *Amount* column.)

Step 7: Select **To be printed**.

Step 8: **Print** the purchase order as follows:

- Click **Print**.
- Select Print on: **Blank paper**.
- If necessary, uncheck **Do not print lines around each field**.
- Click **Print**.

Step 9: Click **Save & New** (or **Next**) to record the purchase order and clear the fields in the *Purchase Order* window.

Step 10: Create and **print** a purchase order for bifold door hardware using the following information.

Vendor	Patton Hardware Supplies
Custom Template	Custom Purchase Order
Date	12/20/2013
Item	Hardware: Bifold knobs
QTY	6

> ☑ ***The purchase order total for bifold door hardware is $36.***

Step 11: Click **Save & Close** to record the purchase order and close the *Purchase Order* window.

RECEIVE INVENTORY

To record inventory items received on 12/22/2013 ordered from the vendor, Kolbe Window & Door, complete the following steps:

Step 1: Click the **Receive Inventory** icon in the *Vendors* section of the Home page.

Step 2: Select: **Receive Inventory without Bill.**

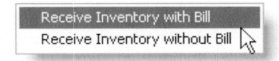

Step 3: In the *Create Item Receipts* window, select vendor: **Kolbe Window & Door**.

Step 4: If a purchase order for the item exists, QuickBooks will display the following *Open POs Exist* window. Click **Yes**.

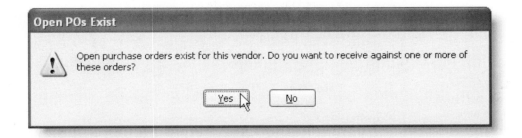

Step 5: When the following *Open Purchase Orders* window appears, select the purchase order for the items received, and then click **OK**.

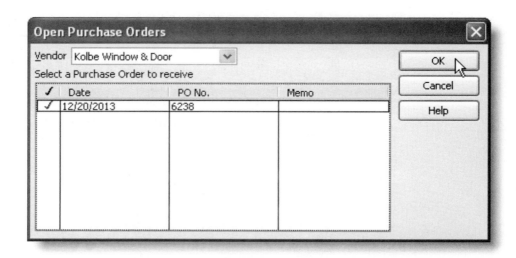

Step 6: The *Create Item Receipts* window will appear with a total of $270. If necessary, change the Date to: **12/22/2013**.

Although Rock Castle Construction ordered 6 bifold doors, only 5 were received. Change the quantity from 6 to **5**.

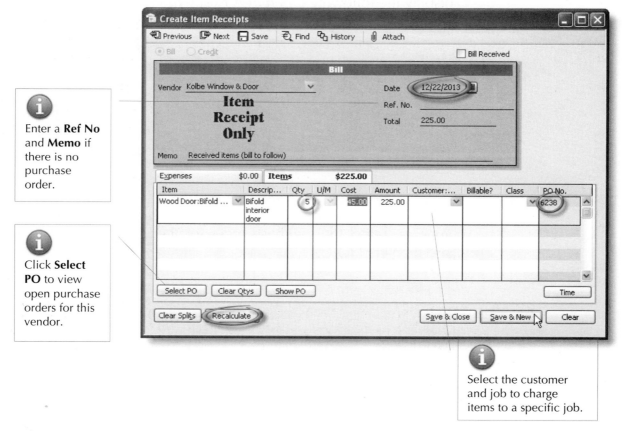

Enter a **Ref No** and **Memo** if there is no purchase order.

Click **Select PO** to view open purchase orders for this vendor.

Select the customer and job to charge items to a specific job.

Step 7: To record expenses associated with the items received, such as freight charges:

- Click the **Expenses** tab in the *Create Item Receipts* window.

- To record $35.00 in freight charges on the bifold doors received, select Account: **54520 Freight & Delivery**.

- Enter Amount: **$35.00**.

- Click the **Recalculate** button.

> ☑ *The Total on the Create Item Receipts window is now $260.00.*

Step 8: Click **Save & New** (or **Next)** to record the bifold doors received and clear the window.

Step 9: Record the receipt of the bifold door hardware using the following information:

Vendor	Patton Hardware Supplies
Date	12/22/2013
PO No.	6239
Item	Bifold door hardware
Qty	6

Step 10: Click **Save & Close** to record the items received and close the *Create Item Receipts* window.

RECEIVE BILLS

You may receive bills at three different times:

	Receive Bill...	Record Using...
1.	You receive a bill for services and no inventory items will be received, as for example, if the bill is for janitorial services.	*Enter Bills*
2.	You receive a bill at the same time you receive inventory items.	*Receive Inventory with Bill*
3.	You receive inventory without a bill, and you receive the bill later.	*a. Receive Inventory without a Bill* *b. Enter Bills Against Inventory*

Later, you will learn how to record bills for situations 1 and 2 above. Next, you will record the bill received for the bifold doors ordered from Kolbe Window & Door (situation 3 above).

ENTER BILLS AGAINST INVENTORY

To enter a bill received after inventory items are received:

Step 1: Click the **Enter Bills Against Inventory** icon on the *Vendors* section of the Home page.

Step 2: When the *Select Item Receipt* window appears:

- Select Vendor: **Kolbe Window & Door**. If necessary, press **Tab**.

- Select the Item Receipt that corresponds to the bill.

- Click **OK**.

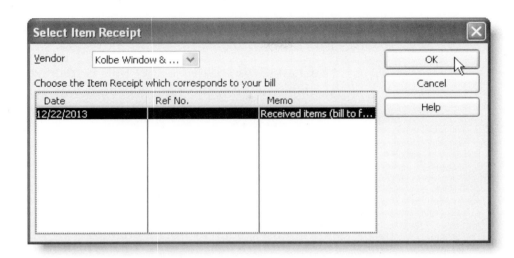

Step 3: The following *Enter Bills* window will appear. Notice that the *Enter Bills* window is the same as the *Create Item Receipts* window except:

1. *Item Receipt Only* stamp does not appear, and

2. Bill Received in the upper right corner is checked.

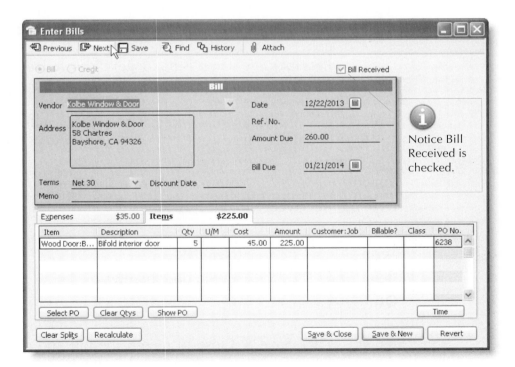

Step 4: At this point, you can make any changes necessary, such as:

- Change the date if the bill is received on a date different from the date the item was received. In this instance, the item and bill are both received on **12/22/2013**.

- Terms

- Ref No.

- Memo

- Expenses, such as freight charges

Step 5: The Amount Due of **$260.00** should agree with the amount shown on the vendor's bill.

Step 6: Click **Next** to advance to the Item Receipt for the bifold door hardware purchased from Patton Hardware Supplies. If asked if you want to record changes, click **Yes**.

Step 7: To record the bill received for the bifold door hardware from Patton Hardware Supplies, check **Bill Received** in the upper right corner of the window. Notice that the *Item Receipt Only* stamp is no longer displayed and the window name changed from *Create Item Receipts* to *Enter Bills*.

Step 8: Use the following information to record the bill for the bifold door hardware.

Vendor	Patton Hardware Supplies
Date Bill Received	12/22/2013
PO No.	6239
Terms	Net 30
Item	Bifold door hardware
Qty	6

Step 9: Click **Save & Close** to record the bill and close the *Enter Bills* window. If asked if you want to change the terms, click **Yes**.

When you enter a bill, QuickBooks automatically adds the bill amount to your Accounts Payable account balance.

PAY BILLS

After receiving the items and entering the bill, the next step is to pay the bill.

To select the bills to pay:

Step 1: Click the **Pay Bills** icon in the *Vendors* section of the Home page.

Step 2: Select Show Bills: **Show all bills**.

You can pay bills by check, credit card, or online.

Check the Ending Balance to avoid over-drawing your checking account.

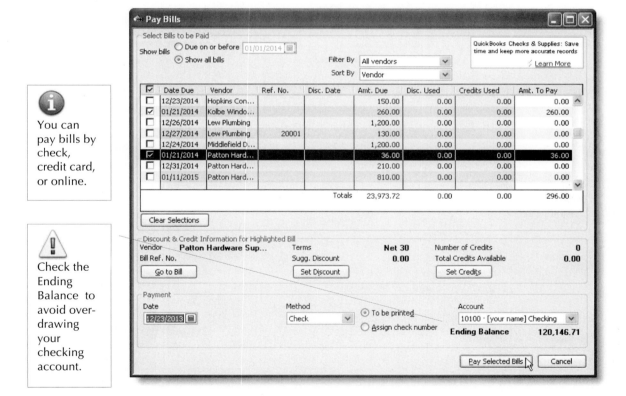

Step 3: Select the bills you want to pay. Typically, you would select the bills that are due first. In this case, however, select **bills that you just recorded for:**

- **Kolbe Window and Door for $260.00**
- **Patton Hardware Supplies for $36.00**

If necessary, scroll down to view these two bills.

Step 4: In the *Payment Method* section, select: **Check**. Then select: **To be printed**.

Step 5: Select Payment Date: **12/23/2013**.

Step 6: Click **Pay Selected Bills**.

 Bills selected for payment total $296.00

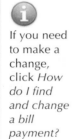

If you need to make a change, click *How do I find and change a bill payment?*

To print the checks, when the *Payment Summary* window appears:

Step 1: Review the information to verify it is correct.

Payment Summary

Payment Details

Payment Date   12/23/2013
Payment Account   10100 · [your name] Checking
Payment Method   Check

Payments have been successfully recorded for the following 2 of 2 bills:

Date Due	Vendor	Amount Paid
01/21/2014	Kolbe Window & Door	260.00
01/21/2014	Patton Hardware Supplies	36.00
	Total	296.00

How do I find and change a bill payment?

You can print checks now, or print them later from Print Forms on the File menu.

[Pay More Bills]   [Print Checks]   [Done]

Step 2: Click **Print Checks**.

Step 3: When the *Select Checks to Print* window appears, select Bank Account: **[your name] Checking**.

Step 4: Select First Check Number: **520**.

To print the checks later, click **Done**. Later, select **File** menu **> Print Forms > Checks**.

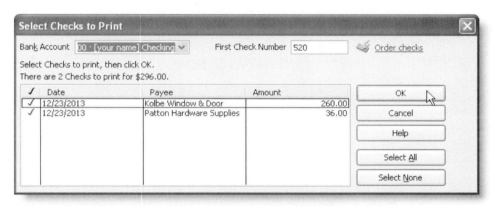

QuickBooks prints one check for each vendor, combining all amounts due to the same vendor.

Step 5: Select the two checks shown above:

- **12/23/2013 Kolbe Window & Door for $260.00**
- **12/23/2013 Patton Hardware Supplies for $36.00**

Step 6: Click **OK**.

If you use Intuit's preprinted check forms, you would now insert the check forms in your printer.

Step 7: Select Check Style: **Standard**. Select: **Print company name and address**.

Step 8: Click **Print**.

RECEIVE INVENTORY WITH BILL

If you receive the inventory item and the bill at the same time (situation 2 mentioned earlier), record both the items and the related bill by completing the following steps:

Step 1: Click the **Receive Inventory** icon in the *Vendors* section of the Home page.

Step 2: Select: **Receive Inventory with Bill**.

Step 3: In the following *Enter Bills* window:

- Enter Vendor: **Wheeler's Tile Etc.**

- Select the open purchase order that corresponds to the bill received: **PO No. 6234**.

- Click **OK**.

- Make any necessary changes to date, quantity or cost. In this case, if necessary change the date to: **12/23/2013**.

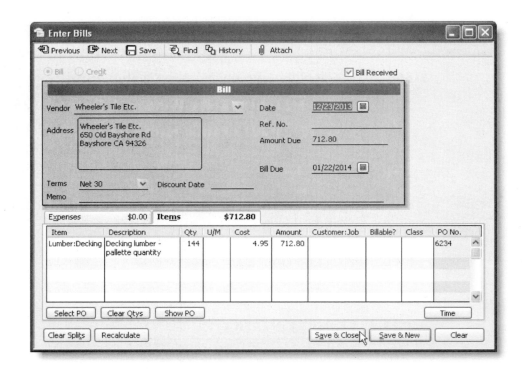

Step 4: Click **Save & Close** to close the *Enter Bills* window.

ENTER BILLS

When you received inventory items from vendors, you recorded those items using either the *Receive Inventory with Bill* option or the *Receive Inventory without Bill* option, entering the bill later.

To record services instead of inventory received, use the Enter Bills icon. Expenses that can be recorded using the *Enter Bills* window include utilities, insurance, and rent.

Recording bills for services, such as utilities, in QuickBooks requires two steps:

1. **Enter Bills.** Record bills received for services.
2. **Pay Bills.** Select bills to pay.

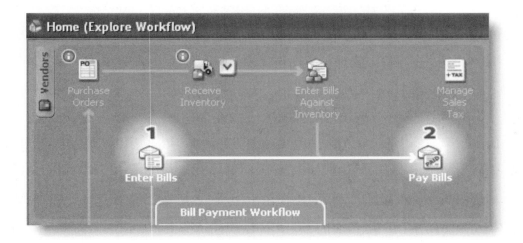

To enter bills for expenses:

Step 1: Click the **Enter Bills** icon in the *Vendors* section of the Home page.

Step 2: The following *Enter Bills* window will appear. Click the **Expenses** tab.

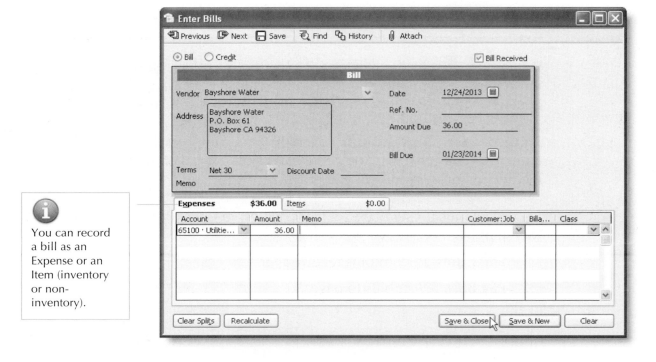

You can record a bill as an Expense or an Item (inventory or non-inventory).

Step 3: Enter the following information for Rock Castle's water bill in the *Enter Bills* window.

Vendor	Bayshore Water
Date	12/24/2013
Amount Due	$36.00
Terms	Net 30
Account	65130: Water

Step 4: Click **Save & Close** to close the *Enter Bills* window.

The next time you pay bills in QuickBooks, the water bill will appear on the list of bills to pay.

PAY SALES TAX

QuickBooks tracks the sales tax that you collect from customers and must remit to governmental agencies. When you set up a new company in QuickBooks, you identify which items and customers are subject to sales tax. In addition, you must specify the appropriate sales tax rate. Then whenever you prepare sales invoices, QuickBooks automatically calculates and adds sales tax to the invoices.

Rock Castle Construction is required to collect sales tax from customers on certain items sold. Rock Castle then must pay the sales tax collected to the appropriate governmental tax agency.

QuickBooks uses a two-step process to remit sales tax:

1. **Pay Sales Tax.** The *Manage Sales Tax* window lists the sales taxes owed and allows you to select the individual sales tax items you want to pay.

2. **Print Checks.** Print the check to pay the sales tax.

To select the sales tax to pay:

Step 1: Click the **Manage Sales Tax** icon in the *Vendors* section of the Home page.

Step 2: When the *Manage Sales Tax* window appears, in the *Pay Sales Tax* section of the window, click the **Pay Sales Tax** button.

Step 3: When the following *Pay Sales Tax* window appears:

- Select Pay From Account: **[your name] Checking**
- Select Check Date: **12/31/2013**.
- Show sales tax due through: **12/31/2013**.
- ✓ Check **To be printed**.

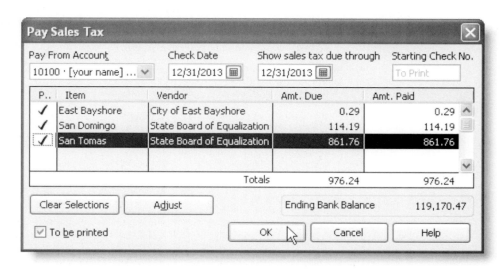

Step 4: Select: **Pay All Tax**.

Step 5: Click **OK**.

Step 6: Click **Close** to close the *Manage Sales Tax* window.

To print the check to pay sales tax to a governmental agency:

Step 1: Click the **Print Checks** icon in the *Banking* section of the Home page.

Step 2: When the following *Select Checks to Print* window appears, select **City of East Bayshore** and **State Board of Equalization**.

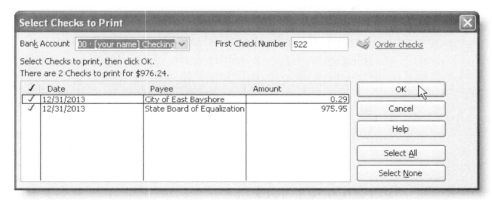

Step 3: Select Bank Account: **[your name] Checking**.

Step 4: Select First Check Number: **522**.

Step 5: Click **OK**.

Step 6: Select print settings, then click **Print**.

VENDOR REPORTS

QuickBooks provides vendor reports to answer the following questions:

- How much do we owe? (Accounts Payable reports)
- How much have we purchased? (Purchase reports)
- How much inventory do we have? (Inventory reports)

QuickBooks offers several different ways to access vendor reports:

1. **Vendor Center.** Summarizes vendor information in one location (Access the Vendor Center by clicking the Vendor Center icon on the Icon bar.)

2. **Report Center.** Permits you to locate reports by type of report (Click the Report Center icon in the Icon bar, then see Vendors & Payables, Purchases, and Inventory reports).

3. **Reports Menu.** Reports are grouped by type of report (See Vendors & Payables, Purchases, and Inventory reports).

VENDOR CENTER

The Vendor Center summarizes vendor information in one convenient location. Display the Vendor Center as follows:

Step 1: From the Icon bar, select **Vendor Center**.

Step 2: Select Vendor: **Kolbe Window & Door**.

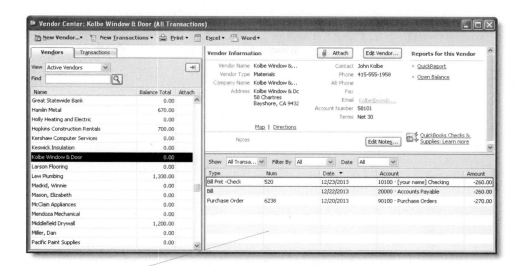

Notice the three transactions for Kolbe Window & Door.

The *Vendor Information* section summarizes information about the vendor selected, including a list of the transactions for the specific vendor. In this case, you recorded three transactions for Kolbe Window & Door:

- Purchase order on 12/20/2013
- Bill received on 12/22/2013
- Bill paid on 12/23/2013

Step 3: Double-click **Bill Pymt – Check** on **12/23/2013** to drill-down and view the check to pay Kolbe Window & Door. After viewing, close the window.

Step 4: With the cursor over the *Vendor Transaction* section of the window, **right-click** to display the following pop-up menu. Select **View as a Report**.

Step 5: 🖨 **Print** the report of all transactions for Kolbe Window & Door for this fiscal year.

Step 6: **Close** the report window.

ACCOUNTS PAYABLE REPORTS: HOW MUCH DO WE OWE?

Accounts Payable consists of amounts that your company is obligated to pay in the future. Accounts Payable reports tell you how much you owe vendors and when amounts are due.

The following Accounts Payable reports provide information useful when tracking amounts owed vendors:

1. Accounts Payable Aging Summary

2. Accounts Payable Aging Detail

3. Unpaid Bills Detail

ACCOUNTS PAYABLE AGING SUMMARY

The Accounts Payable Aging Summary summarizes accounts payable balances by the age of the account. This report helps to track any past due bills as well as provides information about bills that will be due shortly.

Although you can access the vendor reports in several different ways, we will access this report from the Report Center.

To print the A/P Aging Summary report:

Step 1: From the Report Center (List View), select: **Vendors & Payables**.

Step 2: Select: **A/P Aging Summary**.

Step 3: Select Date: **12/22/2013**. Select **Display report** icon.

Step 4: 🖨 **Print** the report using **Portrait** orientation.

Step 5: ✐ **Circle** the vendors and amounts of any account payable that is past due.

Step 6: **Close** the *A/P Aging Summary* window.

☑ ***$3,459.20 is 1-30 days past due.***

ACCOUNTS PAYABLE AGING DETAIL

The Accounts Payable Aging Detail report lists the specific bills that make up the account payable balances.

Double-click on an entry to drill down to the related bill.

To print the A/P Aging Detail report:

Step 1: From the Report Center, select: **Vendors & Payables**.

Step 2: Select: **A/P Aging Detail**.

Step 3: Select Date: **12/22/2013**. Click **Display report** icon.

Step 4: 🖨 **Print** the report using **Portrait** orientation.

Step 5: **Close** the *A/P Aging Detail* window.

PURCHASE REPORTS: HOW MUCH HAVE WE PURCHASED?

Purchase reports provide information about purchases by item, by vendor, or by open purchase orders. Purchase reports include:

1. Open Purchase Orders (Outstanding Purchase Orders)
2. Purchases by Vendor Summary
3. Purchases by Item Summary

OPEN PURCHASE ORDERS REPORT

Open purchase orders are purchase orders for items ordered but not yet received. QuickBooks permits you to view all open purchase orders or just those for a specific vendor.

To print the Open Purchase Orders Report that lists all open purchase orders:

Step 1: From the Report Center, select: **Purchases**.

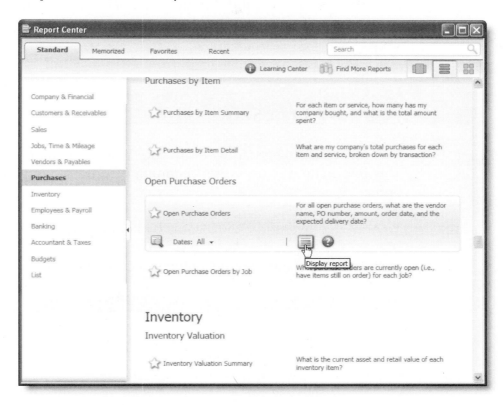

Step 2: Select: **Open Purchase Orders**.

Step 3: Select Dates: **All**. Click **Display report** icon.

Step 4: 🖨 **Print** the report using **Portrait** orientation.

Step 5: **Close** the *Open Purchase Orders* window.

> ☑️ ***Open Purchase Orders equal $19,286.25.***

INVENTORY REPORTS:
HOW MUCH INVENTORY DO WE HAVE?

Inventory reports list the amount and status of inventory. Inventory reports include:

1. Inventory Stock Status by Item
2. Physical Inventory Worksheet

INVENTORY STOCK STATUS BY ITEM

This report lists the quantity of inventory items on hand and on order. This information is useful for planning when and how many units to order.

To print the Inventory Stock Status by Item report:

Step 1: From the Report Center, select: **Inventory**.

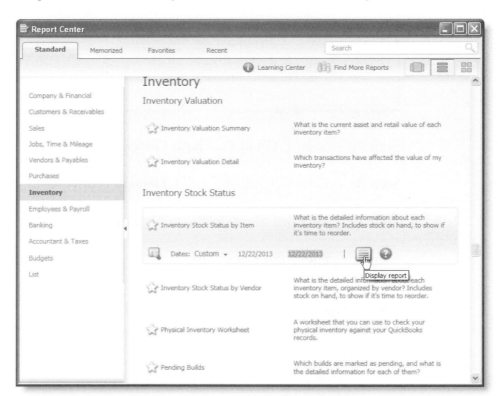

Step 2: Select: **Inventory Stock Status by Item**.

Step 3: Enter Date: From: **12/22/2013** To: **12/22/2013**. Click **Display report** icon.

Step 4: ▣ **Print** the report using **Landscape** orientation.

Step 5: **Close** the *Inventory Stock Status by Item* window.

> ***On 12/22/2013, 5 bifold wood doors are on hand and 1 more is on order.***

PHYSICAL INVENTORY WORKSHEET

The Physical Inventory Worksheet is used when taking a physical count of inventory on hand. The worksheet lists the quantity of inventory items on hand and provides a blank column in which to enter the quantity counted during a physical inventory count. This worksheet permits you to compare your physical inventory count with your QuickBooks records.

To print the Physical Inventory Worksheet:

Step 1: From the Report Center, select: **Inventory**.

Step 2: Select: **Physical Inventory Worksheet**.

Step 3: ▣ **Print** the worksheet using **Portrait** orientation. Use the Fit to Page feature as needed.

Step 4: **Close** the *Physical Inventory Worksheet* window.

QuickBooks offers other additional vendor reports that provide useful information to a business. These reports can also be accessed from the Reports menu or from the Report Center.

SAVE CHAPTER 5

Save a backup of your Chapter 5 file using the file name: **[your name] Chapter 5 Backup.QBB**. See *Appendix B: Back Up & Restore QuickBooks Files* for instructions.

WORKFLOW

If you are using the workflow approach, leave your .QBW file open and proceed directly to Exercise 5.1.

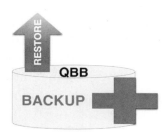

RESTART & RESTORE

If you are using the Restart & Restore approach and are ending your computer session now, close your .QBW file and exit QuickBooks. When you restart, you will restore your backup file to complete Exercise 5.1.

PODCASTS

Watch the Chapter 5 **Podcast** at www.QuickBooksBlog.info to view how to process vendor transactions using QuickBooks. Bookmark www.QuickBooksBlog.info for your future use.

MULTIPLE-CHOICE PRACTICE TEST

A **Multiple-Choice Practice Test** for Chapter 5 is on the *Computer Accounting for QuickBooks Pro* Online Learning Center at www.mhhe.com/kay2010. Try the Practice Test and see how many questions you answer correctly.

EXTRAS!

Section 3: Quick Guide contains quick, easy step-by-step directions for frequently used QuickBooks tasks, including correcting errors. You can find *Quick Guide* at the back of your text or online at www.mhhe.com/kay2010. *Check it out!*

Deliverables Checklist is a list of the reports and documents that you are to deliver to your instructor for grading. You can find the Deliverables Checklist at the end of the chapter or online at www.mhhe.com/kay2010. Staying organized saves time. Use the checklist to organize your reports, checking off the reports as completed. Then include the checklist with your reports for grading.

Appendix D: Electronic Deliverables shows you how to save your QuickBooks reports electronically. Also, watch the Electronic Deliverables Podcast at www.QuickBooksBlog.info. Check with your instructor to see if you should deliver your reports electronically.

Join the QuickBooks Student Community to ask questions and share tips @ www.QuickBooksBlog.info.

LEARNING ACTIVITIES

Important: Ask your instructor whether you should complete the following assignments by printing requested reports or creating electronic deliverables (see Appendix D: Electronic Deliverables).

EXERCISE 5.1: PURCHASE INVENTORY

SCENARIO

Mr. Castle tosses you a document as he charges past your cubicle, shouting over his shoulder, *"That's info about our new supplier. From now on, Rock Castle will install closet shelving instead of waiting on unreliable subcontractors. We do a better job and we get it done on time!"*

Vendor:	Joseph's Closets
Contact:	Joseph
Address:	13 Rheims Road
	Bayshore, CA 94326
Phone:	415-555-5813
E-mail:	joseph@closet.com
Account:	58127
Type:	Materials
Terms:	Net 30
Vendor 1099:	No

New Inventory Item: Closet Materials   Income Acct 40140

New Subitems:

6' Closet Shelving	Cost: $11.00	Sales Price: $15.00
12' Closet Shelving	Cost: $18.00	Sales Price: $25.00
Closet Installation Kit	Cost: $ 5.00	Sales Price: $ 8.00

TASK 1: OPEN COMPANY FILE

WORKFLOW

If you are using the Workflow approach, you will use the same .QBW file.

If your QBW file is not already open, open it by selecting **File > Open Previous Company**. Select your **.QBW file.**

Change the company name to **[your name] Exercise 5.1** by selecting **Company** menu > **Company Information.**

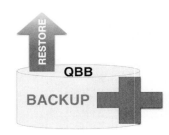

RESTART & RESTORE

If you are not using the same computer, you must use the Restart and Restore approach.

Restore your **Chapter 5 Backup.QBB** file using the directions in *Appendix B: Back Up & Restore QuickBooks Files.*

After restoring the file, change the company name to **[your name] Exercise 5.1** by selecting **Company** menu > **Company Information.**

TASK 2: ADD NEW VENDOR

Add a new vendor from the *Vendor Center.*

Add Joseph's Closets as a new vendor.

TASK 3: ADD NEW INVENTORY ITEM

Step 1: Add the new inventory item, Closet Materials, to the Items List for Rock Castle Construction.

Item Name/Number	Closet Materials
Item Type	Inventory Part
Item Description	Closet Materials
COGS Account	50100 – Cost of Goods Sold
Income Account	40140 – Materials Income
Asset Account	12100 – Inventory Asset
Tax Code	Tax

Step 2: Add the following three new inventory parts as subitems to Closet Materials. Use **Joseph's Closets** as the preferred vendor.

Item Name	6' Closet Shelving
Item Description	6' Closet Shelving
Cost	$11.00
Sales Price	$15.00

Item Name	12' Closet Shelving
Item Description	12' Closet Shelving
Cost	$18.00
Sales Price	$25.00

Item Name	Closet Install Kit
Item Description	Closet Installation Kit
Cost	$5.00
Sales Price	$8.00

TASK 4: CREATE PURCHASE ORDER

Step 1: Create a purchase order to order **6** each of the new inventory items from **Joseph's Closets** on **12/23/2013**.

Step 2: 🖶 **Print** the purchase order.

> ☑ *The total amount of the purchase order is $204.00.*

TASK 5: RECEIVE INVENTORY

On **12/24/2013**, record the receipt of the closet inventory items ordered on **12/23/2013**. There are no freight charges.

TASK 6: RECEIVE BILL

Record the receipt of the bill for the closet items on **12/27/2013**. Use the **Enter Bills Against Inventory** icon in the *Vendors* section of the Home page.

TASK 7: PAY BILLS

Pay the bill for the closet materials ordered from Joseph's Closets on **12/28/ 2013** with Check No. **524**. 🖶 **Print** the check.

TASK 8: SAVE EXERCISE 5.1

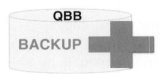

Save a backup of your Exercise 5.1 file using the file name: **[your name] Exercise 5.1 Backup.QBB**. See *Appendix B: Back Up & Restore QuickBooks Files* for instructions.

WORKFLOW

If you are proceeding to Exercise 5.2 and using the same computer, you can leave your .QBW file open and use it for Exercise 5.2.

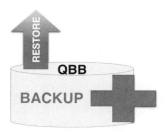

RESTART & RESTORE

If you are stopping your QuickBooks work session and changing computers, you will need to restore your .QBB file when you restart.

EXERCISE 5.2: RECORD SALE (CHAPTER 4 REVIEW)

SCENARIO

"I told you replacing Mrs. Beneficio's door hardware would pay off. She is going to become one of our best customers. Just wait and see." Mr. Castle appears to be in a much better mood today. *"Katrina Beneficio just had us install new closet shelving in her huge walk-in closet. She said she wanted us to do it because we stand by our work."*

TASK 1: OPEN COMPANY FILE

WORKFLOW

If you are using the Workflow approach, you will use the same .QBW file.

If your QBW file is not already open, open it by selecting **File > Open Previous Company**. Select your **.QBW file.**

Change the company name to **[your name] Exercise 5.2** by selecting **Company** menu **> Company Information.**

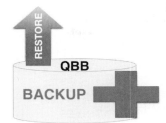

RESTART & RESTORE

If you are using the Restart and Restore approach, restore your backup file using the directions in *Appendix B: Back Up & Restore QuickBooks Files*.

After restoring the file, change the company name to **[your name] Exercise 5.2** by selecting **Company** menu **> Company Information.**

TASK 2: ADD CUSTOMER JOB

Add the Closet Shelving job for Katrina Beneficio to the Customer & Job List. (Hint: From the Customer Center, select **Beneficio**, then **right-click** to display menu, and select **Add Job**.)

Job Name	Closet Shelving
Job Status	Closed
Start Date	12/27/2013
Projected End	12/27/2013
End Date	12/27/2013
Job Description	Replace Closet Shelving
Job Type	Repairs

TASK 3: CREATE INVOICE

Step 1: Create an invoice for the Beneficio closet shelving job using the following information.

Customer: Job	Beneficio, Katrina: Closet Shelving
Custom Template	Rock Castle Invoice
Date	12/27/2013
Invoice No.	1104
Items	(2) 12' Closet Shelves $25.00 each
	(1) 6' Closet Shelves $15.00 each
	(1) Closet Installation Kit $ 8.00 each
	Installation Labor 3 hours

Step 2:   📠 **Print** the invoice.

> ✅ *The invoice for the Closet Shelving job totals $183.66.*

TASK 4: RECEIVE CUSTOMER PAYMENT

Record Katrina Beneficio's payment for the Closet Shelving job (Check No. 625) for the full amount on **12/29/2013**.

TASK 5: RECORD BANK DEPOSIT

Step 1:   Record the bank deposit for Katrina Beneficio's payment on **12/29/2013**.

Step 2:   📠 **Print** a deposit summary.

TASK 6: SAVE EXERCISE 5.2

Save a backup of your Exercise 5.2 file using the file name: **[your name] Exercise 5.2 Backup.QBB**. See *Appendix B: Back Up & Restore QuickBooks Files* for instructions.

WORKFLOW

If you are using the Workflow approach, you can leave your .QBW file open and use it for Exercise 5.3.

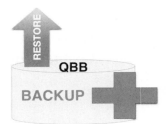

RESTART & RESTORE

If you are stopping your QuickBooks work session and changing computers, you will need to restore your .QBB file when you restart.

EXERCISE 5.3: ENTER BILLS

SCENARIO

When you arrive at work, you decide to sort through the papers stacked in the corner of your cubicle. You discover two unpaid utility bills amid the clutter.

TASK 1: OPEN COMPANY FILE

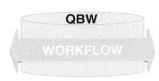

WORKFLOW

If you are using the Workflow approach, you will use the same .QBW file.

If your QBW file is not already open, open it by selecting **File > Open Previous Company**. Select your **.QBW file.**

Change the company name to **[your name] Exercise 5.3** by selecting **Company** menu **> Company Information.**

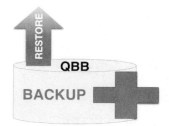

RESTART & RESTORE

If you are using the Restart and Restore approach, restore your backup file using the directions in *Appendix B: Back Up & Restore QuickBooks Files*.

After restoring the file, change the company name to **[your name] Exercise 5.3** by selecting **Company** menu **> Company Information**.

TASK 2: ENTER BILLS

Using the **Enter Bills** icon in the *Vendors* section of the Home page, enter the following two utility bills for Rock Castle Construction.

Vendor	Cal Gas & Electric
Date	12/24/2013
Amount	$87.00
Account	65110: Gas and Electric

Vendor	Cal Telephone
Date	12/24/2013
Amount	$54.00
Account	65120: Telephone

TASK 3: PAY BILLS

On **12/28/2013**, pay the two utility bills that you entered in Task 2. (Hint: Select **Show all bills**.) ▣ **Print** the checks.

 The Amt. To Pay on the Pay Bills window totals $141.00.

TASK 4: SAVE EXERCISE 5.3

Save a backup of your Exercise 5.3 file using the file name: **[your name] Exercise 5.3 Backup.QBB**. See *Appendix B: Back Up & Restore QuickBooks Files* for instructions.

WORKFLOW

If you are using the Workflow approach, you can leave your .QBW file open and use it for Exercise 5.4.

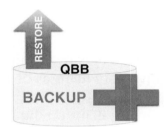

RESTART & RESTORE

If you are stopping your QuickBooks work session and changing computers, you will need to restore your .QBB file when you restart.

EXERCISE 5.4: VENDOR REPORT

In this Exercise, you will print a stock status report for the closet materials inventory and a Trial Balance to verify that your account balances are correct.

TASK 1: OPEN COMPANY FILE

WORKFLOW

If you are using the Workflow approach, you will use the same .QBW file.

If your QBW file is not already open, open it by selecting **File > Open Previous Company**. Select your **.QBW file.**

Change the company name to **[your name] Exercise 5.4** by selecting **Company** menu **> Company Information.**

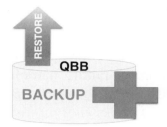

RESTART & RESTORE

If you are using the Restart and Restore approach, restore your backup file using the directions in *Appendix B: Back Up & Restore QuickBooks Files.*

After restoring the file, change the company name to **[your name] Exercise 5.4** by selecting **Company** menu > **Company Information.**

TASK 2: PRINT STOCK STATUS REPORT

Print the stock status report for closet materials inventory.

Step 1: 🖨 **Print** an Inventory Stock Status by Item report to check the status of the closet inventory items as of **12/31/2013.**

Step 2: ✏ **Circle** the closet inventory items on the Inventory Stock Status printout.

Step 3: **Close** the report window.

TASK 3: PRINT TRIAL BALANCE

Next, print a Trial Balance to double check that your accounting system is in balance and that your account balances are correct.

🖨 **Print** the Trial Balance as follows.

Step 1: From the Report Center, select **Accountant and Taxes > Trial Balance**.

Step 2: Select Date From: **12/31/2013** To: **12/31/2013**.

Step 3: 🖨 **Print** the Trial Balance.

Step 4: Compare your printout totals and account balances to the following printout. Correct any errors you find.

| Modify Report... | Memorize... | Print... | E-mail ▾ | Export... | Hide Header | Collapse | Refresh |

Dates Custom   From 12/31/2013 ▦ To 12/31/2013 ▦ Sort By Default

[your name] Exercise 5.4 Rock Castle Construction
Trial Balance
Accrual Basis   As of December 31, 2013

	Dec 31, 13	
	Debit	Credit
10100 · [your name] Checking	119,009.13	
10300 · Savings	17,910.19	
10400 · Petty Cash	500.00	
11000 · Accounts Receivable	93,007.93	
12000 · Undeposited Funds	2,440.00	
12100 · Inventory Asset	30,153.22	
12800 · Employee Advances	832.00	
13100 · Pre-paid Insurance	4,050.00	
13400 · Retainage Receivable	3,703.02	
15000 · Furniture and Equipment	34,326.00	
15100 · Vehicles	78,936.91	
15200 · Buildings and Improvements	325,000.00	
15300 · Construction Equipment	15,300.00	
16900 · Land	90,000.00	
17000 · Accumulated Depreciation		110,344.60
18700 · Security Deposits	1,720.00	
20000 · Accounts Payable		27,885.72
20500 · QuickBooks Credit Card		94.20
20600 · CalOil Credit Card		382.62
24000 · Payroll Liabilities:24010 · Federal Withholding		1,364.00
24000 · Payroll Liabilities:24020 · FICA Payable		2,118.82
24000 · Payroll Liabilities:24030 · AEIC Payable	0.00	
24000 · Payroll Liabilities:24040 · FUTA Payable		100.00
24000 · Payroll Liabilities:24050 · State Withholding		299.19
24000 · Payroll Liabilities:24060 · SUTA Payable		110.00
24000 · Payroll Liabilities:24070 · State Disability Payable		48.13
24000 · Payroll Liabilities:24080 · Worker's Compensation		1,214.31
24000 · Payroll Liabilities:24100 · Emp. Health Ins Payable		150.00
25500 · Sales Tax Payable		5.66
23000 · Loan - Vehicles (Van)		10,501.47
23100 · Loan - Vehicles (Utility Truck)		19,936.91
23200 · Loan - Vehicles (Pickup Truck)		22,641.00
28100 · Loan - Construction Equipment		13,911.32
28200 · Loan - Furniture/Office Equip		21,000.00
28700 · Note Payable - Bank of Anycity		2,693.21
28900 · Mortgage - Office Building		296,283.00
30000 · Opening Bal Equity		38,773.75
30100 · Capital Stock		73,500.00
32000 · Retained Earnings		61,756.76
40100 · Construction Income	0.00	
40100 · Construction Income:40110 · Design Income		36,729.25
40100 · Construction Income:40130 · Labor Income		208,610.42
40100 · Construction Income:40140 · Materials Income		120,233.67
40100 · Construction Income:40150 · Subcontracted Lab...		82,710.35
40100 · Construction Income:40199 · Less Discounts giv...	48.35	
40500 · Reimbursement Income:40520 · Permit Reimbur...		1,223.75
40500 · Reimbursement Income:40530 · Reimbursed Fre...		896.05
50100 · Cost of Goods Sold	15,761.35	
54000 · Job Expenses:54200 · Equipment Rental	1,850.00	
54000 · Job Expenses:54300 · Job Materials	99,648.70	
54000 · Job Expenses:54400 · Permits and Licenses	700.00	
54000 · Job Expenses:54500 · Subcontractors	63,217.95	
54000 · Job Expenses:54520 · Freight & Delivery	877.10	
54000 · Job Expenses:54599 · Less Discounts Taken		201.81
60100 · Automobile:60110 · Fuel	1,588.70	
60100 · Automobile:60120 · Insurance	2,850.24	
60100 · Automobile:60130 · Repairs and Maintenance	2,406.00	
60400 · Selling Expense:60410 · Advertising Expense	200.00	
60600 · Bank Service Charges	145.00	
62100 · Insurance:62110 · Disability Insurance	582.06	
62100 · Insurance:62120 · Liability Insurance	5,885.96	
62100 · Insurance:62130 · Work Comp	13,657.07	
62400 · Interest Expense:62420 · Loan Interest	1,995.65	
62700 · Payroll Expenses:62710 · Gross Wages	110,400.10	
62700 · Payroll Expenses:62720 · Payroll Taxes	8,445.61	
62700 · Payroll Expenses:62730 · FUTA Expense	268.00	
62700 · Payroll Expenses:62740 · SUTA Expense	1,233.50	
63100 · Postage	104.20	
63600 · Professional Fees:63610 · Accounting	250.00	
64200 · Repairs:64210 · Building Repairs	175.00	
64200 · Repairs:64220 · Computer Repairs	300.00	
64200 · Repairs:64230 · Equipment Repairs	1,350.00	
64800 · Tools and Machinery	2,820.68	
65100 · Utilities:65110 · Gas and Electric	1,251.16	
65100 · Utilities:65120 · Telephone	895.15	
65100 · Utilities:65130 · Water	300.00	
70100 · Other Income		146.80
70200 · Interest Income		229.16
TOTAL	**1,156,095.93**	**1,156,095.93**

Step 5: **Close** the *Trial Balance* report window.

TASK 4: PRINT JOURNAL

🖶 **Print** the Journal as follows.

Step 1: From the Report Center, select **Accountant and Taxes > Journal**.

Step 2: Select Dates From: **12/20/2013** To: **12/29/2013**.

Step 3: 🖶 **Print** the Journal.

TASK 5: SAVE EXERCISE 5.4

Save a backup of your Exercise 5.4 file using the file name: **[your name] Exercise 5.4 Backup.QBB**. See *Appendix B: Back Up & Restore QuickBooks Files* for instructions.

WORKFLOW

If you are using the Workflow approach, you can leave your .QBW file open and use it for the next chapter.

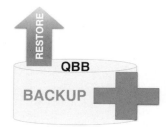

RESTART & RESTORE

If you are stopping your QuickBooks work session and changing computers, you will need to restore your .QBB file when you restart.

EXERCISE 5.5: WEB QUEST

Online bill paying services can be used by small businesses to pay their bills using the Internet.

Step 1: Search www.quickbooks.intuit.com, the QuickBooks website, to discover more information about Intuit QuickBooks Bill Pay Service.

Step 2: ✍ Using word processing or e-mail software, write an e-mail to Mr. Castle summarizing the advantages and disadvantages of online bill paying, including features and benefits, how it works, pricing, and security. Include your recommendations regarding whether Rock Castle Construction should use online bill paying and why.

DELIVERABLES CHECKLIST CHAPTER 5
NAME:

INSTRUCTIONS:
1. CHECK OFF THE DELIVERABLES YOU HAVE COMPLETED.
2. TURN IN THIS PAGE WITH YOUR DELIVERABLES.

CHAPTER 5
- ☐ Vendor List
- ☐ Item List
- ☐ Purchase Order No. 6238 & 6239
- ☐ Checks No. 520-521
- ☐ Check No. 522-523 for Sales Tax
- ☐ Vendor Transaction Report
- ☐ A/P Aging Summary Report
- ☐ A/P Aging Detail Report
- ☐ Open Purchase Orders Report
- ☐ Inventory Stock Status by Item Report
- ☐ Physical Inventory Worksheet

EXERCISE 5.1
- ☐ Task 4: Purchase Order 6240
- ☐ Task 7: Check No. 524

EXERCISE 5.2
- ☐ Task 3: Customer Invoice No. 1104
- ☐ Task 5: Bank Deposit Summary

EXERCISE 5.3
- ☐ Task 3: Checks No. 525-526

EXERCISE 5.4
- ☐ Task 2: Inventory Stock Status By Item Report
- ☐ Task 3: Trial Balance
- ☐ Task 4: Journal

EXERCISE 5.5
- ☐ E-mail: Online Bill Paying Recommendation

REFLECTION: A WISH AND A STAR ★

Reflection improves learning and retention. Reflect on what you have learned after completing Chapter 5 that you did not know before you started the chapter.

A Star:

What did you like best that you learned about QuickBooks in Chapter 5?

A Wish:

If you could pick one thing, what do you wish you knew more about when using QuickBooks?

NOTES:

CHAPTER 6
EMPLOYEES AND PAYROLL

SCENARIO

The next morning on your way to your cubicle, two employees ask you if their paychecks are ready yet. Apparently, Rock Castle employees expect their paychecks today?!

Deciding that you do not want all the employees upset with you if paychecks are not ready on time, you take the initiative and ask Mr. Castle about the paychecks.

His reply: *"Oops! I was so busy I almost forgot about paychecks."* He hands you another stack of documents. *"Here—you will need these. I'm sure you won't have any trouble using QuickBooks to print the paychecks. And don't forget to pay yourself!"* he adds with a chuckle as he rushes out the door.

CHAPTER 6
LEARNING OBJECTIVES

In Chapter 6, you will learn about the following QuickBooks features:

INTRODUCTION

Employees complete Form W-4 when hired. Form W-2 summarizes annual wages and tax withholdings.

In Chapter 6 you will focus on recording employee and payroll transactions. Payroll involves preparing employee paychecks, withholding the appropriate amount in taxes, and paying the company's share of payroll taxes.

To assist in processing payroll, QuickBooks offers a time-tracking feature that permits you to track the amount of time worked. QuickBooks uses time tracked to:

1. Calculate employee paychecks.

2. Transfer time to sales invoices to bill customers for work performed.

No tax withholdings are necessary for independent contractors. Tax Form 1099-MISC summarizes payments.

Although this chapter focuses on time worked by employees, work can be performed by employees, subcontractors, or owners. The time-tracking feature can be used to track time worked by any of the three. How you record the payment, however, depends upon who performs the work: employee, subcontractor, or business owner.

If a stockholder is also an employee, wages are recorded as payroll. If not wages, then payment to the stockholder is a dividend.

Status	Pay Using QB Window	Home Page Section
Employee	*Pay Employees* window	Employee
Subcontractor (Vendor)	*Enter Bills* window *Pay Bills* window	Vendor
Owner	*Write Checks* window	Banking

It is important that you determine the status of the individual performing work. The status determines whether you record payments to the individual as an employee paycheck, vendor payment, or owner withdrawal.

Start QuickBooks by clicking on the **QuickBooks desktop icon** or click **Start > Programs > QuickBooks > QuickBooks Pro 2010**.

WORKFLOW

Use the Workflow approach if you are using the same computer and the same .QBW file from the prior chapter.

Step 1:   If your .QBW file is not already open, open it by selecting **File > Open Previous Company**. Select your **.QBW file.**

Step 2:   Change the company name to **[your name] Chapter 6** by selecting **Company** menu **> Company Information.**

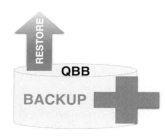

RESTART & RESTORE

Use the Restart & Restore approach if you are restarting your work session.

Step 1:   Restore the **Backup.QBB** file using the directions in *Appendix B: Back Up & Restore QuickBooks Files*.

You can restore your .QBB file from the previous chapter (Exercise 5.4) or the Chapter 6 Backup.QBB data file that comes with the *Computer Accounting with QuickBooks* text (available on CD or download from the Online Learning Center).

If the *QuickBooks Login* window appears with the User Name **Admin**:

- Leave the *User Name* field as **Admin**.
- Leave the *Password* field **blank**.
- Click **OK**.

Step 2:   After restoring the file, change the company name to **[your name] Chapter 6** by selecting **Company** menu **> Company Information.**

PAYROLL SETUP

Payroll setup in QuickBooks is accessed from the Employees menu. (From the Employees menu, click Payroll Setup). The following *QuickBooks Payroll Setup* window summarizes the steps to set up QuickBooks payroll and time tracking.

Payroll accounts for Rock Castle Construction have already been established. To learn more about payroll setup, see Chapter 11.

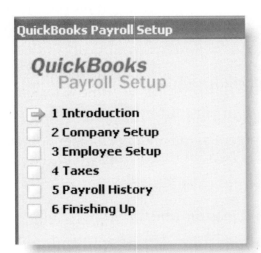

The following table summarizes the steps to set preferences and customize the payroll feature of QuickBooks.

QuickBooks automatically creates a Chart of Accounts with payroll liability and payroll expense accounts. Payroll Items track supporting detail for the payroll accounts.

QuickBooks Time Tracking and Payroll Roadmap

Action	Using QuickBooks...
1. Set up payroll.	Employees menu, Payroll Setup
2. Turn on time tracking.	Edit menu, Preferences, Time & Expenses
3. Turn on payroll, enter Payroll and Employee Preferences.	Edit menu, Preferences, Payroll & Employees
4. Enter customer and jobs on which time is worked.	Customer & Job List
5. Record labor as a service item.	Item List
6. Enter employees and nonemployees whose time will be tracked: ▸ Employee information ▸ Subcontractors ▸ Owners	 Employee List Vendor List Other Names List

In this chapter, we will focus on customizing payroll using preferences and recording employee and payroll transactions. To track time and process payroll in QuickBooks, you will use the *Employees* section of the Home page.

EMPLOYEE NAVIGATION

If necessary, click the **Home** page icon to view the *Employees* section.

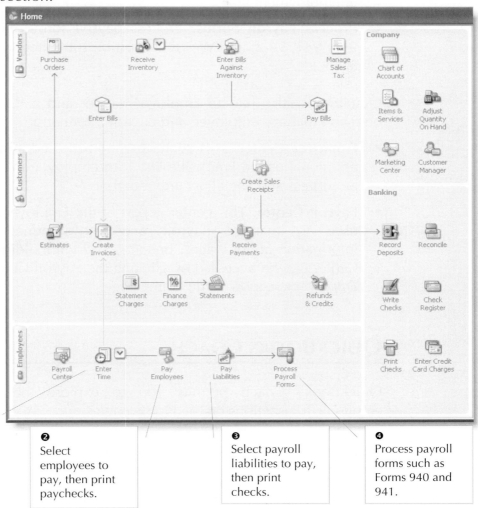

❶ Enter time worked. If the time-tracking feature is turned off, this icon will not appear.

❷ Select employees to pay, then print paychecks.

❸ Select payroll liabilities to pay, then print checks.

❹ Process payroll forms such as Forms 940 and 941.

The *Employees* section of the Home page is a flowchart of payroll transactions. As the flowchart indicates, there are four main steps to processing payroll using QuickBooks:

❶ Enter Time. QuickBooks Pro and QuickBooks Premier permit you to track employee time worked to use in processing payroll and billing customers.

❷ Pay Employees. Select employees to pay and create their paychecks.

❸ **Pay Payroll Liabilities**. Pay payroll tax liabilities due governmental agencies such as the IRS. Payroll tax liabilities include federal income taxes withheld, state income taxes withheld, FICA (Social Security and Medicare), and unemployment taxes.

❹ **Process Payroll Forms**. Process payroll forms including Forms 940, 941, W-2, and W-3 that must be submitted to governmental agencies.

QuickBooks also has an Employee Center and a Payroll Center to help you manage employee and payroll information.

▪ **Employee Center**. This center can be accessed from the Icon bar and contains the Employee List with employee information, such as address and Social Security number.

▪ **Payroll Center**. This center is part of the Employee Center and is used to manage payroll and tax information, including information about wages, benefits, and withholding. The Payroll Center can be accessed by clicking the Payroll Center icon in the *Employees* section of the Home page.

QUICKBOOKS COACH

QuickBooks Coach permits you to explore the workflow for employee transactions on the Home page.

To view the Coach Tips and Payroll Workflow:

Step 1: From the right side of the Home page, click **Show Coach Tips**.

Step 2:   To spotlight the workflow for entering time and payroll, click the **Coach** icon 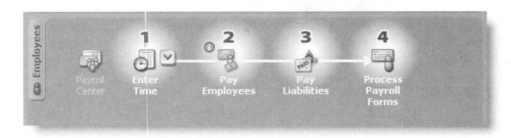 beside **Enter Time**.

Step 3:   Although you can leave the Explore Workflow and Coach Tips displayed while using QuickBooks, if you prefer to hide the Coach Tips, click **Hide Coach Tips** in the *QuickBooks Coach* window.

Next, you will set QuickBooks preferences for time tracking and payroll.

CUSTOMIZE QUICKBOOKS PAYROLL

Use QuickBooks Preferences to customize time tracking and payroll to suit your company's specific needs. There are two types of preferences that affect payroll:

1. Time-tracking preferences.

2. Payroll and employees preferences.

TIME-TRACKING PREFERENCES

To turn on the QuickBooks time-tracking feature, complete the following steps:

Step 1:   From the Menu bar, click **Edit > Preferences**.

Step 2:   When the *Preferences* window appears, select **Time & Expenses** from the left scrollbar.

Step 3:   If necessary, select the **Company Preferences** tab.

Step 4:   Select Do you track time?: **Yes**. Select First Day of Work Week: **Monday**.

Step 5:   Leave the *Preferences* window open.

PAYROLL AND EMPLOYEES PREFERENCES

Next, select QuickBooks payroll and employees preferences for your company.

With the *Preferences* window open:

Step 1: From the left scrollbar of the *Preferences* window, click on the **Payroll & Employees** icon.

Step 2: Select the **Company Preferences** tab.

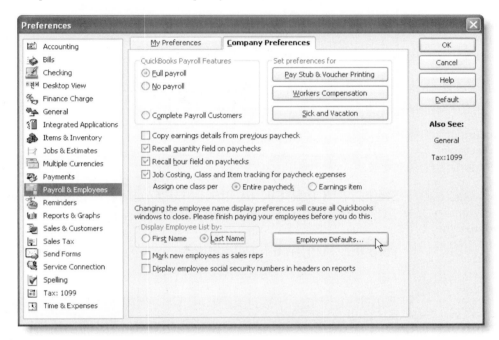

Step 3: Select QuickBooks Payroll Features: **Full payroll**.

Step 4: Select Display Employee List by: **Last Name**.

Step 5: Click the **Employee Defaults** button to select payroll defaults.

Step 6: Select the checkbox: **Use time data to create paychecks**. Now QuickBooks will automatically use tracked time to calculate payroll.

To save time, enter information common to most employees (such as a deduction for health insurance) as an employee default. QuickBooks then records the information for all employees. Later, you can customize the information as needed for a specific employee.

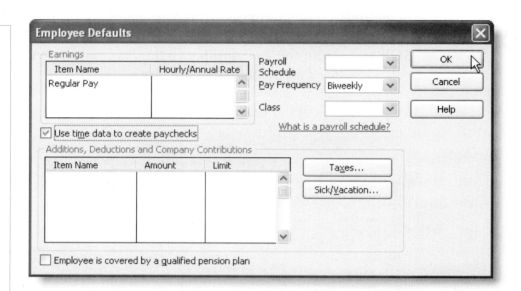

Step 7: Click **OK** to close the *Employee Defaults* window. Click **OK** again to close the *Preferences* window.

Step 8: When the following warning message appears, click **OK**.

Now that the time-tracking and payroll preferences are set, you will edit and print the Employee List.

EMPLOYEE LIST

The Employee List contains employee information such as address, telephone, salary or wage rate, and Social Security number.

To view the Employee List for Rock Castle Construction:

Step 1: Click the **Employee Center** icon on the Icon bar or click the **Employees** button on the Home page to display the Employee Center.

Step 2: Click the **Employees** tab to display a list of employees.

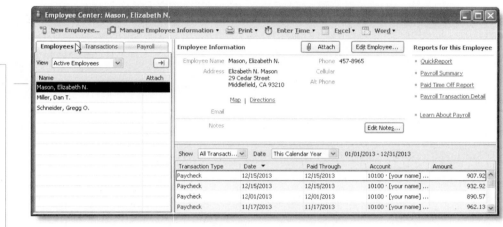

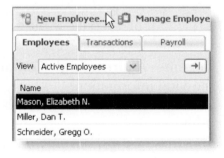

To view or edit employee information, double-click the employee's name.

ADD NEW EMPLOYEE

To enter your name as a new employee in the Employee List:

Step 1: Click the **New Employee** button at the top of the Employee Center.

Step 2: When the following blank *New Employee* window appears, select **Personal Info** in the *Change tabs* field.

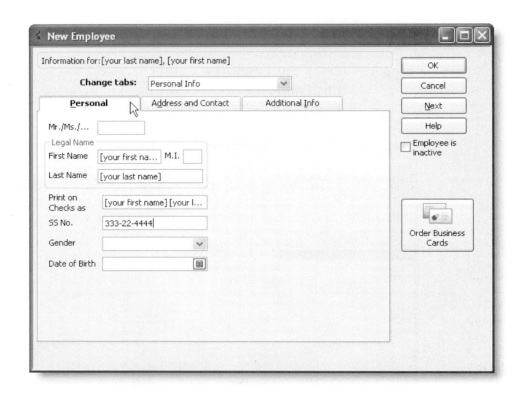

- Click the **Personal** tab and enter the following information.

Personal:	
First Name	[Enter your first name]
Last Name	[Enter your last name]
SS No.	333-22-4444
Gender	[Enter gender]
Date of birth	[Enter a date of birth]

- Click the **Address and Contact** tab, then enter the following information.

Address and Contact:	
Address	555 Lakeview Lane Bayshore, CA 94326
Phone	415-555-6677
E-mail	[Enter your E-mail address]

- Click the **Additional Information** tab, then enter the following information.

Additional Info:	
Employee ID No.	333-22-4444
B-Day	[Enter a birth date]

Step 3: In the *Change Tabs* field, select: **Payroll and Compensation Info**, then enter the following payroll information.

Payroll Info:	
Earnings Name	Regular Pay
Hourly/Annual Rate	10.00
Use time data to create paychecks	Yes
Pay Frequency	Biweekly
Deductions	Health Insurance
Amount	-25.00
Limit	-1200.00

If you receive a message that you must update QuickBooks before you can use payroll, update QuickBooks, then proceed.

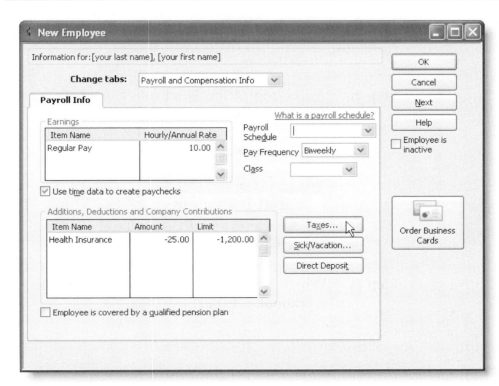

New employees complete Form W-4 to indicate filing status and allowances.

If you start using QuickBooks midyear, enter year-to-date amounts for payroll *before* you start using QuickBooks to process paychecks.

Step 4:   Click the **Taxes** button to view federal, state, and other tax information related to your employment, such as filing status and allowances. Enter the following:

- Filing Status: **Single**.
- Allowances for **Federal: 1**.
- Allowances for **State**: **1**.
- Click **OK** to close the *Taxes* window.

Step 5:   Click **OK** again to add your name to Rock Castle Construction's Employee List.

Step 6:   When asked if you want to set up payroll information for sick leave and vacation, click **Leave As Is** to use the employee default information for these items.

Step 7:   Leave the *Employee Center* window open.

PRINT EMPLOYEE LIST

🖨 **Print** the Employee List as follows:

Step 1:   Click the **Name** bar to sort employee names in alphabetical order.

Step 2:   At the top of the Employee Center, select **Excel > Export Employee List**.

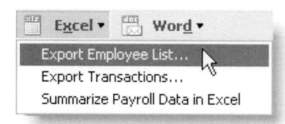

Step 3:   When the *Export* window appears, select **a new Excel workbook** > **Export**.

Step 4: 🖨 **Print** the report from Excel using **Fit to Page** and **Landscape** orientation.

Step 5: ✏ **Circle** your information on the Employee List printout.

Step 6: **Close** the *Employee Center* window.

For more information about payroll setup, see Chapter 11. The remainder of this chapter will cover time tracking, payroll processing, and payroll reports.

TIME TRACKING

QuickBooks Pro and QuickBooks Premier permit you to track time worked on various jobs. As mentioned earlier, time can be tracked for employees, subcontractors, or owners.

When employees use time tracking, the employee records the time worked on each job. The time data is then used to:

1. Prepare paychecks.

2. Bill customers for time worked on specific jobs.

QuickBooks Pro and QuickBooks Premier provide three different ways to track time.

To learn more about online timesheets, from the *Employees* section of the Home page, select **Enter Time > Let Your Employees Enter Time**.

1. **Time Single Activity**. Use the Stopwatch to time an activity and enter the time data. QuickBooks automatically records the time on the employee's weekly timesheet.

2. **Weekly Timesheet**. Use the weekly timesheet to enter time worked by each employee on various jobs during the week.

3. **Online Timesheets**. Enter billable hours from any Internet-connected computer. Download the timesheets into QuickBooks to process paychecks.

TIME SINGLE ACTIVITY

You will use the QuickBooks Stopwatch feature to time how long it takes you to complete payroll activities in this chapter.

To start the Stopwatch:

Step 1:   From the *Employees* section of the Home page, click the **Enter Time** icon.

Step 2:   From the pop-up menu, select: **Time/Enter Single Activity**.

Let Your Employees Enter Time...
Use Weekly Timesheet
Time / Enter Single Activity

Step 3:   When the following window appears:

- Select Date: **12/15/2013**.

- Select Name: **Your Name**.

- If the work was for a particular job or customer, you would enter the job or customer name and the service item, then click Billable. In this case, your time is not billable to a particular customer's job, so **uncheck Billable**.

- Select Payroll Item: **Regular Pay**.

- Enter Notes: **Process payroll**.

You can use the Stopwatch to time activities only for today's date. However, for this activity, use the programmed date for the sample company: 12/15/2013.

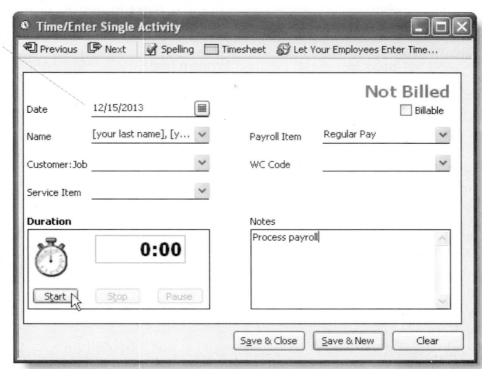

Step 4: Click the **Start** button to start the stopwatch.

Step 5: Leave the window open while you complete the following payroll activities.

TIMESHEET

Rock Castle Construction pays employees biweekly. Checks are issued on Friday for the biweekly pay period ending that day.

Use the timesheet to enter the hours you worked for Rock Castle Construction during the last pay period.

To use QuickBooks timesheet feature:

Step 1: In the *Employees* section of the Home page, select **Enter Time > Use Weekly Timesheet**.

Step 2:   If necessary, click the **Next** button to change the date to the Week Of: **Dec 16 to Dec 22, 2013**.

Step 3:   Select Name: **[your name]**.

Step 4:   From the Payroll Item drop-down list, select **Regular Pay**.

If your time was billable to a specific customer or job, then select Customer: Job name and the Service Item.

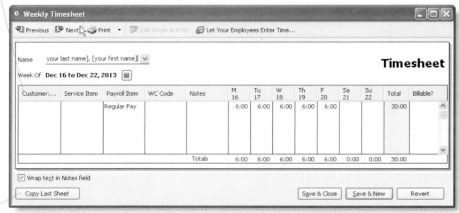

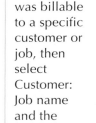

Use Copy Last Sheet if the timesheet does not change much from week to week.

Step 5:   Because your time is not billable to a specific customer or job, **uncheck** the **Billable?** field in the last column to indicate these charges will not be transferred to an invoice.

Step 6:   Enter **6** hours for each of the following dates for a total of 30 hours for the week:

- **Monday (December 16)**
- **Tuesday (December 17)**
- **Wednesday (December 18)**
- **Thursday (December 19)**
- **Friday (December 20)**

Step 7:   Click the **Next** button in the upper left corner of the *Weekly Timesheet* window to advance to the timesheet for the week of **Dec 23 to Dec 29, 2013**.

Remember to enter **Regular Pay** and uncheck **Billable?** to mark your hours as nonbillable.

Step 8:   Enter **6** hours of **nonbillable Regular Pay** for your timesheet on the following dates for a total of 30 hours:

- **Monday (December 23)**
- **Tuesday (December 24)**
- **Wednesday (December 25)**
- **Thursday (December 26)**
- **Friday (December 27)**

Step 9: Click **Save & New** to record your hours and display a new timesheet.

If time is billable to a specific customer or job, this is indicated on the weekly timesheet. For example, Elizabeth Mason, a Rock Castle Construction employee, worked on the Teschner sun room; therefore, her hours are billable to the Teschner sun room job.

To enter billable hours on Elizabeth Mason's weekly timesheet:

Step 1: On the new timesheet, select Employee Name: **Elizabeth N. Mason**.

Step 2: Click the **Previous** button in the upper left corner of the *Weekly Timesheet* window to change the timesheet dates to **Dec 16 to Dec 22, 2013**.

Step 3: To record time billable to a specific customer:

- Select Customer: Job: **Teschner, Anton: Sun Room**.

- Select Service Item: **Framing**.

Step 4: Enter the following hours into the weekly timesheet to record time Elizabeth worked framing the sunroom:

Monday, December 16	8 hours
Tuesday, December 17	8 hours
Wednesday, December 18	8 hours
Thursday, December 19	6 hours

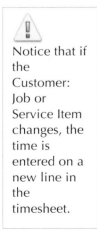

Notice that if the Customer: Job or Service Item changes, the time is entered on a new line in the timesheet.

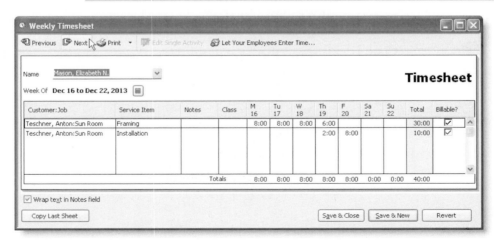

Step 5: ✓ Check: **Billable?**

Step 6: Move to the next line in the timesheet to enter the installation work that Elizabeth performed on the Teschner sun room.

- Select Customer: Job: **Teschner, Anton: Sun Room**.
- Select Service Item: **Installation**.
- Enter hours worked:

Thursday, December 19	2 hours
Friday, December 20	8 hours

Step 7: Click the **Next** button to record Elizabeth N. Mason's hours and display a new timesheet.

Step 8: Record **8** hours for each of the following dates that Elizabeth worked on **installing** the Teschner sun room:

- **Monday (December 23)**
- **Tuesday (December 24)**
- **Wednesday (December 25)**
- **Thursday (December 26)**
- **Friday (December 27)**

Step 9: ✓ Check: **Billable?**

Step 10: Leave the *Weekly Timesheets* window open.

To print the weekly timesheets for yourself and Elizabeth N. Mason, complete the following steps:

Step 1: From the *Weekly Timesheet* window, click the **Print** button.

Step 2: When the following *Select Timesheets to Print* window appears, select Dated: **12/16/2013** thru **12/22/2013**. If necessary, press **Tab**.

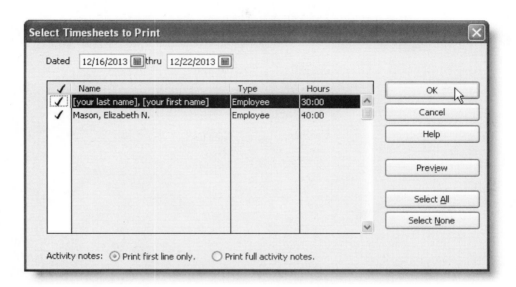

Step 3: Select **Your Name** and **Elizabeth N. Mason**. Click **OK**.

Step 4: 🖶 **Print** the timesheets.

Step 5: ✏ **Sign** the timesheets.

Step 6: Click **Save & Close** to close the *Weekly Timesheet* window.

TRANSFER TIME TO SALES INVOICES

Billable time can be transferred to a specific customer's invoice. This is shown in the Home page by an arrow going from the Enter Time icon to the Create Invoices icon.

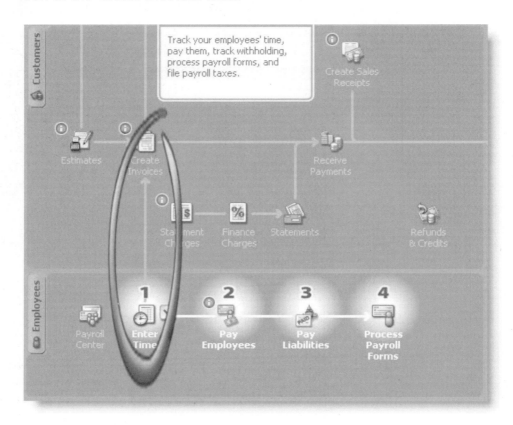

First, you must enter time worked, then open the *Create Invoices* window for the customer, and select the time billable to that specific customer.

For the Teschner sun room job, you have already entered Elizabeth Mason's time. To transfer billable time to the Teschner invoice:

Step 1: Open the *Create Invoices* window by clicking the **Create Invoices** icon in the *Customers* section of the Home page.

Step 2: From the *Create Invoices* window, select the customer job to be billed. In this instance, select Customer: Job: **Teschner, Anton: Sun Room**.

Step 3: If the following *Billable Time/Costs* window appears:

- Select: **Select the outstanding billable time and costs to add to this invoice?**

- Click **OK**.

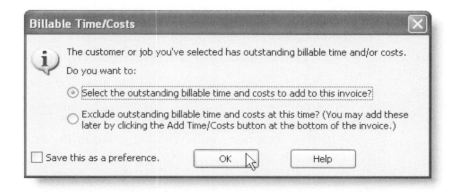

Step 4: When the *Choose Billable Time and Costs* window appears, click the **Time** tab.

Notice that items, expenses, and mileage can also be tracked and billed to specific customer jobs.

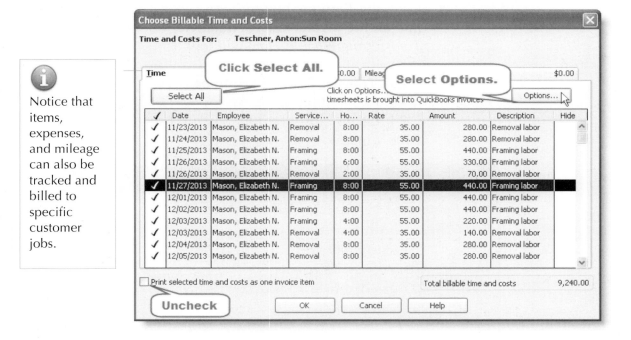

Step 5: Click the **Select All** button to select all the billable times listed for the Teschner sun room job.

☑ ***Total billable time is $9,240.***

Step 6: You can transfer time to an invoice in three different ways:

1. Combine all the selected times and costs into *one* entry on the invoice.

2. List a *subtotal* for each *service* item on the invoice.

3. List a separate invoice line item for each *activity* you check.

In this instance, you will list a separate invoice line item for each activity you check, so:

- *Uncheck* **Print selected time and costs as one invoice item** in the lower left corner of the *Choose Billable Time and Costs* window.

- Click the **Options** button, then select **Enter a separate line on the invoice for each activity** on the *Options for Transferring Billable Time* window.

- Select **Transfer item descriptions**.

- Click **OK** to close the *Options for Transferring Billable Time* window.

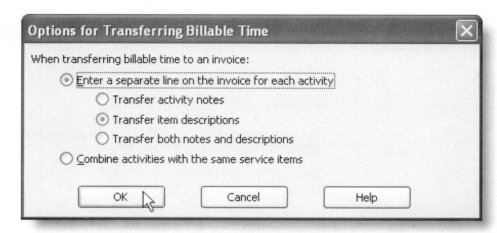

Step 7: Click **OK** to close the *Choose Billable Time and Costs* window and add the labor cost to the Teschner invoice.

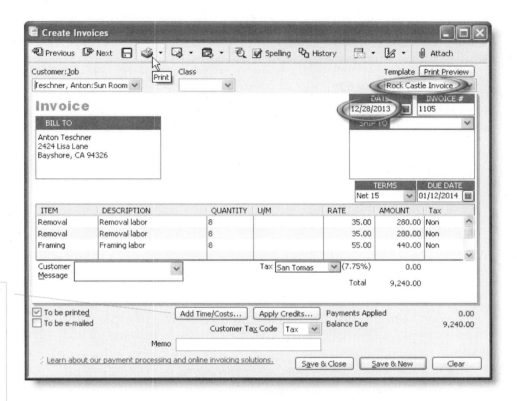

If you had not entered the billable time when you opened the invoice, you can click the **Add Time/Costs** button to add billable time later.

Step 8: Select Template: **Rock Castle Invoice**.

Step 9: Select Invoice Date: **12/28/2013**.

Step 10: 🖨 **Print** the invoice. Select **blank paper** and **print lines around fields**.

Step 11: Click **Save & Close** to record the invoice and close the *Create Invoices* window.

Stop the Stopwatch now by clicking the **Stop** button and then clicking **Clear. Close** the *Stopwatch* window**.**

If a message appears about updating QuickBooks before using payroll, update QuickBooks and then proceed. If you are not able to use QuickBooks payroll tax tables, then enter amounts shown on the following pages manually in the *Create Paychecks* window.

When using a QuickBooks payroll service, turn on the auto update feature of QuickBooks to ensure you have the latest tax tables.

QUICKBOOKS PAYROLL

After entering time worked, the next step is to create employee paychecks.

There are two ways that a company can perform payroll calculations.

1. Use QuickBooks payroll services:

    - Basic Payroll

    - Enhanced Payroll

    - Enhanced Payroll for Accountants

    - Assisted Payroll

2. Manually calculate payroll taxes.

QUICKBOOKS PAYROLL SERVICES

QuickBooks offers three levels of payroll services for the entrepreneur: QuickBooks Basic, Enhanced, or Assisted Payroll. When you subscribe to a payroll service, QuickBooks requires that you have an Internet connection. Then QuickBooks automatically calculates payroll tax deductions.

Features of the three levels of payroll services for entrepreneurs are summarized as follows.

Basic Payroll	• Create paychecks using automatic calculation of payroll tax deductions.
	• Tax forms for filings are not automatically prepared. Entrepreneur must complete the tax forms or work with an accountant on payroll tax filings.
Enhanced Payroll	• Create paychecks using automatic calculation of payroll tax deductions.
	• Generate payroll tax forms for filings automatically.
	• File and pay taxes electronically.
Assisted Payroll	• Pay employees using QuickBooks.
	• Intuit processes payroll taxes and filings for the entrepreneur.

Chapter 6 covers payroll using QuickBooks payroll service. Chapter 11 covers QuickBooks manual payroll option.

CALCULATE PAYROLL TAXES MANUALLY

If you do not use a QuickBooks payroll service, you must calculate tax withholdings and payroll taxes manually using IRS Publication 15 (Circular E) Employer's Tax Guide. Then enter the amounts in QuickBooks to process payroll.

CREATE AND PRINT PAYCHECKS

The QuickBooks payroll service is active for the sample company file, Rock Castle Construction.

To create paychecks for Rock Castle Construction using the QuickBooks payroll service:

Step 1:   From the *Employees* section of the Home page, click the **Pay Employees** icon to display the *Employee Center: Payroll Center* window.

Notice that the following three sections in the Payroll Center correspond to the icons in the *Employee* section of the Home page:

- Pay Employees.

- Pay Schedules Liabilities.

- File Tax Forms.

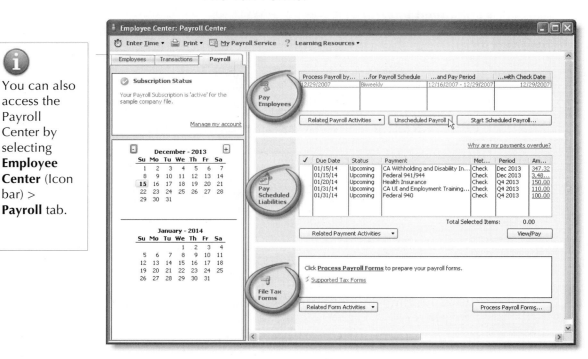

You can also access the Payroll Center by selecting **Employee Center** (Icon bar) > **Payroll** tab.

Step 2: In the *Pay Employees* section, select: **Unscheduled Payroll**.

Step 3: When the *Enter Payroll Information* window appears, notice there are three steps listed at the top of the window: Enter Payroll Information -> Review & Create Paychecks -> Print and Distribute Paychecks.

Select Pay Period Ends: **12/31/2013**. This is the last day of this pay period.

If the *Pay Period Change* window appears, click **No** to change the date without updating the hours worked.

Step 4: Select Check Date: **12/31/2013**. This date will print on each check.

Step 5: Select Employee: **Elizabeth N. Mason**. Click **Continue**.

If you use a QuickBooks payroll service, payroll taxes and deductions would be calculated automatically and appear in the *Review and Create Paychecks* window.

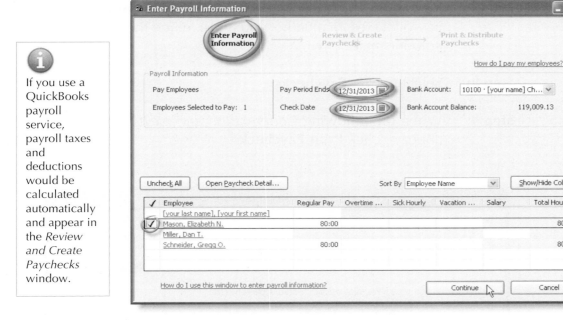

Step 6: When the following *Review and Create Paychecks* window appears, select **Print paychecks from QuickBooks**.

If you planned to handwrite payroll checks instead, select Assign check numbers to handwritten checks.

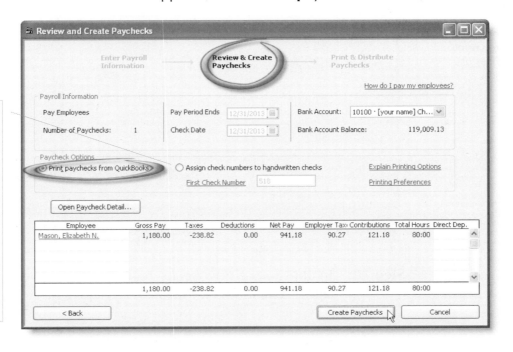

Some businesses use a separate Payroll Checking account instead of using the regular Checking account.

Step 7:   Select Bank Account: **[your name] Checking**. Notice that the tax withholding amounts appear automatically because Rock Castle uses a payroll service. If you are calculating payroll taxes manually, you must enter the withholding amounts manually.

Step 8:   Select **Create Paychecks**.

Step 9:   When the following *Confirmation and Next Steps* window appears, click **Print Paychecks**.

Subcontractors are considered vendors, not employees. Subcontractor payments are entered using the *Enter Bills* window.

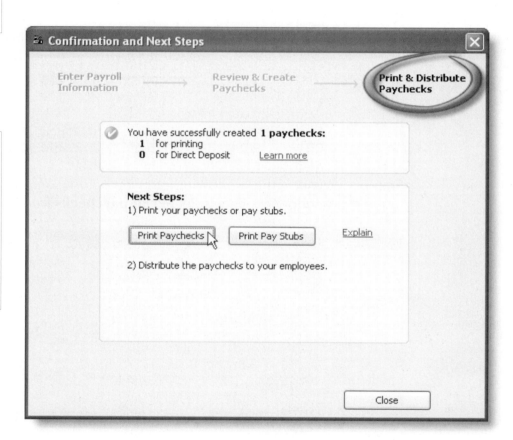

Step 10:   In the *Select Paychecks to Print* window shown below, select: **Elizabeth N. Mason (12/31/2013)**.

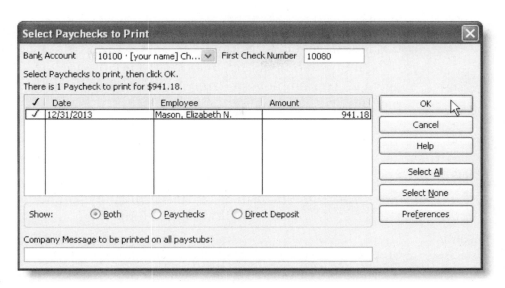

Step 11: Select Bank Account: **[your name] Checking**. Select First Check Number: **10080**. Click **OK**.

Step 12: Select Check Style: **Voucher**. Check **Print company name and address**.

Step 13: 🖶 Click **Print**.

Step 14: **Close** the *Confirmation and Next Steps* window.

 Mason's net pay is $941.18. (Note: This amount may vary depending upon your payroll update.)

PAY PAYROLL LIABILITIES

Payroll liabilities include amounts for:

To help keep
track of filing
dates, see the
IRS Tax
Calendar at
www.irs.gov.

- Federal income taxes withheld from employee paychecks.

- State income taxes withheld from employee paychecks.

- FICA (Social Security and Medicare, including both the employee and the employer portions).

- Unemployment taxes.

Federal income taxes, state income taxes, and the employee portion of FICA are withheld from the employee, and the company has an obligation (liability) to remit these amounts to the appropriate tax agency. The employer share of FICA and unemployment taxes are payroll taxes the employer owes.

You will process payroll liability payments in the exercises for Chapter 6.

To pay the payroll tax liability:

Step 1: If the *Employee Center: Payroll Center* window is not already displayed, select the **Pay Liabilities** icon in the *Employees* section of the Home page.

Step 2: In the *Pay Scheduled Liabilities* section of the *Employee Center: Payroll Center* window, you can view the upcoming scheduled payments for payroll liabilities. If any payments were due, you would select the payroll liabilities to pay, then click View/Pay. In the Due Date column, you can see that no payments are currently due for Rock Castle Construction.

Step 3: Leave open the *Employee Center: Payroll Center* window.

FILE PAYROLL TAX FORMS

Notice that the third section of the Payroll Center is File Tax Forms. When Rock Castle's payroll forms are due, you will click Process Payroll Forms to prepare the payroll forms. Basically, the payroll forms summarize the amount of payroll withholdings that have been collected and remitted.

Payroll tax forms include:

You will process payroll tax forms in the exercises for Chapter 6.

- **Federal Form 940: Employer's Annual Federal Unemployment (FUTA) Tax Return.** This form summarizes the amount of unemployment tax paid and due by the enterprise.

- **Federal Form 941: Employer's Quarterly Federal Tax Return.** Filed with the IRS, this form summarizes the amount of federal income tax, Social Security, and Medicare withheld from employee paychecks for the quarter.

- **Federal Form 944: Employer's Annual Federal Tax Return.** Filed with the IRS, this form summarizes the amount of federal income tax, Social Security, and Medicare withheld from employee paychecks for the year. Form 944 is used by very small employers instead of filing Form 941 each quarter.

- **Form W-2: Wage and Tax Statement.** Before the end of January, an employer must provide W-2s to employees that summarize amounts paid for salaries, wages, and withholdings for the year.

- **Form W-3: Transmittal of Wage and Tax Statements.** Filed with the Social Security Administration, this form is a summary of all your W-2 forms.

Close the *Employee Center: Payroll Center* window.

PAYROLL REPORTS

In addition to providing assistance with filing payroll tax forms with federal, state, and local governmental agencies, QuickBooks also provides payroll reports for owners and managers to use to answer the following questions:

- How much did we pay our employees and pay in payroll taxes? (Payroll reports)

- How much time did we spend classified by employee and job? (Project reports)

Payroll reports can be accessed in the following ways:

1. **Reports menu.** (Select **Reports** menu > **Employees & Payroll.**)

2. **Report Center.** (Select **Report Center** (Icon bar) > **Employees & Payroll.**)

3. **Employee Center.** (Select **Employee Center** (Icon bar) > **Reports for this Employee.**)

PAYROLL REPORTS: HOW MUCH DID WE PAY FOR PAYROLL?

The payroll reports list the amounts paid to employees and the amounts paid in payroll taxes.

To print the Payroll Summary report:

Step 1:   From the *Report Center* window using List View, select **Employees & Payroll > Payroll Summary.**

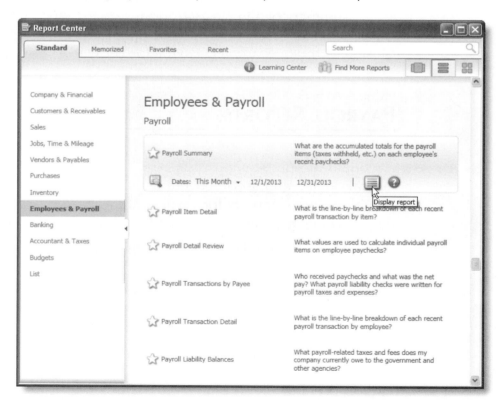

Step 2: Select Dates: **This Month** From: **12/01/2013** To: **12/31/2013**. Click **Display report** icon.

Step 3: **Print** using **Landscape** orientation.

Step 4: Close the *Payroll Summary Report* window.

☑ ***Net pay for Dan Miller for December was $3,974.90.***

PROJECT REPORTS: HOW MUCH TIME DID WE USE?

Four different project reports are available in QuickBooks:

1. **Time by Job Summary**. Lists time spent on each job.

2. **Time by Job Detail**. Lists time by category spent on each job.

3. **Time by Name Report**. Lists the amount of time worked by each employee.

4. **Time by Job Detail Report**. Lists the time worked on a particular job by service.

Project reports are accessed as follows:

Step 1: From the Report Center, select: **Jobs, Time & Mileage > Time By Job Summary**.

To create a report detailing time spent on a specific job:
1. Report Center
2. Jobs & Time
3. Time by Job Detail
4. Filter for Customer & Job

Step 2: **Print** the Time by Job Summary report for **This Month** from **12/01/2013** To: **12/31/2013**. Select **Portrait** orientation.

Step 3: 🖉 Circle the job requiring the most time for December 2013.

SAVE CHAPTER 6

Save a backup of your Chapter 6 file using the file name: **[your name] Chapter 6 Backup.QBB**. See *Appendix B: Back Up & Restore QuickBooks Files* for instructions.

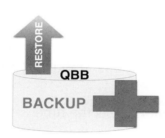

WORKFLOW

If you are using the workflow approach, leave your .QBW file open and proceed directly to Exercise 6.1.

RESTART & RESTORE

If you are using the Restart & Restore approach and are ending your computer session now, close your .QBW file and exit QuickBooks.

When you restart, you will restore your backup file to complete Exercise 6.1.

PODCASTS

Watch the Chapter 6 **Podcast** at www.QuickBooksBlog.info. View the podcast to learn about QuickBooks payroll.

MULTIPLE-CHOICE PRACTICE TEST

A **Multiple-Choice Practice Test** for Chapter 6 is on the *Computer Accounting for QuickBooks Pro* Online Learning Center at www.mhhe.com/kay2010. Try the Practice Test and see how many questions you answer correctly.

EXTRAS!

Section 3: Quick Guide contains quick, easy step-by-step directions for frequently used QuickBooks tasks, including correcting errors. You can find *Quick Guide* at the back of your text or online at www.mhhe.com/kay2010. *Check it out!*

Deliverables Checklist is a list of the reports and documents that you are to deliver to your instructor for grading. You can find the Deliverables Checklist at the end of the chapter or online at www.mhhe.com/kay2010. Staying organized saves time. Use the checklist to organize your reports, checking off the reports as completed. Then include the checklist with your reports for grading.

Appendix D: Electronic Deliverables shows you how to save your QuickBooks reports electronically. Also, watch the Electronic Deliverables Podcast at www.QuickBooksBlog.info. Check with your instructor to see if you should deliver your reports electronically.

Join the QuickBooks Student Community to ask questions and share tips @ www.QuickBooksBlog.info.

LEARNING ACTIVITIES

Important: Ask your instructor whether you should complete the following assignments by printing requested reports or creating electronic deliverables (see Appendix D: Electronic Deliverables).

EXERCISE 6.1: TRACK TIME AND PRINT PAYCHECKS

SCENARIO

When sorting through the payroll documents that Mr. Castle gave you, you find the following timesheets for Dan Miller and Gregg Schneider.

Timesheet						
Dan Miller	**Salary**	**Dec 16**	**Dec 17**	**Dec 18**	**Dec 19**	**Dec 20**
Cook: 2nd Story	Installation	8	8	2		4
Pretell: 75 Sunset	Framing			6	7	4
Dan Miller	**Salary**	**Dec 23**	**Dec 24**	**Dec 25**	**Dec 26**	**Dec 27**
Pretell: 75 Sunset	Framing	8	8	8	8	3
Pretell: 75 Sunset	Installation					5

Timesheet						
Gregg Schneider	**Regular Pay**	**Dec 16**	**Dec 17**	**Dec 18**	**Dec 19**	**Dec 20**
Jacobsen: Kitchen	Installation	8	8	8	2	
Pretell: 75 Sunset	Framing				6	8
Gregg Schneider	**Regular Pay**	**Dec 23**	**Dec 24**	**Dec 25**	**Dec 26**	**Dec 27**
Pretell: 75 Sunset	Framing	8	8	8	8	
Pretell: 75 Sunset	Installation					8

TASK 1: OPEN COMPANY FILE

WORKFLOW

If you are using the Workflow approach, you will use the same .QBW file.

If your QBW file is not already open, open it by selecting **File > Open Previous Company**. Select your **.QBW file.**

Change the company name to **[your name] Exercise 6.1** by selecting **Company** menu > **Company Information.**

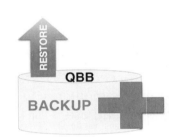

RESTART & RESTORE

If you are not using the same computer, you must use the Restart and Restore approach.

Restore your **Chapter 6 Backup.QBB** file using the directions in *Appendix B: Back Up & Restore QuickBooks Files.*

After restoring the file, change the company name to **[your name] Exercise 6.1** by selecting **Company** menu > **Company Information.**

TASK 2: TIMESHEET

See the Scenario on the previous page for information to complete Tasks 2 and 3.

Step 1: Enter the hours employee **Dan T. Miller** worked using QuickBooks weekly timesheet.

Step 2: Enter the hours **Gregg Schneider** worked using QuickBooks weekly timesheet.

Step 3: 🖨 **Print** and sign the timesheets for Dan Miller and Gregg Schneider.

TASK 3: PRINT PAYCHECKS

Rock Castle Construction uses a different series of check numbers for its payroll checks than it does for all other checks.

Print and sign paychecks using voucher checks for **Dan Miller** and **Gregg Schneider** dated **12/29/2013** for pay period ending **12/29/2013** (Checks No. 10081 and 10082).

TASK 4: SAVE EXERCISE 6.1

Save a backup of your Exercise 6.1 file using the file name: **[your name] Exercise 6.1 Backup.QBB**. See *Appendix B: Back Up & Restore QuickBooks Files* for instructions.

WORKFLOW

If you are proceeding to Exercise 6.2 and using the same computer, you can leave your .QBW file open and use it for Exercise 6.2.

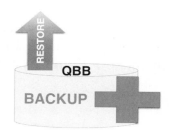

RESTART & RESTORE

If you are stopping your QuickBooks work session and changing computers, you will need to restore your .QBB file when you restart.

EXERCISE 6.2: TRANSFER TIME TO SALES INVOICE

SCENARIO

"By the way, did I mention that I need a current sales invoice for the Jacobsen Kitchen job? Make sure all labor charges have been posted to the invoice," Mr. Castle shouts over the top of your cubicle as he rushes past.

TASK 1: OPEN COMPANY FILE

WORKFLOW

If you are using the Workflow approach, you will use the same .QBW file.

If your QBW file is not already open, open it by selecting **File > Open Previous Company**. Select your **.QBW file.**

Change the company name to **[your name] Exercise 6.2** by selecting **Company** menu > **Company Information.**

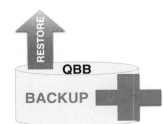

RESTART & RESTORE

If you are using the Restart and Restore approach, restore your backup file using the directions in *Appendix B: Back Up & Restore QuickBooks Files*.

After restoring the file, change the company name to **[your name] Exercise 6.2** by selecting **Company** menu > **Company Information.**

TASK 2: TRANSFER TIME TO SALES INVOICE

Step 1: From the *Customers* section of the Home page, click the **Create Invoices** icon.

Step 2: Transfer billable time and items to a sales invoice dated **12/24/2013** for the Jacobsen Kitchen job.

Step 3: From the *Choose Billable Time & Costs* window, click the **Time** tab, then click the **Select All** button to transfer employee time worked to the invoice. Select the option: **Combine activities with the same service item and rate**.

Step 4: 🖨 **Print** the invoice.

 Billable time totals $2,380.

TASK 3: SAVE EXERCISE 6.2

Save a backup of your Exercise 6.2 file using the file name: **[your name] Exercise 6.2 Backup.QBB**. See *Appendix B: Back Up & Restore QuickBooks Files* for instructions.

WORKFLOW

If you are using the Workflow approach, you can leave your .QBW file open and use it for Exercise 6.3.

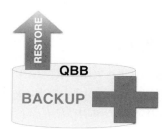

RESTART & RESTORE

If you are stopping your QuickBooks work session and changing computers, you will need to restore your .QBB file when you restart.

EXERCISE 6.3: PAYROLL LIABILITIES AND FORMS

SCENARIO

"Payroll tax forms always gives me a headache," Mr. Castle rubs his temples, muttering as he rushes past your cubicle, *"You can take care of those this year, can't you?"* he shouts over your cubicle wall.

You nod and reply confidently, *"No problem, Mr. Castle,"* to the back of his head as he rushes to his next appointment.

TASK 1: OPEN COMPANY FILE

WORKFLOW

If you are using the Workflow approach, you will use the same .QBW file.

If your QBW file is not already open, open it by selecting **File > Open Previous Company**. Select your **.QBW file**.

Change the company name to **[your name] Exercise 6.3** by selecting **Company** menu **> Company Information**.

RESTART & RESTORE

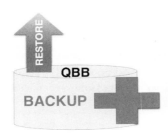

If you are using the Restart and Restore approach, restore your backup file using the directions in *Appendix B: Back Up & Restore QuickBooks Files*. After restoring the file, change the company name to **[your name] Exercise 6.3** by selecting **Company** menu **> Company Information**.

TASK 2: PAY PAYROLL LIABILITIES

To pay the payroll tax liability related to federal Forms 941/944:

Step 1:   Select the **Pay Liabilities** icon in the *Employees* section of the Home page.

Step 2:   In the *Pay Scheduled Liabilities* section of the Employee Center: Payroll Center, select the payroll liabilities for **Federal 941/944** due **01/15/14**.

Step 3:   Click the **View/Pay** button.

Step 4:   When the following check appears on your screen, confirm that check is payable to Great Statewide Bank and displays a Payroll Liabilities tab. Select Date: **12/31/2013**.

Step 5:   Click **Save & Close**.

 Payroll liabilities for Form 941/944 total $4,433.72 (Note: This amount may vary slightly depending upon your payroll update.)

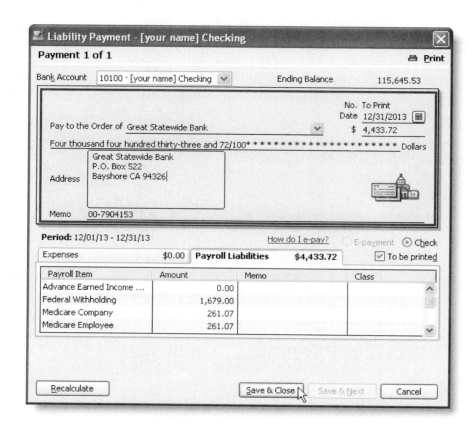

Step 6: When the *Payroll Liability Payment Summary* window appears, click **Print Checks**. Use Check Number **10083** and print using a voucher check.

Step 7: Close the *Payroll Liability Payment Summary* window.

TASK 3: PRINT PAYROLL FORMS

To print the federal Forms 941/944:

Step 1: Select the **Process Payroll Forms** icon in the *Employees* section of the Home page.

> ⚠
> If a warning appears, click **OK** to close the warning window and proceed.

Step 2: Select **Federal form > OK**.

Step 3: Select **Quarterly Form 941/Sch.B – Employer's Quarterly Federal Tax Return > Last Calendar Quarter >**

09/30/2013 > OK.

Step 4: When the *Payroll Tax Form* window appears, select **No** when asked if you need a Schedule B. Click **Next.**

Step 5: Select **Print for Your Records > Tax forms only > 1 Copy.** Select **Printer Setup** to select the printer to use. Click **Print.**

Step 6: Click **Save and Close.**

Step 7: **Sign** Form 941.

TASK 4: PRINT FORM W-2

To print federal Form W-2 that summarizes wages and withholdings for employees:

Step 1: Select the **Process Payroll Forms** icon in the *Employees* section of the Home page.

Step 2: Select **Federal form > OK.**

Step 3: Select **Annual Form W-2/W-3 – Wage and Tax Statement/Transmittal > All Employees > Year 2013 > OK.** If a warning appears, click **OK** to close the window.

Step 4: When the *Select Employees for Form W-2/W-3* window appears, select **Print/E-file.**

Step 5: If a warning appears, select **View Errors.** Select Error **1** at the top of the *Payroll Tax Form* window. In the *Special Situations* section of the form, select **No.**

Step 6: Select **Print for Your Records.** If another warning appears that your form is not complete, select **Yes** to print the form.

Step 7: Select **Blank/Perforated Paper > W-2 forms > 3 per page > Print.**

Step 8: Click **Close Window > Don't Send > Save and Close.**

When printing actual 1099s, you must insert preprinted 1099 forms before printing.

TASK 5: PRINT FORM 1099

Subcontractors are considered vendors, not employees. Thus, subcontractors do not receive W-2s, but in some circumstances you may be required to send a subcontractor a Form 1099 to summarize the amount of payments you have made to the vendor.

To print federal Form 1099 for payments made to each subcontractor:

Subcontractors are considered vendors, not employees. Subcontractor payments are entered using the *Enter Bills* window.

Step 1:   Select **Vendors** menu > **Print 1099s/1096** > **Print 1099s** (Step 4).

Step 2:   Select **This Calendar Year** (01/01/2013 to 12/31/2013) > **OK**.

Step 3:   Select **Print 1099**. Select 1 copy and appropriate print options to print 1099s.

TASK 6: SAVE EXERCISE 6.3

Save a backup of your Exercise 6.3 file using the file name: **[your name] Exercise 6.3 Backup.QBB**. See *Appendix B: Back Up & Restore QuickBooks Files* for instructions.

WORKFLOW

If you are using the Workflow approach, you can leave your .QBW file open and use it for the next chapter.

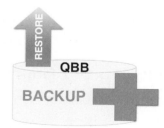

RESTART & RESTORE

If you are stopping your QuickBooks work session and changing computers, you will need to restore your .QBB file when you restart.

EXERCISE 6.4: QUICKBOOKS PAYROLL SERVICES

To learn more about the payroll services offered by QuickBooks:

Step 1: Go to www.payroll.intuit.com. Read about QuickBooks payroll options. ▣ **Print** information summarizing the differences between the QuickBooks Basic, Enhanced, and Assisted Payroll Services.

Step 2: ▤ Using word processing or e-mail software, prepare and ▣ **print** a short e-mail to Mr. Castle with your recommendation regarding which payroll service Rock Castle Construction should use.

EXERCISE 6.5: WEB QUEST

The IRS prepares Publication 15 (Circular E), Employer's Tax Guide, as well as other information about payroll taxes.

To view a copy of Forms 940 and 941 and instructions:

Step 1: Go to the www.irs.gov website.

Step 2: Search the IRS site to find information about Form 940 and Form 941.

Step 3: ▣ **Print** blank Forms 940 and 941.

EXERCISE 6.6: WEB QUEST

When hiring individuals to perform work for a business, it is important to identify the status of the individual as either an employee or independent contractor. For an employee, your business must withhold taxes and provide a W-2. For an independent contractor, your business does not have to withhold taxes. Instead of a W-2, you provide a contractor with a Form 1099-MISC. To learn more about whether a worker is classified for tax purposes as an employee or independent contractor, visit the IRS website.

Step 1: Go to the www.irs.gov website and locate Publication 15-A.

Step 2: Search for requirements that determine employee status and contractor status.

Step 3: 🖶 **Print** your search results.

DELIVERABLES CHECKLIST CHAPTER 6
NAME:

INSTRUCTIONS:
1. **CHECK OFF THE DELIVERABLES YOU HAVE COMPLETED.**
2. **TURN IN THIS PAGE WITH YOUR DELIVERABLES.**

CHAPTER 6
☐ Employee List
☐ Timesheets
☐ Invoice No. 1105
☐ Paycheck (Voucher Check) No. 10080
☐ Payroll Summary Report
☐ Time by Job Summary Report

EXERCISE 6.1
☐ Task 2: Timesheets
☐ Task 3: Paychecks (Voucher Checks) Nos. 10081 and 10082

EXERCISE 6.2
☐ Task 2: Customer Invoice No. 1106

EXERCISE 6.3
☐ Task 2: Payroll Liabilities Check No. 10083
☐ Task 3: Form 941
☐ Task 4: Form W-2
☐ Task 5: Form 1099

EXERCISE 6.4
☐ QuickBooks Payroll Service Printouts
☐ E-mail: QuickBooks Payroll Service Recommendation

EXERCISE 6.5
☐ IRS Forms 940 and 941

EXERCISE 6.6

☐ IRS Printouts for Employee Status and Independent Contractor

REFLECTION: A WISH AND A STAR ★

Reflection improves learning and retention. Reflect on what you have learned after completing Chapter 6 that you did not know before you started the chapter.

A Star:

What did you like best that you learned about QuickBooks in Chapter 6?

A Wish:

If you could pick one thing, what do you wish you knew more about when using QuickBooks?

CHAPTER 7
REPORTS AND GRAPHS

SCENARIO

"I need an income tax summary report ASAP—" Mr. Castle barks as he races past your cubicle. In a few seconds he charges past your cubicle again. *"Don't forget to adjust the accounts first. You'll need to use those confounded debits and credits!*

"Also, I need a P&L, balance sheet, and cash flow statement for my meeting with the bankers this afternoon. Throw in a graph or two if it'll make us look good."

CHAPTER 7
LEARNING OBJECTIVES

In Chapter 7, you will learn about the following QuickBooks features:

THE ACCOUNTING CYCLE

The accounting cycle is a series of activities that a business performs each accounting period.

Financial reports are the end result of the accounting cycle. The accounting cycle usually consists of the following steps:

Chart of Accounts

The Chart of Accounts is a list of all accounts used to accumulate information about assets, liabilities, owners' equity, revenues, and expenses. Create a Chart of Accounts when the business is established and modify the Chart of Accounts as needed over time.

Transactions

During the accounting period, record transactions with customers, vendors, employees, and owners.

Trial Balance

A Trial Balance lists each account and the account balance at the end of the accounting period. Prepare a Trial Balance to verify that the accounting system is in balance—total debits should equal total credits. An *unadjusted* Trial Balance is a Trial Balance prepared *before* adjustments.

An accounting period can be one month, one quarter, or one year.

Adjustments

At the end of the accounting period before preparing financial statements, make any adjustments necessary to bring the accounts up to date. Adjustments are entered in the Journal using debits and credits.

Adjusted Trial Balance

Prepare an *Adjusted Trial Balance* (a Trial Balance *after* adjustments) to verify that the accounting system still balances. If additional account detail is required, print the general ledger (the collection of all the accounts listing the transactions that affected the accounts).

Financial Reports

Prepare financial statements for external users (Profit & Loss, Balance Sheet, and Statement of Cash Flows). Prepare income tax summary reports and reports for managers.

Three types of reports that a business prepares are:

The objective of financial reporting is to provide information to external users for decision making.

1. **Financial statements**. Financial statements are reports used by investors, owners, and creditors to make decisions. A banker might use the financial statements to decide whether to make a loan to a company. A prospective investor might use the financial statements to decide whether to invest in a company.

   The three financial statements most frequently used by external users are:

   - The Profit & Loss (also called the Income Statement) that lists income and expenses.

   - The Balance Sheet listing assets, liabilities, and owners' equity.

   - The Statement of Cash Flows that lists cash flows from operating, investing, and financing activities.

Financial statements can be prepared monthly, quarterly, or annually. Always make adjustments *before* preparing financial statements.

2. **Tax forms**. The objective of the tax form is to provide information to federal and state tax authorities. When preparing tax returns, a company uses different rules from those used to prepare financial statements. When preparing a federal tax return, use the Internal Revenue Code.

   Tax forms include the following:

   - Federal income tax return.

   - State tax return.

   - Forms 940, 941, W-2, W-3, 1099.

3. **Management reports**. Financial reports used by internal users (managers) to make decisions regarding company operations. These reports do not have to follow a particular set of rules and can be created to satisfy a manager's information needs.

   Examples of reports that managers use include:

   - Cash forecast.

   - Cash budget.

   - Accounts receivable aging summary.

In Chapter 6, you prepared several tax forms and reports, including W-2s, 1099s, and Form 941. In this chapter, you will prepare some other reports for Rock Castle Construction. First, you will prepare a Trial Balance and adjustments.

Start QuickBooks by clicking on the **QuickBooks desktop icon** or click **Start > Programs > QuickBooks > QuickBooks Pro 2010**.

WORKFLOW

Use the Workflow approach if you are using the same computer and the same .QBW file from the prior chapter.

Step 1: If your .QBW file is not already open, open it by selecting **File > Open Previous Company**. Select your **.QBW file.**

Step 2: Change the company name to **[your name] Chapter 7** by selecting **Company** menu **> Company Information.**

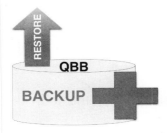

RESTART & RESTORE

Use the Restart & Restore approach if you are restarting your work session.

Step 1: Restore the **Backup.QBB** file using the directions in *Appendix B: Back Up & Restore QuickBooks Files*.

You can restore your .QBB file from the previous chapter or the Chapter 7 Backup.QBB data file that comes with the *Computer Accounting with QuickBooks* text (available on CD or download from the Online Learning Center).

If the *QuickBooks Login* window appears with the User Name **Admin**:

- Leave the *User Name* field as **Admin**.
- Leave the *Password* field **blank**.
- Click **OK**.

Step 2: After restoring the file, change the company name to **[your name] Chapter 7** by selecting **Company** menu > **Company Information**.

TRIAL BALANCE

A Trial Balance is a listing of all of a company's accounts and the ending account balances. A Trial Balance is often printed both before and after making adjustments. The purpose of the Trial Balance is to verify that the accounting system balances.

On a Trial Balance, all debit ending account balances are listed in the *debit* column and credit ending balances are listed in the *credit* column. If the accounting system balances, total debits equal total credits.

To print the Trial Balance for Rock Castle Construction:

Step 1: Click the **Report Center** icon on the Icon bar. Select **List View**.

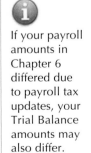

If necessary, display account numbers by selecting **Edit** menu > **Preferences > Accounting > Company Preferences > Use Account Numbers**.

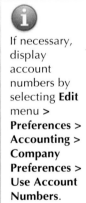

If your payroll amounts in Chapter 6 differed due to payroll tax updates, your Trial Balance amounts may also differ.

Step 2: Select: **Accountant & Taxes > Trial Balance**.

Step 3: Select Date Range: **This Fiscal Quarter** From: **10/01/2013** To: **12/31/2013**. Click **Display report** icon.

Step 4: ▣ **Print** the report using a **Portrait** print setting. Compare your answers to the amounts shown on the following page.

Step 5: To memorize the report, click the **Memorize** button. In the *Name* field, enter: **Trial Balance**, then click **OK**.

Step 6: **Close** the *Trial Balance* window.

Modify Report...	Memorize...	Print...	E-mail ▼	Export...		Hide Header	Collapse	Refresh

Dates | This Fiscal Quarter ▼ | From 10/01/2013 ▦ | To 12/31/2013 ▦ | Sort By | Default ▼

[your name] Chapter 7 Rock Castle Construction
Trial Balance

Accrual Basis   As of December 31, 2013

	Dec 31, 13	
	Debit	**Credit**
10100 · [your name] Checking	111,211.81	
10300 · Savings	17,910.19	
10400 · Petty Cash	500.00	
11000 · Accounts Receivable	104,627.93	
12000 · Undeposited Funds	2,440.00	
12100 · Inventory Asset	30,153.22	
12800 · Employee Advances	832.00	
13100 · Pre-paid Insurance	4,050.00	
13400 · Retainage Receivable	3,703.02	
15000 · Furniture and Equipment	34,326.00	
15100 · Vehicles	78,936.91	
15200 · Buildings and Improvements	325,000.00	
15300 · Construction Equipment	15,300.00	
16900 · Land	90,000.00	
17000 · Accumulated Depreciation		110,344.60
18700 · Security Deposits	1,720.00	
20000 · Accounts Payable		27,885.72
20500 · QuickBooks Credit Card		94.20
20600 · CalOil Credit Card		382.62
24000 · Payroll Liabilities:24010 · Federal Withholding	0.00	
24000 · Payroll Liabilities:24020 · FICA Payable	0.00	
24000 · Payroll Liabilities:24030 · AEIC Payable	0.00	
24000 · Payroll Liabilities:24040 · FUTA Payable		100.00
24000 · Payroll Liabilities:24050 · State Withholding		373.60
24000 · Payroll Liabilities:24060 · SUTA Payable		110.00
24000 · Payroll Liabilities:24070 · State Disability Payable		120.82
24000 · Payroll Liabilities:24080 · Worker's Compensation		1,614.71
24000 · Payroll Liabilities:24100 · Emp. Health Ins Payable		162.50
25500 · Sales Tax Payable		5.66
23000 · Loan - Vehicles (Van)		10,501.47
23100 · Loan - Vehicles (Utility Truck)		19,936.91
23200 · Loan - Vehicles (Pickup Truck)		22,641.00
28100 · Loan - Construction Equipment		13,911.32
28200 · Loan - Furniture/Office Equip		21,000.00
28700 · Note Payable - Bank of Anycity		2,693.21
28900 · Mortgage - Office Building		296,283.00
30000 · Opening Bal Equity		38,773.75
30100 · Capital Stock		73,500.00
32000 · Retained Earnings		61,756.76
40100 · Construction Income	0.00	
40100 · Construction Income:40110 · Design Income		36,729.25
40100 · Construction Income:40130 · Labor Income		220,230.42
40100 · Construction Income:40140 · Materials Income		120,233.67
40100 · Construction Income:40150 · Subcontracted Lab...		82,710.35
40100 · Construction Income:40199 · Less Discounts giv...	48.35	
40500 · Reimbursement Income:40520 · Permit Reimbur...		1,223.75
40500 · Reimbursement Income:40530 · Reimbursed Fre...		896.05
50100 · Cost of Goods Sold	15,761.35	
54000 · Job Expenses:54200 · Equipment Rental	1,850.00	
54000 · Job Expenses:54300 · Job Materials	99,648.70	
54000 · Job Expenses:54400 · Permits and Licenses	700.00	
54000 · Job Expenses:54500 · Subcontractors	63,217.95	
54000 · Job Expenses:54520 · Freight & Delivery	877.10	
54000 · Job Expenses:54599 · Less Discounts Taken		201.81
60100 · Automobile:60110 · Fuel	1,588.70	
60100 · Automobile:60120 · Insurance	2,850.24	
60100 · Automobile:60130 · Repairs and Maintenance	2,406.00	
60400 · Selling Expense:60410 · Advertising Expense	200.00	
60600 · Bank Service Charges	145.00	
62100 · Insurance:62110 · Disability Insurance	582.06	
62100 · Insurance:62120 · Liability Insurance	5,885.96	
62100 · Insurance:62130 · Work Comp	14,057.47	
62400 · Interest Expense:62420 · Loan Interest	1,995.65	
62700 · Payroll Expenses:62710 · Gross Wages	114,556.25	
62700 · Payroll Expenses:62720 · Payroll Taxes	8,763.56	
62700 · Payroll Expenses:62730 · FUTA Expense	268.00	
62700 · Payroll Expenses:62740 · SUTA Expense	1,233.50	
63100 · Postage	104.20	
63600 · Professional Fees:63610 · Accounting	250.00	
64200 · Repairs:64210 · Building Repairs	175.00	
64200 · Repairs:64220 · Computer Repairs	300.00	
64200 · Repairs:64230 · Equipment Repairs	1,350.00	
64800 · Tools and Machinery	2,820.68	
65100 · Utilities:65110 · Gas and Electric	1,251.16	
65100 · Utilities:65120 · Telephone	895.15	
65100 · Utilities:65130 · Water	300.00	
70100 · Other Income		146.80
70200 · Interest Income		229.16
TOTAL	**1,164,793.11**	**1,164,793.11**

ADJUSTING ENTRIES

In QuickBooks, the Journal is used to record adjustments (and corrections). Adjustments are often necessary to bring the accounts up to date at the end of the accounting period.

If you are using the accrual basis to measure profit, the following five types of adjusting entries may be necessary.

See your accountant for more information about calculating depreciation for tax purposes or see IRS Publication 946.

1. **Depreciation**. Depreciation has several different definitions. When conversing with an accountant it is important to know which definition of depreciation is being used. See the table on the following page for more information about depreciation.

2. **Prepaid items**. Items that are prepaid, such as prepaid insurance or prepaid rent. An adjustment may be needed to record the amount of the prepaid item that has not expired at the end of the accounting period. For example, an adjustment may be needed to record the amount of insurance that has not expired as Prepaid Insurance (an asset with future benefit).

3. **Unearned revenue**. If a customer pays in advance of receiving a service, such as when a customer makes a deposit, your business has an obligation (liability) to either provide the service in the future or return the customer's money. An adjustment may be necessary to bring the revenue account and unearned revenue (liability) account up to date.

4. **Accrued expenses**. Expenses that are incurred but not yet paid or recorded. Examples of accrued expenses include accrued interest expense (interest expense that you have incurred but have not yet paid).

5. **Accrued revenues**. Revenues that have been earned but not yet collected or recorded. Examples of accrued revenues include interest revenue that has been earned but not yet collected or recorded.

Depreciation

The accounting definitions of depreciation differ from the popular definition of depreciation as a decline in value.

Depreciation Listed on….	Report Objective	Reporting Rules	Definition of Depreciation	Depreciation Calculation
Financial statements: Profit & Loss, Balance Sheet, Statement of Cash Flows	Provide information to external users (bankers and investors)	GAAP (Generally Accepted Accounting Principles)	*Financial Accounting Definition:* Allocation of asset's cost to periods used	Straight-line depreciation = (Cost − Salvage)/ Useful life
Income tax returns	Provide information to the Internal Revenue Service	Internal Revenue Code	*Tax Definition:* Recovery of asset's cost through depreciation deductions on return	MACRS (See IRS Publication 946 on depreciation)

RECORD ADJUSTING JOURNAL ENTRIES

QuickBooks: Premier Accountant Edition 2010 features a Fixed Asset Manager to record depreciation entries for fixed assets.

Adjusting entries are dated the last day of the accounting period. Some enterprises maintain accounting records using QuickBooks and then hire an outside accountant to prepare adjusting entries at year-end. You can create a copy of your QuickBooks company file for your accountant to use when making adjustments. For more information about creating an Accountant's Copy, see Chapter 12.

At December 31, Rock Castle Construction needs to make an adjustment to record $3,000 of depreciation expense on its truck.

To make the adjusting journal entry in QuickBooks:

Step 1: From the **Company** menu, select **Make General Journal Entries**.

QuickBooks uses onscreen forms to record transactions, and the Journal is used to record adjustments and corrections.

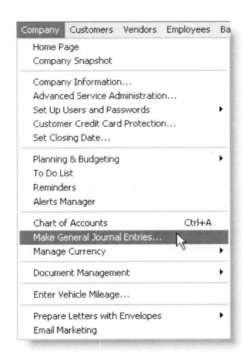

Step 2: When the following *Make General Journal Entries* window appears, select Date: **12/31/2013**.

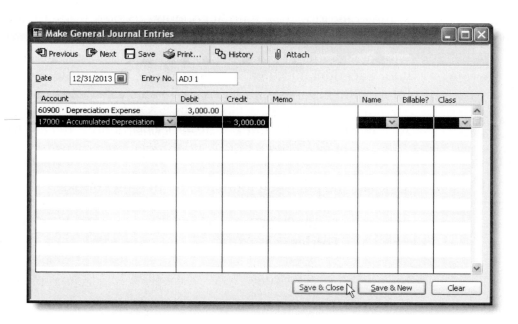

 Type the Account No. **60900** and QuickBooks will automatically complete the account title.

Memorize the journal entry to reuse each accounting period:
1. With the Journal Entry displayed, click **Edit** menu.
2. Select **Memorize General Journal**.

To use the memorized transaction, select **Lists** menu > **Memorized Transaction List**.

Step 3: Enter Entry No: **ADJ 1**.

Step 4: Select Account to debit: **60900 Depreciation Expense**.

Step 5: Enter Debit amount: **3000.00**.

Step 6: Select Account to credit: **17000 Accumulated Depreciation**.

Step 7: If it does not appear automatically, enter Credit amount: **3000.00**.

Step 8: Click **Save & Close** to record the journal entry and close the *Make General Journal Entries* window. FYI: If a message regarding the Fixed Asset List appears, click OK.

PRINT JOURNAL ENTRIES

To view the journal entry you just recorded, display the Journal. The Journal also contains journal entries for all transactions recorded using onscreen forms, such as sales invoices. QuickBooks automatically converts transactions recorded in onscreen forms into journal entries with debits and credits.

To display and print the General Journal:

Step 1: Click the **Report Center** icon in the Icon bar.

Step 2: Select: **Accountant & Taxes > Journal**.

Step 3: Select Dates From: **12/24/2013** To: **12/31/2013**. Click **Display report**.

Notice that the sales invoice you recorded on 12/24/2013 for the Jacobsen Kitchen job (Chapter 6) has now been converted to a journal entry.

Notice the adjusting entry for depreciation.

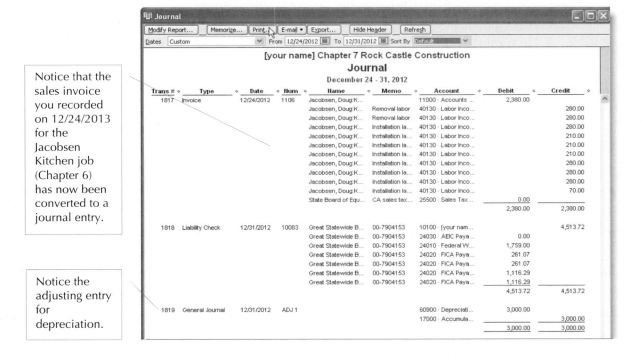

Step 4: 🖶 **Print** the Journal using **Portrait** orientation.

Step 5: **Close** the *Journal* window.

ADJUSTED TRIAL BALANCE

The Adjusted Trial Balance is prepared to verify that the accounting system still balances after adjusting entries are made. The Adjusted Trial Balance is printed in the same way as the Trial Balance except it is printed after adjusting entries have been made.

To print an Adjusted Trial Balance:

Step 1:   Select **Report Center > Accountant & Taxes > Trial Balance**.

Step 2:   Select Date: **12/31/2013**. Click **Display report**.

Step 3:   Modify the report heading by selecting **Modify Report > Header/Footer**. In the *Report Title* field enter the word **Adjusted** so the report title appears as Adjusted Trial Balance. Click **OK** to close the *Modify Report* window.

Step 4:   🖨 **Print** the Adjusted Trial Balance using **Portrait** orientation.

Step 5:   ✏ **Circle** the account balances that are different from the Trial Balance amounts.

 Total debits and total credits equal $1,167,793.11.

GENERAL LEDGER

The general ledger is a collection of all of the company's accounts and account activity. While the Trial Balance lists only the ending balance for each account, the general ledger provides detail about all transactions affecting the account during a given period.

Each account in the general ledger lists:

- Beginning balance.
- Transactions that affected the account for the selected period.
- Ending balance.

Normally, the general ledger is not provided to external users, such as bankers. However, the general ledger can provide managers with supporting detail needed to answer questions bankers might ask about the financial statements.

To print the general ledger:

Step 1: If the Report Center is not open, click the **Report Center** icon on the Icon bar.

Step 2: Select: **Accountant & Taxes > General Ledger**.

Step 3: Select Date Range: **This Fiscal Quarter**. Click **Display report**.

Step 4: The General Ledger report lists each account and all the transactions affecting the account. **Double-click on a transaction listed in the Checking account** to drill down to the original source document, such as a check or an invoice. **Close** the source document window.

Step 5: Use a filter to view only selected accounts in the general ledger. For example, to view only bank accounts, complete the following steps:

- Select **Modify Report > Filters**.
- Select Filter: **Account**.

- Select Account: **All bank accounts**.

Select a specific account or select from these choices for accounts to filter.

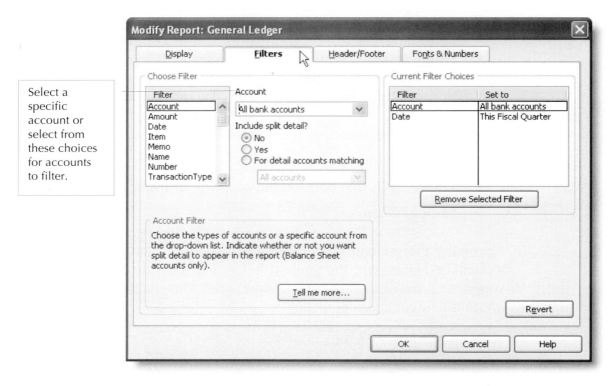

Step 6: To omit accounts with zero balances in the General Ledger report, from the *Modify Report* window:

- Click the **Display** tab > **Advanced** button.
- Select Include: **In Use**.
- Click **OK**.

Step 7: Click **OK** to close the *Modify Report* window.

Step 8: 🖼 **Print** the selected general ledger account using **Portrait** orientation and **Fit to 1 page(s) wide**.

Step 9: **Close** the *General Ledger* window.

FINANCIAL STATEMENTS

Financial statements are standardized financial reports given to bankers and investors. The three main financial statements are the Profit & Loss, Balance Sheet, and Statement of Cash Flows. The statements are prepared following Generally Accepted Accounting Principles (GAAP).

PROFIT AND LOSS

The Profit and Loss Statement is also called P&L or Income Statement.

The Profit and Loss Statement lists sales (sometimes called revenues) and expenses for a specified accounting period. Profit, or net income, can be measured two different ways:

1. **Cash basis**. A sale is recorded when cash is collected from the customer. Expenses are recorded when cash is paid.

2. **Accrual basis**. Sales are recorded when the good or service is provided regardless of whether the cash is collected from the customer. Expenses are recorded when the cost is incurred or expires, even if the expense has not been paid.

GAAP requires the accrual basis for the Profit and Loss Statement because it provides a better matching of income and expenses.

QuickBooks permits you to prepare the Profit and Loss Statement using either the accrual or the cash basis. QuickBooks also permits you to prepare Profit and Loss Statements monthly, quarterly, or annually.

To prepare a quarterly Profit and Loss Statement for Rock Castle Construction using the accrual basis:

Step 1: From the Report Center, select **Company & Financial > Profit & Loss Standard**.

Step 2: Select Dates: **This Fiscal Quarter**. Click **Display report**.

Step 3: Click the **Modify Report** button. Click the **Display** tab, and then select Report Basis: **Accrual**. Click **OK**.

Step 4: **Print** the Profit and Loss Statement using **Portrait** orientation.

Step 5: **Close** the *Profit and Loss* window.

☑ *Net Income equals $42,449.48.*

INCOME AND EXPENSE GRAPH

QuickBooks provides you with the ability to easily graph profit and loss information. A graph is simply another means to communicate financial information.

To create an Income and Expense Graph for Rock Castle Construction:

Step 1: From the Report Center, select: **Company & Financial > Income & Expense Graph**.

Step 2: Select Dates: **This Fiscal Quarter** to display the following *QuickInsight: Income and Expense Graph* window.

Step 3: Click the **By Account** button. The income and expense graph depicts a bar chart of income and expense for the three months in the fiscal quarter. The pie chart in the lower section of the window displays the relative proportion of each expense as a percentage of total expenses.

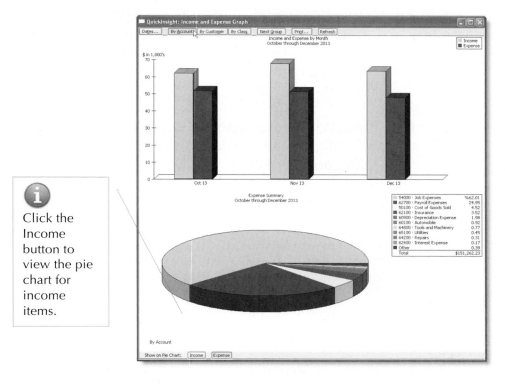

Click the Income button to view the pie chart for income items.

Step 4: ⊟ **Print** the income and expense graph.

Step 5: **Close** the *QuickInsight: Income and Expense Graph* window.

BALANCE SHEET

The Balance Sheet presents a company's financial position on a particular date. The Balance Sheet can be prepared at the end of a month, quarter, or year. The Balance Sheet lists:

1. **Assets**. What a company owns. On the Balance Sheet, assets are recorded at their historical cost, the amount you paid for the asset when you purchased it. Note that historical cost can be different from the market value of the asset, which is the amount the asset is worth now.

2. **Liabilities**. What a company owes. Liabilities are obligations that include amounts owed vendors (accounts payable) and bank loans (notes payable).

3. **Owner's equity**. The residual that is left after liabilities are satisfied. This is also called net worth. Owners' equity is increased by the owners' contributions and net income. Owners' equity is decreased by the owners' withdrawals (or dividends) and net losses.

To prepare a Balance Sheet for Rock Castle Construction at 12/31/2013:

Step 1:   From the Report Center, select **Company & Financial > Balance Sheet Standard**.

Step 2:   Select Dates: **This Fiscal Quarter**. Click **Display report**.

Step 3:   🖶 **Print** the Balance Sheet using **Portrait** orientation.

Step 4:   **Close** the *Balance Sheet* window.

Step 5:   ✎ **Circle** the single largest asset listed on the Balance Sheet.

✔ ***Total Assets equal $707,366.48.***

STATEMENT OF CASH FLOWS

The Statement of Cash Flows summarizes cash inflows and cash outflows for a business over a period of time. Cash flows are grouped into three categories:

1. **Cash flows from operating activities**. Cash inflows and outflows related to the company's primary business, such as cash flows from sales and operating expenses.

2. **Cash flows from investing activities**. Cash inflows and outflows related to acquisition and disposal of long-term assets.

3. **Cash flows from financing activities**. Cash inflows and outflows to and from investors and creditors (except for interest payments). Examples include: loan principal repayment and investments by owners.

To print the Statement of Cash Flows for Rock Castle Construction:

Step 1: From the Report Center, select **Company & Financial > Statement of Cash Flows**.

Step 2: Select Date: **This Fiscal Quarter**. Click **Display report**.

Step 3: Print the Statement of Cash Flows using **Portrait** orientation.

Step 4: **Close** the *Statement of Cash Flows* window.

Step 5: Circle Net Cash Provided by Operating Activities listed on the Statement of Cash Flows.

 Net cash increase for period equals $55,448.78.

TAX REPORTS

QuickBooks provides two different approaches that you can use when preparing your tax return.

1. Print QuickBooks income tax reports and then manually enter the tax information in your income tax return.

2. Export your QuickBooks accounting data to tax software, such as TurboTax software, and then use TurboTax to complete your income tax return.

Three different income tax reports are provided by QuickBooks:

1. **Income Tax Preparation report**. Lists the assigned tax line for each account.

2. **Income Tax Summary report**. Summarizes income and expenses that should be listed on a business income tax return.

3. **Income Tax Detail report**. Provides more detailed information about the income or expense amount appearing on each tax line of the Income Tax Summary report.

INCOME TAX PREPARATION REPORT

Before printing the Income Tax Summary report, check your QuickBooks accounts to see that the correct Tax Line is selected for each account. An easy way to check the Tax Line specified for each account is to print the Income Tax Preparation report as follows.

Step 1: From the Report Center, select: **Accountant & Taxes > Income Tax Preparation**.

Step 2: Select Date: **Today**. Click **Display report**.

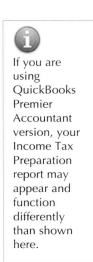

If you are using QuickBooks Premier Accountant version, your Income Tax Preparation report may appear and function differently than shown here.

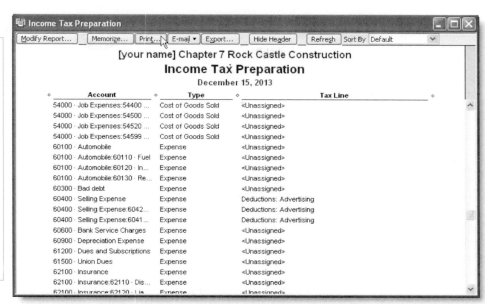

Step 3: 🖨 **Print** the Income Tax Preparation report.

Step 4: ✏ **Circle** the Tax Line for the Selling Expense accounts you added in Chapter 2. Notice that the Tax Line is Deductions: Advertising.

Step 5: Leave the *Income Tax Preparation* window open.

To determine if the correct tax line has been entered for each account, compare the tax lines listed on the Income Tax Preparation report with your business income tax return.

For example, if you wanted to change the Tax Line for the Bad Debt account from Unassigned to the appropriate Tax Line:

Step 1: From the *Income Tax Preparation* window, double-click on the account: **60300 Bad Debt**.

Step 2: When the following *Edit Account* window appears, change the Tax-Line Mapping to: **Deductions: Bad debts**.

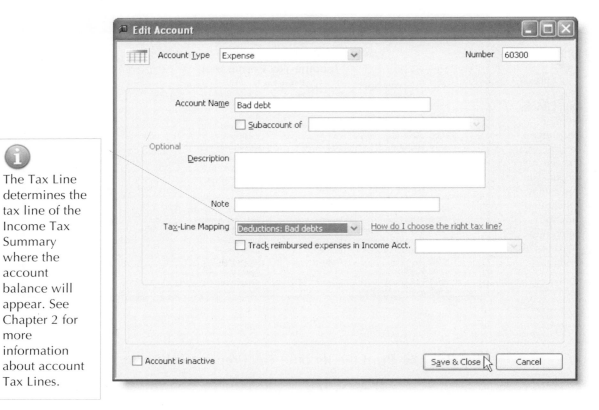

The Tax Line determines the tax line of the Income Tax Summary where the account balance will appear. See Chapter 2 for more information about account Tax Lines.

Step 3: To save the changes, click **Save and Close**. Close the Income Tax Preparation report.

INCOME TAX SUMMARY REPORT

After you confirm that the Tax Line for each account is correct, you are ready to print an Income Tax Summary report. The Income Tax Summary report lists sales and expenses that should appear on the business federal tax return filed with the IRS.

A business can use the information on the Income Tax Summary report to manually complete its income tax return. A sole proprietorship files Schedule C (attached to the owner's personal 1040 tax return). A corporation files Form 1120; a subchapter S corporation files Form 1120S.

INCOME TAX DETAIL REPORT

If you want to view detail for the line items shown on the Income Tax Summary report, you could display the Income Tax Detail report.

EXPORT TO TURBOTAX

Another approach to preparing a tax return is to export the account information from QuickBooks into TurboTax software. TurboTax for Home and Business is used for a sole proprietorship Schedule C.

TurboTax for Business is for corporations, S corporations, and partnerships.

To import your QuickBooks tax data into TurboTax software:

Step 1: Make a copy of your QuickBooks company data file.

Step 2: Start TurboTax software.

Step 3: Import your QuickBooks company file into TurboTax. In TurboTax, from the File menu, click Import.

MANAGEMENT REPORTS

Reports used by management do not have to follow a specified set of rules such as GAAP or the Internal Revenue Code. Instead, management reports are prepared as needed to provide management with information for making operating and business decisions.

Management reports include:

1. Cash flow forecast.
2. Budgets (See Chapter 12).
3. Accounts receivable aging (See Chapter 4).
4. Accounts payable aging (See Chapter 5).
5. Inventory reports (See Chapter 5).

CASH FLOW FORECAST

QuickBooks permits you to forecast cash flows. This enables you to project whether you will have enough cash to pay bills when they are due. If it appears that you will need additional cash, then you can arrange for a loan or line of credit to pay your bills. The Cash Flow Forecast report lists projected cash inflows and cash outflows.

To print a Cash Flow Forecast report for Rock Castle Construction:

Step 1: From the Report Center, select: **Company & Financial > Cash Flow Forecast**.

Step 2: Select Dates: **Next 4 Weeks** to display the *Cash Flow Forecast* window.

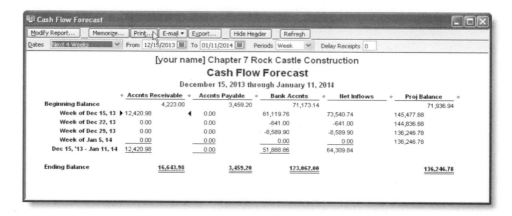

Step 3: 🖨 **Print** the Cash Flow Forecast report using **Portrait** orientation.

Step 4: Leave the *Cash Flow Forecast* window open.

EXPORT REPORTS TO MICROSOFT® EXCEL®

QuickBooks permits you to export a report to Microsoft Excel spreadsheet software. In order to use this feature of QuickBooks, you must have Microsoft Excel software installed on your computer.

To export the Cash Flow Forecast report to Excel:

Step 1: With the *Cash Flow Forecast* window still open, click the **Export** button at the top of the window.

Step 2: When the following *Export Report* window appears, select Export QuickBooks report to: **a new Excel workbook**.

To export to an existing Excel spreadsheet, select the **Export** button > **Basic** tab > **an existing Excel spreadsheet** > **Browse** to select the file.

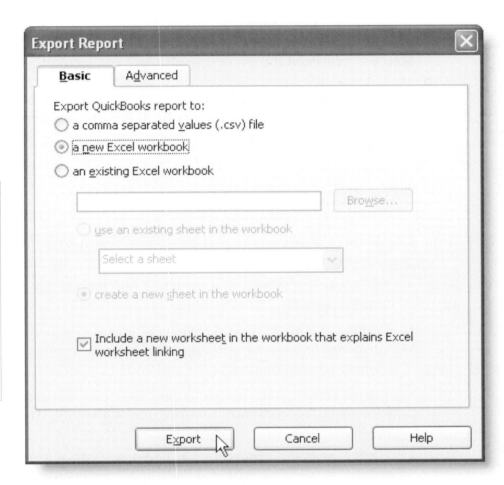

Step 3: Then click **Export** to export the QuickBooks report to Excel.

Step 4: Excel will automatically open. When the spreadsheet appears on your screen, **click on the cell that contains the Ending Balance of Accounts Receivable**. Notice that Excel has already entered a formula into the cell.

Step 5: To save the Excel file:
- In Excel, click the **save** icon.
- Select **Save As**.
- Select the drive to which you are saving (C drive or USB drive).
- Enter File name: **Cash Forecast**.
- Click **Save**.

Step 6: 🖨 **Print** the Excel spreadsheet.

Step 7: **Close** the Cash Forecast Excel workbook, then **close** Excel software by clicking the ⊠ in the upper right corner of the *Excel* window.

SAVE REPORTS TO ELECTRONIC FILES

QuickBooks also permits you to save a report to a file instead of printing the report. You can select from the following file formats:

- ASCII text file. After saving as a text file, the file can be used with word processing software.

- Comma delimited file. Comma delimited files can be imported into word processing, spreadsheet, or database software. Commas identify where columns begin and end.

- Tab delimited file. Tab delimited files can be used with word processing or database software. Tabs identify where columns begin and end.

- Adobe PDF file. This is a portable document file that permits reports to be e-mailed. See Appendix D for more information about using PDF files as electronic deliverables.

SAVE CHAPTER 7

Save a backup of your Chapter 7 file using the file name: **[your name] Chapter 7 Backup.QBB**. See *Appendix B: Back Up & Restore QuickBooks Files* for instructions.

WORKFLOW

If you are using the workflow approach, leave your .QBW file open and proceed directly to Exercise 7.1.

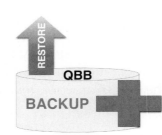

RESTART & RESTORE

If you are using the Restart & Restore approach and are ending your computer session now, close your .QBW file and exit QuickBooks.

When you restart, you will restore your backup file to complete Exercise 7.1.

PODCASTS

Watch the Chapter 7 **Podcast** at www.QuickBooksBlog.info to learn more about QuickBooks reports.

MULTIPLE-CHOICE PRACTICE TEST

A **Multiple-Choice Practice Test** for Chapter 7 is on the *Computer Accounting for QuickBooks Pro* Online Learning Center at www.mhhe.com/kay2010. Try the Practice Test and see how many questions you answer correctly.

EXTRAS!

Section 3: Quick Guide contains quick, easy step-by-step directions for frequently used QuickBooks tasks, including correcting errors. You can find *Quick Guide* at the back of your text or online at www.mhhe.com/kay2010. *Check it out!*

Deliverables Checklist is a list of the reports and documents that you are to deliver to your instructor for grading. You can find the Deliverables Checklist at the end of the chapter or online at www.mhhe.com/kay2010. Staying organized saves time. Use the checklist to organize your reports, checking off the reports as completed. Then include the checklist with your reports for grading.

Appendix D: Electronic Deliverables shows you how to save your QuickBooks reports electronically. Also, watch the Electronic Deliverables Podcast at www.QuickBooksBlog.info. Check with your instructor to see if you should deliver your reports electronically.

Join the QuickBooks Student Community to ask questions and share tips @ www.QuickBooksBlog.info.

LEARNING ACTIVITIES

Important: Ask your instructor whether you should complete the following assignments by printing requested reports or creating electronic deliverables (see Appendix D: Electronic Deliverables).

EXERCISE 7.1: PROFIT & LOSS: VERTICAL ANALYSIS

SCENARIO

You vaguely recall from your college accounting course that performing financial statement analysis can reveal additional useful information. Since Mr. Castle asked for whatever additional information he might need, you decide to print a vertical analysis of the Profit and Loss Statement using QuickBooks.

TASK 1: OPEN COMPANY FILE

WORKFLOW

If you are using the Workflow approach, you will use the same .QBW file.

If your QBW file is not already open, open it by selecting **File > Open Previous Company**. Select your **.QBW file.**

Change the company name to **[your name] Exercise 7.1** by selecting **Company** menu > **Company Information.**

RESTART & RESTORE

If you are not using the same computer, you must use the Restart and Restore approach.

Restore your **Chapter 7 Backup.QBB** file using the directions in *Appendix B: Back Up & Restore QuickBooks Files*.

After restoring the file, change the company name to **[your name] Exercise 7.1** by selecting **Company** menu **> Company Information.**

TASK 2: PROFIT & LOSS: VERTICAL ANALYSIS

Prepare a customized Profit and Loss Statement that shows each item on the statement as a percentage of sales (income):

Step 1:   From the Report Center, select **Company & Financial > Profit & Loss Standard.**

Step 2:   Select Dates: **This Fiscal Quarter**. Click **Display report.**

Step 3:   To customize the report, click the **Modify Report** button.

Step 4:   When the following *Modify Report* window appears, select **Display** tab. Select: **% of Income.** Click **OK.**

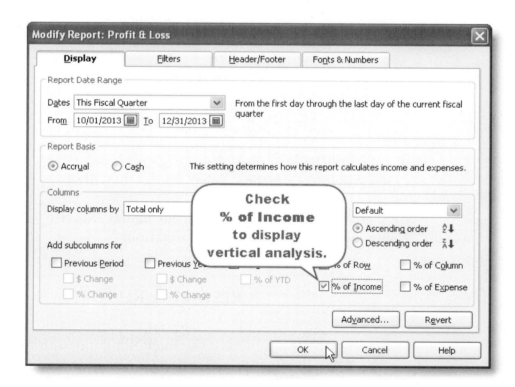

Step 5: ⊟ Click the **Print** button to print the report using **Portrait** orientation.

Step 6: ✎ On the printout, **circle** or highlight the single largest expense as a percentage of income.

Step 7: ✎ On the printout, **circle** or highlight the profit margin (net income as a percentage of sales).

TASK 3: WORKFLOW

Leave your QuickBooks company file open to complete the next exercise.

EXERCISE 7.2: BALANCE SHEET: VERTICAL ANALYSIS

SCENARIO

You decide to also prepare a customized Balance Sheet that displays each account on the Balance Sheet as a percentage of total assets. This vertical analysis indicates the proportion of total assets that each asset represents. For example, inventory might be 30 percent of total assets. Vertical analysis also helps to assess the percentage of assets financed by debt versus owners' equity.

TASK 1: CHANGE COMPANY NAME

Change the company name to: **[your name] Exercise 7.2 Rock Castle Construction**.

TASK 2: BALANCE SHEET: VERTICAL ANALYSIS, EXPORT TO EXCEL

Prepare a customized Balance Sheet that shows each account as a percentage of total assets.

Step 1: From the Report Center, select: **Company & Financial > Balance Sheet Standard**.

Step 2: Select Dates: **This Fiscal Quarter**. Click **Display report**.

Step 3: Click the **Modify Report** button and select: **% of Column**.

Step 4: 🖨 **Print** the customized Balance Sheet using the **Portrait** orientation.

Step 5: ✏ On the printout, **circle** or highlight the asset that represents the largest percentage of assets.

Step 6: ✏ On the printout, **circle** or highlight the percentage of assets financed with debt. (Hint: What is the percentage of total liabilities?)

Step 7: Export the customized Balance Sheet to Excel by clicking the **Export** button in the *Balance Sheet* window. 🖨 **Print** the Excel spreadsheet and compare it to your QuickBooks printout.

TASK 3: WORKFLOW

Leave your QuickBooks company file open to complete the next exercise.

EXERCISE 7.3: ANALYSIS

SCENARIO

"Last year, the bank told us we had money in the bank, but QuickBooks told us we were broke and had no money in our Checking account to pay bills." Mr. Castle casts you a look as he rushes past your cubicle—a look that warns you to be ready to answer a QuickBooks question.

"We had to hire an accountant last year to find the missing cash in QuickBooks." Rock Castle now pauses as you anticipated the upcoming question. *"Will we need to hire an accountant this year to find the missing cash or can you show me the money?"*

Rapidly, you reply, *"No problem, Mr. Castle. This year we know where all our cash is."* When you look up to show him some QuickBooks reports, Mr. Castle is already back in his office on the phone.

TASK 1: CHANGE COMPANY NAME

Change the company name to: **[your name] Exercise 7.3 Rock Castle Construction**.

TASK 2: GENERAL LEDGER: SHOW ME THE MONEY

To show Mr. Castle the money, complete the following steps.

Step 1: Display a General Ledger report for Rock Castle Construction for December 15 to December 31, 2013, listing all **asset** accounts in use with a balance.

Step 2: Find the account on your General Ledger report where the accountant found the missing cash last year. **Print** only that specific account using a filter.

Step 3: 📝 Prepare a brief e-mail explaining to Rock Castle the purpose of this account and what you plan to do this year so there is no problem. Present your findings of how including this account changes the analysis of Rock Castle Construction's cash position.

TASK 3: RATIOS

In addition to the QuickBooks reports you will be providing Mr. Castle, you decide that preparing ratio analysis for him will provide additional insight into Rock Castle Construction operations.

Using your QuickBooks reports from this chapter, calculate the following ratios.

Step 1: The Current Ratio is used as a measure of how well current assets cover the current liabilities that will be due within the next year. A general rule of thumb for the current ratio is that an enterprise should have $2 in current assets for each $1 in current liabilities which is stated as 2:1.

Calculate the Current Ratio (Current Assets/Current Liabilities) for Rock Castle Construction. _____:_____

Step 2: The debt ratio focuses on the percentage of company's assets financed with debt as opposed to equity. For example, a debt ratio of 40% indicates that 40 percent of the enterprise's assets are financed with debt. Too high a debt ratio can indicate increased risk of default on the debt.

Calculate the Debt Ratio (Total Liabilities/Total Assets) for Rock Castle Construction. _____%

Step 3: The profit margin shows the percentage of each sales dollar that is left in profit. For example a profit margin of 10% indicates that on average, 10 cents of each dollar of sales is profit. Profit margin varies greatly by industry with some industries, such as discount stores, having low profit margins.

Calculate the Profit Margin (Net Income or Net Profit/Total Sales) for Rock Castle Construction. _____%

Step 4: ✍ Prepare a brief email to Rock Castle summarizing the results of your ratio analysis and outlining your conclusions, comments, or recommendations based on your analysis.

TASK 4: SAVE EXERCISE 7.3

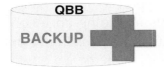

Save a backup of your Exercise 7.3 file using the file name: **[your name] Exercise 7.3 Backup.QBB**. See *Appendix B: Back Up & Restore QuickBooks Files* for instructions.

EXERCISE 7.4: YEAR-END GUIDE

QuickBooks provides a Year-End Guide to assist in organizing the tasks that a business must complete at the end of its accounting period.

Print the Year-End Guide as follows:

Step 1: Select **Help** menu > **Year-End Guide**.

Step 2: ✓ **Check** the items that you have already completed for Rock Castle Construction.

Step 3: 🖨 **Print** the Year-End Guide by clicking the **Print** icon at the top of the window.

EXERCISE 7.5: WEB QUEST

To learn more information about TurboTax software, visit Intuit's TurboTax website.

Step 1: Go to www.turbotax.com website.

Step 2: Prepare a short e-mail to Mr. Castle summarizing the difference between TurboTax Home & Business and TurboTax Business. Which TurboTax would you recommend for Rock Castle Construction?

EXERCISE 7.6: WEB QUEST

Publicly traded companies (companies that sell stock to the public) are required to provide an annual report to stockholders. The annual report contains financial statements including an Income Statement, Balance Sheet, and Statement of Cash Flows. Many publicly traded companies now post their financial statements on their websites. Print financial statements for Intuit, the company that sells QuickBooks software.

Step 1: Go to www.intuit.com website. Click **About Intuit.**

Step 2: Click **Investor Relations**. Click **Annual Reports**. Select **2007 Annual Report**.

Step 3: In the Consolidated Financial Statements, **Print** Intuit's Consolidated Statements of Operations which shows results for three years.

Step 4: **Circle** net income for the year Intuit was most profitable.

DELIVERABLES CHECKLIST CHAPTER 7
NAME:

INSTRUCTIONS:
1. CHECK OFF THE DELIVERABLES YOU HAVE COMPLETED.
2. TURN IN THIS PAGE WITH YOUR DELIVERABLES.

CHAPTER 7

- ☐ Trial Balance
- ☐ Journal
- ☐ Adjusted Trial Balance
- ☐ General Ledger
- ☐ Profit & Loss
- ☐ Income and Expense Graph
- ☐ Balance Sheet
- ☐ Statement of Cash Flows
- ☐ Income Tax Preparation Report
- ☐ Cash Flow Forecast
- ☐ Excel Spreadsheet Cash Flow Forecast

EXERCISE 7.1

- ☐ Task 2: Profit & Loss: Vertical Analysis

EXERCISE 7.2

- ☐ Task 2: Balance Sheet: Vertical Analysis and Excel Spreadsheet

EXERCISE 7.3

- ☐ Task 2: General Ledger Account
- ☐ Task 3: Ratios

EXERCISE 7.4

- ☐ Year-End Guide Printout

EXERCISE 7.5
☐ E-mail: TurboTax Recommendation

EXERCISE 7.6
☐ Statement of Operations for Intuit, Inc.

REFLECTION: A WISH AND A STAR

Reflection improves learning and retention. Reflect on what you have learned after completing Chapter 7 that you did not know before you started the chapter.

A Star:

What did you like best that you learned about QuickBooks in Chapter 7?

A Wish:

If you could pick one thing, what do you wish you knew more about when using QuickBooks?

SECTION 2
QUICKBOOKS
ACCOUNTING FOR ENTREPRENEURS

CHAPTER 8
NEW COMPANY SETUP

SCENARIO

Lately, you've considered starting your own business and becoming an entrepreneur. You have been looking for a business opportunity that would use your talents to make money.

While working at Rock Castle Construction, you have overheard conversations that some of the customers have been dissatisfied with the quality of the paint jobs. In addition, you believe there is a demand for custom painting. You know that Rock Castle Construction lost more than one job because it could not find a subcontractor to do custom painting.

One morning when you arrive at work, you hear Mr. Castle's voice booming throughout the office. *"That's the second time this month!"* he roars into the telephone. *"How are we supposed to finish our jobs on time when the painting subcontractor doesn't show up?!"* Mr. Castle slams down the phone.

That morning you begin to seriously consider the advantages and disadvantages of starting your own painting service business. Perhaps you could pick up some work from Rock Castle Construction. You could do interior and exterior painting for homes and businesses, including custom-painted murals while continuing to work part-time for Rock Castle Construction maintaining its accounting records. Now that you have learned QuickBooks, you can quickly enter transactions and create the reports Mr. Castle needs, leaving you time to operate your own painting service business.

When you return from lunch, you notice Katrina Beneficio in Mr. Castle's office. Then you overhear Mr. Castle telling her, *"We would like to help you, Mrs. Beneficio, but we don't have anyone who can do a custom-painted landscape on your dining room wall. If I hear of anyone who does that type of work, I will call you."*

You watch as the two of them shake hands and Mrs. Beneficio walks out the front door. Sensing a window of opportunity, you pursue Mrs. Beneficio into the parking lot. *"Mrs. Beneficio—"*

She stops and turns to look at you. *"Mrs. Beneficio—I understand that you are looking for someone to paint a landscape mural in your home. I would like to bid on the job."*

With a sparkle in her eye, Mrs. Beneficio asks, *"How soon can you start?"*

"As soon as I get off work this afternoon!" you reply as the two of you shake hands. *"Would you like a bid on the job?"*

Without hesitation, Mrs. Beneficio replies, *"I trust you will be fair to your first customer."*

When you reenter the office building, Mr. Castle is waiting for you. You can feel Mr. Castle's gaze as you debate how best to tell him about your business plans.

Finally, Mr. Castle speaks. *"Give Tom Whalen a call. He would like you to do marble faux painting in his home's foyer."*

"Thanks, Mr. Castle. I'll do that right away," you reply as you head toward your cubicle, wondering how Mr. Castle knew about your business plans.

Walking back to your cubicle, you quickly make start-up decisions:
1. To use the sole proprietorship form of business.
2. To name your business Paint Palette.
3. To use environmentally friendly paints and European painting techniques (faux and murals) for competitive advantage.
4. To invest in a computer so that you can use QuickBooks to maintain the accounting records for your business.

Now you will have two sources of income:
- Wages from Rock Castle Construction reported on your W-2 and attached to your 1040 tax return.
- Income from your painting business reported on a Schedule C attached to your 1040 tax return.

CHAPTER 8
LEARNING OBJECTIVES

In Chapter 8, you will learn about the following QuickBooks features:

INTRODUCTION

In this chapter, you will set up a new service company in QuickBooks by completing the following steps:

---

1. EasyStep Interview

Use the EasyStep Interview to enter information and preferences for the new company. Based on the information entered, QuickBooks automatically creates a Chart of Accounts.

---

2. Customize the Chart of Accounts

Modify the Chart of Accounts to customize it for your business.

---

3. Customer List

In the Customer List, enter information about customers to whom you sell products and services.

---

4. Vendor List

In the Vendor List, enter information about vendors from whom you buy products, supplies, and services.

---

5. Item List

In the Item List, enter information about (1) products and services you *sell to customers* and (2) products and services you *buy from vendors*.

If you hired employees, you would also enter information into the Employee List. In this case, Paint Palette has no employees.

To begin Chapter 8, start QuickBooks software by clicking on the **QuickBooks** desktop icon or click **Start > Programs > QuickBooks > QuickBooks Pro 2010**.

SET UP A NEW COMPANY

To create a new company data file in QuickBooks, use the EasyStep Interview. The EasyStep Interview asks you a series of questions about your business. Then QuickBooks uses the information to customize QuickBooks to fit your business needs.

Open the EasyStep Interview as follows:

Step 1:   Select the **File** menu.

Step 2:   Select **New Company**. The following *EasyStep Interview* window will appear.

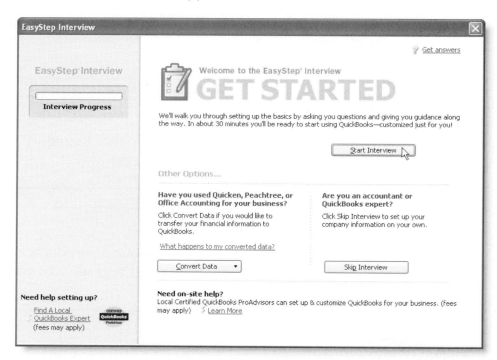

Step 3:   Click **Start Interview**.

Your DBA (Doing Business As) name is used to identify your company for sales, advertising, and marketing.

Your company's Legal Name is used on all legal documents, such as contracts, tax returns, licenses, and patents.

For a Federal Tax ID number:
1. A sole proprietorship uses the owner's Social Security number.
2. A corporation uses an EIN (Employer Identification Number).

Your company is a sole proprietorship, with business income reported on Schedule C attached to a 1040 tax return. Accordingly, your Social Security number is the business federal Tax ID number.

Step 4: When the following *Enter Your Company Information* window appears:

- Enter Company Name: **[your name] Paint Palette**.

- Press the **Tab** key, and QuickBooks will automatically enter the company name in the *Legal name* field. Since your company will do business under its legal name, the *Company name* and *Legal name* fields are the same.

- Enter the following information, then click **Next**.

Tax ID	333-22-4444
Address	127 Asheur Boulevard
City	Bayshore
State	CA
Zip	94326
Phone	800-555-1358
E-mail	<Enter your e-mail address>

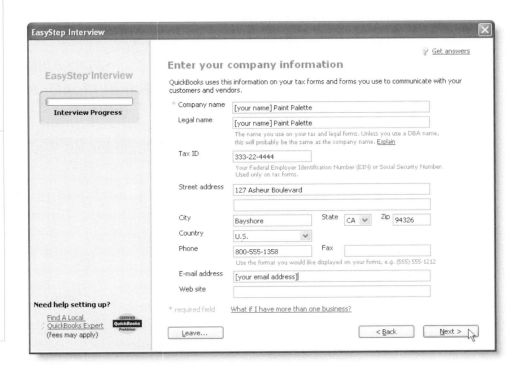

Step 5: In the *Select Your Industry* window, select **General Service-based Business > Next**.

Step 6: When the *How Is Your Company Organized?* window appears, select **Sole Proprietorship > Next**.

How your business entity is organized (Sole Proprietorship, Partnership, Limited Liability Partnership (LLP), Limited Liability Company (LLC), C Corporation, S Corporation, or Non-Profit) determines which tax form and tax lines you use.

Step 7: Select the first month of your fiscal year: **January > Next**.

Write your password on the inside front cover of your text.

Step 8: In the *Set Up Your Administrator Password* window:

- Enter your administrator password.

- Retype the password.

- Click **Next.**

Step 9: When the *Create Your Company File* window appears, click **Next** to choose a file name and location to save your company file.

Step 10: When the *Filename for New Company* window appears:

- Enter File name: **[Your Name] Chapter 8.**

- Click **Save**.

If you are using removable media such as a USB drive or external hard drive to save the .QBW file, ascertain there is enough disk space on the drive and then specify that drive for the location to save the .QBW file.

The default location for saving a QuickBooks company is: *C:\Document and Settings\All Users\(Shared) Documents\Intuit\QuickBooks\Company Files.*

Step 11: Click **Next** when the *Customizing QuickBooks For Your Business* window appears.

Step 12: When the *What Do You Sell* window appears:
- Select: **Services only**.
- Click **Next**.

Step 13: When asked "Do you charge sales tax?"
- Select: **No**.
- Click **Next**.

Step 14: When asked "Do you want to create estimates in QuickBooks?"
- Select **Yes**.
- Click **Next**.

Step 15: When the *Sales Receipts* window appears:
- "Do you want to use sales receipts in QuickBooks?" Select: **Yes**.
- Click **Next**.

Step 16: When the *Using Statements in QuickBooks* window appears:
- "Do you want to use billing statements in QuickBooks?" Select: **Yes**.
- Click **Next**.

Step 17: When the *Using Progress Invoicing* window appears:
- "Do you want to use progress invoicing?" Select: **No**.
- Click **Next**.

Step 18: When the *Managing Bills You Owe* window appears:

- "Do you want to keep track of bills you owe?" Select: **Yes**.
- Click **Next**.

Step 19: When the *Do You Print Checks?* window appears:

- Select: **I print checks**.
- Click **Next**.

Step 20: When the *Credit Card* window appears:

- "Do you accept credit cards?" Select: **I don't currently accept credit cards, but I would like to**.
- Click **Next**.

Step 21: When the *Tracking Time in QuickBooks* window appears:

- "Do you want to track time in QuickBooks?" Select: **Yes**.
- Click **Next**.

You are not considered an employee because you are the owner.

Step 22: When the *Employee* window appears:

- "Do you have employees?" Select: **No**.
- Click **Next**.

Step 23: When the *Tracking Multiple Currencies in QuickBooks* window appears:

- "Do you want to track multiple currencies in QuickBooks?" Select: **No**.
- Click **Next**.

Step 24: Read the *Using Accounts in QuickBooks* window. Click **Next**.

Step 25: When the *Select a Date to Start Tracking Your Finances* window appears:

- Select: **Use today's date or the first day of the quarter or month**.

▪ Enter Start Date: **01/01/2014**.

▪ Click **Next**.

Step 26: When *the Add Your Bank Account* window appears:

▪ "Would you like to add an existing bank account?" Select: **Yes**.

▪ Click **Next**.

Step 27: When the *Enter Your Bank Account Information* window appears:

▪ Enter Bank Account Name: **[your name] Checking**.

▪ Enter Bank Account Number: **5555555555**

▪ Enter Bank Routing Number: **888888888**

▪ "When did you open this bank account?" Select: **On or after 01/01/2014**.

▪ Click **Next**.

Step 28: Read the *About Your Account Balance* window. Click **Next**.

Step 29: When the *Review Bank Accounts* window appears:

▪ Select **No** when asked if you want to add another bank account.

▪ Click **Next**.

Step 30: When the *Review Income and Expense Accounts* window appears, click **Next**.

Step 31: When the following *Congratulations!* window appears, click **Finish**.

Step 32: If the *QuickBooks Coach* window appears on your screen, click **Start Working.**

Step 33: The *QuickBooks Coach* window should now appear on the right side of your screen with Explore Workflow view of the Home page.

HOME PAGE

Notice that the Home page for Paint Palette differs from the Home page for Rock Castle Construction in the following ways:

1. The *Vendors* section of the Home page for Paint Palette does not include Purchase Order, Receive Inventory, and Enter Bills Against Inventory icons. During the company setup, you indicated that Paint Palette was a service company. Since you will not be selling a product, you will not be tracking inventory for resale.

2. Also notice that the *Employees* section does not include the Pay Employees and Pay Liabilities icons. During the company setup, you indicated that there were no employees so these icons are not needed for Paint Palette.

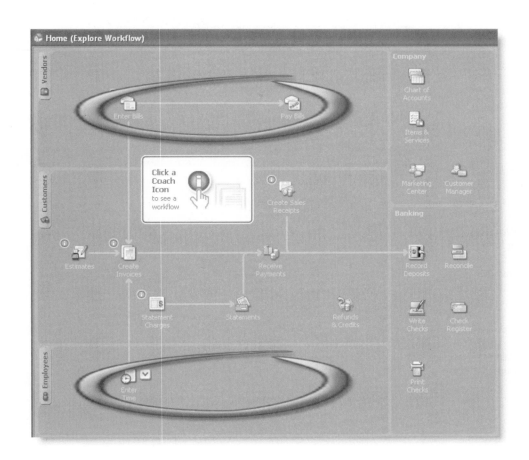

COMPLETE COMPANY SETUP

After the EasyStep Interview is finished, use the following checklist to complete the company setup:

☐ Complete the company information.

☐ Customize the Chart of Accounts.

☐ Add customers.

☐ Add vendors.

☐ Add products and services as items.

ENTER COMPANY INFORMATION

To enter additional company information:

Step 1:   From **Company** menu > **Company Information**.

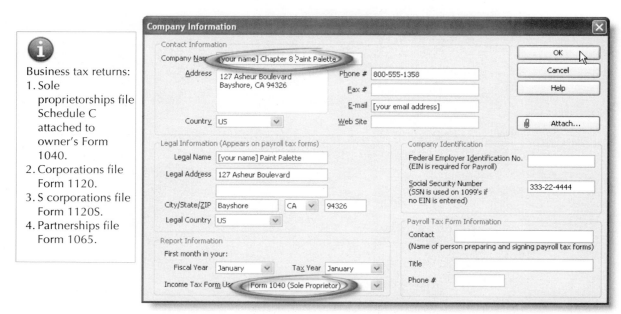

Business tax returns:
1. Sole proprietorships file Schedule C attached to owner's Form 1040.
2. Corporations file Form 1120.
3. S corporations file Form 1120S.
4. Partnerships file Form 1065.

Step 2:   Change the Company Name: **[Your Name] Chapter 8 Paint Palette**.

Step 3:   Verify Income Tax Form Used: **Form 1040 (Sole Proprietor)**.

Step 4:   Click **OK** to close the *Company Information* window.

CUSTOMIZE QUICKBOOKS

You will customize QuickBooks for Paint Palette by customizing preferences and by customizing the Chart of Accounts. First, to customize preferences:

Step 1:   Select **Edit** menu > **Preferences** > **General** > **My Preferences**.

Step 2: Select Default Date to Use for New Transactions: **Use the last entered date as default**.

Step 3: Click **OK**.

CUSTOMIZE CHART OF ACCOUNTS

The Chart of Accounts is a list of all the accounts Paint Palette will use when maintaining its accounting records. The Chart of Accounts is like a table of contents for accounting records.

In the EasyStep Interview, when you selected General Service-based Business as the type of industry, QuickBooks automatically created a Chart of Accounts for Paint Palette. Then QuickBooks permits you to customize the Chart of Accounts to fit your accounting needs.

DISPLAY CHART OF ACCOUNTS

To display the following *Chart of Accounts* window, click **Chart of Accounts** in the *Company* section of the Home page.

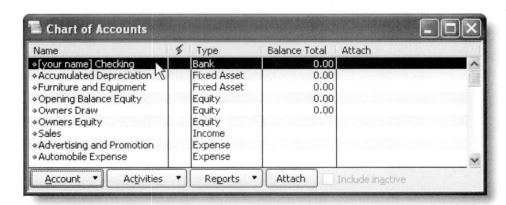

DISPLAY ACCOUNT NUMBERS

Notice that the Chart of Accounts does not list the account numbers. Display account numbers in the Chart of Accounts by completing the following steps:

Step 1: Select **Edit** menu > **Preferences**.

Step 2: When the following *Preferences* window appears:

- Select the **Accounting** icon on the left scrollbar.
- Select the **Company Preferences** tab.
- Select **Use account numbers**.
- Uncheck **Warn if transactions are 30 day(s) in the future.**

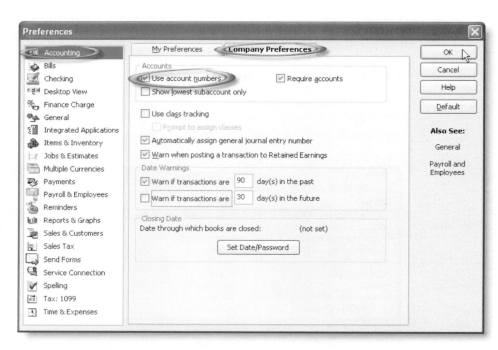

Step 3: Click **OK** to close the *Preferences* window.

The Chart of Accounts should now display account numbers.

ADD NEW ACCOUNTS

The Paint Palette will be purchasing a new computer. To account for the computer, you will need to add the following three accounts to the Chart of Accounts:

Account	Computer
Subaccount	Computer Cost
Subaccount	Accumulated Depreciation Computer

The Computer Cost subaccount contains the original cost of the computer. The Accumulated Depreciation subaccount for the computer accumulates all depreciation recorded for the computer over its useful life. The parent account, Computer, will show the net book value of the computer (cost minus accumulated depreciation).

To add new accounts to the Chart of Accounts for Paint Palette:

Step 1: From the following *Chart of Accounts* window:

- **Right-click** to display the popup menu.
- Select **New**.

If your business has a large number of fixed asset accounts, you can use the Fixed Asset Item List to track fixed asset information.

The Chart of Accounts now lists account numbers.

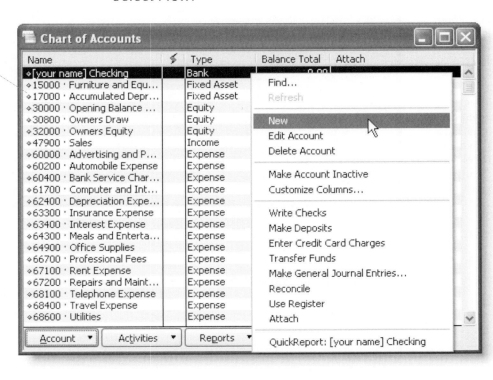

Step 2: From the *Add New Account: Choose Account Type* window, select **Fixed Asset (major purchases)**. Click **Continue**.

Step 3: When the following *Add New Account* window appears:

- Select Account Type: **Fixed Asset**.
- Enter Account Number: **14100**.
- Enter Account Name: **Computer**.
- Enter Description: **Computer**.
- Select Tax Line: **<Unassigned>**.

The Tax Line determines where QuickBooks lists the account balance on the Income Tax Summary report. Because only income and expense accounts are listed on Schedule C of the tax return, an Unassigned Tax Line is used for other accounts not appearing on the tax return.

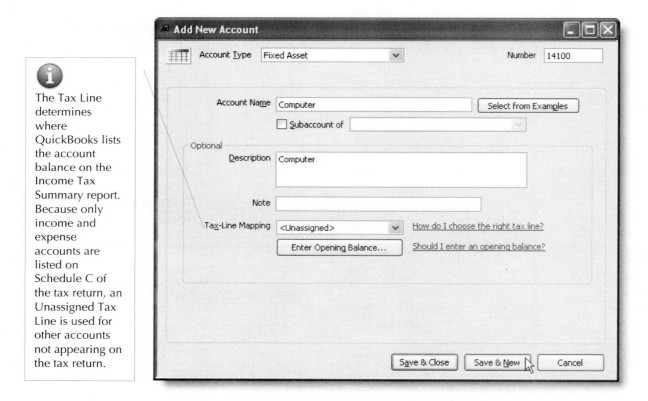

Step 4: Click **Save & New** to enter another account.

To enter new subaccounts, complete the following steps.

Step 1: Add the Computer Cost subaccount by entering the following information when a blank *Add New Account* window appears:

- Select Account Type: **Fixed Asset**.
- Enter Account Number: **14200**.
- Enter Account Name: **Computer Cost**.
- Check ✓ Subaccount of: **14100 – Computer**.
- Enter Description: **Computer Cost**.
- Select Tax Line: **<Unassigned>**.

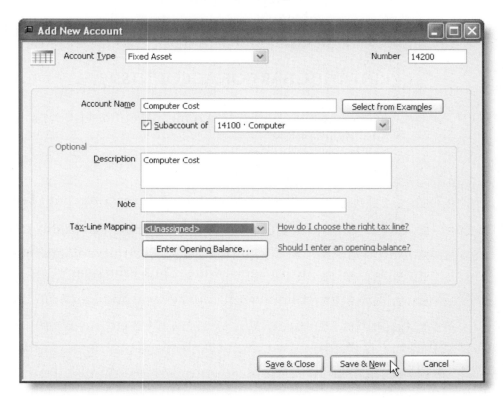

Step 2: Click **Save & New** to add another subaccount.

Step 3: Add the Accumulated Depreciation Computer subaccount by entering the following information in the *Add New Account* window:

Account No.	14300
Account Type	Fixed Asset
Account Name	Accumulated Depr Computer
Subaccount of	14100 Computer
Account Description	Accumulated Depreciation Computer
Tax Line	Unassigned

Step 4: Click **Save & Close** to close the *Add New Account* window.

PRINT THE CHART OF ACCOUNTS

To 🖷 **print** the Chart of Accounts (Account Listing) report, complete the following steps:

Step 1: From the *Report Center:*

- Select: **Accountant & Taxes > Account Listing**.

- Select Date: **01/01/2014**. Click **Display report**.

- 🖷 Click **Print**. Select **Portrait** orientation and **Fit report to 1 page(s) wide**. Click **Print** again.

- **Close** the *Account Listing* and *Report Center* windows.

Step 2: **Close** the *Chart of Accounts* window.

CREATE A CUSTOMER LIST

You can import list information using Excel. See QuickBooks Help for more information.

As you learned in Chapter 4, the Customer List contains information about the customers to whom you sell services. In addition, the Customer List also contains information about jobs or projects for each customer.

Paint Palette has two customers:

1. Katrina Beneficio, who wants a custom landscape mural painted on her dining room wall.

2. Tom Whalen, who wants marble faux painting in his home's foyer.

To add a new customer to Paint Palette's Customer List:

Step 1: Click the **Customer Center** icon on the Icon bar.

Step 2: To add a new customer, select **New Customer & Job > New Customer.**

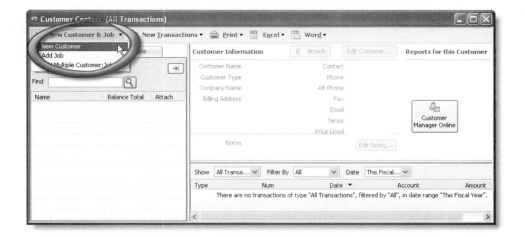

Step 3: When the *New Customer* window appears, enter the following information about your first customer, Katrina Beneficio.

Customer	Beneficio, Katrina
Opening Balance	0.00
As of	01/01/2014
Address Info:	
Mr./Ms./...	Mrs.
First Name	Katrina
Last Name	Beneficio
Contact	Katrina Beneficio
Phone	415-555-0013
Alt. Phone	415-555-3636
Address	10 Pico Blvd Bayshore, CA 94326

Additional Info:	
Type	Referral
Terms	Net 30

Payment Info:	
Account	1001
Preferred Payment Method	Check

Step 4: Click **OK** to close the *New Customer* window.

Step 5: To add a new job, select Katrina Beneficio in the Customer List, then **right-click** to display the popup menu. Select **Add Job**.

Job Info:	
Job Name	Dining Room
Opening Balance	0.00
As of	01/01/2014
Job Status	Awarded
Start Date	01/03/2014
Job Description	Dining Room Landscape Mural
Job Type	Mural

Select **Add New**.

Step 6: Click **OK** to save.

Step 7: Export the Customer List to Excel and then print.

- Click the **Excel** button at the top of the Customer Center.

- Click **Export Customer List**.

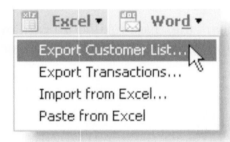

- **Export** and then **save** the Excel file.
- **Print** the Customer List using Excel.

Step 8: **Close** the Customer Center.

CREATE A VENDOR LIST

As you learned in Chapter 5, the Vendor List contains information about vendors from whom you buy products and services.

To add vendors to the Vendor List for Paint Palette:

Step 1: Click the **Vendor Center** icon on the Icon bar.

Step 2: To add a new vendor, click the **New Vendor** button.

Step 3: When the *New Vendor* window appears, enter the following information about Brewer Paint Supplies.

Vendor Name	Brewer Paint Supplies
Opening Balance	0.00
As of	01/01/2014
Address Info:	
Company Name	Brewer Paint Supplies
Address	200 Spring Street Bayshore, CA 94326
Contact	Ella Brewer
Phone	415-555-6070
Print on Check as	Brewer Paint Supplies

Additional Info:	
Account	2012
Type	Supplies
Terms	Net 30
Credit Limit	3000.00
Tax ID	37-7832541

Step 4: Click **OK** to close the *New Vendor* window.

Step 5: ☐ **Export** the Vendor List to Excel and **print**.

Step 6: **Close** the Vendor Center.

CREATE AN ITEM LIST

As you learned in Chapter 5, the Item List contains information about service items, inventory items, and non-inventory items sold to customers. Paint Palette plans to sell four different service items to customers:

1. Labor: mural painting
2. Labor: faux painting
3. Labor: interior painting
4. Labor: exterior painting

To add a service item to the Item List:

Step 1: Click the **Items & Services** icon in the *Company* section of the Home page.

Step 2: When the *Item List* window appears, click the **Item** button.

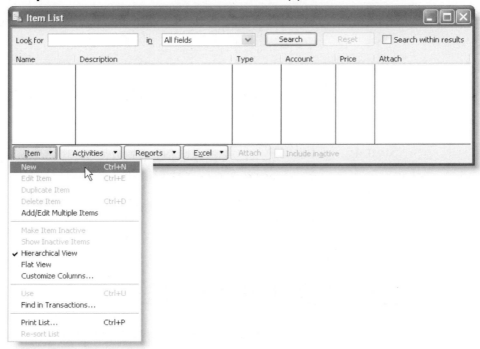

Step 3: Click **New** to add new items to the Items List.

Step 4: When the following *New Item* window appears:

- Enter Type: **Service**

- Enter Item Name: **Labor**

- Enter Description: **Painting Labor**

- Select Account: **47900 - Sales**

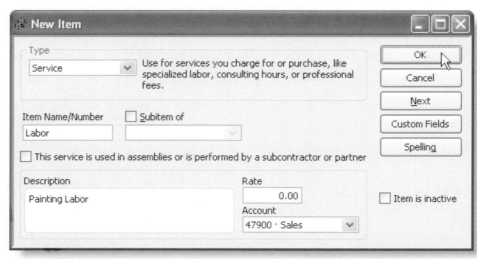

Step 5: Click **OK** to close the *New Item* window.

Step 6: **Export** the Item List to Excel and **print**.

Step 7: **Close** the *Item List* window.

SAVE CHAPTER 8

 Save a backup of your Chapter 8 file using the file name: **[your name] Chapter 8 Backup.QBB**. See *Appendix B: Back Up & Restore QuickBooks Files* for instructions.

 ### WORKFLOW

If you are using the workflow approach, leave your .QBW file open and proceed directly to Exercise 8.1.

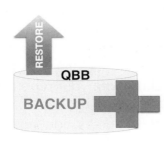 ### RESTART & RESTORE

If you are using the Restart & Restore approach and are ending your computer session now, close your .QBW file and exit QuickBooks.

When you restart, you will restore your backup file to complete Exercise 8.1.

PODCASTS

Watch the Chapter 8 **Podcast** at www.QuickBooksBlog.info to view how to set up a new company in QuickBooks.

MULTIPLE-CHOICE PRACTICE TEST

A **Multiple-Choice Practice Test** for Chapter 8 is on the *Computer Accounting for QuickBooks Pro* Online Learning Center at www.mhhe.com/kay2010. Try the Practice Test and see how many questions you answer correctly.

EXTRAS!

Section 3: Quick Guide contains quick, easy step-by-step directions for frequently used QuickBooks tasks, including correcting errors. You can find *Quick Guide* at the back of your text or online at www.mhhe.com/kay2010. *Check it out!*

Deliverables Checklist is a list of the reports and documents that you are to deliver to your instructor for grading. You can find the Deliverables Checklist at the end of the chapter or online at www.mhhe.com/kay2010. Staying organized saves time. Use the checklist to organize your reports, checking off the reports as completed. Then include the checklist with your reports for grading.

Appendix D: Electronic Deliverables shows you how to save your QuickBooks reports electronically. Also, watch the Electronic Deliverables Podcast at www.QuickBooksBlog.info. Check with your instructor to see if you should deliver your reports electronically.

Join the QuickBooks Student Community to ask questions and share tips @ www.QuickBooksBlog.info.

LEARNING ACTIVITIES

Important: Ask your instructor whether you should complete the following assignments by printing requested reports or creating electronic deliverables (see Appendix D: Electronic Deliverables).

EXERCISE 8.1: CHART OF ACCOUNTS, CUSTOMER LIST, VENDOR LIST, AND ITEM LIST

In this exercise, you will add new accounts and subaccounts to Paint Palette's Chart of Accounts and add new customers and vendors.

TASK 1: OPEN COMPANY FILE

WORKFLOW

If you are using the Workflow approach, you will use the same .QBW file.

If your QBW file is not already open, open it by selecting **File > Open Previous Company**. Select your **.QBW file.**

Change the company name to [**your name**] **Exercise 8.1 Paint Palette** by selecting **Company** menu > **Company Information.**

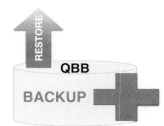

RESTART & RESTORE

If you are not using the same computer, you must use the Restart and Restore approach.

Restore your **Chapter 8 Backup.QBB** file using the directions in *Appendix B: Back Up & Restore QuickBooks Files*. After restoring the file, change the company name to [**your name**] **Exercise 8.1 Paint Palette** by selecting **Company** menu > **Company Information.**

TASK 2: ADD ACCOUNTS

Step 1: Add the following new accounts and subaccounts to the Chart of Accounts for Paint Palette. Click **Save & New** after entering each account.

If necessary, select **Other Account Type**, then select **Accounts Receivable**.

Account No.	11000
Account Type	Accounts Receivable
Account Name	Accounts Receivable
Account Description	Accounts Receivable
Tax Line	Unassigned

Account No.	13000
Account Type	Other Current Asset
Account Name	Paint Supplies
Account Description	Paint Supplies
Tax Line	Unassigned

Account No.	14400
Account Type	Fixed Asset
Account Name	Equipment
Account Description	Equipment
Tax Line	Unassigned

Account No.	14500
Account Type	Fixed Asset
Account Name	Equipment Cost
Account Description	Equipment Cost
Subaccount of	14400 Equipment
Tax Line	Unassigned

Account No.	14600
Account Type	Fixed Asset
Account Name	Accum Depr-Equipment
Account Description	Accum Depr-Equipment
Subaccount of	14400 Equipment
Tax Line	Unassigned

Account No.	21000
Account Type	Accounts Payable
Account Name	Accounts Payable
Account Description	Accounts Payable
Tax Line	Unassigned

Account No.	65300
Account Type	Expense
Account Name	Depr Expense-Computer
Account Description	Depr Expense-Computer
Tax Line	Unassigned

Account No.	65600
Account Type	Expense
Account Name	Depr Expense-Equipment
Account Description	Depr Expense-Equipment
Tax Line	Unassigned

Account No.	64800
Account Type	Expense
Account Name	Paint Supplies Expense
Account Description	Paint Supplies Expense
Tax Line	Sch C: Supplies (not from COGS)

Step 2: 📠 **Print** the Chart of Accounts (Click **Reports > Account Listing**).

TASK 3: ADD CUSTOMER

Step 1: Add Tom Whalen to Paint Palette's Customer List.

Customer	Whalen, Tom
Opening Balance	0.00
As of	01/01/2014
Address Info:	
Mr./Ms./…	Mr.
First Name	Tom
M.I.	M
Last Name	Whalen
Contact	Tom Whalen
Phone	415-555-1234
Alt. Phone	415-555-5678
Alt. Contact	Work phone
Address	100 Sunset Drive Bayshore, CA 94326

Additional Info:	
Type	Referral
Terms	Net 30

Payment Info:	
Account	1002
Preferred Payment	Check

Step 2: Click **OK** to close the *New Customer* window.

TASK 4: ADD JOB

Step 1: To add a new job, select: **Tom Whalen**.

Step 2: **Right-click** to display popup menu. Select **Add Job**.

Step 3: After entering the following job information, **close** the *New Job* window.

Job Info:	
Job Name	Foyer
Opening Balance	0.00
As of	01/01/2014
Job Status	Pending
Job Description	Foyer Marbled Faux Painting
Job Type	Faux Painting

Select
Add New.

Step 4: 🖨 **Export** the Customer List to Excel and **print**.

Step 5: **Close** the Customer Center.

TASK 5: ADD VENDORS

Step 1: Add the following vendors to the Vendor List for Paint Palette.

Vendor	Cornell Computers
Opening balance	0.00
As of	01/01/2014
Address Info:	
Company Name	Cornell Computers
Address	72 Business Parkway Bayshore, CA 94326

Contact	Becky Cornell
Phone	415-555-7507
Additional Info:	
Account	2002
Type	Supplies
Terms	Net 30
Credit Limit	3000.00
Tax ID	37-4356712

Step 2:   Click **Next** to add another vendor.

Vendor	Hartzheim Leasing
Opening balance	0.00
As of	01/01/2014
Address Info:	
Company Name	Hartzheim Leasing
Address	13 Appleton Drive Bayshore, CA 94326
Contact	Joseph Hartzheim
Phone	415-555-0412
Additional Info:	
Account	2003
Type	Leasing
Terms	Net 30
Tax ID	37-1726354

Step 3:   📇 **Export** the Vendor List to Excel and **print**.

TASK 6: ADD ITEMS

Step 1:   Add the following items to Paint Palette's Item List. Click **Next** after entering each item.

Item Type	Service
Item Name	Labor Mural
Subitem of	Labor
Description	Labor: Mural Painting
Rate	40.00
Account	47900 – Sales

Item Type	Service
Item Name	Labor Faux
Subitem of	Labor
Description	Labor: Faux Painting
Rate	40.00
Account	47900 – Sales

Item Type	Service
Item Name	Labor Interior
Subitem of	Labor
Description	Labor: Interior Painting
Rate	20.00
Account	47900 – Sales

Item Type	Service
Item Name	Labor Exterior
Subitem of	Labor
Description	Labor: Exterior Painting
Rate	30.00
Account	47900 - Sales

Step 2:   **Export** the Item List to Excel and **print**.

TASK 7: SAVE EXERCISE 8.1

Save a backup of your Exercise 8.1 file using the file name: **[your name] Exercise 8.1 Backup.QBB**. See *Appendix B: Back Up & Restore QuickBooks Files* for instructions.

WORKFLOW

If you are using the Workflow approach, you can leave your .QBW file open and use it for the following chapter which is a continuation of this exercise.

RESTART & RESTORE

If you are stopping your QuickBooks work session and changing computers, you will need to restore your .QBB file when you restart Chapter 9.

EXERCISE 8.2: NEW COMPANY SETUP

SCENARIO

Villa Floor & Carpet, a start-up business, provides custom hardwood floor cleaning and refinishing. In addition, the business provides specialized cleaning of fine oriental rugs.

First, set up a new QuickBooks company file for Villa Floor & Carpet using the EasyStep Interview. Then create the Customer List, Vendor List, and the Item List for the new company.

TASK 1: NEW COMPANY SETUP

Step 1: Create a new company in QuickBooks for Villa Floor & Carpet. Use the following information.

Company name	[your name] Exercise 8.2 Villa Floor & Carpet
Legal name	[your name] Exercise 8.2 Villa Floor & Carpet
Tax ID	130-13-3636
Address	1958 Rue Grand
City	Bayshore
State	CA
Zip	94326
Phone	415-555-1313
E-mail	[enter your own e-mail address]
Industry	General Service-based Business
Type of organization	Sole Proprietorship
First month of fiscal year	January
File name	[your name] Exercise 8.2
What do you sell?	Services only
Sales tax	No
Estimates	No
Sales receipts	Yes
Billing statements	Yes
Progress invoicing	No
Track bills you owe	Yes
Print checks	Yes
Accept credit cards	I don't currently accept credit cards and I don't plan to.
Track time	Yes
Employees	No
Multiple currencies	No
Start date	01/01/2014

Add a bank account	Yes
Bank account name	[your name] Checking
Bank account opened	On or after 01/01/2014
Use recommended income and expense accounts	Yes

Step 2: Click **Finish** to exit the EasyStep Interview.

Step 3: To verify the income tax form used, from the Company menu, select **Company Information**. Verify Income Tax Form Used: **Form 1040 (Sole Proprietor)**.

Step 4: Click **OK** to close the *Company Information* window.

TASK 2: ADD ACCOUNTS

Step 1: Display account numbers.

Step 2: Add the following new accounts and subaccounts to the Chart of Accounts for Villa Floor & Carpet. Click **Save & New** after entering each account.

Account No.	13000
Account Type	Other Current Asset
Account Name	Cleaning Supplies
Account Description	Cleaning Supplies
Tax Line	Unassigned

Account No.	14400
Account Type	Fixed Asset
Account Name	Cleaning Equipment
Account Description	Cleaning Equipment
Tax Line	Unassigned

Account No.	14500
Account Type	Fixed Asset
Account Name	Cleaning Equipment Cost
Account Description	Cleaning Equipment Cost
Subaccount of	14400 Cleaning Equipment
Tax Line	Unassigned

Account No.	14600
Account Type	Fixed Asset
Account Name	Accum Depr-Cleaning Equipment
Account Description	Accum Depr-Cleaning Equipment
Subaccount of	14400 Cleaning Equipment
Tax Line	Unassigned

Account No.	21000
Account Type	Accounts Payable
Account Name	Accounts Payable
Account Description	Accounts Payable
Tax Line	Unassigned

Account No.	64800
Account Type	Expense
Account Name	Supplies Expense
Account Description	Supplies Expense
Tax Line	Sch C: Supplies (not from COGS)

Step 3:   📰 **Print** the Chart of Accounts.

TASK 3: ADD CUSTOMER & JOB

Step 1:   Add Thomas Dent to Villa Floor & Carpet Customer List.

Customer	Dent, Thomas
Address Info:	
First Name	Thomas
Last Name	Dent
Contact	Thomas Dent
Phone	415-555-4242
Address	36 Penny Lane Bayshore, CA 94326

Additional Info:	
Type	Residential
Terms	Net 15

Payment Info:	
Account	1005
Preferred Payment	Check

Step 2:   Click **OK** to close the *New Customer* window.

Step 3:   To add a new job, select Thomas Dent in the Customer List, then **right-click** to display popup menu. Select **Add Job**.

Job Info:	
Job Name	Oriental Rugs
Job Status	Pending
Job Description	Oriental rug cleaning
Job Type	Residential

Step 4: 🖨 **Print** the Customer List.

- Click the **Print** button at the top of the Customer Center.

- Select **Customer & Job List**.

- Select **Portrait** orientation **> Print**.

Step 5: **Close** the Customer Center.

TASK 4: ADD VENDORS

Step 1: Add the following vendor to the Vendor List for Villa Floor & Carpet.

Vendor	Blumer Cleaning Supplies
Opening balance	0.00
As of	01/01/2014
Address Info:	
Company Name	Blumer Cleaning Supplies
Address	72 St. Charles Blvd Bayshore, CA 94326
Contact	Charlie Blumer
Phone	415-555-7272
Additional Info:	
Account	2004
Type	Supplies
Terms	Net 30
Tax ID	37-6543219

Step 2: 🖨 **Print** the Vendor List.

TASK 5: ADD ITEMS

Step 1: Add the following items to Villa Floor & Carpet. Click **Next** after entering each item.

Item Type	Service
Item Name	Rug Cleaning
Description	Oriental Rug Cleaning
Account	47900 – Sales

Item Type	Service
Item Name	3x5 Rug Cleaning
Subitem of	Rug Cleaning
Description	3x5 Oriental Rug Cleaning
Rate	50.00
Account	47900 – Sales

Item Type	Service
Item Name	5x7 Rug Cleaning
Subitem of	Rug Cleaning
Description	5x7 Oriental Rug Cleaning
Rate	100.00
Account	47900 – Sales

Item Type	Service
Item Name	8x10 Rug Cleaning
Subitem of	Rug Cleaning
Description	8x10 Oriental Rug Cleaning
Rate	150.00
Account	47900 - Sales

Step 2: 🖨 **Print** the Item List.

TASK 6: SAVE EXERCISE 8.2

Save a backup of your Exercise 8.2 file using the file name: **[your name] Exercise 8.2 Backup.QBB**. See *Appendix B: Back Up & Restore QuickBooks Files* for instructions.

WORKFLOW

If you are using the Workflow approach, you can leave your .QBW file open and use it to complete Exercise 9.6.

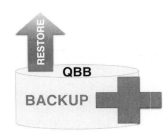

RESTART & RESTORE

If you are stopping your QuickBooks work session and changing computers, you will need to restore your .QBB file when you restart.

EXERCISE 8.3: WEB QUEST

The Small Business Administration (SBA) summarizes. government resources to assist the small business owner. When starting a new business, an entrepreneur is faced with numerous decisions. As a result, planning becomes crucial for business success. The SBA website provides information about how to write a successful business plan.

The websites used in the Web Quests are subject to change due to website updates.

Step 1: Go to www.sba.gov website.

Step 2: At the top of the Small Business Administration website, click **Small Business Planner**.

Step 3: Click **Plan Your Business**. Click and then read **Write a Business Plan > Writing The Business Plan**.

- 🖨 **Print** the page.

- ✏ Place a ✓ by the business plan Financial Data Items that QuickBooks could help you prepare.

DELIVERABLES CHECKLIST CHAPTER 8
NAME:

INSTRUCTIONS:
1. CHECK OFF THE DELIVERABLES YOU HAVE COMPLETED.
2. TURN IN THIS PAGE WITH YOUR DELIVERABLES.

CHAPTER 8
☐ Chart of Accounts (Account Listing)
☐ Customer List
☐ Vendor List
☐ Item List

EXERCISE 8.1
☐ Task 2: Chart of Accounts
☐ Task 4: Customer List
☐ Task 5: Vendor List
☐ Task 6: Item List

EXERCISE 8.2
☐ Task 2: Chart of Accounts
☐ Task 3: Customer List
☐ Task 4: Vendor List
☐ Task 5: Item List

EXERCISE 8.3
☐ Business Plan Deliverables

REFLECTION: A WISH AND A STAR ★

Reflection improves learning and retention. Reflect on what you have learned after completing Chapter 8 that you did not know before you started the chapter.

A Star:

What did you like best that you learned about QuickBooks in Chapter 8?

A Wish:

If you could pick one thing, what do you wish you knew more about when using QuickBooks?

CHAPTER 9
ACCOUNTING FOR A SERVICE COMPANY

SCENARIO

Preferring to use your savings rather than take out a bank loan, you invest $6,000 of your savings to launch Paint Palette.

You prepare the following list of items your business will need.

Computer & printer $1,500

Paint equipment (ladder, drop cloths, etc.) $500

Paint supplies (paint brushes rollers, etc.) $300

Van lease $200/month

Chapter 9
Learning Objectives

In Chapter 9, you will learn about the following QuickBooks features:

INTRODUCTION

In this chapter, you will enter business transactions for Paint Palette's first year of operations. These include transactions with the owner, customers, and vendors.

To begin Chapter 9, first start QuickBooks by clicking on the **QuickBooks desktop icon** or click **Start > Programs > QuickBooks > QuickBooks Pro 2010**.

WORKFLOW

Use the Workflow approach if you are using the same computer and the same .QBW file from the prior chapter.

Step 1: If your .QBW file is not already open, open it by selecting **File > Open Previous Company**. Select your previous **Paint Palette .QBW file.**

Step 2: Change the company name to **[your name] Chapter 9** by selecting **Company** menu **> Company Information.**

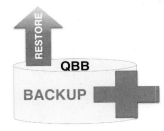

RESTART & RESTORE

Use the Restart & Restore approach if you are restarting your work session.

Step 1: Restore the **Backup.QBB** file using the directions in *Appendix B: Back Up & Restore QuickBooks Files*.

You can restore your .QBB file for Exercise 8.1 from the previous chapter or the Chapter 9 Backup.QBB data file that comes with the *Computer Accounting with QuickBooks* text (available on CD or download from the Online Learning Center).

If the *QuickBooks Login* window appears with the User Name **Admin**:

- Leave the *User Name* field as **Admin**.
- Leave the *Password* field **blank**.
- Click **OK**.

Step 2: After restoring the file, change the company name to **[your name] Chapter 9** by selecting **Company** menu > **Company Information.**

RECORD OWNER'S INVESTMENT

To launch your new business, you invest $6,000 in Paint Palette. In order to keep business records and your personal records separate, you open a business Checking account at the local bank for Paint Palette. You then deposit your personal check for $6,000 in the business Checking account.

In Chapters 3 and 4 you recorded deposits using the Record Deposits icon in the *Banking* section of the Home page. You can also record deposits directly in the Check Register. QuickBooks then transfers the information to the *Make Deposits* window.

To record the deposit to Paint Palette's Checking account using the *Make Deposits* window, complete the following steps:

Step 1: Click the **Record Deposits** icon in the *Banking* section of the Home page.

Step 2:   Enter the following information in the *Make Deposits* window:

- Date: **01/01/2014**.

- On the *Received From* drop-down list, select **<Add New>**. Select **Other**, then click **OK**. Enter Name: **[Your Name]**. Click **OK**.

- Account: **30000: Opening Balance Equity**. Press the **Tab** key.

- Memo: **Invested $6,000 in business**.

- Check No.: **1001**.

- Payment Method: **Check**.

- Amount: **6000.00**.

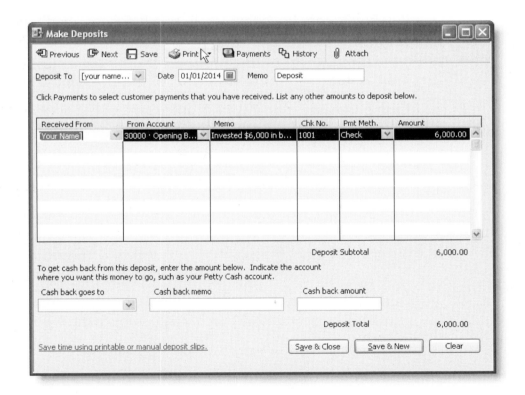

Step 3: 🖨 To **print** the deposit slip:

- Select **Print** arrow > **Deposit Summary**.

> Deposit Slip...
> Deposit Summary...
> Order Deposit Slips...

- Select **Portrait** orientation > **Print**.

Step 4: Click **Save & Close** to close the *Make Deposits* window.

RECORD PURCHASE TRANSACTIONS

Purchases can be either cash purchases or credit purchases on account.

Transaction	Description	Record Using...
Cash purchase	Pay cash at the time of purchase	*Write Checks* window
Credit purchase	Pay for purchase at a later time	1. *Enter Bills* window 2. *Pay Bills* window 3. Print checks

Paint Palette purchased a computer, painting equipment, and paint supplies. To record these purchases, complete the following steps.

RECORD CASH PURCHASES
USING THE WRITE CHECKS WINDOW

Paint Palette first purchased a computer and printer for $1,500 cash. Because Paint Palette paid cash for the purchase, you can use the *Write Checks* window to record the purchase.

To record the computer and printer purchase using the *Write Checks* window:

Step 1: Click the **Write Checks** icon in the *Banking* section of the Home page.

Step 2: Enter the following information in the *Write Checks* window:

- Date: **01/01/2014**.
- Pay to the Order of: **Cornell Computers**.
- Amount: **1500.00**.

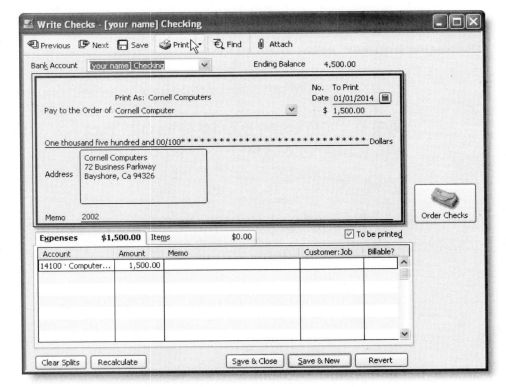

- Check: **To be printed**.

- Select Account: **14200 Computer Cost**.

Step 3:  **Print** the check as follows:

- Click the **Print** button.

- When the *Print Check* window appears, enter Check No. **501**, then click **OK**.

> If a *Future Transactions* window appears, click Yes to save your transaction.

- Select **Print company name and address**.

- Select Check Style: **Standard**

- Click **Print**.

- When asked if the check(s) printed OK, select **OK**.

Step 4: Click **Save & Close** to record Check No. 501 and close the *Write Checks* window.

RECORD CREDIT PURCHASES USING THE ENTER BILLS WINDOW

When items are purchased on credit, a two-step process is used to record the purchase in QuickBooks.

	Action	Record Using...	Result
1	**Enter bill when received**	*Enter Bills* window	QuickBooks records an expense (or asset) and records an obligation to pay the bill later (Accounts Payable).
2	**Pay bill when due**	1. *Pay Bills* window 2. Print Checks	QuickBooks reduces cash and reduces Accounts Payable.

Next, you will enter bills for items Paint Palette purchased on credit. The first bill is for paint and supplies that Paint Palette purchased for the Beneficio job.

Step 1: Click the **Enter Bills** icon in the *Vendors* section of the Home page.

Step 2: Enter the following information in the *Enter Bills* window:

- Select **Bill**.
- Enter Date: **01/03/2014**.
- Select Vendor: **Brewer Paint Supplies**.
- Enter Amount Due: **300.00**.
- Select Terms: **Net 30**.

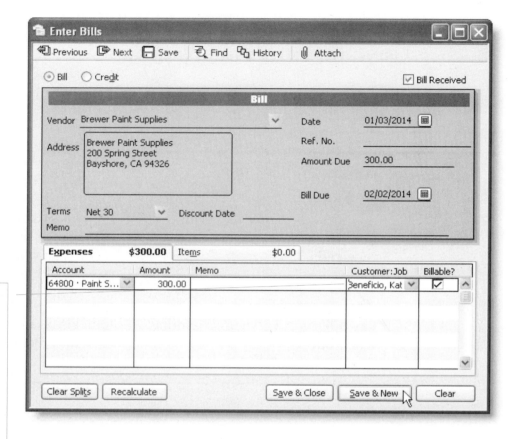

Select customer and job to charge. Later, you can transfer these costs to the customer's invoice.

- Click the **Expenses** tab.

- Select Account: **64800 Paint Supplies Expense**.

- Select Customer & Job: **Beneficio, Katrina: Dining Room**.

- Verify that **Billable** is ✓ checked.

Step 3: Click **Save & New** to enter another bill.

Step 4: Paint Palette made a credit purchase of painting equipment including ladders and drop cloths. The painting equipment is recorded as an asset because it will benefit more than one accounting period. The painting equipment will be depreciated over the useful life of the equipment.

Enter the following bill for paint equipment purchased on account.

Date	01/04/2014
Vendor	Brewer Paint Supplies
Amount Due	500.00
Terms	Net 30
Account	14500 Equipment Cost
Memo	Purchased paint equipment

Step 5: Click **Save & Close** to record the bill and close the *Enter Bills* window.

QuickBooks records these bills as accounts payable, indicating that Paint Palette has an obligation to pay these amounts to vendors. QuickBooks increases liabilities (accounts payable) on the company's Balance Sheet.

 Total fixed assets equal $2,000 (consisting of the Computer account of $1,500 and the Equipment account of $500).

RECORD A MEMORIZED TRANSACTION

Often a transaction is recurring, such as monthly rent or utility payments. QuickBooks' memorized transaction feature permits you to memorize or save recurring transactions.

Paint Palette leases a van for a monthly lease payment of $200. You will use a memorized transaction to reuse each month to record the lease payment.

To create a memorized transaction:

Step 1: First, enter the transaction in QuickBooks. You will enter the bill for the van lease payment for Paint Palette.

- Click the **Enter Bills** icon in the *Vendors* section of the Home page.

- Enter the following information about the van lease bill.

Date	01/04/2014
Vendor	Hartzheim Leasing
Amount Due	200.00
Terms	Net 30
Account	67100 Rent Expense
Memo	Van lease

Step 2: With the *Enter Bills* window still open, click **Edit** on the Menu bar.

Step 3: Click **Memorize Bill** on the *Edit* menu.

Step 4: When the following *Memorize Transaction* window appears:

- Select **Remind Me**.

- Select How Often: **Monthly**.

- Enter Next Date: **02/01/2014**.

- Click **OK** to record the memorized transaction.

Step 5: Click **Save & Close** to close the *Enter Bills* window and record the van lease.

To use the memorized transaction at a later time:

Step 1: Select **Lists** menu **> Memorized Transaction List**.

Step 2: When the following *Memorized Transaction List* window appears, **double-click** the memorized transaction you want to use.

Step 3: QuickBooks displays the *Enter Bills* window with the memorized transaction data already entered. You can make any necessary changes on the form, such as changing the date. To record the bill in QuickBooks, you would click Save & Close.

At this time, **close the *Enter Bills* window without saving**. Then **close** the *Memorized Transaction List* window. Later, you will use the memorized transaction in **Exercise 9.1** at the end of the chapter.

PAY BILLS

To pay bills already entered:

Step 1: Click the **Pay Bills** icon in the *Vendors* section of the Home page.

Step 2: When the following *Pay Bills* window appears:

  ▪ Select Show Bills: **Due on or before 02/04/2014**, then press the **Tab** key.

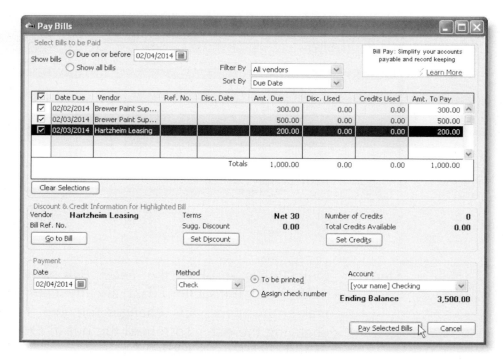

  ▪ Select the three bills listed to pay.

  ▪ Select Payment Account: **[your name] Checking**.

  ▪ Select Payment Method: **Check**.

  ▪ Select **To be printed**.

  ▪ Enter Payment Date: **02/04/2014**.

Step 3: Click **Pay Selected Bills** to record the bills selected for payment and close the *Pay Bills* window.

PRINT CHECKS

You can buy preprinted check forms to use with QuickBooks software.

After using the *Pay Bills* window to select bills for payment, the next step is to print checks.

 To print checks for the bills selected for payment:

Step 1:   When the following *Payment Summary* window appears, select: **Print Checks**.

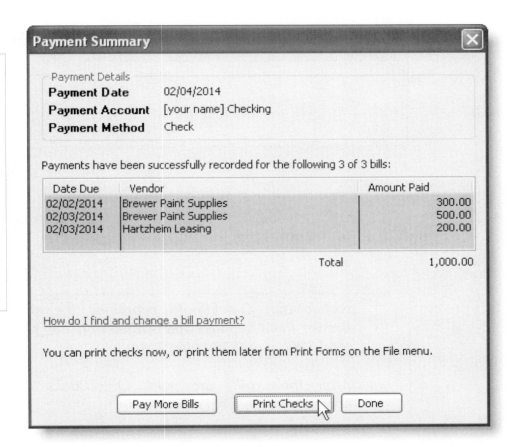

You can also print checks by selecting **File** menu > **Print Forms** > **Checks** or clicking the **Print Checks** icon in the *Banking* section of the Home page.

Step 2: When the *Select Checks to Print* window appears:

- Select Bank Account: **[your name] Checking**.
- First Check No.: **502**.
- Click the **Select All** button.
- Click **OK**.

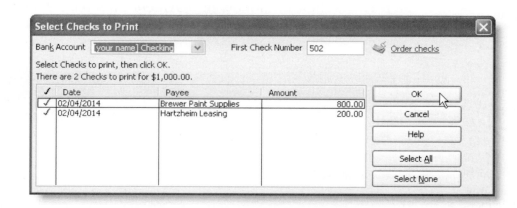

- Select print settings and standard checks, then click **Print**.

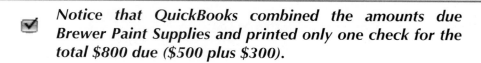 *Notice that QuickBooks combined the amounts due Brewer Paint Supplies and printed only one check for the total $800 due ($500 plus $300).*

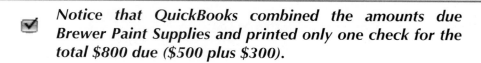 *After these bills are paid, QuickBooks reduces the accounts payable balance to zero.*

ADDITIONAL PURCHASE TRANSACTIONS

See **Exercise 9.1** for additional purchase transactions for Paint Palette.

RECORD SALES TRANSACTIONS

When using QuickBooks, sales transactions are recorded using three steps.

	Action	Record Using…	Result
1	**Prepare invoice to record charges for services provided customer**	*Invoice* window	The invoice is used to bill the customer for services. QuickBooks records the services provided on credit as an account receivable (an amount to be received in the future).
2	**Receive customer payment**	*Receive Payments* window	QuickBooks reduces accounts receivable and increases undeposited funds.
3	**Record bank deposit**	*Make Deposits* window	QuickBooks transfers the amount from undeposited funds to the bank account.

To create an invoice to record painting services provided by Paint Palette to Katrina Beneficio during January:

Step 1: Click the **Create Invoices** icon in the *Customers* section of the Home page.

Step 2: Select Customer & Job: **Beneficio, Katrina: Dining Room**.

Step 3: When the *Billable Time/Costs* window appears to remind you the job has outstanding billable time, click **Select the outstanding billable time and costs to add to this invoice?** and click **OK**.

Step 4: Select billable costs to apply to the Beneficio invoice as follows:

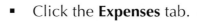

Be sure to enter %, otherwise $40 will be the markup.

- Click the **Expenses** tab.

- Enter Markup Amount: **40.0%**. Select Markup Account: **47900 – Sales**.

- Check ✓ to select: **Brewer Paint Supplies**.

- Click **OK** to bill the Paint Supplies cost.

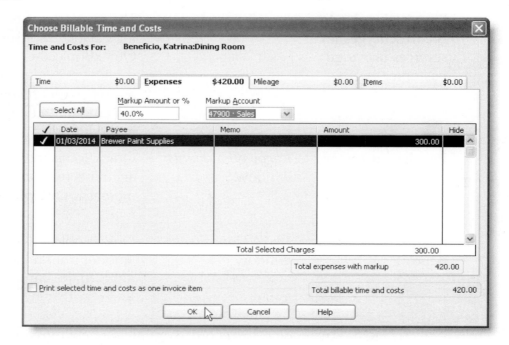

Step 5: Select Template: **Intuit Service Invoice**.

Step 6: Enter Date: **01/31/2014**.

Step 7: The Beneficio invoice will list Total Reimbursable Expenses of $420.00. Enter the service provided in the *Create Invoices* window as follows:

- Select Item: **Labor Mural**.

- Enter Quantity: **82** (hours).

Step 8: Click the **Print** button and print the invoice.

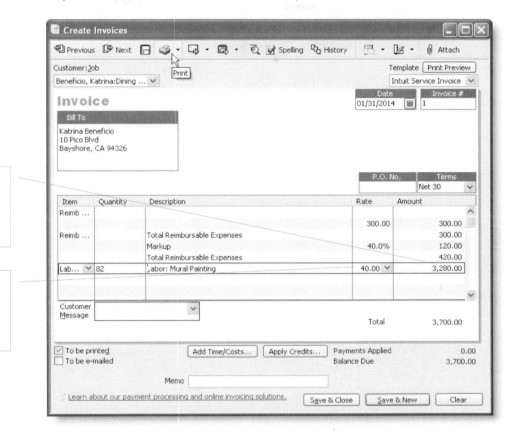

The Amount column will automatically display 3,280.00.

The Rate column will automatically display 40.00.

Step 9: To e-mail an invoice:

For purposes of this exercise, e-mail the invoice to yourself.

- Click the **Send** arrow at the top of the *Invoices* window. Select **E-mail Invoice**.

- If Outlook is enabled on your computer, complete the onscreen instructions and e-mail the invoice to yourself. Otherwise, select Send by: **E-mail** and complete the process for e-mailing invoices using QuickBooks. If you are not able to establish an Internet connection, select **Send Later**, close the open windows and proceed to the next section.

Step 10: Click **Save & Close** to record the invoice and close the *Create Invoices* window.

If a message appears regarding payment methods, select No.

To record Katrina Beneficio's payment for the $3,700.00 invoice:

Step 1: From the *Customers* section of the Home page, click the **Receive Payments** icon.

Step 2: Select Received From: **Beneficio, Katrina: Dining Room**.

Step 3: Select Date: **02/04/2014**.

Step 4: Enter Amount: **3700.00**. A check mark will appear by the outstanding invoice listed.

Step 5: Select Payment Method: **Check**.

Step 6: Enter Check No. **555**.

QuickBooks automatically applies the payment to the outstanding invoice.

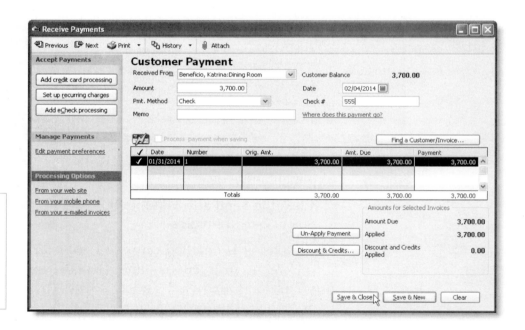

Step 7: Click **Save & Close** to record the payment and close the *Receive Payments* window.

When a customer makes a payment, the customer's account receivable is reduced by the amount of the payment. In this case, Beneficio's account receivable is reduced by $3,700.

To record the deposit of the customer's payment in the bank:

Step 1: From the *Banking* section of the Home page, click the **Record Deposits** icon. The following *Payments to Deposit* window will appear.

The *Payments to Deposit* window lists undeposited funds that have been received, but not yet deposited in the bank.

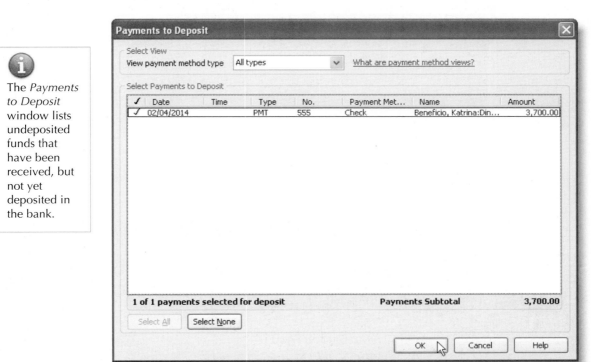

Step 2: Select the payment from Katrina Beneficio for deposit.

Step 3: Click **OK** and the following *Make Deposits* window appears.

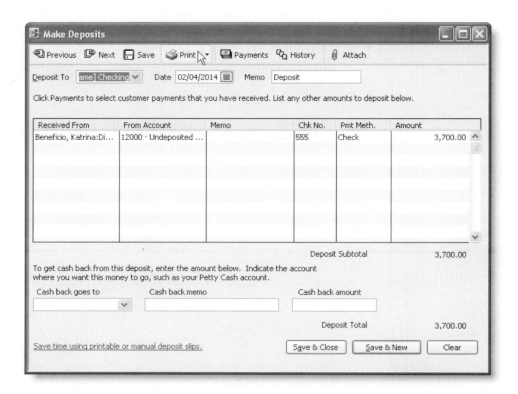

Step 4: Select Deposit To: **[your name] Checking**.

Step 5: Select Date: **02/04/2014**.

Step 6: Click **Print**.

Step 7: When the *Print Deposits* window appears, select **Deposit summary only > OK**.

Step 8: Select printer settings, then click **Print**.

Step 9: Click **Save & Close** to record the deposit and close the *Make Deposits* window.

ADDITIONAL SALES TRANSACTIONS

See **Exercise 9.2** for additional sales transactions for Paint Palette.

MAKE ADJUSTING ENTRIES

> ⚠
> Before making adjusting entries, prepare a trial balance to see if the accounting system is in balance (debits equal credits).

At the end of Paint Palette's accounting period, December 31, 2014, it is necessary to record adjustments to bring the company's accounts up to date as of year-end.

The following adjustments are necessary for Paint Palette at December 31, 2014:

1. Record depreciation expense for the computer for the year.

2. Record depreciation expense for the painting equipment for the year. (Complete in **Exercise 9.3**.)

3. Record the amounts of paint supplies that are still on hand at year-end. Unused paint supplies should be recorded as assets because they have future benefit. (Complete in **Exercise 9.3**.)

Use the *Make General Journal Entries* window to record the adjusting entry for depreciation expense on the computer for Paint Palette at December 31, 2014. The $1,500 computer cost will be depreciated over a useful life of three years.

Step 1: Select **Company** menu > **Make General Journal Entries**.

If a message about numbering journal entries appears, click **OK**.

Step 2:   Record the entry for depreciation on the computer equipment in the General Journal.

- Select Date: **12/31/2014**.

- Entry No.: **ADJ 1**.

- Enter Account: **65300**. Press the **Tab** key to advance the cursor to the *Debit* column.

- Next, use QuickMath calculator to calculate the amount of depreciation expense.

  - With the cursor in the *Debit* column, press the **=** key to display the QuickMath calculator.

  - Enter **1500.00**.

  - Press **/**.

  - Enter **3** to divide by the 3-year useful life.

  - Press the **Enter** key. $500 should now appear in the *Debit* column.

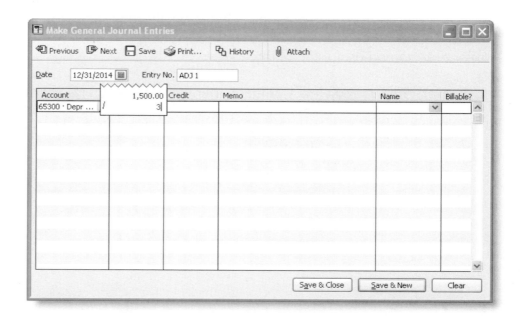

- Enter Account: **14300**. Credit: **500.00**. Your journal entry should appear as shown below.

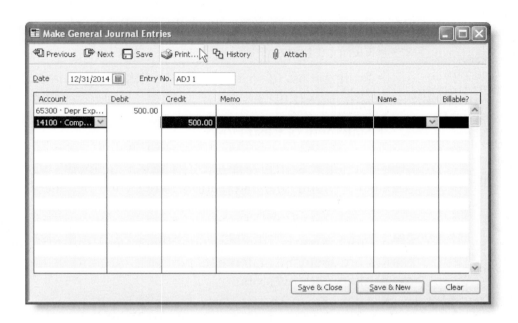

To print the entire Journal instead of just one entry from Report Center, select: **Accountant & Taxes > Journal**.

Step 3:   🖨 To **print** the adjusting journal entry, click the **Print** button and follow the onscreen instructions.

Step 4:   Click **Save & Close** to close the *Make General Journal Entries* window.

PRINT REPORTS

To print the General Ledger, from Report Center, select: **Accountant & Taxes > General Ledger**.

The next step in the accounting cycle is to print financial reports. Usually, a company prints the following financial reports for the year:

- General Ledger
- Profit & Loss (also known as the P & L or Income Statement)
- Balance Sheet
- Statement of Cash Flows

The General Ledger report lists each account with its opening balance, ending balance, and changes to the account during the period.

To print financial statements, from Report Center, select: **Company & Financial**.

The Profit & Loss, the Balance Sheet, and the Statement of Cash Flows are financial statements typically given to external users, such as bankers and investors.

You will print financial statements for Paint Palette for the year 2014 in **Exercise 9.4**.

CLOSE THE ACCOUNTING PERIOD

When using a manual accounting system, closing entries are made in the General Journal to close the temporary accounts (revenues, expenses, and withdrawals or dividends). Closing entries are used in order to start the new year with a zero balance in the temporary accounts.

QuickBooks automatically closes temporary accounts to start each new year with $-0- balances in all temporary accounts (revenues, expenses, and dividends).

To prevent changes to prior periods, QuickBooks permits you to restrict access to the accounting records for past periods that have been closed. See **Exercise 9.5** for instructions on closing the accounting period in QuickBooks.

SAVE CHAPTER 9

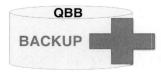

Save a backup of your Chapter 9 file using the file name: **[your name] Chapter 9 Backup.QBB**. See *Appendix B: Back Up & Restore QuickBooks Files* for instructions.

WORKFLOW

If you are using the workflow approach, leave your .QBW file open and proceed directly to Exercise 9.1.

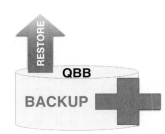

RESTART & RESTORE

If you are using the Restart & Restore approach and are ending your computer session now, close your .QBW file and exit QuickBooks. When you restart, you will restore your backup file to complete Exercise 9.1.

PODCASTS

Watch the Chapter 9 **Podcast** at www.QuickBooksBlog.info.

MULTIPLE-CHOICE PRACTICE TEST

A **Multiple-Choice Practice Test** for Chapter 9 is on the *Computer Accounting for QuickBooks Pro* Online Learning Center at www.mhhe.com/kay2010. Try the Practice Test and see how many questions you answer correctly.

EXTRAS!

Section 3: Quick Guide contains quick, easy step-by-step directions for frequently used QuickBooks tasks, including correcting errors. You can find *Quick Guide* at the back of your text or online at www.mhhe.com/kay2010. *Check it out!*

Deliverables Checklist is a list of the reports and documents that you are to deliver to your instructor for grading. You can find the Deliverables Checklist at the end of the chapter or online at www.mhhe.com/kay2010. Staying organized saves time. Use the checklist to organize your reports, checking off the reports as completed. Then include the checklist with your reports for grading.

Appendix D: Electronic Deliverables shows you how to save your QuickBooks reports electronically. Also, watch the Electronic Deliverables Podcast at www.QuickBooksBlog.info. Check with your instructor to see if you should deliver your reports electronically.

Join the QuickBooks Student Community to ask questions and share tips @ www.QuickBooksBlog.info.

LEARNING ACTIVITIES

Important: Ask your instructor whether you should complete the following assignments by printing requested reports or creating electronic deliverables (see Appendix D: Electronic Deliverables).

EXERCISE 9.1: PURCHASE TRANSACTIONS

In this exercise, you will enter purchase transactions for Paint Palette.

TASK 1: OPEN COMPANY FILE

WORKFLOW

If you are using the Workflow approach, you will use the same .QBW file.

If your QBW file is not already open, open it by selecting **File > Open Previous Company**. Select your **.QBW file.**

Change the company name to **[your name] Exercise 9.1** by selecting **Company** menu > **Company Information.**

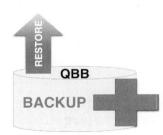

RESTART & RESTORE

If you are not using the same computer, you must use the Restart and Restore approach.

Restore your **Chapter 9 Backup.QBB** file using the directions in *Appendix B: Back Up & Restore QuickBooks Files*.

After restoring the file, change the company name to **[your name] Exercise 9.1** by selecting **Company** menu > **Company Information.**

TASK 2: RECORD PURCHASE TRANSACTIONS

Record the following purchase transactions for Paint Palette during the year 2014. Print checks as appropriate.

<table>
<tr><td rowspan="3">For memorized transactions select **Lists** menu > **Memorized Transaction List**.

To view the van lease bill, select **Show All Bills** in the *Pay Bills* window.</td></tr>
</table>

Date	Purchase Transaction
02/01/2014	Use the memorized transaction to record the $200 bill for the February van lease to be paid later.
02/28/2014	Paid van lease for February.
03/01/2014	Received $200 bill for van lease for March.
03/30/2014	Paid van lease for March. (Due: 03/31/2014)
04/01/2014	Received $200 bill for van lease for April.
04/04/2014	Purchased $50 of paint supplies on account from Brewer Paint Supplies. Record as Paint Supplies Expense.
04/30/2014	Paid van lease for April. (Due: 05/01/2014) Paid for paint supplies purchased on April 4.
05/01/2014	Received $200 bill for van lease for May.
05/30/2014	Paid van lease for May. (Due: 05/31/2014)
06/01/2014	Received $200 bill for van lease for June.
06/30/2014	Paid van lease for June. (Due: 07/01/2014)
07/01/2014	Purchased $100 of paint supplies on account from Brewer Paint Supplies.
07/01/2014	Received $200 bill for van lease for July.

Record as **Paint Supplies Expense**.

07/30/2014	Paid van lease for July. (Due: 07/31/2014)
	Paid for paint supplies purchased on July 1.
08/01/2014	Received $200 bill for van lease for August.
08/30/2014	Paid van lease for August. (Due: 08/31/2014)
09/01/2014	Received $200 bill for van lease for September.
09/02/2014	Purchased $75 of paint supplies on account from Brewer Paint Supplies.
09/30/2014	Paid September van lease. (Due: 10/01/2014).
	Paid for paint supplies purchased on 09/02/2014.
10/01/2014	Received $200 bill for van lease for October.
10/30/2014	Paid van lease for October. (Due: 10/31/2014)
11/01/2014	Received $200 bill for van lease for November.
11/30/2014	Paid van lease for November. (Due: 12/01/2014)
12/01/2014	Received $200 bill for van lease for December.
12/20/2014	Purchased $50 of paint supplies on account from Brewer Paint Supplies.
12/30/2014	Paid van lease for December. (Due: 12/31/2014)

Record **as Paint Supplies Expense**. These items are not chargeable to a specific job.

TASK 3: SAVE EXERCISE 9.1

Save a backup of your Exercise 9.1 file using the file name: **[your name] Exercise 9.1 Backup.QBB**. See *Appendix B: Back Up & Restore QuickBooks Files* for instructions.

WORKFLOW

Use the Workflow approach and leave your .QBW file open to use for the following exercise.

EXERCISE 9.2: SALES TRANSACTIONS

In this exercise, you will record sales transactions for Paint Palette.

TASK 1: CHANGE COMPANY NAME

WORKFLOW

Since you are using the Workflow approach, you will use the same .QBW file.

If your QBW file is not already open, open it by selecting **File > Open Previous Company**. Select your **.QBW file.**

Change the company name to **[your name] Exercise 9.2** by selecting **Company** menu > **Company Information.**

TASK 2:
SALES TRANSACTIONS AND DEPOSIT SUMMARIES

🖶 **Print** invoices and deposit summaries for the following sales transactions for Paint Palette during the year 2014.

When necessary, add a new job. For more information about adding jobs, see Chapter 4.

Date	02/28/2014
Customer	Katrina Beneficio
Job	Dining Room
Item	Labor: Mural
Hours	86
Payment Received & Deposited	03/15/2014
Check No.	675

Date	03/31/2014
Customer	Katrina Beneficio
Job	Dining Room
Item	Labor: Mural
Hours	84
Payment Received & Deposited	04/15/2014
Check No.	690

Date	04/30/2014
Customer	Tom Whalen
Job	Foyer
Item	Labor: Faux
Hours	80
Payment Received & Deposited	05/15/2014
Check No.	432

Date	05/31/2014
Customer	Tom Whalen
Job	Foyer
Item	Labor: Faux
Hours	75
Payment Received & Deposited	06/15/2014
Check No.	455

Date	06/30/2014
Customer	Katrina Beneficio
Job	Vaulted Kitchen
Item	Labor: Mural
Hours	100
Payment Received & Deposited	07/15/2014
Check No.	733

Date	07/31/2014
Customer	Katrina Beneficio
Job	Vaulted Kitchen
Item	Labor: Mural
Hours	90
Payment Received & Deposited	08/15/2014
Check No.	750

Date	08/31/2014
Customer	Katrina Beneficio
Job	Vaulted Kitchen
Item	Labor: Mural
Hours	92
Payment Received & Deposited	09/15/2014
Check No.	782

Date	10/31/2014
Customer	Tom Whalen
Job	Screen Porch
Item	Labor: Mural
Hours	85
Payment Received & Deposited	11/15/2014
Check No.	685

Date	11/30/2014
Customer	Tom Whalen
Job	Screen Porch
Item	Labor: Mural
Hours	87
Payment Received & Deposited	12/15/2014
Check No.	725

TASK 3: SAVE EXERCISE 9.2

Save a backup of your Exercise 9.2 file using the file name: **[your name] Exercise 9.2 Backup.QBB**. See *Appendix B: Back Up & Restore QuickBooks Files* for instructions.

WORKFLOW

Use the Workflow approach and leave your .QBW file open to use for the following exercise.

EXERCISE 9.3: YEAR-END ADJUSTMENTS

In this exercise, you will first print a Trial Balance and then record adjusting entries for Paint Palette.

TASK 1: CHANGE COMPANY NAME

WORKFLOW

Since you are using the Workflow approach, you will use the same .QBW file.

If your QBW file is not already open, open it by selecting **File > Open Previous Company**. Select your **.QBW file.**

Change the company name to **[your name] Exercise 9.3** by selecting **Company** menu > **Company Information.**

The purpose of the Trial Balance is to determine whether the accounting system is in balance (debits equal credits).

TASK 2: PRINT TRIAL BALANCE

📠 **Print** a Trial Balance for Paint Palette at December 31, 2014.

Step 1: From the Report Center select **Accountant & Taxes > Trial Balance**.

Step 2: Select Dates From: **01/01/2014** To: **12/31/2014**.

Step 3: 📠 **Print** the Trial Balance for The Paint Palette.

Step 4: **Close** the *Trial Balance* window.

☑ *Total debits equal $41,110.*

TASK 3: RECORD ADJUSTING ENTRIES

At the end of the accounting period, it is necessary to make adjusting entries to bring a company's accounts up to date as of year-end. Three adjusting entries are needed for Paint Palette as of December 31, 2014:

This adjusting entry was recorded in Chapter 9.

1. Record depreciation expense for the computer for the year.

2. Record depreciation expense for the painting equipment for the year. The $500 paint equipment cost is depreciated using straight-line depreciation over five years with no salvage value.

For convenience entrepreneurs often record supplies as supplies expense when originally purchased. At year end, the supplies are often used or what is left on hand is an immaterial amount.

3. On December 31, 2014, you take an inventory of unused paint supplies on hand to learn that all the paint supplies had been used as of that date. Thus, no adjusting entry is needed since the supplies had been recorded as supplies expense when originally purchased.

Enter the adjusting entry at 12/31/2014 to record depreciation expense for the painting equipment for the year in the Journal.

TASK 4: PRINT ADJUSTING ENTRIES

🖶 **Print** the two adjusting entries recorded on December 31, 2014, for Paint Palette.

Step 1: From the Report Center, select **Accountant & Taxes > Journal**.

Step 2: Select Dates From: **12/31/2014** To: **12/31/2014**.

Step 3: 🖶 **Print** the Journal report using **Portrait** orientation.

Step 4: **Close** the *Journal Report* window.

TASK 5: PRINT ADJUSTED TRIAL BALANCE

An adjusted trial balance is simply a trial balance printed after adjusting entries are made.

Step 1: 🖶 **Print** an Adjusted Trial Balance at December 31, 2014. Change the report title to: **Adjusted Trial Balance** by selecting **Modify Report > Header/Footer**. Use **Portrait** orientation.

Step 2: ✎ On the Adjusted Trial Balance, **circle** the accounts affected by the adjusting entries.

TASK 6: SAVE EXERCISE 9.3

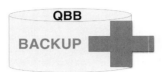

Save a backup of your Exercise 9.3 file using the file name: **[your name] Exercise 9.3 Backup.QBB**. See *Appendix B: Back Up & Restore QuickBooks Files* for instructions.

WORKFLOW

Use the Workflow approach and leave your .QBW file open to use for the following exercise.

EXERCISE 9.4: FINANCIAL REPORTS

In this exercise, you will print out financial statements for Paint Palette for the year 2014.

TASK 1: CHANGE COMPANY NAME

WORKFLOW

Since you are using the Workflow approach, you will use the same .QBW file.

To eliminate the 0.00 appearing for accounts with zero balances, from the *General Ledger* report window, select **Modify Report** button > **Advanced** > **In Use**.

If your QBW file is not already open, open it by selecting **File > Open Previous Company**. Select your **.QBW file.**

Change the company name to **[your name] Exercise 9.4** by selecting **Company** menu > **Company Information.**

TASK 2: GENERAL LEDGER

🖨 **Print** the General Ledger report for Paint Palette for the year 2014.

TASK 3: FINANCIAL STATEMENTS

Print the following financial statements for Paint Palette for the year 2014.

- Profit & Loss, Standard
- Balance Sheet, Standard
- Statement of Cash Flows

 Net income for the year 2014 is $31,285.

WORKFLOW

Use the Workflow approach and leave your .QBW file open to use for the following exercise.

EXERCISE 9.5: CLOSE THE ACCOUNTING PERIOD

Complete Exercise 9.5 only after you have completed Exercise 9.4.

To prevent changes to prior periods, QuickBooks permits you to restrict access to the accounting records for past periods that have been closed.

The QuickBooks Administrator can restrict user access to closed periods either at the time a new user is set up or later.

WORKFLOW

Since you are using the Workflow approach, you will use the same .QBW file.

If your QBW file is not already open, open it by selecting **File > Open Previous Company**. Select your **.QBW file.**

TASK 1: CLOSE THE ACCOUNTING PERIOD

To enter the closing date in QuickBooks:

The QuickBooks Administrator has access to all areas of QuickBooks and is established when a new company is set up. For more information about the QuickBooks Administrator, see Chapter 2.

Step 1: Select **Company** menu > **Set Up Users and Passwords**.

Step 2: Select **Set Up Users**.

Step 3: If necessary, enter information for the QuickBooks Administrator, then click **OK**.

Step 4: When the following *User List* window appears, click the **Closing Date** button.

Write your password on the inside of your text cover. You will not be able to access your company file without your password.

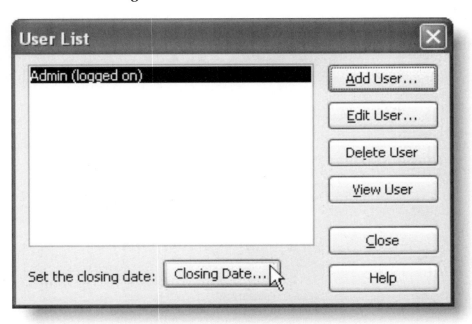

If the *User List* window is not open, open the *User List* window by clicking **Company > Set Up Users and Passwords > Set up Users**.

Step 5: Enter the closing date: **12/31/2014**.

Step 6: Click **OK** to close the *Set Closing Date and Password* window.

TASK 2: SAVE EXERCISE 9.5

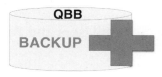

Save a backup of your Exercise 9.5 file using the file name: **[your name] Exercise 9.5 Backup.QBB**. See *Appendix B: Back Up & Restore QuickBooks Files* for instructions.

WORKFLOW

Chapter 12 is a continuation of Exercise 9.5.

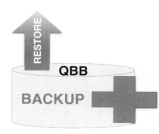

RESTART & RESTORE

If you use the restart and restore approach, you will restore your .QBB file when you restart in Chapter 12.

EXERCISE 9.6:
VILLA FLOOR & CARPET TRANSACTIONS

This exercise is a continuation of Exercise 8.2. In Exercise 8.2 you created a new company file for Villa Floor & Carpet. In this exercise, you will enter transactions for the new company.

TASK 1: OPEN COMPANY FILE

WORKFLOW

If you are using the Workflow approach, you will use the same .QBW file you used for Exercise 8.2.

If your QBW file is not already open, open it by selecting **File > Open Previous Company**. Select your **.QBW file.**

Change the company name to **[your name] Exercise 9.6** by selecting **Company** menu **> Company Information.**

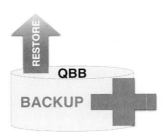

RESTART & RESTORE

If you are not using the same computer, you must use the Restart and Restore approach.

Restore your **Exercise 8.2 Backup.QBB** file using the directions in *Appendix B: Back Up & Restore QuickBooks Files.*

After restoring the file, change the company name to **[your name] Exercise 9.6** by selecting **Company** menu **> Company Information.**

TASK 2: RECORD PURCHASE TRANSACTIONS

During January, Villa Floor & Carpet entered into the transactions listed below. Record the transactions. 🖨 **Print** invoices, checks, and deposit summaries as appropriate.

Use *Make Deposits* window.

Use *Write Checks* window.

Use *Enter Bills* window to record Supplies Expense.

Date	Transaction
01/01/2014	Ashley Villa invested $5,000 cash in the business.
01/02/2014	Purchased cleaning equipment for $900 from Blumer Cleaning Supplies (Check No. 5001).
01/05/2014	Purchased $100 of cleaning supplies on account from Blumer Cleaning Supplies.
01/09/2014	Cleaned oriental rugs for Tom Dent on account: ▪ (2) 3 x 5 ▪ (3) 5 x 7 ▪ (4) 8 x 10
01/20/2014	Paid Blumer Cleaning Supply bill.
01/29/2014	Collected Tom Dent payment for cleaning services (Check No. 580). Print the deposit summary.

TASK 3: ADJUSTING ENTRIES

Step 1: Make an adjusting entry for Villa Floor & Carpet at January 31, 2014, to record one month of depreciation for the cleaning equipment. The cleaning equipment cost $900 and has a three-year (36-month) life and no salvage value.

Step 2: 🖨 **Print** the Journal report for the year to date.

TASK 4: FINANCIAL REPORTS

🖨 **Print** the following reports for Villa Floor & Carpet for January.

- Adjusted Trial Balance. Since this report is printed after adjusting entries are recorded, change the report title to Adjusted Trial Balance by selecting **Modify Report > Header/Footer**.

- General Ledger from 01/01/2014 to 01/31/2014. Eliminate unused accounts with zero balances by selecting **Modify Report > Display > Advanced > In Use**.

- Profit & Loss, Standard

- Balance Sheet, Standard

- Statement of Cash Flows

TASK 5: SAVE EXERCISE 9.6

Save a backup of your Exercise file using the file name: **[your name] Exercise 9.6 Backup.QBB**. See *Appendix B: Back Up & Restore QuickBooks Files* for instructions.

EXERCISE 9.7 WEB QUEST

The Internal Revenue Service (IRS) provides tax information useful for the small business. A sole proprietorship must file Form 1040 Schedule C for the annual tax return. If a sole proprietorship meets certain criteria, it may file a simplified Schedule C-EZ.

Step 1: Go to the www.irs.gov website.

Step 2: Search for Schedule C-EZ on the IRS website. 🖨 **Print** the Schedule C-EZ.

Step 3: ✏ **Circle** the information about whether you may use Schedule C-EZ instead of Schedule C.

DELIVERABLES CHECKLIST CHAPTER 9
NAME:

INSTRUCTIONS:
1. **CHECK OFF THE DELIVERABLES YOU HAVE COMPLETED.**
2. **TURN IN THIS PAGE WITH YOUR DELIVERABLES.**

CHAPTER 9
- ☐ Deposit Summary
- ☐ Check No. 501
- ☐ Check No. 502
- ☐ Check No. 503
- ☐ Invoice No. 1
- ☐ Deposit Summary
- ☐ Adjusting Entry

EXERCISE 9.1
- ☐ Task 2: Checks

EXERCISE 9.2
- ☐ Task 2: Invoices and Deposit Summaries

EXERCISE 9.3
- ☐ Task 2: Trial Balance
- ☐ Task 4: Adjusting Entries
- ☐ Task 5: Adjusted Trial Balance

EXERCISE 9.4
- ☐ Task 2: General Ledger
- ☐ Task 3: Financial Statements

EXERCISE 9.6
- ☐ Task 2: Villa Invoices, Checks & Deposit Summaries
- ☐ Task 3: Journal

□ Task 4: Adjusted Trial Balance
□ Task 4: General Ledger
□ Task 4: Profit & Loss
□ Task 4: Balance Sheet
□ Task 4: Statement of Cash Flows

EXERCISE 9. 7
□ Schedule C-EZ

REFLECTION: A WISH AND A STAR ☆

Reflection improves learning and retention. Reflect on what you have learned after completing Chapter 9 that you did not know before you started the chapter.

A Star:

What did you like best that you learned about QuickBooks in Chapter 9?

A Wish:

If you could pick one thing, what do you wish you knew more about when using QuickBooks?

QUICKBOOKS PROJECT 9.1
TUSCANY LANDSCAPES

SCENARIO

Your friend and entrepreneur, Tomaso Moltissimo, is starting a new landscape care business, Tuscany Landscapes, to help pay his college expenses. Consistent with consumer demand for more environmentally friendly lawn and landscape care, Tomaso decides to specialize in the maintenance and landscape care of native plantings.

You and Tomaso reach an agreement: you will help Tomaso with his accounting records and provide customer referrals, and he will help you with your painting business.

TASK 1: SET UP A NEW COMPANY

Step 1: Create a new company in QuickBooks for Tuscany Landscapes. Use the following information.

Company name	[your name] Project 9.1 Tuscany Landscapes
Legal name	[your name] Project 9.1 Tuscany Landscapes
Tax ID	314-14-7878
Address	2300 Olive Boulevard
City	Bayshore
State	CA
Zip	94326
E-mail	[enter your own e-mail address]
Industry	Lawn Care or Landscaping
Company organized?	Sole Proprietorship
First month of fiscal year?	January
File name	[your name] Project 9.1

What do you sell?	Services only
Sales tax	No
Estimates	No
Sales receipts	Yes
Billing statements	Yes
Invoices	Yes
Progress billing	No
Track bills you owe	Yes
Print checks?	Yes
Accept credit cards	I don't currently accept credit cards and I don't plan to.
Track time	Yes
Employees	No
Multiple currencies	No
Start date	01/01/2014
Add a bank account?	Yes
Bank account name	[your name] Checking
Bank account opened	On or after 01/01/2014
Use recommended income and expense accounts?	Yes

Step 2: Click **Finish** to exit the EasyStep Interview.

Step 3: Select Tax Form: Form 1040 (Sole Proprietor). (From the **Company** menu, select **Company Information**. Select Income Tax Form Used: **Form 1040 (Sole Proprietor)**.

To display account numbers, select **Edit** menu > **Preferences** > **Accounting** > **Company Preferences** > **Use account numbers.**

TASK 2: CUSTOMIZE THE CHART OF ACCOUNTS

Customize the Chart of Accounts for Tuscany Landscapes as follows:

Step 1: Display account numbers in the Chart of Accounts.

Step 2: Add the following accounts to the Chart of Accounts. Abbreviate account titles as necessary.

Account No.	14000
Account Type	Fixed Asset
Account Name	Mower
Account Description	Mower
Tax Line	Unassigned
Opening Balance	0 as of 01/01/2014

Account No.	14100
Account Type	Fixed Asset
Account Name	Mower Cost
Subaccount of	Mower
Account Description	Mower Cost
Tax Line	Unassigned
Opening Balance	0 as of 01/01/2014

Account No.	14200
Account Type	Fixed Asset
Account Name	Accumulated Depreciation-Mower
Account Description	Accumulated Depreciation-Mower
Subaccount of	Mower
Tax Line	Unassigned
Opening Balance	0 as of 01/01/2014

Account No.	18000
Account Type	Fixed Asset
Account Name	Trimmer Equipment
Account Description	Trimmer Equipment
Tax Line	Unassigned
Opening Balance	0 as of 01/01/2014

Account No.	18100
Account Type	Fixed Asset
Account Name	Trimmer Equipment Cost
Account Description	Trimmer Equipment Cost
Subaccount of	Trimmer Equipment
Tax Line	Unassigned
Opening Balance	0 as of 01/01/2014

Account No.	18200
Account Type	Fixed Asset
Account Name	Accumulated Depr Trimmer
Account Description	Accumulated Depr Trimmer
Subaccount of	Trimmer Equipment
Tax Line	Unassigned
Opening Balance	0 as of 01/01/2014

Account No.	64800
Account Type	Expense
Account Name	Supplies Expense
Account Description	Supplies Expense
Tax Line	Sch C: Supplies (not from COGS)

Step 3: 🖨 **Print** the Chart of Accounts report for Tuscany Landscapes.

TASK 3: CUSTOMER LIST

Step 1: Create a Customer List for Tuscany Landscapes using the following information.

Customer	Beneficio, Katrina
Opening Balance	0 as of 01/01/2014
Address Info:	
First Name	Katrina
Last Name	Beneficio
Contact	Katrina Beneficio
Phone	415-555-1818
Alt. Phone	415-555-3636
Address	10 Pico Blvd Bayshore, CA 94326

Select **Add New**.

Additional Info:	
Type	Residential
Terms	Net 30

Payment Info:	
Account No.	3001
Preferred Payment Method	Check

Step 2: Add a job for Katrina Beneficio.

Job Info:	
Job Status	Awarded
Job Description	Mow/Trim Lawn
Job Type	Lawn

Select **Add New**.

Step 3: Add another customer.

Customer	Whalen, Tom
Opening balance	0 as of 01/01/2014
Address Info:	
First Name	Tom
Last Name	Whalen
Contact	Tom Whalen
Phone	415-555-1234
Alt. Phone	415-555-5678
Alt. Contact	Work phone
Address	100 Sunset Drive Bayshore, CA 94326

Additional Info:	
Type	Residential
Terms	Net 30

Payment Info:	
Account	3002
Preferred Payment Method	Check

Step 4: Add a job for Tom Whalen.

Job Info:	
Job Status	Awarded
Job Description	Mow/Trim Lawn
Job Type	Lawn

Step 5:   Add a new customer.

Customer	Rock Castle Construction
Opening balance	0 as of 01/01/2014
Address Info:	
Company Name	Rock Castle Construction
First Name	Rock
Last Name	Castle
Contact	Rock Castle
Phone	415-555-7878
Alt. Phone	415-555-5679
Address	1735 County Road Bayshore, CA 94326

Additional Info:	
Type	Commercial
Terms	Net 30

Payment Info:	
Account No.	3003
Preferred Payment Method	Check

Step 6:   Add a new job for Rock Castle Construction.

Job Info:	
Job Status	Awarded
Job Description	Mow/Trim Lawn & Shrubs
Job Type	Lawn & Shrubs

Step 7:   🖨 **Print** the Customer List.

TASK 4: VENDOR LIST

Step 1: Create a Vendor List for Tuscany Landscapes using the following information.

Vendor	AB Gas Station
Opening Balance	0 as of 01/01/2014
Address Info:	
Company Name	AB Gas Station
Address	100 Manchester Road Bayshore, CA 94326
Contact	Norm
Phone	415-555-7844
Print on Check as	AB Gas Station

Additional Info:	
Account	4001
Type	Fuel
Terms	Net 30
Credit Limit	500.00
Tax ID	37-8910541

Vendor	Mower Sales & Repair
Opening Balance	0 as of 01/01/2014
Address Info:	
Company Name	Mower Sales & Repair
Address	650 Manchester Road Bayshore, CA 94326
Contact	Teresa
Phone	415-555-8222
Print on Check as	Mower Sales & Repair

Additional Info:	
Account	4002
Type	Mower
Terms	Net 30
Credit Limit	1000.00
Tax ID	37-6510541

Step 2: 🖨 **Print** the Vendor List.

TASK 5: ITEM LIST

Step 1: Create an Item List for Tuscany Landscapes using the following information.

Item Type	Service
Item Name	Mowing
Description	Lawn Mowing
Rate	25.00
Account	45700 – Maintenance Services

Item Type	Service
Item Name	Trim Shrubs
Description	Trim Shrubs
Rate	30.00
Account	45700 – Maintenance Services

Step 2: **Print** the Item List.

TASK 6: CUSTOMIZE INVOICE TEMPLATE

Create a Custom Invoice Template with a *Service Date* column. This permits Tuscany Landscapes to bill customers once a month for all services provided during the month, listing each service date separately on the invoice.

To create a Custom Invoice Template, complete the following steps:

Step 1: Click the **Create Invoices** icon in the *Customers* section of the Home page.

Step 2: Click the **Customize** icon on the upper right of the *Create Invoices* window.

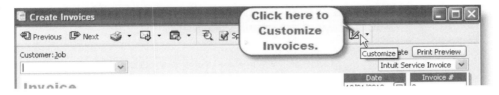

Step 3: When the following *Basic Customization* window appears, select **Manage Templates**.

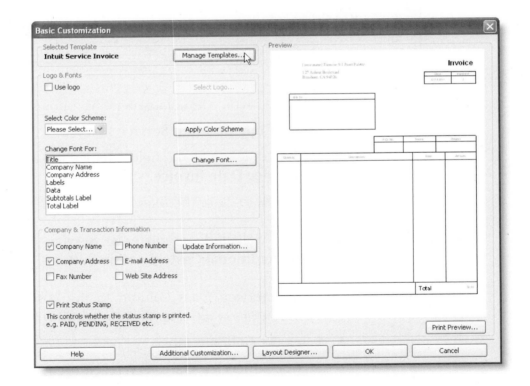

Step 4: In the *Manage Templates* window, select **Intuit Service Invoice**. Then click **Copy**.

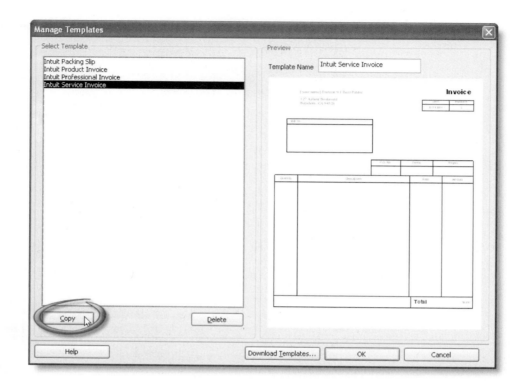

Step 5: Change the invoice template name as follows:

- Select **Copy of: Intuit Service Invoice**.

- In the Template Name field, change the template name to: **Service Date Invoice**.

- Click **OK** to close the *Manage Templates* window.

Step 6: Verify the Selected Template is: **Service Date Invoice**. Click the **Additional Customization** button.

Step 7: To add a *Service Date* column to the custom template, when the *Additional Customization* window appears:

- Click the **Columns** tab.

- ✓ Check **Service Date: Screen**. If the Layout Designer message appears, click OK.

- ✓ Check **Service Date: Print**.

- ✓ Check **Item: Print**. If an Overlapping Fields message appears, click Continue.

- Enter Title for Service Date: **Date**.

- Renumber the Order so they appear as shown below.

- Click the **Layout Designer** button and adjust the field sizes as needed.

- Click **OK** to close the *Additional Customization* window. Click **OK** again to close the *Basic Customization* window.

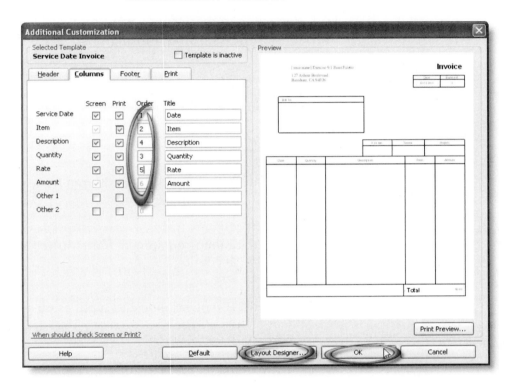

Step 8: To view the custom invoice:

- If necessary, from the *Create Invoices* window, select Template: **Service Date Invoice**.

- Notice that the first column of the invoice is now the *Date* column.

Step 9: **Close** the *Create Invoices* window.

Task 7: Record Transactions

During the year, Tuscany Landscapes entered into the transactions listed below.

Step 1: Record the following transactions for Tuscany Landscapes. Customers are billed monthly. ⊟ **Print** invoices, checks, and deposit summaries as appropriate. Use memorized transactions for recurring transactions.

Use *Make Deposits* window.

Use *Write Checks* window.

Use *Enter Bills* window.

Record Supplies Expense.

Select **Show All Bills** in the *Pay Bills* window.

Date	Transaction		
01/01/2014	Tomaso Moltissimo invested $1,500 cash in the business.		
2/01/2014	Purchased a mower for $800 cash from Mower Sales & Repair (Check No. 501).		
02/20/2014	Purchased trimming equipment from Mower Sales & Repair for $200 on account.		
03/01/2014	Purchased $100 of gasoline and supplies on account from AB Gas Station.		
03/20/2014	Paid $200 on the account with Mower Sales & Repair. Paid $100 on the account with AB Gas Station.		
04/30/2014	Printed and mailed invoices to customers for the following work performed in April. Use the Service Date Invoice to record all work performed for the same customer on **one** invoice, indicating the date of service in the *DATE* column.		
	04/01/2014	Mowed Katrina Beneficio's lawn	6 hrs
	04/15/2014	Mowed Katrina Beneficio's lawn	6 hrs
	04/04/2014	Mowed R.C. Construction's lawn	8 hrs
	04/19/2014	Mowed R.C. Construction's lawn	8 hrs
	04/08/2014	Mowed Tom Whalen's lawn	4 hrs
	04/22/2014	Mowed Tom Whalen's lawn	4 hrs

05/01/2014	Purchased $100 of gasoline and supplies on account from AB Gas Station.		
05/15/2014	Received payments from Beneficio (Check No. 755), Whalen (Check No. 645), and Rock Castle Construction (Check No. 1068) for April invoices.		
05/30/2014	Paid AB Gas Station bill.		
05/30/2014	Mailed invoices to customers for the following services provided during May.		
	05/01/2014	Mowed Katrina Beneficio's lawn	6 hrs
	05/15/2014	Mowed Katrina Beneficio's lawn	6 hrs
	05/04/2014	Mowed R.C. Construction's lawn	8 hrs
	05/19/2014	Mowed R.C. Construction's lawn	8 hrs
	05/08/2014	Mowed Tom Whalen's lawn	4 hrs
	05/22/2014	Mowed Tom Whalen's lawn	4 hrs
06/01/2014	Purchased $100 of gasoline and supplies on account from AB Gas Station.		
06/15/2014	Received payments from Beneficio (Check No. 895), Whalen (Check No. 698), and Rock Castle Construction (Check No. 1100) for May services.		
06/30/2014	Paid AB Gas Station bill.		
06/30/2014	Mailed invoices to customers for the following services provided during June.		
	06/01/2014	Mowed Katrina Beneficio's lawn	6 hrs
	06/02/2014	Trimmed Katrina Beneficio's shrubs	7 hrs
	06/15/2014	Mowed Katrina Beneficio's lawn	6 hrs
	06/04/2014	Mowed R. C. Construction's lawn	8 hrs
	06/05/2014	Trimmed R.C. Construction's shrubs	9 hrs
	06/19/2014	Mowed R. C. Construction's lawn	8 hrs
	06/08/2014	Mowed Tom Whalen's lawn	4 hrs
	06/09/2014	Trimmed Tom Whalen's shrubs	3 hrs
	06/22/2014	Mowed Tom Whalen's lawn	4 hrs

07/01/2014	Purchased $100 of gasoline and supplies on account from AB Gas Station.		
07/15/2014	Received payments from Beneficio (Check No. 910), Whalen (Check No. 715), and Rock Castle Construction (Check No. 1200) for June services.		
07/31/2014	Paid AB Gas Station bill.		
07/31/2014	Mailed invoices to customers for the following services provided during July.		
	07/01/2014	Mowed Katrina Beneficio's lawn	6 hrs
	07/15/2014	Mowed Katrina Beneficio's lawn	6 hrs
	07/04/2014	Mowed R.C. Construction's lawn	8 hrs
	07/19/2014	Mowed R.C. Construction's lawn	8 hrs
	07/08/2014	Mowed Tom Whalen's lawn	4 hrs
	07/22/2014	Mowed Tom Whalen's lawn	4 hrs
08/01/2014	Purchased $100 of gasoline and supplies on account from AB Gas Station.		
08/15/2014	Received payments from Beneficio (Check No. 935), Whalen (Check No. 742), and Rock Castle Construction (Check No. 1300) for July services.		
08/31/2014	Paid AB Gas Station bill.		
08/31/2014	Mailed invoices to customers for the following services provided during August.		
	08/01/2014	Mowed Katrina Beneficio's lawn	6 hrs
	08/15/2014	Mowed Katrina Beneficio's lawn	6 hrs
	08/04/2014	Mowed R.C. Construction's lawn	8 hrs
	08/19/2014	Mowed R.C. Construction's lawn	8 hrs
	08/08/2014	Mowed Tom Whalen's lawn	4 hrs
	08/22/2014	Mowed Tom Whalen's lawn	4 hrs

09/01/2014	Purchased $100 of gasoline and supplies on account from AB Gas Station.		
09/15/2014	Received payments from Beneficio (Check No. 934), Whalen (Check No. 746), and Rock Castle Construction (Check No. 1400) for August services.		
09/30/2014	Paid AB Gas Station bill.		
09/30/2014	Mailed invoices to customers for the following services provided during September.		
	09/01/2014	Mowed Katrina Beneficio's lawn	6 hrs
	09/15/2014	Mowed Katrina Beneficio's lawn	6 hrs
	09/04/2014	Mowed R.C. Construction's lawn	8 hrs
	09/19/2014	Mowed R.C. Construction's lawn	8 hrs
	09/08/2014	Mowed Tom Whalen's lawn	4 hrs
	09/22/2014	Mowed Tom Whalen's lawn	4 hrs
10/01/2014	Purchased $50 of gasoline on account from AB Gas Station.		
10/15/2014	Received payments from Beneficio (Check No. 956), Whalen (Check No. 755), and Rock Castle Construction (Check No. 1500) for September services.		
10/31/2014	Paid AB Gas Station bill.		
10/31/2014	Mailed invoices to customers for the following services provided during October.		
	10/01/2014	Mowed Katrina Beneficio's lawn	6 hrs
	10/02/2014	Trimmed Katrina Beneficio's shrubs	7 hrs
	10/15/2014	Mowed Katrina Beneficio's lawn	6 hrs
	10/04/2014	Mowed R. C. Construction's lawn	8 hrs
	10/05/2014	Trimmed R.C. Construction's shrubs	9 hrs
	10/19/2014	Mowed R. C. Construction's lawn	8 hrs
	10/08/2014	Mowed Tom Whalen's lawn	4 hrs
	10/09/2014	Trimmed Tom Whalen's shrubs	3 hrs
	10/22/2014	Mowed Tom Whalen's lawn	4 hrs

11/15/2014	Received payments from Beneficio (Check No. 967), Whalen (Check No. 765), and Rock Castle Construction (Check No. 1600) for October services.

Step 2: 🖨 **Print** the Check Register for January 1, 2014, to December 31, 2014.

TASK 8: ADJUSTING ENTRIES

Step 1: Make adjusting entries for Tuscany Landscapes at December 31, 2014, using the following information.

- The mowing equipment cost $800 and has a four-year life and no salvage value.

- The trimming equipment cost $200 and has a two-year life and no salvage value.

Step 2: 🖨 **Print** the Journal for the year.

TASK 9: FINANCIAL REPORTS

🖨 **Print** the following reports for Tuscany Landscapes.

- General Ledger (Remember to omit unused accounts with zero balances from the deliverable.)

- Profit & Loss, Standard

- Balance Sheet, Standard

- Statement of Cash Flows

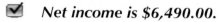 *Net income is $6,490.00.*

TASK 10: SAVE PROJECT 9.1

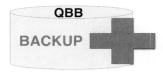

Save a backup of your Project 9.1 file using the file name: **[your name] Project 9.1 Backup.QBB**. See *Appendix B: Back Up & Restore QuickBooks Files* for instructions.

WORKFLOW

If you are using the workflow approach, leave your .QBW file open and proceed to Project 12.1.

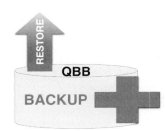

RESTART & RESTORE

If you are using the Restart & Restore approach and are ending your computer session now, close your .QBW file and exit QuickBooks. When you restart, you will restore your backup file to complete Project 12.1.

TASK 11: ANALYSIS AND RECOMMENDATIONS

Step 1:   Analyze the financial performance of Tuscany Landscapes.

Step 2:   What are your recommendations to improve the company's financial performance in the future?

DELIVERABLES CHECKLIST PROJECT 9.1
NAME:

INSTRUCTIONS:
1. **CHECK OFF THE DELIVERABLES YOU HAVE COMPLETED.**
2. **TURN IN THIS PAGE WITH YOUR DELIVERABLES.**

PROJECT 9.1

- ☐ Chart of Accounts
- ☐ Customer List
- ☐ Vendor List
- ☐ Item List
- ☐ Invoices
- ☐ Checks
- ☐ Deposit Summaries
- ☐ Check Register
- ☐ General Journal
- ☐ General Ledger
- ☐ Profit & Loss
- ☐ Balance Sheet
- ☐ Statement of Cash Flows

REFLECTION: A WISH AND A STAR ⭐

Reflection improves learning and retention. Reflect on what you have learned after completing Project 9.1 that you did not know before you started the project.

A Star:

What did you like best that you learned about QuickBooks in Project 9.1?

A Wish:

If you could pick one thing, what do you wish you knew more about when using QuickBooks?

NOTES

CHAPTER 10
MERCHANDISING CORPORATION: SALES, PURCHASES & INVENTORY

Home   Company Snapshot   Customer Center   Vendor Center   Employee Center   Report Center

SCENARIO

After only one year of operation, your painting service is growing as more customers learn of your custom murals. You often suggest that your customers buy their paint from a small paint store owned and operated by Wil Miles because he provides excellent customer service. In addition, Wil will deliver paint to a job when you run short.

To your dismay, you discover that Wil Miles is planning to sell the store and retire, taking his first vacation since he opened the store 15 years ago. After your initial disappointment, however, you see a business opportunity.

Lately, you've noticed increased demand for custom paint colors to coordinate with furniture, fabrics, and various decorating accessories. If you owned the paint store, you could make a profit on the markup from paint sales made to Paint Palette customers. In addition, you are certain you could land three large commercial customers for whom you have worked: Cara Interiors, Decor Centre, and Rock Castle Construction. You could also sell paint to other customers, including paint contractors and homeowners.

Convinced there is a profitable market for custom-mixed paint, you approach Wil Miles about purchasing his store. Wil agrees to sell the business to you for

$11,000 cash. In addition, you agree to assume a $1,000 bank loan as part of the purchase agreement. You have some extra cash you can invest, and you decide to seek other investors to finance the remainder.

Two of Rock Castle Construction's subcontractors, John of Kolbe Window & Door, and Joseph of Joseph's Closets are long-time customers of the paint store. When they learn of your plans to buy the paint store, both eagerly offer to invest.

John suggests that you investigate incorporating the new business to provide limited liability to the owners. You vaguely recall discussion of limited liability in your college accounting class and decide to e-mail your college accounting professor, Kim Temme, for more information.

Professor Temme's e-mail reply:

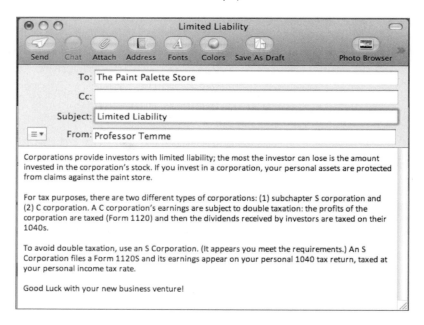

John, Joseph, and you form an S Corporation. John and Joseph each buy $3,000 of stock, and you buy $5,000 of stock. The stock proceeds are used to purchase the business from Wil Miles. Until you can hire a store manager, you will manage the store.

You prepare the following list of planned expenditures to launch the business:

THE PAINT PALETTE STORE

Color Match Computer Equipment $1,000

Supplies $600

Store Building & Fixtures Rent $1,000/month

The Paint Palette Store opens for business on January 1, 2015.

CHAPTER 10
LEARNING OBJECTIVES

In Chapter 10, you will learn about the following QuickBooks activities:

INTRODUCTION

A company can sell customers either (1) a product or (2) a service. In Chapters 8 and 9, you maintained accounting records for a company that sells a service to customers. In this chapter, you will maintain an accounting system for a company that sells a product. In Chapter 10, you will complete the following:

---

1. Easy Step Interview

Use the EasyStep Interview to enter information and preferences for the new company. Based on the information entered, QuickBooks automatically creates a Chart of Accounts.

---

2. Create Lists

Enter information in the following lists:
- Customer List. Enter information about customers to whom you sell.
- Vendor List. Enter information about vendors from whom you buy.
- Item List. Enter information about products (inventory) you buy and resell to customers.
- Employee List. Enter information about employees.

---

3. Customize the Chart of Accounts

Customize the Chart of Accounts for your business. Enter beginning account balances. Make opening adjustments.

---

4. Record Transactions

Enter business transactions in QuickBooks using onscreen forms and the onscreen Journal.

---

5. Reports

After preparing adjusting entries, print financial reports.

To begin Chapter 10, start QuickBooks software by clicking on the QuickBooks desktop icon or click **Start > Programs > QuickBooks Pro > QuickBooks Pro 2010.**

SET UP A NEW COMPANY

To create a new company data file in QuickBooks, use the EasyStep Interview. The EasyStep Interview will ask you a series of questions about your business. QuickBooks then uses the information to customize QuickBooks to fit your business needs.

Open the EasyStep Interview as follows:

Step 1:   Select **File** menu **> New Company**.

Step 2:   Click **Start Interview.** Enter the following information for The Paint Palette Store in the EasyStep Interview.

You can create a company in QuickBooks and skip the interview questions, by clicking **Skip Interview**.

Write your password on the inside front cover of your text.

Company name	[your name] Chapter 10 Paint Palette Store
Legal name	[your name] Chapter 10 Paint Palette Store
Federal tax ID	37-9875602
Address	2301 Olive Boulevard
City	Bayshore
State	CA
Zip	94326
E-mail	[enter your own e-mail address]
Industry	Retail Shop or Online Commerce
Company organized?	S Corporation
First month of fiscal year?	January
File name	[your name] Chapter 10
What do you sell?	Products only
Enter sales	Record each sale individually
Sell products online?	I don't sell online, but I may want to someday.

Sales tax	Yes
Estimates	No
Sales receipts	Yes
Billing statements	No
Invoices	Yes
Progress invoicing	No
Track bills you owe	Yes
Print checks?	Yes
Track inventory in QuickBooks?	Yes
Accept credit cards	I accept credit cards and debit cards.
Track time	Yes
Employees	No
Multiple currencies	No
Start date	01/01/2015
Add a bank account?	Yes
Bank account name	[your name] Checking
Bank account opened	On or after 01/01/2015

Step 4:   Click **Finish** to exit the EasyStep Interview.

COMPLETE COMPANY SETUP

After the EasyStep Interview is finished, use the following checklist to complete the company setup:

☐ Customize QuickBooks.

☐ Add customers.

☐ Add vendors.

☐ Add products and services as items.

☐ Customize Chart of Accounts.

☐ Opening adjustments.

CUSTOMIZE QUICKBOOKS

You will customize QuickBooks for The Paint Palette Store by customizing preferences and by customizing the Chart of Accounts.

First, to customize preferences:

Step 1: Select **Edit** menu **> Preferences > General > My Preferences**.

Step 2: Select Default Date to Use for New Transactions: **Use the last entered date as default**.

Step 3: Select **Accounting > Company Preferences**.

- Select **Use account numbers**.

- Verify that **Use class tracking** is *not* selected.

- Uncheck **Warn if transactions are 30 day(s) in the future.**

Step 4: Select **Desktop View > My Preferences > Color Scheme**. Select the color scheme of your choice.

Step 5: Select **Desktop View > Company Preferences**. Verify the following preference settings: Estimates (off), Sales Tax (on), Inventory (on), Payroll (off), and Time Tracking (on). To change the settings for these preferences in the future, you would return to this screen.

Step 6: Click **OK** to save your customized preference settings.

After customizing QuickBooks preferences, since The Paint Palette Store is an existing company as opposed to a new company, the next steps are to enter information into lists for customers, vendors, and items.

CREATE A CUSTOMER LIST

Next, enter customer information in the Customer List. When using QuickBooks to account for a merchandising company that sells a product to customers, you must indicate whether the specific customer is charged sales tax.

The Paint Palette Store will sell to:

1. Retail customers, such as homeowners who must pay sales tax.

2. Wholesale customers, such as Decor Centre, who resell the product and do not pay sales tax.

Step 1: Create a Customer List for The Paint Palette Store using the following information.

Customer	Beneficio, Katrina
Opening Balance	0.00 as of 01/01/2015
Address Info:	
Mr./Ms./…	Mrs.
First Name	Katrina
Last Name	Beneficio
Contact	Katrina Beneficio
Phone	415-555-1818
Alt. Phone	415-555-3636
Address	10 Pico Blvd Bayshore, CA 94326

Select **Add New**.

Additional Info:	
Type	Residential
Terms	Net 30
Tax Code	Tax
Tax Item	State Tax

Payment Info:	
Account	3001

Job Info:	
Job Status	Awarded
Job Description	Custom Paint
Job Type	Custom Paint

Select **Add New**.

Customer	Decor Centre
Opening Balance	0.00 as of 01/01/2015
Address Info:	
Company Name	Decor Centre
Contact	Vicki
Phone	415-555-9898
Address	750 Clayton Road Bayshore, CA 94326

Additional Info:	
Type	Commercial
Terms	Net 30
Tax Code	Non

Payment Info:	
Account	3005

Job Info:	
Job Status	Awarded
Job Description	Custom & Stock Paint
Job Type	Custom & Stock Paint

Customer	Rock Castle Construction
Opening Balance	0.00 as of 01/01/2015
Address Info:	
Company Name	Rock Castle Construction
Mr./Ms./…	Mr.
First Name	Rock
Last Name	Castle
Contact	Rock Castle
Phone	415-555-7878
Alt. Phone	415-555-5679
Address	1735 County Road Bayshore, CA 94326

Additional Info:	
Type	Commercial
Terms	Net 30
Tax Code	Non

Payment Info:	
Account	3003

Job Info:	
Job Status	Awarded
Job Description	Custom Paint
Job Type	Custom Paint

Customer	Cara Interiors
Opening Balance	0.00 as of 01/01/2015
Address Info:	
Company Name	Cara Interiors
Contact	Cara
Phone	415-555-4356
Address	120 Ignatius Drive Bayshore, CA 94326

Additional Info:	
Type	Commercial
Terms	Net 30
Tax Code	Non

Payment Info:	
Account	3004

Job Info:	
Job Status	Awarded
Job Description	Custom & Stock Paint
Job Type	Custom & Stock Paint

Customer	Whalen, Tom
Opening Balance	0.00 as of 01/01/2015
Address Info:	
Mr./Ms./...	Mr.
First Name	Tom
Last Name	Whalen
Contact	Tom Whalen
Phone	415-555-1234
Address	100 Sunset Drive Bayshore, CA 94326

Additional Info:	
Type	Residential
Terms	Net 30
Tax Code	Tax
Tax Item	State Tax

Payment Info:	
Account	3002

Job Info:	
Job Status	Awarded
Job Description	Custom Paint
Job Type	Custom Paint

Step 2: 🖶 **Print** The Paint Palette Store Customer List using Excel.

CREATE A VENDOR LIST

Step 1: Create a Vendor List for The Paint Palette Store using the following information.

Vendor	Brewer Paint Supplies
Opening Balance	0.00 as of 01/01/2015
Address Info:	
Company Name	Brewer Paint Supplies
Address	200 Spring Street Bayshore, CA 94326
Contact	Ella Brewer
Phone	415-555-6070
Print on Check as	Brewer Paint Supplies

Select **Add New**.

Additional Info:	
Account	4001
Type	Paint
Terms	Net 30
Credit Limit	15,000.00
Tax ID	37-7832541

Vendor	Hartzheim Leasing
Opening Balance	0.00 as of 01/01/2015
Address Info:	
Company Name	Hartzheim Leasing
Address	13 Appleton Drive Bayshore, CA 94326
Contact	Joseph
Phone	415-555-0412

Select **Add New**.

Additional Info:	
Account	4002
Type	Leasing
Terms	Net 30
Tax ID	37-1726354

Vendor	Shades of Santiago
Opening Balance	0.00 as of 01/01/2015
Address Info:	
Company Name	Shades of Santiago
Address	650 Chile Avenue Bayshore, CA 94326
Contact	Juan
Phone	415-555-0444

Additional Info:	
Account	4003
Type	Inventory
Terms	Net 30
Tax ID	37-1726355

Step 2:   🖶 **Print** The Paint Palette Store Vendor List using Excel.

CREATE AN INVENTORY LIST

Each of the inventory items that The Paint Palette Store sells is entered in the QuickBooks Item List. The Paint Palette Store will stock and sell paint inventory to both retail and wholesale customers. The Paint Palette Store will charge retail customers the full price and charge wholesale customers a discounted price for the paint. Because the sales price varies depending upon the type of customer, instead of entering the sales price in the Item List, you will enter the sales price on the invoice at the time of sale.

Step 1: Create an Item List for The Paint Palette Store inventory using the following information.

Item Type	Inventory Part
Item Name	Paint Base
Description	Paint Base
COGS Account	50000 – Cost of Goods Sold
Income Account	46000 – Merchandise Sales
Asset Account	12100 – Inventory Asset
Qty on Hand	0.00 as of 01/01/2015

Item Type	Inventory Part
Item Name	IntBase 1 gal
Subitem of	Paint Base
Description	Interior Paint Base (1 gallon)
Cost	10.00
COGS Account	50000 – Cost of Goods Sold
Taxable	Tax
Income Account	46000 – Merchandise Sales
Asset Account	12100 – Inventory Asset
Qty on Hand	0.00 as of 01/01/2015

Item Type	Inventory Part
Item Name	ExtBase 1 gal
Subitem of	Paint Base
Description	Exterior Paint Base (1 gallon)
Cost	10.00
COGS Account	50000 – Cost of Goods Sold
Taxable	Tax
Income Account	46000 – Merchandise Sales
Asset Account	12100 – Inventory Asset
Qty on Hand	0.00 as of 01/01/2015

Item Type	Inventory Part
Item Name	Paint Color
Description	Paint Color
COGS Account	50000 – Cost of Goods Sold
Income Account	46000 – Merchandise Sales
Asset Account	12100 – Inventory Asset
Qty on Hand	0.00 as of 01/01/2015

Item Type	Inventory Part
Item Name	Stock Color
Subitem of	Paint Color
Description	Stock Paint Color
Cost	2.00
COGS Account	50000 – Cost of Goods Sold
Taxable	Tax
Income Account	46000 – Merchandise Sales
Asset Account	12100 – Inventory Asset
Qty on Hand	0.00 as of 01/01/2015

Item Type	Inventory Part
Item Name	Custom Color
Subitem of	Paint Color
Description	Custom Paint Color
Cost	8.00
COGS Account	50000 – Cost of Goods Sold
Taxable	Tax
Income Account	46000 – Merchandise Sales
Asset Account	12100 – Inventory Asset
Qty on Hand	0.00 as of 01/01/2015

Step 2: 🖨 **Print** the Item List for inventory using Excel.

CREATE A SALES TAX ITEM

A merchandiser selling products to consumers must charge sales tax. A sales tax item is created in the Item List with the rate and tax agency information.

To enter a sales tax item:

Step 1: In the *Item List* window, double-click on **State Tax**.

Step 2: When the *Edit Item* window appears:

- Enter Tax Rate: **7.75**%.

- Enter Tax Agency: **California State Board of Equalization**.

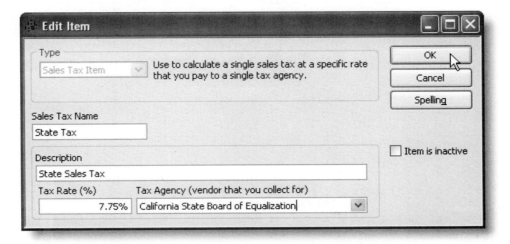

Step 3: Click **OK**.

Step 4: When the *Vendor Not Found* window appears, select: **Quick Add**. If necessary, click **OK** again to close the *Edit Item* window.

CUSTOMIZE CHART OF ACCOUNTS

Based on your answers in the EasyStep Interview, QuickBooks automatically creates a Chart of Accounts for The Paint Palette Store. You can customize the Chart of Accounts to suit your specific business needs.

Because you are purchasing an existing business, some accounts have opening balances. Opening balances for The Paint Palette Store at January 1, 2015, appear as follows.

Enter opening balances when you customize the Chart of Accounts.

You purchased $5,000 in stock and John and Joseph each purchased $3,000 in stock for a total of $11,000.

THE PAINT PALETTE STORE
Balance Sheet

Assets:
Checking $2,400
Supplies on hand $600
Store fixtures $5,000
Paint mixing equipment $4,000
Total assets $12,000

Liabilities & equity:
Notes payable $1,000
Capital stock (opening balance equity) $11,000
Total liabilities & equity $12,000

Customize the Chart of Accounts and enter opening balances as follows:

To display account numbers select **Edit** menu > **Preferences > Accounting > Company Preferences > Use account numbers**.

Step 1: If needed, display account numbers in the Chart of Accounts.

Step 2: Enter the opening balance for the company Checking account:

- To open the Chart of Accounts, click the **Chart of Accounts** icon in the *Company* section of the Home page.

- Select **[your name] Checking** account. **Right-click** to display the popup menu.

- Select **Edit Account**.

- When the *Edit Account* window for the Checking account appears, enter Account No.: **10100**.

- Select **Enter Opening Balance**. Enter Statement Ending Balance: **$2,400**. Statement Ending Date: **01/01/2015**. Click **OK**.

- Click **Save & Close** to close the *Edit Account* window.

Step 3: Add the following accounts and opening balances to the Chart of Accounts. Abbreviate account titles as necessary.

Account No.	26000
Account Type	Other Current Liability
Account Name	Notes Payable
Account Description	Notes Payable
Tax Line	B/S-Liabs/Eq.: Other current liabilities
Opening Balance	$1,000 as of 01/01/2015

Account No.	12500
Account Type	Other Current Asset
Account Name	Supplies on Hand
Account Description	Supplies on Hand
Tax Line	B/S-Assets: Other current assets
Opening Balance	$600 as of 01/01/2015

Account No.	14000
Account Type	Fixed Asset
Account Name	Store Fixtures
Account Description	Store Fixtures
Tax Line	B/S-Assets: Buildings/oth. depr. assets
Opening Balance	$0 as of 01/01/2015

Account No.	14100
Account Type	Fixed Asset
Account Name	Store Fixtures Cost
Subaccount of	Store Fixtures
Account Description	Store Fixtures Cost
Tax Line	B/S-Assets: Buildings/oth. depr. assets
Opening Balance	$5,000 as of 01/01/2015

Account No.	14200
Account Type	Fixed Asset
Account Name	Accumulated Depr-Store Fixtures
Subaccount of	Store Fixtures
Account Description	Acc Depr-Store Fixtures
Tax Line	B/S-Assets: Buildings/oth. depr. assets
Opening Balance	$0 as of 01/01/2015

Account No.	14300
Account Type	Fixed Asset
Account Name	Paint Mixing Equipment
Account Description	Paint Mixing Equipment
Tax Line	B/S-Assets: Buildings/oth. depr. assets
Opening Balance	$0 as of 01/01/2015

Account No.	14400
Account Type	Fixed Asset
Account Name	Paint Mixing Equipment Cost
Subaccount of	Paint Mixing Equipment
Account Description	Paint Mixing Equipment Cost
Tax Line	B/S-Assets: Buildings/oth. depr. assets
Opening Balance	$4,000 as of 01/01/2015

Account No.	14500
Account Type	Fixed Asset
Account Name	Acc Depr-Paint Mixing Equipment
Subaccount of	Paint Mixing Equipment
Account Description	Acc Depr-Paint Mixing Equipment
Tax Line	B/S-Assets: Buildings/oth. depr. assets
Opening Balance	$0 as of 01/01/2015

Account No.	14600
Account Type	Fixed Asset
Account Name	Color Match Equipment
Account Description	Color Match Equipment
Tax Line	B/S-Assets: Buildings/oth. depr. assets
Opening Balance	$0 as of 01/01/2015

Account No.	14700
Account Type	Fixed Asset
Account Name	Color Match Equipment Cost
Subaccount of	Color Match Equipment
Account Description	Color Match Equipment Cost
Tax Line	B/S-Assets: Buildings/oth. depr. assets
Opening Balance	$0 as of 01/01/2015

Account No.	14800
Account Type	Fixed Asset
Account Name	Acc Depr-Color Match Equipment
Subaccount of	Color Match Equipment
Account Description	Acc Depr-Color Match Equipment
Tax Line	B/S-Assets: Buildings/oth. depr. assets
Opening Balance	$0 as of 01/01/2015

Account No.	64800
Account Type	Expense
Account Name	Supplies Expense
Account Description	Supplies Expense
Tax Line	Other Deductions: Supplies

Step 4: 🖨 **Print** the Chart of Accounts report with opening balances for The Paint Palette Store.

QuickBooks Opening Adjustments

As discussed in Chapter 1, accounting systems use double-entry accounting where each entry must balance. In general, when an existing company with opening balances is set up in QuickBooks accounting software, as accounts receivable, accounts payable, and item balances are entered, QuickBooks offsets these entries with a balancing effect to other accounts.

For example, as customer accounts receivable opening balances are entered, QuickBooks offsets these to an Uncategorized Income account. As vendor accounts payable opening balances are entered, QuickBooks offsets these to an Uncategorized Expense account. As item opening balances are entered, QuickBooks offsets these to an Opening Balance Equity account. When opening balances are entered for all other accounts in the Chart of Accounts, QuickBooks offsets these to the Opening Balance Equity account.

For new start-up companies, the opening balances are zero. For existing companies that have opening balances, QuickBooks offsets these opening balances. Thus, when setting up existing companies in QuickBooks, the following opening adjustments must be recorded using journal entries.

1. When accounts receivable opening balances create Uncategorized Income, use an opening adjustment to transfer the Uncategorized Income to the Opening Balance Equity account.

2. When accounts payable opening balances create Uncategorized Expenses, use an opening adjustment to transfer the Uncategorized Expenses to the Opening Balance Equity account.

3. Opening balances for inventory items and all other accounts are offset by QuickBooks in the Opening Balance Equity account. At this point the balance in the Opening Balance Equity account consists of the transfers from Uncategorized Income and Uncategorized Expenses plus offsets from Inventory items and all other accounts. Use an opening adjustment to transfer the balance in the Opening Balance Equity account to the Capital Stock account.

The following summarizes the transfer of offsets used for opening balances in QuickBooks.

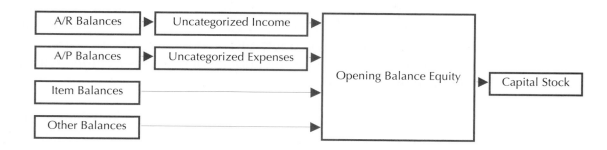

Next, you will prepare the opening adjustments for The Paint Palette Store.

Step 1: 🖶 **Print** a Trial Balance report for The Paint Palette Store dated **01/01/2015**. Compare your Trial Balance report to the following check figures to verify your account balances are correct. Note that QuickBooks records the offsetting amount to the opening account balances in an Opening Balance Equity account. Since The Paint Palette Store did not have any opening balances for customers or vendors, there was no Uncategorized Income or Uncategorized Expense accounts shown on the Trial Balance report.

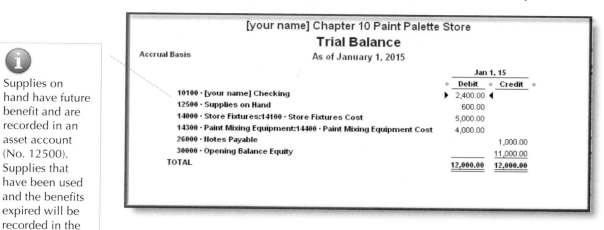

> ℹ️ Supplies on hand have future benefit and are recorded in an asset account (No. 12500). Supplies that have been used and the benefits expired will be recorded in the Supplies Expense account (No. 64800).

Step 2: Transfer the Opening Balance Equity account balance to the Capital Stock account using a journal entry.

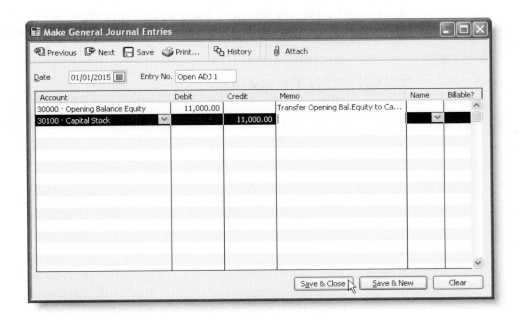

Step 3: Reprint the Trial Balance after the opening adjustment was made to verify that the Opening Balance Equity account balance was transferred to the Capital Stock account.

[your name] Chapter 10 Paint Palette Store
Trial Balance

Accrual Basis   As of January 1, 2015

	Jan 1, 15	
	Debit	Credit
10100 · [your name] Checking	2,400.00	
12500 · Supplies on Hand	600.00	
14000 · Store Fixtures:14100 · Store Fixtures Cost	5,000.00	
14300 · Paint Mixing Equipment:14400 · Paint Mixing Equi...	4,000.00	
26000 · Notes Payable		1,000.00
30000 · Opening Balance Equity	0.00	
30100 · Capital Stock		11,000.00
TOTAL	12,000.00	12,000.00

Step 4: ▣ **Print** a Balance Sheet (standard) for The Paint Palette Store dated **01/01/2015**.

RECORD PURCHASE TRANSACTIONS

EQUIPMENT PURCHASES

On January 1, 2015, The Paint Palette Store purchased computerized paint color matching equipment from Brewer Paint Supplies for $1,000 cash.

Step 1: Record the purchase using the *Write Checks* window. Record the color match equipment in Account No. 14700. If asked, add the equipment to the Fixed Asset List.

Step 2: 🖨 **Print** the check (Check No. 401) using the standard check style.

THE PURCHASING TRANSACTION CYCLE

The purchasing transaction cycle for a merchandising company consists of the following transactions:

1. Create a purchase order to order inventory.
2. Receive the inventory items ordered and update the inventory account.
3. Enter the bill in QuickBooks when the bill is received.
4. Pay the bill.
5. Print the check.

Next, you will record each of the above transactions in the purchasing cycle for The Paint Palette Store.

CREATE A PURCHASE ORDER

The first step in the purchasing cycle is to create a purchase order which is sent to the vendor to order inventory. The purchase order provides a record of the type and quantity of item ordered.

The Paint Palette Store needs to order 50 gallons of Interior Base Paint. To order the paint, The Paint Palette Store must create a purchase order indicating the item and quantity desired.

To create a purchase order in QuickBooks:

Step 1: Click the **Purchase Orders** icon in the *Vendors* section of the Home page.

Step 2: Select Vendor: **Brewer Paint Supplies**.

Step 3: Select Template: **Custom Purchase Order**.

Step 4: Enter Date: **01/03/2015**.

Step 5: Enter the item ordered:
- Select Item: **Interior Paint Base (1 gallon)**.
- Enter Quantity: **50**.

Step 6: Select: **To be printed**.

$10.00 will automatically appear in the *Rate* column.

After entering 50 in the Quantity column, $500.00 will appear in the *Amount* column.

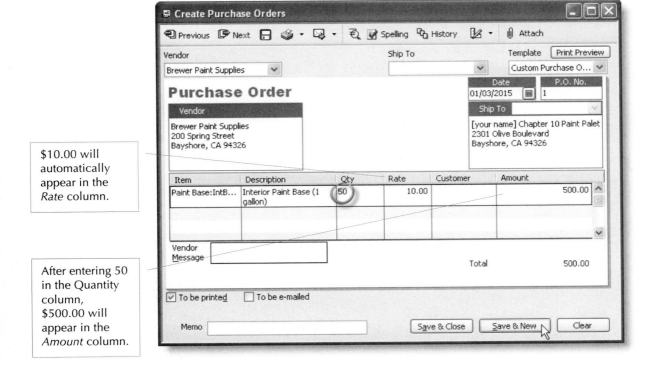

Step 7: Click **Save & New** to record the purchase order and advance to a blank purchase order.

Step 8: Create purchase orders for the following inventory items for The Paint Palette Store.

Vendor	Brewer Paint Supplies
Date	01/05/2015
Item	Exterior Paint Base (1 gallon)
Quantity	40

Vendor	Shades of Santiago
Date	01/10/2015
Item	Custom Color
Quantity	25 (cartons)
Item	Stock Color
Quantity	5 (cartons)

Vendor	Brewer Paint Supplies
Date	01/12/2015
Item	Stock Color
Quantity	10 (cartons)

Step 9: Click **Save & Close** to record the last purchase order and close the *Purchase Order* window.

Step 10: 🖶 **Print** the purchase orders as follows:

- Select **File** menu > **Print Forms** > **Purchase Orders**.
- Select the purchase orders to print and click **OK**.

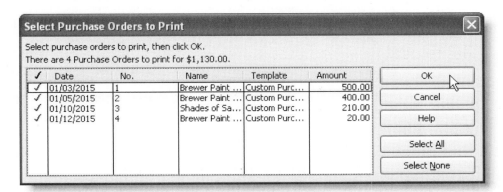

- Select print settings: **Blank paper** and uncheck **Do not print lines around each field**.
- Click **Print**.

RECEIVE INVENTORY ITEMS

When the inventory items that have been ordered are received, record their receipt in QuickBooks. QuickBooks will then add the items received to the Inventory account.

On January 12, 2015, The Paint Palette Store received 40 gallons of interior paint base from Brewer Paint Supplies.

To record the inventory items received from Brewer Paint Supplies:

Step 1: Click the **Receive Inventory** icon in the *Vendors* section of the Home page. Select **Receive Inventory without Bill**.

Step 2: When the *Create Item Receipts* window appears, select Vendor: **Brewer Paint Supplies**.

Step 3: If a purchase order for the item exists, QuickBooks displays the following *Open POs Exist* window.

- Click **Yes** to receive against an open purchase order for Brewer Paint Supplies.

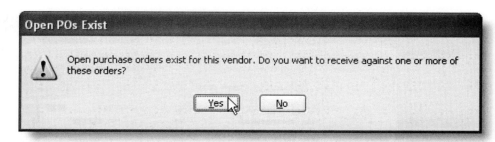

- When the following *Open Purchase Orders* window appears, select **Purchase Order No. 1** dated **01/03/2015**, then click **OK**.

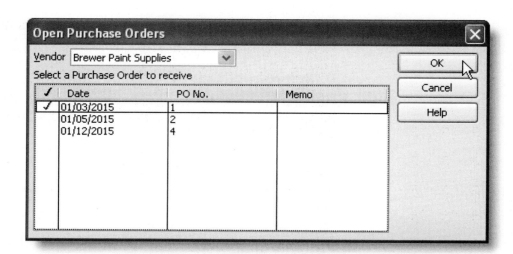

Step 4: The following *Create Item Receipts* window will appear. The quantity received (40 gallons) differs from the quantity ordered (50 gallons). Enter Quantity: **40**.

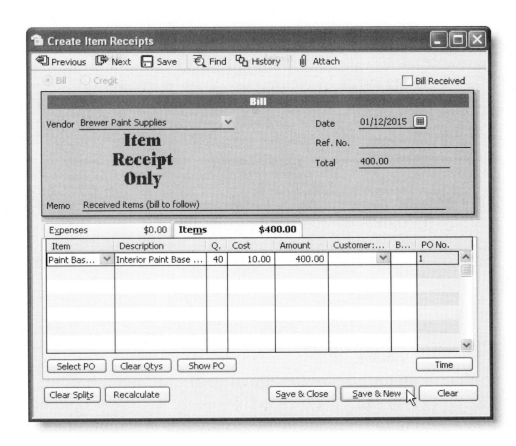

☑ *Total for items received is $400.00.*

Step 5: Click **Save & New** on the *Create Item Receipts* window to record the paint received and advance to a blank screen.

Step 6: Record the following inventory items received.

Vendor	Brewer Paint Supplies
Date	01/13/2015
PO No.	2
Item	1 gallon Exterior Paint Base
Quantity	40

Vendor	Brewer Paint Supplies
Date	01/14/2015
PO No.	4
Item	Stock Color
Quantity	10 (cartons)

Vendor	Shades of Santiago
Date	01/15/2015
PO No.	3
Item	Custom Color
Quantity	25 (cartons)
Item	Stock Color
Quantity	5 (cartons)

Step 7: Click **Save & Close** to record the items received and close the *Create Item Receipts* window.

Step 8: 🖶 **Print** the Item List showing the quantity on hand for each item in inventory.

ENTER BILLS

Bills can be entered in QuickBooks when the bill is received or when the bill is paid. (For more information, see Chapter 5.)

The Paint Palette Store will enter bills in QuickBooks when bills are received. At that time, QuickBooks records an obligation to pay the bill later (account payable). QuickBooks tracks bills due. If you use the reminder feature, QuickBooks will even remind you when it is time to pay bills.

The Paint Palette Store previously received 40 1-gallon cans of Interior Paint Base. To record the bill when it is received:

Step 1: Click the **Enter Bills Against Inventory** icon in the *Vendors* section of the Home page.

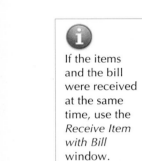

If the items and the bill were received at the same time, use the *Receive Item with Bill* window.

Step 2: The following *Select Item Receipt* window will appear.

- Select Vendor: **Brewer Paint Supplies**.

- Select Item Receipt corresponding to the bill (**Date: 01/12/2015**).

- Click **OK**.

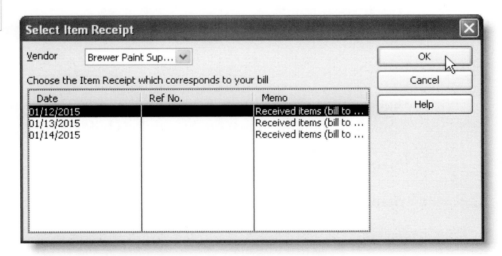

Step 3: When the following *Enter Bills* window appears, make any necessary changes. In this case, change the date to **01/15/2015** (the date the bill was received).

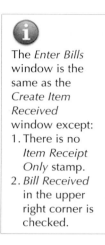

The *Enter Bills* window is the same as the *Create Item Received* window except:
1. There is no *Item Receipt Only* stamp.
2. *Bill Received* in the upper right corner is checked.

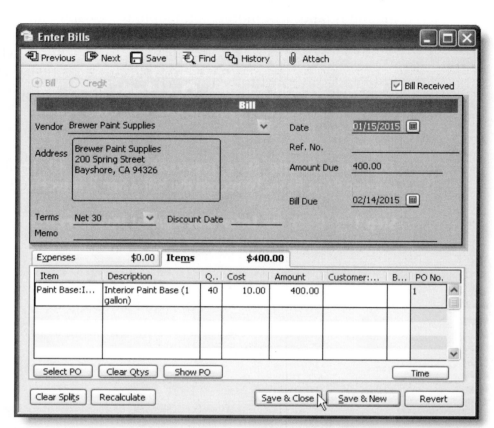

Step 4: The Amount Due of $400.00 should agree with the amount shown on the vendor's bill received.

Step 5: Click **Save & Close**.

Step 6: Record the following bills that The Paint Palette Store received.

Vendor	Brewer Paint Supplies
Date Bill Received	01/16/2015
Terms	Net 30
PO No.	2
Item	Exterior Paint Base (1 gallon)
Quantity	40
Vendor	Shades of Santiago
Date Bill Received	01/16/2015
Terms	Net 30
PO No.	3
Item	Custom Color
Quantity	25 cartons
Item	Stock Color
Quantity	5 cartons

> You could also use the *Enter Bills* window because there was no Purchase Order for the transaction.

Step 7: Click **Next** to enter the Hartzheim Leasing bill for January rent.

> Click the **Expenses** tab to record.

Vendor	Hartzheim Leasing
Date Bill Received	01/16/2015
Terms	Net 30
Amount Due	$1,000.00
Account	67100 Rent Expense
Memo	Rent

> With the *Enter Bills* window still open, click **Edit** menu > **Memorize Bill**.

Step 8: Record the bill for rent as a memorized transaction.

Step 9: Click **Save & Close** to record the bill and close the *Enter Bills* window.

When you enter bills, QuickBooks automatically adds the amount of the bill to Accounts Payable, reflecting your obligation to pay the bills later.

PAY BILLS

After receiving an inventory item and entering the bill in QuickBooks, the next step is to pay the bill when due. To pay the bill, select bills to pay, then 🖨 **print** the checks.

The Paint Palette Store will pay the bills for paint and paint color that have been received and recorded.

To pay bills in QuickBooks:

Step 1: Click the **Pay Bills** icon in the *Vendors* section of the Home page.

Step 2: When the *Pay Bills* window appears:
- Select: **Show All Bills**.
- Select bills from **Brewer Paint Supplies** and **Shades of Santiago**.
- Select **Checking** account.
- Select Payment Method: **To be Printed**.
- Select Payment Date: **01/31/2015**.

Step 3: Click **Pay Selected Bills** to close the *Pay Bills* window.

PRINT CHECKS

After selecting bills to pay, you can prepare checks in two different ways:

1. Write the checks manually, or

2. ▣ **Print** the checks using QuickBooks. If you use QuickBooks to print checks, preprinted check forms are inserted in the printer before printing.

If the *Payment Summary* window does not appear automatically, to print checks:

QuickBooks prints one check for each vendor, combining all amounts due the same vendor.

Step 1: Select **File** menu **> Print Forms > Checks**.

Step 2: Select **Checking** account.

Step 3: First Check No.: **402**.

Step 4: Select checks to print: **Brewer Paint Supplies** and **Shades of Santiago**. Then click **OK**.

Step 5: Select printer settings, then click **Print**.

RECORD SALES TRANSACTIONS

The sales cycle for a merchandising company consists of the following transactions:

1. Create an invoice to record the sale and bill the customer.

2. Receive the customer payments.

3. Deposit the customer payments in the bank.

Next, you will record each of these transactions in QuickBooks for The Paint Palette Store.

CREATE INVOICES

When inventory is sold to a customer, the sale is recorded on an invoice in QuickBooks. The invoice lists the items sold, the quantity, and the price. In addition, if the product is sold to a retail customer, sales tax is automatically added to the invoice.

To create an invoice:

Step 1: Click the **Create Invoices** icon in the *Customers* section of the Home page.

Step 2: Create and **print** invoices for the following sales made by The Paint Palette Store.

Sale of 3 gallons of custom color interior paint to Katrina Beneficio:

Date	01/20/2015
Customer	Katrina Beneficio
Terms	Net 30
Quantity	3 gallons
Item Code	Interior Paint Base (1 gallon)
Price Each	25.00
Quantity	3
Item Code	Custom Color
Price Each	6.00
To Be Printed	Yes
Tax Code	State Tax

> ☑ *The invoice total for Katrina Beneficio is $100.21.*

Sale of 10 gallons of stock color interior paint to Decor Centre.

Date	01/22/2015
Customer	Decor Centre
Terms	Net 30
Quantity	10 gallons
Item Code	Interior Paint Base (1 gallon)
Price Each	20.00
Quantity	10
Item Code	Stock Color
Price Each	3.50
To Be Printed	Yes
Tax Code	Non

Sale of 5 gallons stock color interior paint and 2 gallons customer color exterior paint to Cara Interiors:

Date	01/25/2015
Customer	Cara Interiors
Terms	Net 30
Quantity	5 gallons
Item Code	Interior Paint Base (1 gallon)
Price Each	20.00
Quantity	5
Item Code	Stock Color
Price Each	3.50
Quantity	2 gallons
Item Code	Exterior Paint Base (1 gallon)
Price Each	22.00
Quantity	2
Item Code	Custom Color
Price Each	5.00
To Be Printed	Yes
Tax Code	Non

If a customer pays cash at the time of sale, it is recorded using the *Sales Receipts* window.

RECEIVE PAYMENTS

When a credit sale is recorded, QuickBooks records an account receivable at the time the invoice is created. The account receivable is the amount that The Paint Palette Store expects to receive from the customer later.

To record a payment received from a customer:

Step 1: Click the **Receive Payments** icon in the *Customers* section of the Home page.

Step 2: Record the following payments received by The Paint Palette Store from customers.

Date Received	01/30/2015
Customer	Katrina Beneficio
Amount Received	100.21
Payment Method	Check
Check No.	1001

Date Received	01/31/2015
Customer	Cara Interiors
Amount Received	171.50
Payment Method	Check
Check No.	4567

MAKE DEPOSITS

When the customer's payment is deposited in The Paint Palette Store's Checking account, record the bank deposit in QuickBooks.

To record a bank deposit:

Step 1: Click the **Record Deposits** icon in the *Banking* section of the Home page.

Step 2: On January 31, 2015, record the deposit of customer payments received from **Katrina Beneficio** and **Cara Interiors**. Select Deposit To: **[Your Name] Checking**.

Step 3: 🖶 **Print** the deposit summary.

MAKE ADJUSTING ENTRIES

Before preparing financial statements for The Paint Palette Store for January, print a Trial Balance and make adjusting entries to bring the accounts up to date.

Step 1: 🖶 **Print** the Trial Balance for The Paint Palette Store at January 31, 2015.

Step 2: Make adjusting entries for The Paint Palette Store at January 31, 2015, using the following information:

- The store fixtures cost of $5,000 will be depreciated over a 10-year useful life with no salvage value. Depreciation expense is $42 per month.

- The paint mixing equipment cost of $4,000 will be depreciated over a 5-year useful life with no salvage value. Depreciation expense is $67 per month.

- The computer paint color match equipment cost of $1,000 will be depreciated over a four-year useful life with no salvage value. Depreciation expense is $21 per month.

- A count of supplies on hand at the end of January totaled $400. The Supplies on Hand account balance before adjustment is $600. Therefore, reduce (credit) the Supplies on Hand account by $200 and increase (debit) Account No. 64800 Supplies Expense by $200.

Step 3: 🖶 **Print** the Journal (including adjusting entries) for The Paint Palette Store for January 2015.

Step 4: 🖶 **Print** the Adjusted Trial Balance for The Paint Palette Store at January 31, 2015. Change the report title to Adjusted Trial Balance.

Step 5: ✏ On the Adjusted Trial Balance, **circle** the account balances affected by the adjusting entries.

> ☑ **Total debits on the Adjusted Trial Balance equal $13,656.71.**

PRINT REPORTS

To eliminate the 0.00 appearing for accounts with zero balances, from the *General Ledger* report window, select **Modify Report** button **> Advanced > In Use**.

🖨 **Print** the following reports for The Paint Palette Store for the month of January 2015.

- General Ledger
- Profit and Loss, Standard
- Balance Sheet, Standard
- Statement of Cash Flows

After reviewing the financial statements for The Paint Palette Store, what are your recommendations to improve financial performance?

SAVE CHAPTER 10

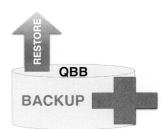

Save a backup of your Chapter 10 file using the file name: **[your name] Chapter 10 Backup.QBB**. See *Appendix B: Back Up & Restore QuickBooks Files* for instructions.

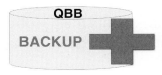

WORKFLOW

If you are using the workflow approach, leave your .QBW file open and proceed to Chapter 11.

RESTART & RESTORE

If you are using the Restart & Restore approach and are ending your computer session now, close your .QBW file and exit QuickBooks. When you restart, you will restore your backup file to complete Chapter 11.

PODCASTS

Watch the Chapter 10 **Podcast** at www.QuickBooksBlog.info to learn more about recording accounting transactions using QuickBooks.

MULTIPLE-CHOICE PRACTICE TEST

A **Multiple-Choice Practice Test** for Chapter 10 is on the *Computer Accounting for QuickBooks Pro* Online Learning Center at www.mhhe.com/kay2010. Try the Practice Test and see how many questions you answer correctly.

EXTRAS!

Section 3: Quick Guide contains quick, easy step-by-step directions for frequently used QuickBooks tasks, including correcting errors. You can find *Quick Guide* at the back of your text or online at www.mhhe.com/kay2010. *Check it out!*

Deliverables Checklist is a list of the reports and documents that you are to deliver to your instructor for grading. You can find the Deliverables Checklist at the end of the chapter or online at www.mhhe.com/kay2010. Staying organized saves time. Use the checklist to organize your reports, checking off the reports as completed. Then include the checklist with your reports for grading.

Appendix D: Electronic Deliverables shows you how to save your QuickBooks reports electronically. Also, watch the Electronic Deliverables Podcast at www.QuickBooksBlog.info. Check with your instructor to see if you should deliver your reports electronically.

Join the QuickBooks Student Community to ask questions and share tips @ www.QuickBooksBlog.info.

LEARNING ACTIVITIES

Important: Ask your instructor whether you should complete the following assignments by printing requested reports or creating electronic deliverables (see Appendix D: Electronic Deliverables).

EXERCISE 10.1: MUJERES YARNS

SCENARIO

Chel, owner of Mujeres Yarns, has asked you if you would be interested in maintaining the accounting records for her yarn shop. She would like to begin using accounting software for her accounting records, converting from her current manual accounting system. After reaching agreement on your fee, Chel gives you the following information to enter into QuickBooks.

TASK 1: NEW COMPANY SETUP

Step 1: Create a new company in QuickBooks for Mujeres Yarns using the following information.

Company name	[your name] Exercise 10.1 Mujeres Yarns
Legal name	[your name] Exercise 10.1 Mujeres Yarns
Federal tax ID	37-1872613
Address	13 Isla Boulevard
City	Bayshore
State	CA
Zip	94326
E-mail	[enter your own e-mail address]
Industry	Retail Shop or Online Commerce
Company organized as?	S Corporation

First month of fiscal year?	January
File name	[your name] Exercise 10.1
What do you sell?	Products only
Enter sales	Record each sale individually
Sell products online?	I don't sell online, but I may want to someday.
Sales tax	Yes
Estimates	No
Sales receipts	Yes
Billing statements	No
Invoices	Yes
Progress invoicing	No
Track bills you owe	Yes
Print checks?	Yes
Track inventory in QuickBooks?	Yes
Accept credit cards	I accept credit cards and debit cards.
Track time	Yes
Employees	No
Multiple currencies	No
Start date	01/01/2015
Add a bank account?	Yes
Bank account name	[your name] Checking
Bank account opened	On or after 01/01/2015
Use recommended income and expense accounts?	Yes

Step 2: Click **Finish** to exit the EasyStep Interview.

Step 3: From the **Company** menu, select **Company Information**. Select Income Tax Form Used: **Form 1120S (S Corporation)**.

TASK 2: ADD CUSTOMER & JOB

Step 1:   Add Ella Brewer to Mujeres Yarns Customer List.

Customer	Brewer, Ella
Address Info:	
First Name	Ella
Last Name	Brewer
Contact	Ella Brewer
Phone	415-555-3600
Address	18 Spring Street Bayshore, CA 94326

Additional Info:	
Terms	Net 15
Tax Code	Tax
Tax Item	State Tax

Payment Info:	
Account	10000
Preferred Payment	Check

Step 2:   Click **Next** to add Suzanne Counte to Mujeres Yarns Customer List.

Customer	Counte, Suzanne
Address Info:	
First Name	Suzanne
Last Name	Counte
Contact	Suzanne Counte
Phone	415-555-2160
Address	220 Johnson Avenue Bayshore, CA 94326

Additional Info:	
Terms	Net 15
Tax Code	Tax
Tax Item	State Tax

Payment Info:	
Account	12000
Preferred Payment	Check

Step 3: Click **OK**.

Step 4: 🖨 **Print** the Customer List using Excel.

Step 5: **Close** the Customer Center.

TASK 3: ADD VENDORS

Step 1: Add the following vendors to the Vendor List for Mujeres Yarns.

Vendor	Shahrzad Enterprises
Opening Balance	$0.00 as of 01/01/2015
Address Info:	
Company Name	Shahrzad Enterprises
Address	720 Yas Avenue Bayshore, CA 94326
Contact	Shahrzad
Phone	415-555-1270
Additional Info:	
Account	2400
Terms	Net 30
Tax ID	37-3571595

Vendor	Hartzheim Leasing
Opening Balance	$0.00 as of 01/01/2015
Address Info:	
Company Name	Hartzheim Leasing
Address	13 Appleton Drive Bayshore, CA 94326
Contact	Joe Hartzheim
Phone	415-555-0412
Additional Info:	
Account	2500
Type	Leasing
Terms	Net 30
Tax ID	37-1726354

Vendor	Roxanne's Supplies
Opening balance	$0.00 as of 01/01/2015
Address Info:	
Company Name	Roxanne's Supplies
Address	5 Austin Drive Bayshore, CA 94326
Contact	Roxanne
Phone	415-555-1700
Additional Info:	
Account	2600
Terms	Net 30
Tax ID	37-1599515

Step 2: 🖨 **Print** the Vendor List using Excel.

TASK 4: ADD ITEMS

Step 1: Add the following items for Mujeres Yarns using multiple list entries. Click **Next** after entering each item.

Item Type	Inventory Part
Item Name	Alpaca Yarn
Description	Alpaca Yarn 3 ply
Income Account	46000 – Merchandise Sales

Item Type	Inventory Part
Item Name	Alpaca Yarn-Creme Color
Subitem of	Alpaca Yarn
Description	Alpaca Yarn-Creme Color
Sales Price	10.00 (per skein)
Income Account	46000 – Merchandise Sales

Item Type	Inventory Part
Item Name	Alpaca Yarn-Earthen Tweed
Subitem of	Alpaca Yarn
Description	Alpaca Yarn-Earthen Tweed Color
Sales Price	12.00 (per skein)
Income Account	46000 – Merchandise Sales

Item Type	Inventory Part
Item Name	Peruvian Wool
Description	Peruvian Wool Yarn 4 ply
Income Account	46000 – Merchandise Sales

Item Type	Inventory Part
Item Name	Peruvian Wool Yarn-Charcoal
Subitem of	Peruvian Wool
Description	Peruvian Wool Yarn-Charcoal Color
Sales Price	20.00 (per skein)
Income Account	46000 – Merchandise Sales

Item Type	Inventory Part
Item Name	Peruvian Wool Yarn-Black
Subitem of	Peruvian Wool
Description	Peruvian Wool Yarn-Black Color
Sales Price	25.00 (per skein)
Income Account	46000 – Merchandise Sales

Step 2:   From the Item List, enter the 7.75% sales tax rate as follows:

- **Double-click** on **State Tax** in the Item List.

- Enter Tax Rate: **7.75%.**

- Enter Tax Agency: **California State Board of Equalization**.

Step 3:   ▣ **Print** the Item List using Excel.

TASK 5: CUSTOMIZE CHART OF ACCOUNTS

Edit the Chart of Accounts and enter opening balances as follows:

Step 1: Display account numbers in the Chart of Accounts.

Step 2: Enter the opening balance of $1,300 for the company Checking account:

- To open the Chart of Accounts, click the **Chart of Accounts** icon in the *Company* section of the Home page.

- Select **[your name] Checking** account. **Right-click** to display the popup menu.

- Select **Edit Account**.

- When the *Edit Account* window for the Checking account appears, enter Account No.: **10100**.

- Enter Opening Balance: **$1,300** as of **01/01/2015**.

- Click **OK**.

Step 3: Enter the opening balance of **$1,800** for the Inventory Asset account.

Step 4: Add the following Notes Payable account and opening balance of $800 to the Chart of Accounts.

Account No.	26000
Account Type	Other Current Liability
Account Name	Notes Payable
Account Description	Notes Payable
Tax Line	B/S-Liabs/Eq.: Other current liabilities
Opening Balance	$800 as of 01/01/2015

Step 5: 🖨 **Print** the Chart of Accounts report with opening balances for Mujeres Yarns.

Step 6: 🖨 **Print** a Trial Balance report for Mujeres Yarns dated **01/01/2015**. Compare your Trial Balance to the following to verify your account balances are correct.

		Trial Balance	
10100	[your name] Checking	1,300	
12100	Inventory Asset	1,800	
26000	Notes Payable		800
30000	Opening Balance Equity		2,300
	Totals	3,100	3,100

Step 7: Prepare the following opening adjustment using the Journal:
  - Transfer the Opening Balance Equity account balance to the Capital Stock account. Use Entry No. **Open ADJ 1**.

Step 8: 🖨 **Print** the opening Adjusted Trial Balance report for Mujeres Yarns dated **01/01/2015**.

TASK 6: ENTER TRANSACTIONS

Mujeres Yarns entered into the following transactions during January 2015.

- Record all deposits to: [your name] Checking.
- 🖨 **Print** invoices, checks, purchase orders, and deposit summaries as appropriate. Use memorized transactions for recurring transactions.

Record the following transactions for Mujeres Yarns.

Use *Write Checks* window, then create a memorized transaction.

Use *Enter Bills* window to record Office Supplies Expense.

Click **Yes** if asked to update cost.

Use *Create Invoices* window.

Date	Transaction
01/01/2015	Chel paid $600 store rent to Hartzheim Leasing (Check No. 1001).
01/02/2015	Purchased $300 in office supplies on account from Roxanne's Supplies.
01/13/2015	Placed the following order with Shahrzad Enterprises. ▪ 10 skeins of Alpaca creme yarn at a cost of $4 each ▪ 20 skeins of Alpaca earthen tweed yarn at a cost of $4.80 each
01/15/2015	Received Alpaca yarn ordered on 01/13/2015.
01/19/2015	Sold 6 skeins of Alpaca creme yarn to Suzanne Counte on account and 8 skeins of Alpaca earthen tweed yarn.
01/19/2015	Received bill from Shahrzad Enterprises for Alpaca yarn received on 01/15/2015.
01/21/2015	Ordered the following yarn from Shahrzad Enterprises on account. ▪ 20 skeins of Peruvian Wool in Charcoal @ $8 each ▪ 12 skeins of Peruvian Wool in Black @ $10 each
01/23/2015	Received the Peruvian Wool yarn ordered on 01/21/2015.
01/25/2015	Sold 13 skeins of Peruvian Wool Charcoal and 5 skeins of Peruvian Wool Black to Ella Brewer on account.
01/25/2015	Paid Shahrzad Enterprises for bill received on 01/19/2015 for Alpaca yarn (Check No. 1002).
01/25/2015	Received and deposited to the Checking account the customer payment from Suzanne Counte for sale of Alpaca yarn on 01/19/2015 (Check No. 1200).
01/27/2015	Paid $300 bill received from Roxanne's Supplies.

TASK 7: ADJUSTING ENTRIES

Step 1: 🖨 **Print** the Trial Balance report for Mujeres Yarns at January 31, 2015.

Step 2: Make an adjusting entry for Mujeres Yarns at January 31, 2015, using the following information.

- A count of supplies revealed $180 of supplies on hand. Since $300 of supplies were recorded as Office Supplies Expense when purchased and $180 still remain on hand unused, it is necessary to transfer $180 into an asset account, Supplies on Hand.

- Add a new account: **12500 Supplies on Hand**. Account Type: **Other Current Asset**.

- Make the adjusting entry to transfer $180 from the Office Supplies Expense account to the Supplies on Hand, an asset account.

Step 3: 🖨 **Print** the Journal report for January 2015, including the adjusting journal entry.

Step 4: 🖨 **Print** the Adjusted Trial Balance report for Mujeres Yarns at January 31, 2015.

Step 5: ✏ On the Adjusted Trial Balance report, **circle** the accounts affected by the adjusting entry.

TASK 8: FINANCIAL REPORTS

🖨 **Print** the following reports for Mujeres Yarns.

- General Ledger (Remember to omit unused accounts with zero balances from the deliverable.)
- Profit & Loss, Standard
- Balance Sheet, Standard
- Statement of Cash Flows

TASK 9: SAVE EXERCISE 10.1

Save a backup of your Exercise file using the file name: **[your name] Exercise 10.1 Backup.QBB**. See *Appendix B: Back Up & Restore QuickBooks Files* for instructions.

WORKFLOW

Exercise 11.1 is a continuation of Exercise 10.1.

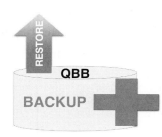

RESTART & RESTORE

If you use the restart and restore approach, you will restore your .QBB file when you restart Exercise 11.1.

EXERCISE 10.2 WHAT'S NEW

To explore new features of QuickBooks Pro 2010:

Step 1: In QuickBooks, click **Help** menu **> Learning Center Tutorials > What's New**.

Step 2: 🖨 **Print** the information about one new item for QuickBooks 2010 that you find most useful.

EXERCISE 10.3: WEB QUEST

When setting up a Chart of Accounts for a business, it is helpful to review the tax form that the business will use. Then accounts can be used to track information needed for the business tax return.

The tax form used by the type of organization is listed below.

Type of Organization	Tax Form
Sole Proprietorship	Schedule C (Form 1040)
Partnership	Form 1065 & Schedule K-1
Corporation	Form 1120
S Corporation	Form 1120S

In this exercise, you will download the tax form for a Subchapter S corporation from the Internal Revenue Service website.

Step 1: Go to the Internal Revenue Service website: www.irs.gov.

Step 2: Using the Forms and Publications link on the IRS website, find and 🖨 **print** Form 1120S: U.S. Income Tax Return for an S Corporation.

Step 3: ✏ **Circle** Advertising Expense on Form 1120S.

DELIVERABLES CHECKLIST CHAPTER 10
NAME:

INSTRUCTIONS:
1. **CHECK OFF THE DELIVERABLES YOU HAVE COMPLETED.**
2. **TURN IN THIS PAGE WITH YOUR DELIVERABLES.**

CHAPTER 10
- ☐ Customer List
- ☐ Vendor List
- ☐ Item List
- ☐ Chart of Accounts (Account Listing)
- ☐ Trial Balance
- ☐ Opening Adjusted Trial Balance
- ☐ Balance Sheet
- ☐ Check No. 401
- ☐ Purchase Orders
- ☐ Item List: Quantity on Hand
- ☐ Check Nos. 402 and 403
- ☐ Invoices
- ☐ Deposit Summary
- ☐ Trial Balance
- ☐ Journal
- ☐ Adjusted Trial Balance
- ☐ General Ledger
- ☐ Profit & Loss
- ☐ Balance Sheet
- ☐ Statement of Cash Flows

EXERCISE 10.1
- ☐ Task 2: Customer List
- ☐ Task 3: Vendor List
- ☐ Task 4: Item List
- ☐ Task 5: Chart of Accounts

☐ Task 5: Trial Balance
☐ Task 5: Opening Adjusted Trial Balance
☐ Task 6: Purchase Orders
☐ Task 6: Checks
☐ Task 6: Invoices
☐ Task 6: Deposit Summary
☐ Task 7: Trial Balance
☐ Task 7: Journal
☐ Task 7: Adjusted Trial Balance
☐ Task 8: General Ledger
☐ Task 8: Profit & Loss
☐ Task 8: Balance Sheet
☐ Task 8: Statement of Cash Flows

EXERCISE 10.2
☐ What's New

EXERCISE 10.3
☐ Form 1120S: U.S. Income Tax Return for an S Corporation

REFLECTION: A WISH AND A STAR ✶

Reflection improves learning and retention. Reflect on what you have learned after completing Chapter 10 that you did not know before you started the chapter.

A Star:

What did you like best that you learned about QuickBooks in Chapter 10?

A Wish:

If you could pick one thing, what do you wish you knew more about when using QuickBooks?

QUICKBOOKS PROJECT 10.1
TOMASO'S MOWERS & MORE

SCENARIO

On March 1, 2015, your friend Tomaso Moltissimo approaches you with another investment opportunity. He asks if you would like to buy stock in a business that sells lawn mowers and equipment. Tomaso would like to buy the business but needs additional investors.

Tomaso plans to invest $10,000 and you agree to invest $5,000 in the business. You also enter into an arrangement with Tomaso whereby you agree to help Tomaso with the accounting records for his new business in exchange for lawn service for your paint store.

TASK 1: SET UP A NEW COMPANY

Step 1: Create a new company in QuickBooks for Tomaso's Mowers & More using the following information.

Company name	[your name] Project 10.1 Tomaso's Mowers & More
Legal name	[your name] Project 10.1 Tomaso's Mowers & More
Federal tax ID	37-7879146
Address	2300 Olive Boulevard
City	Bayshore
State	CA
Zip	94326
E-mail	[enter your own e-mail address]
Industry	Retail Shop
Company organized as?	S Corporation
First month of fiscal year?	January

File name	[your name] Project 10.1
What do you sell?	Products only
Enter sales	Record each sale individually
Sell products online?	I don't sell online, and I am not interested in doing so.
Sales tax	Yes
Estimates	No
Sales receipts	Yes
Billing statements	No
Invoices	Yes
Progress billing	No
Track bills you owe	Yes
Print checks?	Yes
Track inventory in QuickBooks?	Yes
Accept credit cards	I accept credit cards and debit cards.
Track time	Yes
Employees	No
Multiple currencies	No
Start date	03/01/2015
Add a bank account?	Yes
Bank account name	[your name] Checking
Bank account opened	On or after 03/01/2015
Use recommended income and expense accounts?	Yes

Step 2: Click **Finish** to exit the EasyStep Interview.

TASK 2: CUSTOMER LIST

Create and 🖨 **print** a Customer List using Excel for Tomaso.

Customer	Fowler, Gerry
Opening Balance	$200.00 as of 03/01/2015
Address Info:	
First Name	Gerry
Last Name	Fowler
Contact	Gerry Fowler
Phone	415-555-9797
Alt. Phone	415-555-0599
Address	500 Lindell Blvd Bayshore, CA 94326
Additional Info:	
Type	Residential
Terms	Net 30
Tax Code	Tax
Tax Item	State Tax
Payment Info:	
Account	3001

Select **Add New**.

Customer	Stanton, Mike
Opening Balance	$0.00 as of 03/01/2015
Address Info:	
First Name	Mike
Last Name	Stanton
Contact	Mike Stanton
Phone	415-555-7979
Alt. Phone	415-555-0596
Alt. Contact	Work phone
Address	1000 Grand Avenue Bayshore, CA 94326

Additional Info:	
Type	Residential
Terms	Net 30
Tax Code	Tax
Tax Item	State Tax
Payment Info:	
Account	3002

Customer	Grady's Bindery
Opening Balance	$0.00 as of 03/01/2015
Address Info:	
Company Name	Grady's Bindery
First Name	Mike
Last Name	Grady
Contact	Mike Grady
Phone	415-555-7777
Address	700 Laclede Avenue Bayshore, CA 94326
Additional Info:	
Type	Commercial
Terms	Net 30
Tax Code	Tax
Tax Item	State Tax
Payment Info:	
Account	3003

TASK 3: VENDOR LIST

Create and 🖶 **print** a Vendor List using Excel for Tomaso's Mowers & More.

Vendor	Astarte Supply
Address Info:	
Company Name	Astarte Supply
Address	100 Salem Road Bayshore, CA 94326
Contact	Freyja
Phone	415-555-0500
Print on Check as	Astarte Supply

Additional Info:	
Account	4001
Type	Mowers
Terms	Net 30
Credit Limit	20,000.00
Tax ID	37-4327651
Opening Balance	$0 as of 03/01/2015

Vendor	Mower Sales & Repair
Address Info:	
Company Name	Mower Sales & Repair
Address	650 Manchester Road Bayshore, CA 94326
Contact	Mark
Phone	415-555-8222
Print on Check as	Mower Sales & Repair

Additional Info:	
Account	4002
Type	Mowers
Terms	Net 30
Credit Limit	10,000.00
Tax ID	37-6510541
Opening Balance	$0 as of 03/01/2015

Vendor	Hartzheim Leasing
Address Info:	
Company Name	Hartzheim Leasing
Address	13 Appleton Drive Bayshore, CA 94326
Contact	Joseph Hartzheim
Phone	415-555-0412
Print on Check as	Hartzheim Leasing

Additional Info:	
Account	4003
Type	Leasing
Terms	Net 30
Tax ID	37-1726354
Opening Balance	$0 as of 03/01/2015

TASK 4: ITEM LIST

Step 1: From the Item List, enter the 7.75% sales tax rate as follows:

- **Double-click** on **State Tax** in the Item List.

- Enter Tax Rate: **7.75%.**

- Enter Tax Agency: **California State Board of Equalization**.

Step 2: Enter the following items in the Item List for Tomaso's Mowers & More. If necessary, display account numbers.

Item Type	Inventory Part
Item Name	Mowers
Description	Lawn Mowers
COGS Account	50000 – Cost of Goods Sold
Tax Code	Tax
Income Account	46000 – Merchandise Sales
Asset Account	12100 – Inventory Asset
Quantity on Hand	0 as of 03/01/2015

Item Type	Inventory Part
Item Name	Riding Mower
Subitem of	Mowers
Description	48″ Riding Mower
Cost	2,000.00
COGS Account	50000 – Cost of Goods Sold
Tax Code	Tax
Sales Price	3800.00
Income Account	46000 – Merchandise Sales
Asset Account	12100 – Inventory Asset
Quantity on Hand	0 as of 03/01/2015

Item Type	Inventory Part
Item Name	Push Mower
Subitem of	Mowers
Description	Push Mower
Cost	400.00
COGS Account	50000 – Cost of Goods Sold
Tax Code	Tax
Sales Price	780.00
Income Account	46000 – Merchandise Sales
Asset Account	12100 – Inventory Asset
Quantity on Hand	0 as of 03/01/2015

Item Type	Inventory Part
Item Name	Propel Mower
Subitem of	Mowers
Description	Self-Propelled Mower
Cost	600.00
COGS Account	50000 – Cost of Goods Sold
Tax Code	Tax
Sales Price	1150.00
Income Account	46000 – Merchandise Sales
Asset Account	12100 – Inventory Asset
Quantity on Hand	0 as of 03/01/2015

Item Type	Inventory Part
Item Name	Trimmer
Description	Lawn Trimmer
COGS Account	50000 – Cost of Goods Sold
Tax Code	Tax
Income Account	46000 – Merchandise Sales
Asset Account	12100 – Inventory Asset
Quantity on Hand	0 as of 03/01/2015

Item Type	Inventory Part
Item Name	Gas Trimmer
Subitem of	Trimmer
Description	Gas-Powered Trimmer
Cost	300.00
COGS Account	50000 – Cost of Goods Sold
Tax Code	Tax
Sales Price	570.00
Income Account	46000 – Merchandise Sales
Asset Account	12100 – Inventory Asset
Quantity on Hand	0 as of 03/01/2015

Item Type	Inventory Part
Item Name	Battery Trimmer
Subitem of	Trimmer
Description	Rechargeable Battery-Powered Trimmer
Cost	200.00
COGS Account	50000 – Cost of Goods Sold
Tax Code	Tax
Sales Price	390.00
Income Account	46000 – Merchandise Sales
Asset Account	12100 – Inventory Asset
Quantity on Hand	0 as of 03/01/2015

Step 3:   **Print** an Item List using Excel for Tomaso's Mowers & More.

TASK 5: CUSTOMIZE THE CHART OF ACCOUNTS

Customize the Chart of Accounts for Tomaso's Mowers & More as follows:

Step 1: Display account numbers in the Chart of Accounts.

Step 2: Enter the opening balance for the company Checking account:
- To open the Chart of Accounts, click the **Chart of Accounts** icon in the *Company* section of the Home page.
- Select **[your name] Checking** account. **Right-click** to display the popup menu.
- Select **Edit Account**.
- When the *Edit Account* window for the Checking account appears, enter Account No.: **10100**.
- Enter Opening Balance: **$2,400** as of **03/01/2015**.
- Click **OK**.

Step 3: Add the following accounts and opening balances to the Chart of Accounts. Abbreviate account titles as necessary.

This loan will not be paid in one year; therefore, it is a long-term liability.

Account No.	26000
Account Type	Long Term Liability
Account Name	Notes Payable
Account Description	Notes Payable
Tax Line	B/S-Liabs/Eq.:L-T Mortgage/note/bond pay.
Opening Balance	$2,000 as of 03/01/2015

Account No.	12500
Account Type	Other Current Asset
Account Name	Supplies on Hand
Account Description	Supplies on Hand
Tax Line	B/S-Assets: Other current assets
Opening Balance	$500 as of 03/01/2015

Account No.	14000
Account Type	Fixed Asset
Account Name	Store Fixtures
Account Description	Store Fixtures
Tax Line	B/S-Assets: Buildings/oth.depr. assets
Opening Balance	$0 as of 03/01/2015

Account No.	14100
Account Type	Fixed Asset
Account Name	Store Fixtures Cost
Subaccount of	Store Fixtures
Account Description	Store Fixtures Cost
Tax Line	B/S-Assets: Buildings/oth.depr. assets
Opening Balance	$2500 as of 03/01/2015

Account No.	14200
Account Type	Fixed Asset
Account Name	Acc Depr - Store Fixtures
Subaccount of	Store Fixtures
Account Description	Acc Depr - Store Fixtures
Tax Line	B/S-Assets: Buildings/oth.depr. assets
Opening Balance	$0 as of 03/01/2015

Account No.	64800
Account Type	Expense
Account Name	Supplies Expense
Account Description	Supplies Expense
Tax Line	Other Deductions: Supplies

Step 4: 🖨 **Print** the Chart of Accounts (Account Listing) report for Tomaso's Mowers & More.

Step 5: ▣ **Print** a Trial Balance report for Tomaso's Mowers & More dated **03/01/2015**.

Step 6: Prepare the following opening adjustments using the Journal:

- Transfer $200 of Uncategorized Income to the Opening Balance Equity account. Use Entry No. **Open ADJ 1**.

- Transfer the Opening Balance Equity account balance to the Capital Stock account. Use Entry No. **Open ADJ 2**.

Step 7: ▣ **Print** the opening Adjusted Trial Balance report for Tomaso's Mowers & More dated **03/01/2015**.

TASK 6: RECORD TRANSACTIONS

Tomaso's Mowers & More entered into the following transactions during March 2015.

Step 1: Record the following transactions for Tomaso's Mowers & More. Customers are billed monthly. ▣ **Print** checks, purchase orders, invoices, and deposit summaries as appropriate. Use memorized transactions for recurring transactions.

Date	Transaction
03/01/2015	Tomaso Moltissimo invested $10,000 cash in stock of Tomaso's Mowers & More. You invested $5,000 cash in the stock of the business. Deposit the funds into the company Checking account.
03/01/2015	Paid $800 store rent to Hartzheim Leasing (Check No. 601).
03/02/2015	Purchased $300 in supplies on account from Mower Sales & Repair.

Use *Make Deposits* window.

Use *Write Checks* window, then create a memorized transaction.

Use *Enter Bills* window to record Office Supplies Expense.

Use *Create Invoices* window.

03/02/2015	Ordered (2) 48" riding mowers, 2 gas-powered trimmers, and 3 battery-powered trimmers from Astarte Supply.
03/04/2015	Received items ordered from Astarte Supply on 03/02/2015.
03/05/2015	Sold a 48" riding mower and a gas-powered trimmer to Grady's Bindery on account.
03/07/2015	Received bill from Astarte Supply.
03/09/2015	Ordered 2 self-propelled mowers and 1 push mower from Astarte Supply.
03/12/2015	Received only the self-propelled mowers ordered on 03/09/2015 from Astarte Supply.
03/13/2015	Received the bill from Astarte Supply for the self-propelled mowers only.
03/15/2015	Sold 1 self-propelled mower and 1 battery-powered trimmer to Mike Stanton on account.
03/16/2015	Sold a 48" riding mower to Gerry Fowler on account.
03/16/2015	Ordered (2) 48" riding mowers from Astarte Supply to restock inventory.
03/20/2015	Received and deposited the customer payment from Grady's Bindery (Check No. 401).
03/29/2015	Paid bill from Astarte Supply received on 03/07/2015 and due 04/06/2015. Paid $300 bill from Mower Sales & Repairs.
03/31/2015	Received and deposited payment from Mike Stanton (Check No. 3001).

| 03/31/2015 | Paid bill for self-propelled mowers due 04/12/2015. |
| 03/31/2015 | Paid $800 store rent to Hartzheim Leasing. |

Step 2: 🖶 **Print** the Check Register for March 2015.

TASK 7: ADJUSTING ENTRIES

Step 1: 🖶 **Print** the Trial Balance report for Tomaso's Mowers & More at March 31, 2015.

Step 2: Make adjusting entries for Tomaso's Mowers & More at March 31, 2015, using the following information.

- A count of supplies revealed $350 of supplies on hand.
- March depreciation expense for store fixtures was $35.

Step 3: 🖶 **Print** the Journal report for March 2015, including the adjusting journal entries.

Step 4: 🖶 **Print** the Adjusted Trial Balance report for Tomaso's Mowers & More at March 31, 2015.

Step 5: ✏ On the Adjusted Trial Balance report, **circle** the accounts affected by the adjusting entries.

TASK 8: FINANCIAL REPORTS

Step 1: 🖶 **Print** the following reports for Tomaso's Mowers & More.

- General Ledger (Remember to omit unused accounts with zero balances from the deliverable.)
- Profit & Loss, Standard
- Balance Sheet, Standard
- Statement of Cash Flows

- Accounts Receivable Aging Summary

Step 2: Using the financial statements, determine the balance of the Supplies Expense account and explain how the account balance was calculated. $_____

Step 3: Using the Balance Sheet, determine the amount of sales tax that Tomaso's Mowers & More collected and owes to the State Board of Equalization. $_____

Step 4: Discuss how the Accounts Receivable Aging Summary report might be used by a small business.

TASK 9: SAVE PROJECT 10.1

Save a backup of your Project 10.1 file using the file name: **[your name] Project 10.1 Backup.QBB**. See *Appendix B: Back Up & Restore QuickBooks Files* for instructions.

WORKFLOW

If you are using the workflow approach, leave your .QBW file open and proceed to Project 11.1.

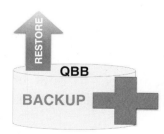

RESTART & RESTORE

If you are using the Restart & Restore approach and are ending your computer session now, close your .QBW file and exit QuickBooks. When you restart, you will restore your backup file to complete Project 11.1.

TASK 10: ANALYSIS AND RECOMMENDATIONS

Step 1: Analyze the financial performance of Tomaso's Mowers & More.

Step 2: What are your recommendations to improve the company's financial performance in the future?

DELIVERABLES CHECKLIST PROJECT 10.1
NAME:

INSTRUCTIONS:
1. **CHECK OFF THE DELIVERABLES YOU HAVE COMPLETED.**
2. **TURN IN THIS PAGE WITH YOUR DELIVERABLES.**

PROJECT 10.1

☐ Task 2: Customer List
☐ Task 3: Vendor List
☐ Task 4: Item List
☐ Task 5: Chart of Accounts
☐ Task 5: Trial Balance
☐ Task 5: Opening Adjusted Trial Balance
☐ Task 6: Invoices
☐ Task 6: Purchase Orders
☐ Task 6: Checks
☐ Task 6: Deposit Summaries
☐ Task 6: Check Register
☐ Task 7: Trial Balance
☐ Task 7: Journal
☐ Task 7: Adjusted Trial Balance
☐ Task 8: General Ledger
☐ Task 8: Profit & Loss
☐ Task 8: Balance Sheet
☐ Task 8: Statement of Cash Flows
☐ Task 8: Accounts Receivable Aging Summary

REFLECTION: A WISH AND A STAR ✮

Reflection improves learning and retention. Reflect on what you have learned after completing Project 10.1 that you did not know before you started the project.

A Star:

What did you like best that you learned about QuickBooks in Project 10.1?

A Wish:

If you could pick one thing, what do you wish you knew more about when using QuickBooks?

NOTES

CHAPTER 11
MERCHANDISING CORPORATION: PAYROLL

SCENARIO

After returning from his vacation, Wil Miles drops by the paint store to visit you and his former business. While the two of you are talking, customers in the store begin asking him for assistance. In cheerful good humor, he offers to tend the store for you while you go to lunch.

When you return after lunch, Wil tells you that Katrina Beneficio called, asking when you will have time to finish a paint job for her. Always ready to help, Wil suggests that you finish the Beneficio job while he watches the store.

When you return later that afternoon, Wil appears to be thoroughly enjoying himself as he restocks the shelves and waits on customers. By closing time, you and Wil have reached an agreement: you will hire him to manage the store full-time, freeing you to return to your painting. Wil has only one condition—he wants one month of vacation every year.

CHAPTER 11
LEARNING OBJECTIVES

In Chapter 11, you will learn about the following QuickBooks features:

INTRODUCTION

Chapter 11 is a continuation of Chapter 10.

In Chapter 11, you will account for payroll for The Paint Palette Store. In Chapter 10, you set up a new merchandising company, The Paint Palette Store, in QuickBooks. In this chapter, you will record a bank loan. Then you will set up payroll and record payroll transactions for The Paint Palette Store.

OPEN COMPANY FILE

To begin Chapter 11, first start QuickBooks software by clicking on the **QuickBooks desktop icon** or click **Start > Programs > QuickBooks > QuickBooks Pro 2010**.

WORKFLOW

Use the Workflow approach if you are using the same computer and the same .QBW file from the prior chapter.

Step 1: If your Chapter 10.QBW file is not already open, open it by selecting **File > Open Previous Company**. Select your **.QBW file.**

Step 2: Change the company name to **[your name] Chapter 11 Paint Palette Store** by selecting **Company** menu **> Company Information.**

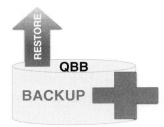

RESTART & RESTORE

Use the Restart & Restore approach if you are restarting your work session.

Step 1: Restore the **Chapter 10 Backup.QBB** file using the directions in *Appendix B: Back Up & Restore QuickBooks Files.*

You can restore your Chapter 10 Backup.QBB file from the previous chapter or use the data file that comes with the *Computer Accounting with QuickBooks* text available on CD or download from the Online Learning Center).

Step 2: After restoring the file, change the company name to **[your name] Chapter 11 Paint Palette Store** by selecting **Company** menu > **Company Information.**

BANK LOAN

Although The Paint Palette Store sales appear to be improving, business has been slower than you anticipated. As a result, you need an operating loan in order to pay your bills and Wil's salary.

The Paint Palette Store takes out a $4,000 operating loan from National Bank. You intend to repay the loan within one year.

Step 1: Create a new loan account: Note Payable: National Bank.

A loan to be repaid within 1 year is classified as Other Current Liability.

- Display the **Chart of Accounts**.

- Right-click to display the popup menu. Select **New**.

- Select Account Type: **Other Current Liability**.

- Enter Account Number: **26100**.

- Enter Account Name: **Note Payable-National Bank**.

- Enter Description: **Note Payable-National Bank**.

- Enter Tax Line: **B/S-Liabs/Eq.: Other current liabilities**.

- Enter Opening Balance: **$0.00** as of **02/01/2015**.

- Click **Save & Close** to save.

Because this loan was not an opening balance, the $4,000 is not recorded when the account is established in Step 1. Instead, it is recorded in a separate transaction in Step 2.

Step 2: When the bank deposits the $4,000 loan amount in your Checking account, record the loan as follows:

- From the *Banking* section of the Home page, select **Record Deposits**.

- Select Deposit To: **[your name] Checking**.

- Select Date: **02/01/2015**.

- Select From Account: **26100: Note Payable-National Bank**.

- Enter Amount: **4,000.00**.

- ▣ **Print** the **deposit summary**.

- Click **Save & Close**.

ENABLE PAYROLL

To enable QuickBooks payroll for The Paint Palette Store, complete the following steps:

Step 1:   Select **Edit** menu > **Preferences** > **Payroll & Employees** > **Company Preferences**.

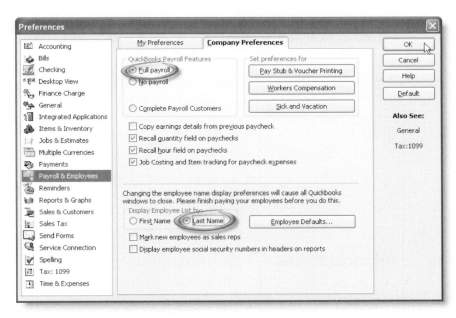

Step 2:   Select **Full payroll** to enable QuickBooks Payroll.

Step 3:   Select Display Employee List by: **Last Name**.

Step 4:   Click **OK** to close the *Preferences* window.

Chapter 6 covers payroll using QuickBooks payroll service. Chapter 11 covers QuickBooks manual payroll option.

QuickBooks Payroll

QuickBooks Pro and QuickBooks Premier provide various ways to process payroll. There are two general ways that a company can perform payroll calculations.

1. Use a QuickBooks payroll service.

2. Manually calculate payroll taxes.

Additional information about each option follows.

QuickBooks Payroll Services

When you subscribe to a QuickBooks payroll service, QuickBooks automatically calculates tax withholdings. To use the payroll services, you must pay a monthly fee and have an Internet connection.

QuickBooks offers three different levels of payroll services:

Basic Payroll	▪ Create paychecks using automatic calculation of payroll tax deductions.
	▪ Tax forms for filings are not automatically prepared. Entrepreneur must complete the tax forms or work with an accountant on payroll tax filings.
Enhanced Payroll	▪ Create paychecks using automatic calculation of payroll tax deductions.
	▪ Generate payroll tax forms for filings automatically.
	▪ File and pay taxes electronically.
Assisted Payroll	▪ Pay employees using QuickBooks.
	▪ Intuit processes payroll taxes and filings for the entrepreneur.

To view more information about each of the QuickBooks payroll services, select **Employees** menu > **Payroll** > **Learn About Payroll Options**.

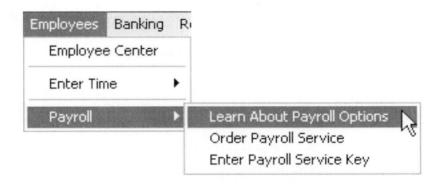

CALCULATE PAYROLL TAXES MANUALLY

If you do not use a QuickBooks payroll service, you must calculate tax withholdings and payroll taxes manually using IRS Circular E (Publication 15, Employer's Tax Guide). Then enter the amounts in QuickBooks to process payroll.

In Chapter 6, you processed payroll with tax deductions calculated automatically by QuickBooks. In this chapter, you will learn how to enter payroll tax amounts manually instead of using a payroll tax service.

PROCESS PAYROLL MANUALLY

Or you can access payroll setup by selecting **Employees** menu > **Payroll** > **Learn About Payroll Options.**

To enable manual paycheck entry:

Step 1: Select **Help** menu > **QuickBooks Help** > **Search** tab.

Step 2: Type **Process Payroll Manually** in the Search field.

Step 3: From the topics listed, select **Process payroll manually (without a subscription to QuickBooks Payroll)**.

Step 4: Select **manual payroll calculations** link.

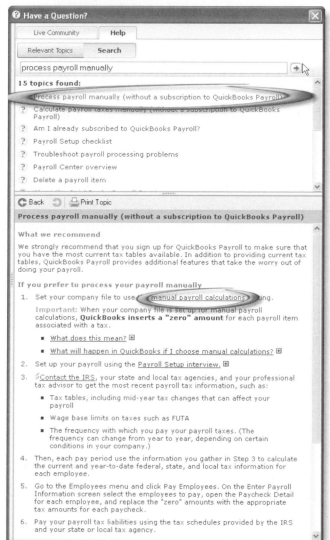

Step 5: When asked Are you sure you want to set your company file to use manual calculations? select **Set my company file to use manual calculations**.

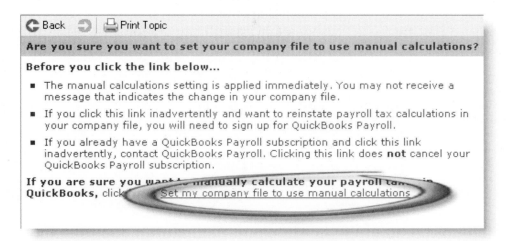

Step 6: Click **OK** when the following QuickBooks Information window appears.

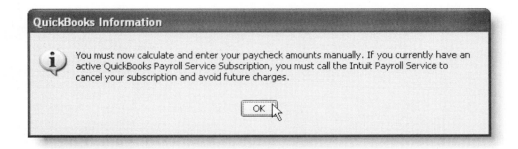

Step 7: Click **Show Coach Tips**. Click the 🛈 icon beside the Enter Time icon. The *Employees* section of the Home page should now appear as below. Notice that the Payroll Forms icon is not displayed when the company file is set to use manual payroll calculations.

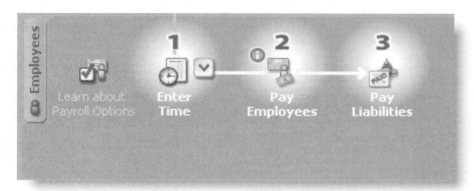

⚠️

If the *Employees* section of your Home page does not appear as shown here, close and then reopen the company file.

Step 8: From the *Employees* section select **Pay Employees**. If the following *QuickBooks Payroll Service* window appears, select **No**.

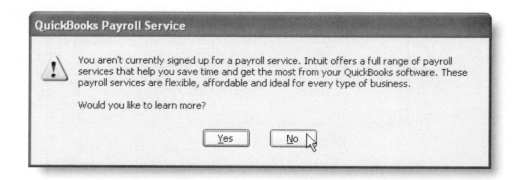

Step 9:   Select: **Go to Payroll Setup**.

Step 10:   If the *Live Community* window appears, click **Close** to close it. After reading the *Welcome to QuickBooks Payroll Setup* window, click **Continue**.

Step 11:   When the *Company Setup: Compensation and Benefits* window appears, click **Continue**.

Step 12: When the *Add New* window appears, select the following options, then click **Finish**.

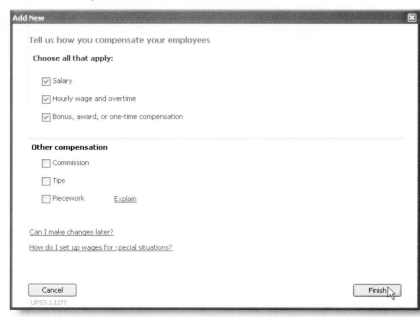

Step 13: Click **Continue** when the following *Compensation list* window appears.

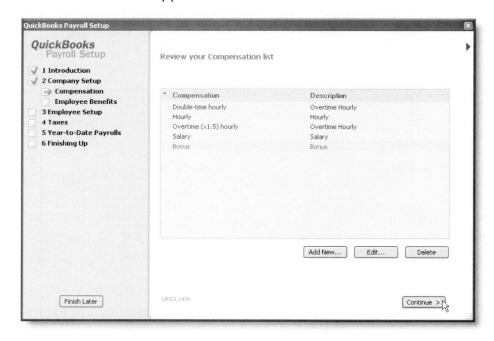

Step 14: Click **Continue** when the *Set up employee benefits* window appears.

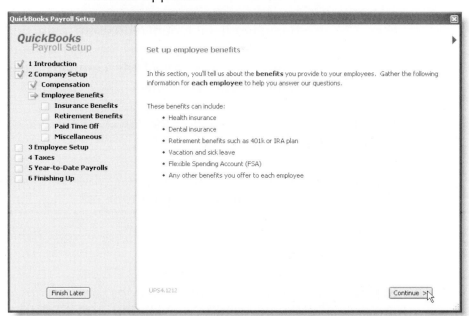

Step 15: If you needed to set up insurance benefits, you would select the appropriate items on this screen. Since you are not providing insurance benefits to your employee, select: **My company does not provide insurance benefits**. Click **Finish**.

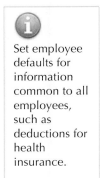

Set employee defaults for information common to all employees, such as deductions for health insurance.

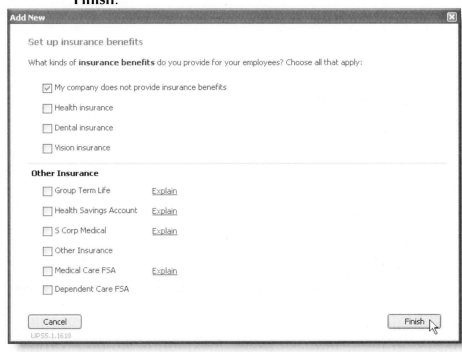

Step 16: Click **Continue** when the *Review your Insurance Benefits list* window appears.

Step 17: If your payroll included retirement plan deductions, you would indicate those items on this screen. Since your company does not, select **My company does not provide retirement benefits > Finish**.

Step 18: Click **Continue** when the *Review your Retirement Benefits list* window appears.

Step 19: When the *Set up paid time off* window appears, select: **My employees do not get paid time off**. Click **Finish**.

Step 20: Click **Continue** when the *Review your Paid Time Off list* window appears**.**

Step 21: When the *Set up additions and deductions* window appears, select: **Donation to charity > Next > Finish**.

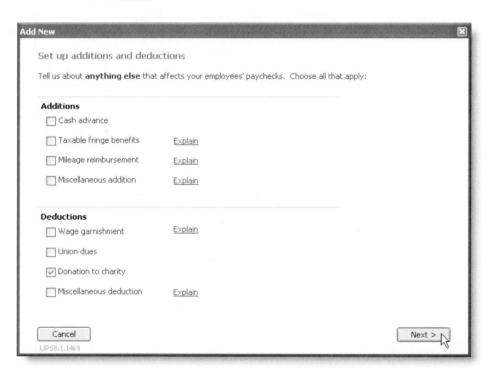

Step 22: Click **Continue** when the *Review your Additions and Deductions list* window appears.

Step 23: Click **Continue** when the *Set up your employees* window appears.

Step 24: When the *New Employee* window appears, enter the following information for Wil Miles. Click **Next**.

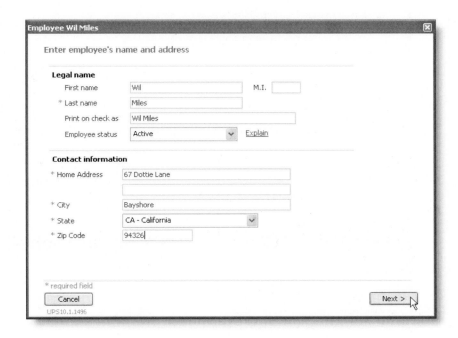

Step 25: Enter Wil Miles hiring information as follows. Click **Next**.

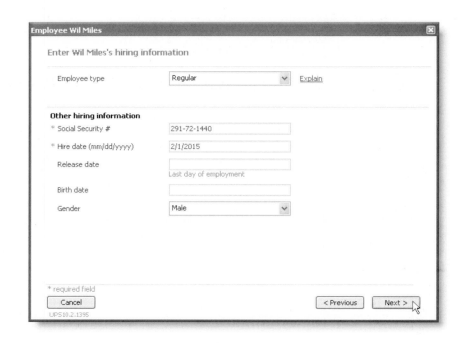

Step 26: Enter Wil Miles compensation information as follows. Click **Next**.

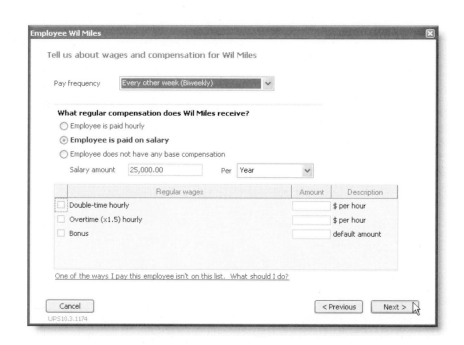

Step 27: When the *Tell us about benefits for Wil Miles* window appears, enter the information as follows. Click **Next**.

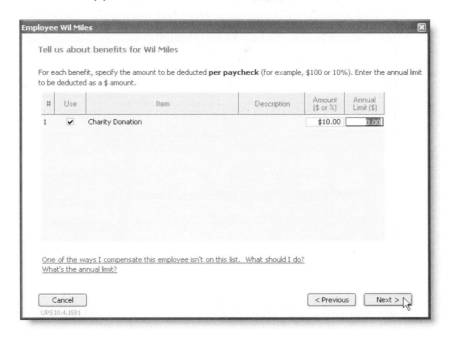

Step 28: When the Wil Miles *Direct Deposit* window appears, leave it **unchecked**, and click **Next**.

Step 29: When the *Tell us where Wil Miles is subject to taxes* window appears, enter the following information. Click **Next**.

Employee Wil Miles

Tell us where Wil Miles is subject to taxes

* State subject to withholding	CA - California ▾ Explain
	Usually where the employee lives
* State subject to unemployment tax	CA - California ▾ Explain
	Usually where the employee works

While working for you in 2009, did Wil Miles live or work in another state?

◉ No
○ Yes

When should an employee be marked as exempt from a tax?

* required field

Cancel   < Previous   Next >

UPS10.8.1605

Step 30: Enter Wil Miles federal tax information as follows. Click **Next**.

Employee Wil Miles

Enter federal tax information for Wil Miles

Filing Status	Married ▾ Explain
Allowances	2 Explain
Extra Withholding	Explain
Nonresident Alien Withholding	Does not apply ▾ Explain

Withholdings and Credits:
Most employees' wages are **subject to** the following withholdings; also, most employees are **not eligible** for the Advance Earned Income Credit. Incorrectly changing the selections below will cause your taxes to be calculated incorrectly, resulting in penalties; be sure to check with your tax agency or accountant if you are unsure.

☑ Subject to Medicare   Explain

☑ Subject to Social Security   Explain

☑ Subject to Federal Unemployment

☐ Subject to Advance Earned Income Credit   Explain

Cancel   < Previous   Next >

UPS10.11.1477

Step 31: Enter Wil Miles state income tax information as follows. Click **Next**.

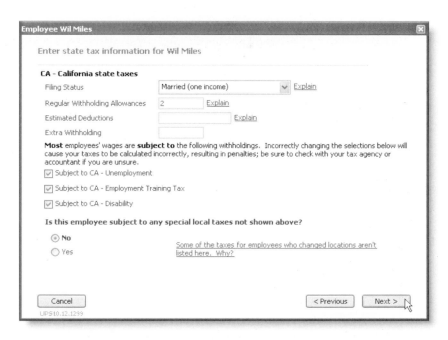

Step 32: When the *Wage Plan* window appears, select Wage Plan Code: **S (State Plan For Both UI and DI)**. Click **Finish**.

Step 33: Review the Employee List, then click **Continue**.

Step 34: When the *Set up your payroll taxes* window appears, click **Continue**.

Step 35: Click **Continue** when the *Here are the federal taxes we set up for you* window appears.

Step 36: When the *Set up state payroll taxes* window appears enter the information as follows. Click **Finish**.

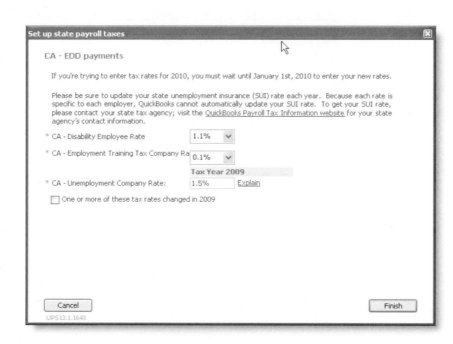

Step 37: Click **Continue** when the *Review your state taxes* window appears.

Step 38: If necessary, click **Next** when the *Schedule your tax payments* window appears.

Step 39: Enter the information as follows in the *Set up payment schedule for Federal 940* window. Click **Next**.

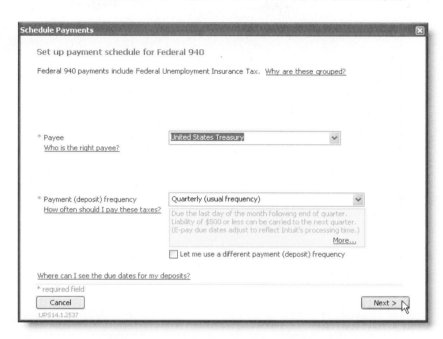

Step 40: When the following *Set up payment schedule for Federal 941/944* window appears, enter the following information. Click **Next**.

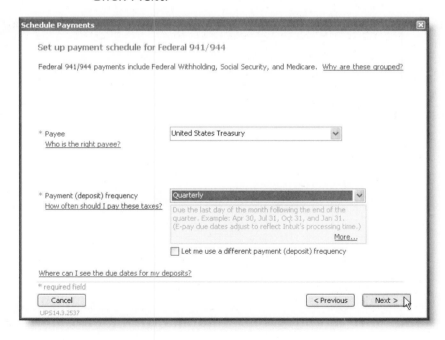

Step 41: Enter the following information in the *Set up payment schedule for CA Withholding and Disability Insurance* window. Click **Next**.

Schedule Payments

Set up payment schedule for CA Withholding and Disability Insurance

CA Withholding payments include Income Tax Withholdings and State Disability Insurance. <u>Why are these grouped?</u>

* Payee — EDD
<u>Who is the right payee?</u>

* CA Employment Development Dept Employer Acct No. — 999-9999-9
<u>What number do I enter?</u>

* Payment (deposit) frequency — Quarterly
<u>How often should I pay these taxes?</u>

Due the last day of the month following the end of the quarter. Example: Apr 30, Jul 31, Oct 31, and Jan 31. (E-pay due dates adjust to reflect Intuit's processing time.)
<u>More...</u>

☐ Let me use a different payment (deposit) frequency

<u>Where can I see the due dates for my deposits?</u>

* required field

Cancel | < Previous | Next >

UPS14.5.2537

Step 42: Enter the following information in the *Set up payment schedule for CA UI and Employment Training Tax* window. Click **Finish**.

Schedule Payments

Set up payment schedule for CA UI and Employment Training Tax

CA UI payments include Unemployment Insurance and Employment Training Tax. <u>Why are these grouped?</u>

* Payee — EDD
<u>Who is the right payee?</u>

* CA Employment Development Dept Employer Acct No. — 999-9999-9
<u>What number do I enter?</u>

* Payment (deposit) frequency — Quarterly (usual frequency)
<u>How often should I pay these taxes?</u>

Due the last day of the month following the end of the quarter. Example: Apr 30, Jul 31, Oct 31, and Jan 31. (E-pay due dates adjust to reflect Intuit's processing time.)
<u>More...</u>

☐ Let me use a different payment (deposit) frequency

<u>Where can I see the due dates for my deposits?</u>

* required field

Cancel | < Previous | Finish

UPS14.7.2537

Step 43: When the *Review your Scheduled Tax Payments list* window appears, click **Continue**.

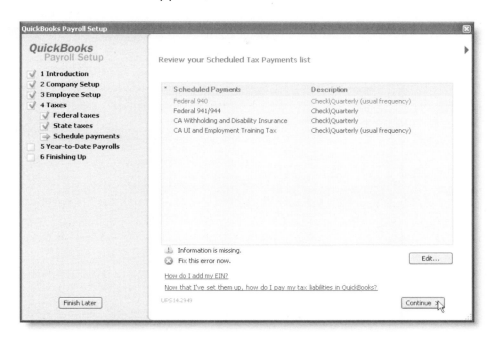

Step 44: Click **Continue** when the *Year-to-date payrolls* window appears.

Step 45: When asked if your company has issued paychecks this year, select **No > Continue**.

Step 46: Click **Go to Payroll Center** when the following *Setup is complete* window appears. The Employee Center should appear.

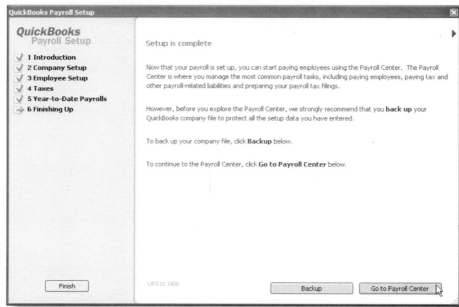

PRINT EMPLOYEE LIST

🖨 **Print** the Employee information as follows:

Step 1: From the Employee Center, select **Excel > Export Employee List**.

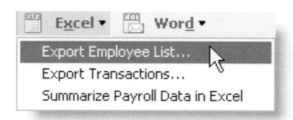

Step 2: 🖨 **Print** the Employee List using Excel.

Step 3: **Close** the Employee Center.

PRINT PAYCHECKS

As you may recall from Chapter 6, processing payroll using QuickBooks involves the following steps:

1. Create paychecks for the employees.

2. Print the paychecks.

3. Pay payroll liabilities, such as federal and state income tax withheld.

4. Print payroll forms and reports.

When you create paychecks using QuickBooks, you must deduct (withhold) the following items from employees' pay:

- Federal income taxes.
- State income taxes.
- Social security (employee portion).
- Medicare (employee portion).

The amounts withheld for taxes are determined by tax tables that change periodically. Intuit offers two different ways for a company to perform payroll calculations:

1. **Use a QuickBooks Payroll Service**. For more information about QuickBooks Payroll Services, select **Employees** menu **> Payroll Service Options > Learn About Payroll Options**.

2. **Manually calculate payroll taxes**. You can manually calculate tax withholdings and payroll taxes using IRS Circular E. Then enter the amounts in QuickBooks to process payroll.

In this chapter, you will learn how to enter payroll tax amounts manually.

Wil Miles was hired by The Paint Palette Store on February 1, 2015. He is paid an annual salary of $25,000. Wil will be paid biweekly, receiving a paycheck every two weeks. Therefore, the first pay period ends on February 14 and Wil is paid February 15.

To create a paycheck for Wil Miles:

Step 1: From the *Employees* section of the Home page, click the **Pay Employees** icon.

Step 2: If the following window appears, click **No**.

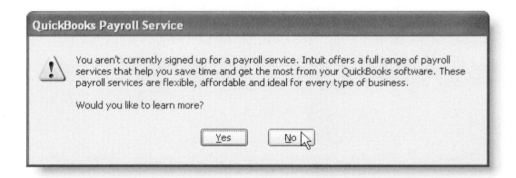

Step 3: When the following *Enter Payroll Information* window appears:

The Check Date (payday) is the day the check is prepared; the Pay Period Ends date is the last day the employee works during the pay period.

- Select Bank Account: **[your name] Checking**.
- Enter Pay Period Ends: **02/14/2015**.
- Enter Check Date: **02/15/2015**.
- Select Employee: **Wil Miles**.
- Click **Continue**.

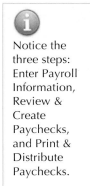

Notice the three steps: Enter Payroll Information, Review & Create Paychecks, and Print & Distribute Paychecks.

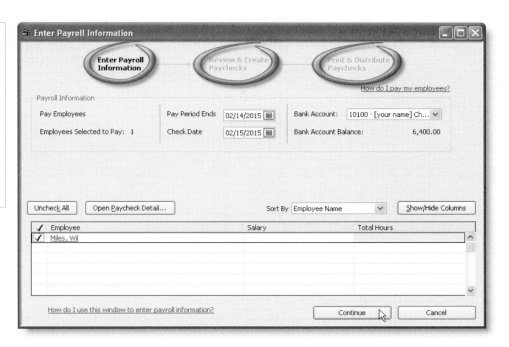

Step 4: When the *Review and Create Paychecks* window appears, select Wil Miles' name and click **Open Paycheck Detail**.

Step 5: In the *Preview Paycheck* window enter the following information:

- In the *Employee Summary* section, the Salary amount of $961.54 and Charity Donation of $-10.00 will automatically appear.

- In the *Employee Summary* section, enter Federal Withholding: **-75.00**.

- In the *Employee Summary* section, enter Social Security Employee: **-60.00**.

- In the *Employee Summary* section, enter Medicare Employee: **-14.00**.

- In the *Company Summary* section, enter Social Security Company: **60.00**.

- In the *Company Summary* section, enter Medicare Company: **14.00**.

- Leave all other amounts at $0.00.

- Click **Save & Close**.

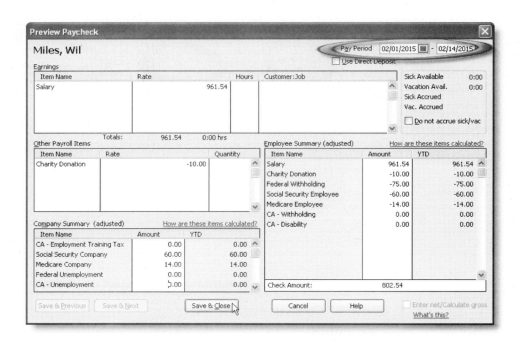

Step 6: When returning to the *Review and Create Paychecks* window:

- Select Paycheck Options: **Print paychecks from QuickBooks**.

- Select **Create Paychecks**.

Step 7: When the *Confirmation and Next Steps* window appears, click **Print Paychecks**.

Step 8: When the *Select Paychecks to Print* window appears, select **Wil Miles**. Enter Check Number **404**. Click **OK**.

When voucher checks are used, paystub information is printed on the voucher. If standard checks are used, print paystubs by clicking **File** menu > **Print Forms** > **Paystubs**.

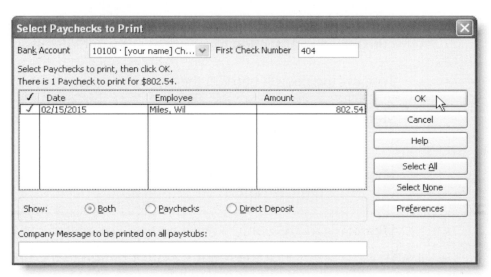

Step 9: Select the following print settings:

- Select **Voucher Checks**.
- Select **Print company name and address**.
- 🖨 Click **Print**.

Step 10: Create and 🖨 **print** paychecks to pay Wil Miles through the end of March 2015.

Check Date	Pay Period
03/01/2015	02/15/2015 – 02/28/2015
03/15/2015	03/01/2015 – 03/14/2015
03/29/2015	03/15/2015 – 03/28/2015

Step 11: Click **Close** to close the *Confirmation and Next Steps* window.

QuickBooks records gross pay (the total amount the employee earned) as salaries expense and records the amounts due tax agencies as payroll tax liabilities.

PRINT PAYROLL JOURNAL ENTRIES

Wil Miles' wages are recorded as payroll expense.

Withholdings from his paycheck, such as amounts owed tax agencies, are payroll liabilities.

Payroll taxes the company must pay, such as employer share of Social Security and Medicare, are recorded as payroll expense.

When QuickBooks records paychecks and payroll tax liabilities, it converts the transaction to a journal entry with debits and credits.

To view the payroll entry in the Journal:

Step 1: From the Report Center, select **Accountant & Taxes > Journal**.

Step 2: Select Dates From: **02/01/2015** To: **02/15/2015**. Click **Display report**.

Step 3: To view only payroll entries, use a filter:

- Click the **Modify Report** button in the upper left corner of the *Journal* window.
- Click the **Filters** tab.
- Choose filter: **Transaction Type**.
- Select Transaction Type: **Paycheck**.
- Click **OK**.

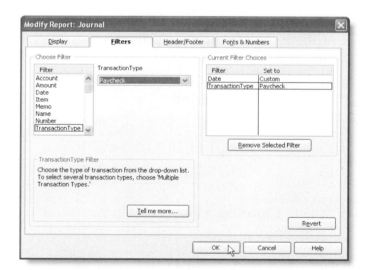

Step 4: 🖶 **Print** the Journal report.

Step 5: **Close** the *Journal* window, then close the Report Center.

PAY PAYROLL LIABILITIES

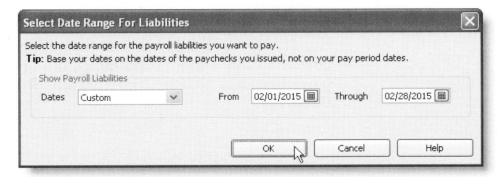

Typically, a small company deposits payroll withholdings and payroll taxes with a local bank. The local bank then remits the amount to the IRS on behalf of the company.

Payroll liabilities include amounts The Paint Palette Store owes to outside agencies including:

- Federal income taxes withheld from employee paychecks.
- State income taxes withheld from employee paychecks.
- FICA (Social Security and Medicare) taxes, both the employee and the employer portions.
- Unemployment taxes.

By the fifteenth of each month, The Paint Palette Store is required to remit federal income tax withheld and the employee and employer portions of Social Security and Medicare taxes from the previous month's paydays. The store plans to make its monthly deposits of these federal taxes by the tenth of each month.

To pay payroll taxes:

Step 1: Click the **Pay Liabilities** icon in the *Employee*s section of the Home page.

Step 2: When the *Select Date Range for Liabilities* window appears, enter dates from **02/01/2015** through **02/28/2015**. Click **OK**.

FYI: QuickBooks calculates payroll liabilities based on check dates rather than the pay period. Accordingly, the March 10 payroll liability check covers obligations arising only from the payroll check dated 02/15/2015.

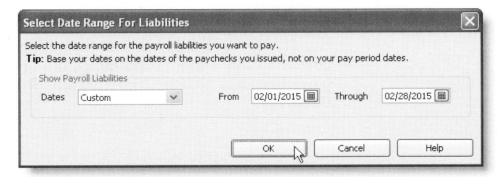

Step 3: When the *Pay Liabilities* window appears:

- Select Checking Account: **[your name] Checking**.

- Select Check Date: **03/10/2015**.

- Check: **To be printed**.

- Select the following amounts to pay:

  ✓ Federal Withholding
  ✓ Medicare Company
  ✓ Medicare Employee
  ✓ Social Security Company
  ✓ Social Security Employee

- Select: **Review liability check to enter expenses/penalties**.

Step 4: Click **Create** to view the check to pay the payroll liabilities selected.

Step 5: To ▤ **print** the check:

- Click the **Print** button at the top of the *Liability Check* window.

- Enter the check number: **408**, then click **OK**.

- Select **Voucher** checks.

- Select **Print company name and address**.

- Click **Print**.

Step 6: Record and ▤ **print** the check to pay payroll liabilities for the pay period **03/01/2015** to **03/31/2015** to be paid on **04/10/2015**.

QuickBooks calculates payroll liabilities based on check dates rather than the pay period. Accordingly, the April 10 payroll liability check covers obligations arising from the payroll checks dated 03/01/2015, 03/15/2015, and 03/29/2015.

PROCESS PAYROLL FORMS

Businesses that have employees and payroll are required to file payroll forms with specific governmental tax agencies. These payroll forms summarize the payroll tax amounts withheld and paid. If you subscribe to a QuickBooks payroll service, you will have a Process Payroll Forms icon in the *Employees* section of the Home page. The QuickBooks payroll service will automatically complete the payroll tax forms.

If you are using a QuickBooks payroll service, the payroll amounts are automatically transferred to the payroll tax form.

If you are using QuickBooks to manually process payroll, then basically there are three steps to processing payroll tax forms:

1. Print the appropriate payroll reports in QuickBooks to obtain the necessary information to complete the payroll tax forms.

2. Find the payroll tax forms (940 and 941) on the IRS website (www.irs.gov).

3. Manually transfer the information from the QuickBooks payroll reports to the IRS payroll tax forms.

The Paint Palette Store is processing payroll manually using QuickBooks. When The Paint Palette Store pays federal payroll taxes, it must file a Form 941 to report the amount of federal income tax withheld and Social Security and Medicare taxes for the quarter. QuickBooks tracks the amounts to report on the Form 941. However, you must manually transfer the amounts from QuickBooks reports into the payroll tax forms.

To complete payroll tax Form 941 (Employer's Quarterly Federal Tax Return) for The Paint Palette Store for the first quarter of 2015:

Step 1: Obtain the amounts to manually prepare your payroll forms:

- Select **Reports** menu > **Employees & Payroll > More Payroll Reports in Excel > Tax Form Worksheets**.

- If necessary, follow the onscreen instructions to enable macros.

- Select **Quarterly 941**.

- Enter Dates: **01/01/2015** To: **03/31/2015**.

- Check **Refresh from QuickBooks**.
- Click the **Create Report** button.

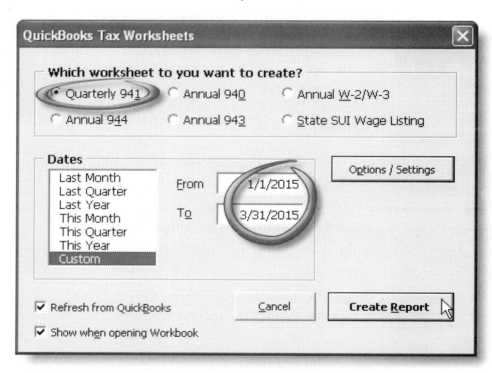

- When the *QuickBooks Tax Worksheets* window appears, click **OK**.

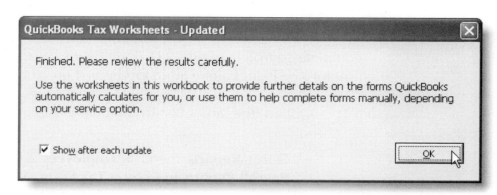

- **Print** the Excel 941 Summary.

Step 2: Find Form 941, Employer's Quarterly Federal Tax Return, on the IRS website at www.irs.gov.

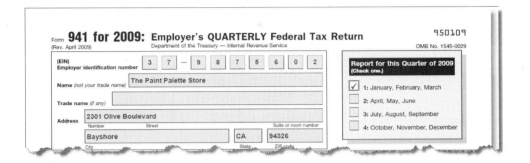

Step 3: Complete Form 941 using amounts from your QuickBooks Tax Worksheet.

You may enter amounts in Form 941 onscreen before printing or print the blank form and enter amounts by hand.

- You may enter amounts in Form 941 onscreen before printing or print the blank form and enter amounts by hand.

- Enter number of employees: **1**.

- Apply any overpayment to the next return.

- Enter state code for California: **CA**.

- Note that the dates on the IRS Form 941 may differ from your QuickBooks report.

Form 941 is filed with the IRS to report the amount of federal income tax and Medicare and Social Security taxes associated with the company's payroll for the first quarter of the year. Form 941 for the first quarter of the year must be filed by April 30.

Processing payroll using a QuickBooks payroll service is also covered in Chapter 6.

If you subscribe to a QuickBooks payroll service, QuickBooks permits you to print Form 941 directly from QuickBooks software. When using a QuickBooks payroll service to print Form 941 (Employer's Quarterly Federal Tax Return), you would complete the following.

Step 1: Click the Process Payroll Forms icon in the *Employees* section of the Home page.

Step 2: Select Payroll Form: Federal Form.

Step 3: When the *Select Payroll Form* window appears:
- Select: Quarterly Form 941/Schedule B.
- Select Quarter.
- Click OK.

Step 4: If a message appears stating that QuickBooks must close all windows or asking if you have downloaded the latest forms, click OK.

Step 5: When asked if you need to file a Schedule B, select No.

Step 6: Enter the state. Click Next.

Step 7: On Form 941 Line 1, enter number of employees.

Step 8: On Form 941, Line 15 Overpayment, select: Apply to next return.

Step 9: Click Check for errors. If QuickBooks tells you there are no errors, then click Print forms to print Form 941.

Step 10: Select: Tax form(s) and filing instructions. Click Print.

Step 11: Click Save & Close to close the *Form 941* window. Read Next Steps if any, then click OK to close the *Next Steps* window.

PRINT PAYROLL REPORTS

QuickBooks provides payroll reports that summarize amounts paid to employees and amounts paid in payroll taxes. Payroll reports can be accessed using the Report Center.

📧 **Print** the Payroll Summary report:

Step 1: From the Report Center select **Employees & Payroll > Payroll Summary**.

Step 2: Select Dates From: **02/01/2015** To: **02/28/2015**. Click **Display report**.

Step 3: 📧 **Print** the Payroll Summary report using **Portrait** orientation.

SAVE CHAPTER 11

Save a backup of your Chapter 11 file using the file name: **[your name] Chapter 11 Backup.QBB**. See *Appendix B: Back Up & Restore QuickBooks Files* for instructions.

PODCASTS

Watch the Chapter 11 **Podcast** at www.QuickBooksBlog.info to view a screencast of QuickBooks payroll features.

MULTIPLE-CHOICE PRACTICE TEST

A **Multiple-Choice Practice Test** for Chapter 11 is on the *Computer Accounting for QuickBooks Pro* Online Learning Center at www.mhhe.com/kay2010. Try the Practice Test and see how many questions you answer correctly.

EXTRAS!

Section 3: Quick Guide contains quick, easy step-by-step directions for frequently used QuickBooks tasks, including correcting errors. You can find *Quick Guide* at the back of your text or online at www.mhhe.com/kay2010. *Check it out!*

Deliverables Checklist is a list of the reports and documents that you are to deliver to your instructor for grading. You can find the Deliverables Checklist at the end of the chapter or online at www.mhhe.com/kay2010. Staying organized saves time. Use the checklist to organize your reports, checking off the reports as completed. Then include the checklist with your reports for grading.

Appendix D: Electronic Deliverables shows you how to save your QuickBooks reports electronically. Also, watch the Electronic Deliverables Podcast at www.QuickBooksBlog.info. Check with your instructor to see if you should deliver your reports electronically.

Join the QuickBooks Student Community to ask questions and share tips @ www.QuickBooksBlog.info.

LEARNING ACTIVITIES

Important: Ask your instructor whether you should complete the following assignments by printing requested reports or creating electronic deliverables (see Appendix D: Electronic Deliverables).

EXERCISE 11.1: MUJERES YARNS TIME TRACKING

SCENARIO

Exercise 11.1 is a continuation of Exercise 10.1.

Chel, the owner of Mujeres Yarns, has a good friend, Roxanne, who enjoys knitting and likes to spend time at the store in the knitting corner. Roxanne agrees to watch the store when Chel is busy or needs to take deposits to the bank. Roxanne will not be paid for her time, but Chel would like to keep track of the hours. You advise Chel that it is possible to permit Roxanne access to the time-tracking feature of QuickBooks but restrict her access to other areas and to closed periods.

TASK 1: OPEN COMPANY FILE

WORKFLOW

Use the Workflow approach if you are using the same computer and the same .QBW file from the prior Exercise 10.1.

Step 1: If your Exercise 10.1.QBW file is not already open, open it by selecting **File > Open Previous Company**. Select your **.QBW file.**

Step 2: Change the company name to **[your name] Exercise 11.1 Mujeres Yarns** by selecting **Company** menu > **Company Information.**

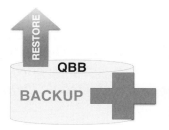

RESTART & RESTORE

Use the Restart & Restore approach if you are restarting your work session.

Step 1: Restore the .QBB file using the directions in *Appendix B: Back Up & Restore QuickBooks Files*.

You can restore your Exercise 10.1 Backup.QBB file from the previous exercise or use the Exercise 11.1.QBB data file that comes with the *Computer Accounting with QuickBooks* text (available on CD or download from the Online Learning Center).

Step 2: After restoring the file, change the company name to **[your name] Exercise 11.1 Mujeres Yarns** by selecting **Company** menu > **Company Information.**

TASK 2: SET UP USER WITH TIME TRACKING

To restrict access when setting up a new user (Roxanne):

Step 1: Select **Company** menu > **Set Up Users and Passwords** > **Set Up Users**.

Step 2: From the *User List* window, click **Add User**.

Step 3: Enter User Name: **Roxanne**.

Step 4: Enter Password: **Time**. Confirm password. Click **Next**.

Step 5: Select: **Selected areas of QuickBooks**. Click **Next**. If necessary, answer no to questions until you arrive at the *Time Tracking* window.

Step 6: For Time Tracking, make the following selections. Click **Next**.

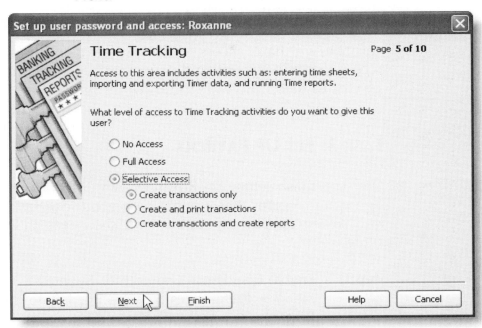

Step 7: Continue selecting No until the following window appears. To restrict access to closed periods, when the following window appears, select: **No** to answer the second question.

Step 8:   Click **Finish** to set up Roxanne as a new user.

Step 9:   **Close** the *User List* window.

Roxanne will have access to time tracking only and will not have access to other accounting functions or accounting periods prior to the closing date.

TASK 3: SET UP PAYROLL

After you finish setting up Roxanne with time-tracking access, Chel, the owner, decides that it might be a good idea for you to proceed with setting up payroll, just in case she needs this feature in the future.

Step 1:   Enable QuickBooks payroll for Mujeres Yarns. (Select **Edit** menu **> Preferences > Payroll & Employees > Company Preferences > Full Payroll**.)

Step 2:   Follow the instructions in Chapter 11 to enable manual payroll and set up payroll for Mujeres Yarns. Skip adding specific employee information at this time by selecting **Finish Later** when the *Set Up Employees* window appears.

TASK 4: SAVE EXERCISE 11.1

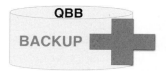

Save a backup of your Exercise 11.1 file using the file name: **[your name] Exercise 11.1 Backup.QBB**. See *Appendix B: Back Up & Restore QuickBooks Files* for instructions.

EXERCISE 11.2: WEB QUEST

Learn more about filing payroll Forms 940 and 941 by visiting the IRS website.

Step 1: Go to the www.irs.gov website.

Step 2: ▣ **Print** instructions for preparing and filing Form 940.

Step 3: ▣ **Print** instructions for preparing and filing Form 941.

Step 4: On the instructions for Form 941, **circle** the address to which Rock Castle Construction located in California would send payroll taxes.

EXERCISE 11.3: WEB QUEST

Employers must give employees Form W-2 each year summarizing wages and withholdings for tax purposes. In addition, employers must file Form W-3 with the Social Security Administration. Form W-3 summarizes the payroll information provided on the W-2 forms.

To learn more about filing Forms W-2 and W-3, visit the IRS website.

Step 1: Go to the www.irs.gov website.

Step 2: ▣ **Print** instructions for preparing and filing Form W-2.

Step 3: ▣ **Print** instructions for preparing and filing Form W-3.

DELIVERABLES CHECKLIST CHAPTER 11
NAME:

INSTRUCTIONS:
1. CHECK OFF THE DELIVERABLES YOU HAVE COMPLETED.
2. TURN IN THIS PAGE WITH YOUR DELIVERABLES.

CHAPTER 11
- ☐ Deposit Summary
- ☐ Employee List
- ☐ Voucher Paychecks
- ☐ Journal
- ☐ Payroll Liability Checks
- ☐ Excel Tax Worksheet
- ☐ Form 941
- ☐ Payroll Summary Report

EXERCISE 11.2
- ☐ Form 940 and Form 941 Instructions

EXERCISE 11.3
- ☐ Form W-2 and Form W-3 Instructions

REFLECTION: A WISH AND A STAR ⭐

Reflection improves learning and retention. Reflect on what you have learned after completing Chapter 11 that you did not know before you started the chapter.

A Star:

What did you like best that you learned about QuickBooks in Chapter 11?

A Wish:

If you could pick one thing, what do you wish you knew more about when using QuickBooks?

QuickBooks Project 11.1
Tomaso's Mowers & More: Payroll

Scenario

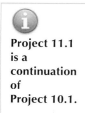

Project 11.1 is a continuation of Project 10.1.

Tomaso's Mowers & More hired Sophia Marcella as an office employee. You maintain the payroll records for Tomaso's Mowers & More and print Sophia's payroll checks.

Task 1: Open Company File

Workflow

Use the Workflow approach if you are using the same computer and the same .QBW file from the prior chapter.

Step 1: If your Project 10.1.QBW file is not already open, open it by selecting **File > Open Previous Company**. Select your **.QBW file.**

Step 2: Change the company name to **[your name] Project 11.1 Tomaso's Mowers & More** by selecting **Company** menu > **Company Information.**

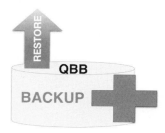

Restart & Restore

Use the Restart & Restore approach if you are restarting your work session.

Step 1: Restore the .QBB file using the directions in *Appendix B: Back Up & Restore QuickBooks Files.*

You can restore your Project 10.1 Backup.QBB file from the chapter or use the Project 11.1.QBB data file that comes with the *Computer Accounting with QuickBooks* text (available on CD or download from the Online Learning Center).

Step 2: After restoring the file, change the company name to **[your name] Project 11.1 Tomaso's Mowers & More** by selecting **Company** menu > **Company Information.**

TASK 2: SET UP PAYROLL

Set up QuickBooks Payroll for Tomaso's Mowers & More by completing the following steps.

Step 1: Enable QuickBooks Payroll for Tomaso's Mowers & More. (From the **Edit** menu, select **Preferences > Payroll & Employees > Company Preferences > Full Payroll.**)

Step 2: Follow the instructions in Chapter 11 to enable manual payroll and set up payroll for Tomaso's Mowers & More using the employee information on the following page.

First Name	Sophia
Last Name	Marcella
SS No.	343-21-6767
Address and Contact Info:	
Address	58 Wise Drive
City	Bayshore
State	CA
ZIP	94326
Phone	415-555-5827
Payroll Info:	
Hourly Regular Rate	$8.00
Pay Period	Weekly
Hired	03/01/2015
Federal and State Filing Status	Single
Allowances	1
State Tax	CA
Federal ID Number	37-7879146
State ID Number	888-8888-8
State Allowances	1
Subject to CA Training Tax?	No

TASK 3: PRINT EMPLOYEE INFORMATION

▣ **Print** the Employee List as demonstrated in Chapter 11.

TASK 4: PRINT PAYCHECKS

Using the following information and instructions in Chapter 11, create and **print** paychecks for Tomaso's Mowers & More employee, Sophia Marcella. Use voucher style checks and paystubs.

To print paystubs select **File** menu > **Print Forms > Pay Stubs**.

Check Date	Payroll Period	Hours Worked*
March 5	March 1-3	12
March 12	March 4-10	30
March 19	March 11-17	32
March 26	March 18-24	28
April 2	March 25-31	31

* Enter hours worked in the *Preview Paycheck* window.

To display the QuickMath Calculator:
1. Place your cursor in the federal withholding field, then press the = key.
2. Enter calculations using the * key to multiply.
3. Press **Enter** to enter the amount into the field.

Assume the following rates for withholdings:

Federal income tax	20.00%
Social Security (employee)	6.20%
Social Security (company)	6.20%
Medicare (employee)	1.45%
Medicare (company)	1.45%
State (CA) income tax	5.00%

Note that the wage base limit will not be exceeded for Social Security.

☑ **Sophia Marcella's March 12th paycheck is $161.64.**

TASK 5: PAY PAYROLL LIABILITY

On April 10, pay the payroll tax liability for federal income tax, Social Security and Medicare taxes, and state income tax as of 03/31/2015. **Print** the payroll liability checks.

TASK 6:
PRINT TAX FORM WORKSHEET FOR FORM 941

🖶 **Print** the Tax Form Worksheet in Excel for Form 941 for Tomaso's Mowers & More for the first quarter of 2015.

TASK 7: SAVE PROJECT 11.1

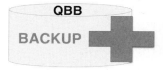

Save a backup of your Project 11.1 file using the file name: **[your name] Project 11.1 Backup.QBB**. See *Appendix B: Back Up & Restore QuickBooks Files* for instructions.

DELIVERABLES CHECKLIST PROJECT 11.1
NAME:

INSTRUCTIONS:
1. CHECK OFF THE DELIVERABLES YOU HAVE COMPLETED.
2. TURN IN THIS PAGE WITH YOUR DELIVERABLES.

PROJECT 11.1
☐ Employee List
☐ Paychecks and Paystubs
☐ Payroll Liability Check
☐ Excel Tax Form Worksheet for Form 941

REFLECTION: A WISH AND A STAR ☆

Reflection improves learning and retention. Reflect on what you have learned after completing Project 11.1 that you did not know before you started the chapter.

A Star:

What did you like best that you learned about QuickBooks in Project 11.1?

A Wish:

If you could pick one thing, what do you wish you knew more about when using QuickBooks?

NOTES

CHAPTER 12
ADVANCED QUICKBOOKS FEATURES FOR ACCOUNTANTS

SCENARIO

During the month of January 2015 you continue to operate your painting service while still managing The Paint Palette Store. You know that you need to budget for the coming year, providing you an opportunity to develop a business plan for the company.

In the new year, several commercial customers have approached you about custom painting for their offices and restaurants. Moreover, you continue to get referrals from your satisfied customers. The new customers want bids and estimates before they award contracts. Also, since some of these new jobs would require months to complete, you want to use progress billing (bill customers as the job progresses) in order to bring in a steady cash flow for your business.

Furthermore, you continue to provide QuickBooks consulting services for a variety of accounting clients. Therefore, to improve customer service for your QuickBooks clients, you continue to expand your knowledge and learn more about other advanced features of QuickBooks designed for the accounting professional.

CHAPTER 12
LEARNING OBJECTIVES

In Chapter 12, you will learn about the following QuickBooks features:

INTRODUCTION

This chapter covers some of the more advanced features of QuickBooks software that are of interest to the accounting professional. These features include setting up budgets, progress billing, multiple currencies, remote access for accountants, the accountant's copy of the company file, and the audit trail. Chapter 12 will use the Paint Palette service company file from Chapter 9.

OPEN COMPANY FILE

Chapter 12 is a continuation of Exercise 9.5.

To begin Chapter 12, first start QuickBooks software by clicking on the **QuickBooks desktop icon** or click **Start > Programs > QuickBooks > QuickBooks Pro 2010**.

WORKFLOW

Use the Workflow approach if you are using the same computer and the same .QBW file from Exercise 9.5.

Step 1: If your Exercise 9.5.QBW file is not already open, open it by selecting **File > Open Previous Company**. Select your **.QBW file.**

Step 2: Change the company name to **[your name] Chapter 12 Paint Palette** by selecting **Company** menu **> Company Information.**

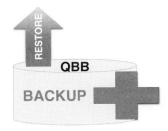

RESTART & RESTORE

Use the Restart & Restore approach if you are restarting your work session on a different computer.

Step 1: Restore the .QBB file using the directions in *Appendix B: Back Up & Restore QuickBooks Files.*

You can restore your Exercise 9.5 Backup.QBB file or the Chapter 11.QBB data file that comes with the *Computer Accounting with QuickBooks* text (available on CD or download from the Online Learning Center).

Step 2: After restoring the file, change the company name to **[your name] Chapter 12 Paint Palette** by selecting **Company** menu > **Company Information.**

BUDGETS

As Paint Palette enters its second year of operation, planning for future expansion is important to its continued success. You develop the following budget for 2015.

- January sales are expected to be $3,000. Sales are expected to increase by 5% each month thereafter.

- Paint supplies expense is budgeted at $60 per month.

- The van lease will increase to $300 per month. (Use Account No. 67100.)

To prepare budgets for Paint Palette using QuickBooks:

Step 1: Select **Company** menu > **Planning & Budgeting** > **Set Up Budgets**.

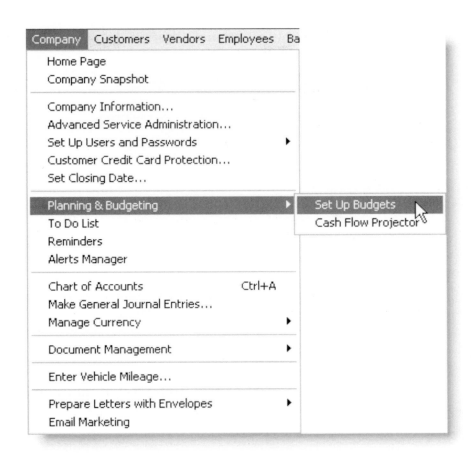

Step 2:   In the *Create New Budget* window, select the year: **2015**.

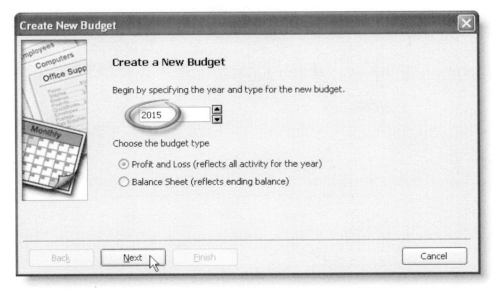

Step 3:   Select budget type: **Profit and Loss > Next**.

Step 4:   Select **No additional criteria > Next**.

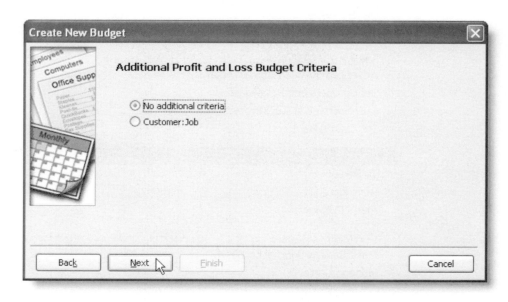

Step 5:   Select **Create budget from scratch**. Click **Finish**.

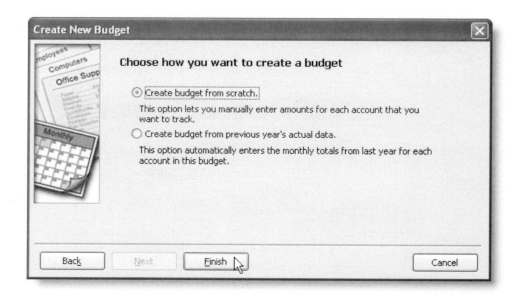

Step 6: When the following *Set Up Budgets* window appears, enter **3000.00** for 47900 Sales account in the *Jan15* column.

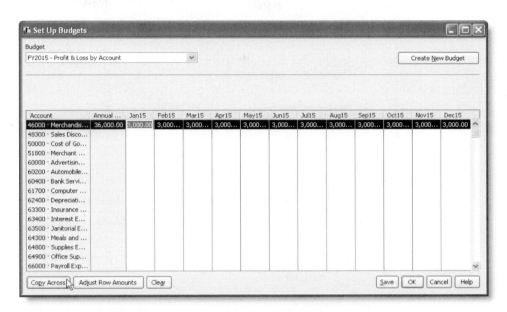

Step 7: Click the **Copy Across** button.

Step 8: Click the **Adjust Row Amounts** button.

Step 9: When the following *Adjust Row Amounts* window appears:

- Select Start at: **Currently selected month**.
- Select: **Increase each remaining monthly amount in this row by this dollar amount or percentage**.
- Enter **5.0%**.
- Check: **Enable compounding**.
- Click **OK**.

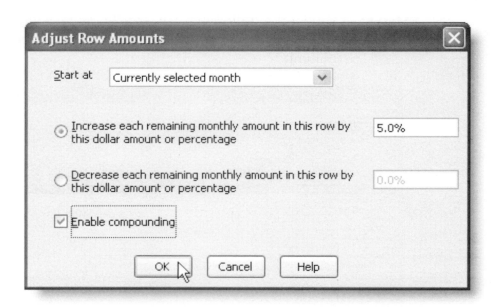

Step 10: The *Set Up Budgets* window should now appear as follows.

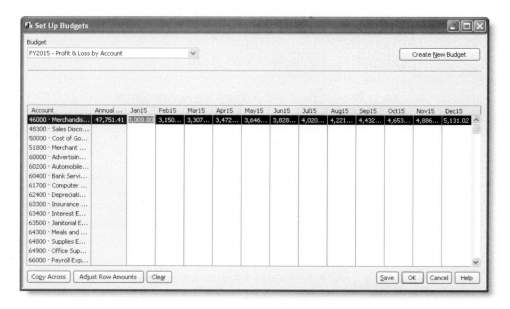

Use the **Copy Across** button to fill in the budget amounts for each month.

Step 11: Enter budget amounts for Paint Supplies Expense ($60 per month) and Rent Expense for the van ($300 per month).

Step 12: Click **OK** to close the *Set Up Budgets* window.

🖺 **Print** the budgets you created for Paint Palette:

Step 1: From the Report Center select **Budgets > Budget Overview**.

Step 2: Select Dates: **01/01/2015** To: **12/31/2015**. Click **Display report**.

Step 3: Select: **FY2015 – Profit and Loss by Account > Next**.

Step 4: Select Report Layout: **Account by Month > Next > Finish**.

Step 5: 🖨 **Print** the Budget Overview report using **Landscape** orientation.

Step 6: **Close** the *Budget Overview* window.

ESTIMATES

Often customers ask for a bid or estimate of job cost before awarding a contract. Paint Palette needs to estimate job costs that are accurate in order not to *overbid* and lose the job or *underbid* and lose money on the job.

To prepare a job cost estimate for Paint Palette:

Step 1: Click the **Estimates** icon in the *Customers* section of the Home page.

If the Estimates icon does not appear on your screen, select **Edit** menu > **Preferences > Jobs and Estimates > Company Preferences**. Select **Yes** to indicate you create estimates.

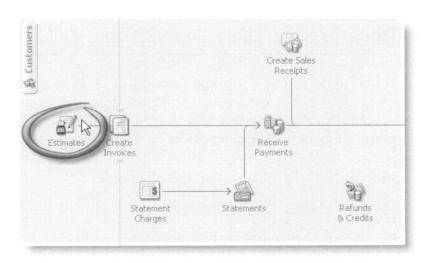

Step 2: When the *Create Estimates* window appears, add a new customer as follows:

- From the drop-down Customer List, select: **<Add New>**.

- Enter Customer Name: **Grandprey Cafe**.

- Enter Address: **10 Montreal Blvd., Bayshore, CA 94326**.

- Enter Contact: **Milton**.

- Click the **Job Info** tab, then enter Job Status: **Pending**.

- Click **OK** to close the *New Customer* window.

> The estimate can be given to a customer when bidding on a job. You can also e-mail estimates to customers using QuickBooks.

Step 3: Next, enter estimate information in the *Create Estimates* window:

- Select Template: **Custom Estimate**.

- Select Date: **01/05/2015**.

- Enter Item: **Labor: Exterior Painting**.

- Enter Quantity **40**.

- Enter a second item: **Labor: Interior Painting**.

- Enter Quantity: **65**.

Step 4: 🖨 **Print** the estimate, then click **Save & Close** to close the *Create Estimates* window.

PROGRESS BILLING

When undertaking a job that lasts a long period of time, a business often does not want to wait until the job is completed to receive payment for its work. The business often incurs expenses in performing the job that must be paid before the business receives payment from customers. This can create a cash flow problem. One solution to this problem is progress billing.

Progress billing permits a business to bill customers as the job progresses. Thus, the business receives partial payments from the customer before the project is completed.

After you give Grandprey Cafe your estimate of the paint job cost, Milton awards you the contract. The job will last about three weeks. However, instead of waiting three weeks to bill Milton, you bill Milton every week so that you will have cash to pay your bills.

To use progress billing in QuickBooks, first you must turn on the preference for progress invoicing.

To select the preference for progress invoicing:

Step 1:   Select **Edit** menu > **Preferences > Jobs & Estimates > Company Preferences**.

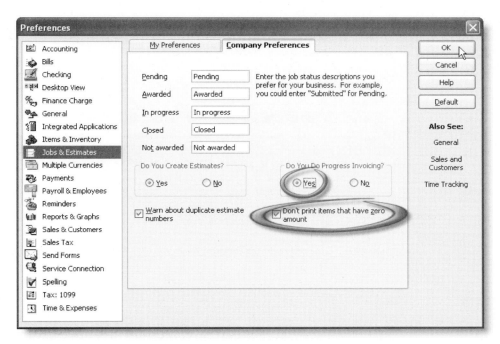

Step 2:   Select **Yes** to indicate you want to use Progress Invoicing.

Step 3:   ✓ Check **Don't print items that have zero amount**.

Step 4:   Click **OK** to save the Progress Invoicing preference and close the *Preferences* window. Click **OK** if a warning window appears.

After selecting the Progress Invoicing preference, the Progress Invoice template is now available in the *Create Invoices* window.

To create a progress invoice:

Step 1: Click the **Create Invoices** icon in the *Customers* section of the Home page.

Step 2: When the *Create Invoices* window appears, select Customer: **Grandprey Cafe**.

Step 3: Select the **Grandprey Cafe** estimate to invoice, then click **OK**.

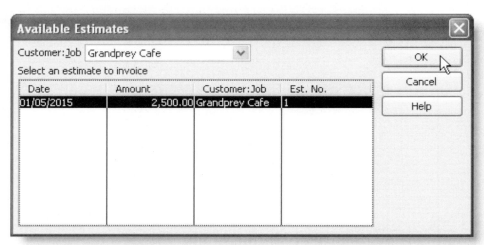

Step 4: When the *Create Progress Invoice Based on Estimate* window appears:

- Select: **Create invoice for the entire estimate (100%)**.
- Click **OK**.

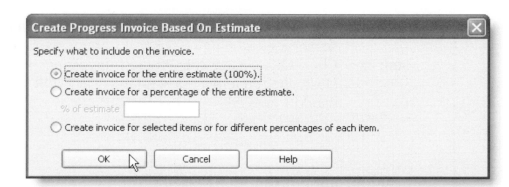

Step 5: When the following *Create Invoices* window appears, the template should now be: **Progress Invoice**.

When you selected Create invoice for the entire estimate, QuickBooks automatically entered the items and estimated amounts for the entire job on the progress invoice.

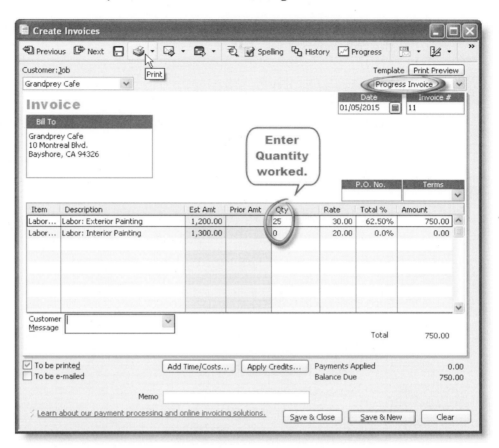

Step 6: Enter the number of hours actually worked on the Grandprey Cafe job.

- Enter Exterior Painting Labor Quantity: **25**.

- Enter Interior Painting Labor Quantity: **0**.

Step 7: 🖨 **Print** the progress invoice.

Step 8: Click **Save & Close** to close the *Create Invoices* window. If a message appears, click **Yes** to record changes to the invoice.

The following week you complete the exterior painting for Grandprey Cafe and work 6.5 hours on interior painting.

Create another progress invoice for Grandprey Cafe by completing the following steps.

Step 1: Display the *Create Invoices* window.

Step 2: Select Customer: **Grandprey Cafe**.

Step 3: Select the **Grandprey Cafe** estimate to invoice, then click **OK**.

Step 4: When the following *Create Progress Invoice Based on Estimate* window appears:

- Select **Create invoice for selected items or for different percentages of each item**.
- Click **OK**.

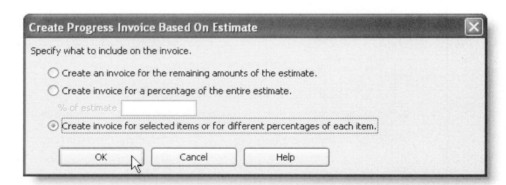

Step 5: When the following *Specify Invoice Amounts for Items on Estimate* window appears:

- ✓ Check: **Show Quantity and Rate**.
- ✓ Check: **Show Percentage**.
- Enter Exterior Painting Quantity: **15**.
- Enter Interior Painting Quantity: **6.5**.
- Click **OK** to record these amounts on the progress invoice.

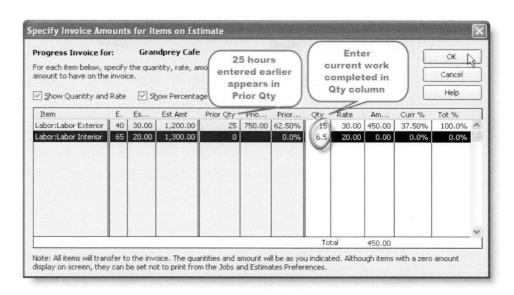

Step 6: When the *Create Invoices* window appears, change the date of the progress invoice to: **01/12/2015**.

Step 7: 🖨 **Print** the invoice.

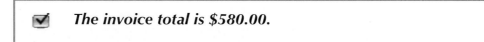

☑ *The invoice total is $580.00.*

Step 8: Click **Save & Close** to record the progress invoice and close the *Create Invoices* window.

Customer payments received on progress invoices are recorded in the same manner as customer payments for standard invoices (See Chapter 4).

CREDIT CARD SALES

As a convenience to your customers, you agree to accept credit cards as payment for services you provide. Grandprey Cafe would like to make its first payment using a VISA credit card.

In QuickBooks, you record credit card payments in the same manner that you record a payment by check; however, instead of selecting Check as the payment method, you select the type of credit card used.

To record a credit card sale using QuickBooks:

Step 1: Click the **Receive Payments** icon in the *Customers* section of the Home page.

Step 2: If you want to complete the Payment Interview, select Yes. Otherwise, select **No** and close the *Payment Interview* window.

Step 3: When the *Receive Payments* window appears, select Received From: **Grandprey Cafe**. QuickBooks will automatically display any unpaid invoices for Grandprey Cafe.

> If the specific credit card is not listed on the Payment Method List, select **Add New**, then enter the name of the credit card.

Step 4: Enter the Date: **01/30/2015**.

Step 5: Enter Amount: **750.00**.

Step 6: Select Payment Method: **Visa**.

Step 7: Enter Card No.: **19585858581958**. Enter Exp. Date: **12/2015**.

Step 8: If not already selected, select outstanding Invoice No. **11**, dated **01/05/2015**.

Step 9: Your *Receive Payments* window should appear as follows. To record the customer payment and close the *Receive Payments* window, click **Save & Close**.

Banks will accept bank credit card payments, such as Visa or MasterCard, the same as a cash or check deposit. You can record the credit card payment as a deposit to your checking account.

Step 10: Since you are not using the Merchant Account Services, when the credit card payment is deposited at the bank on 01/30/2015, record the deposit just as you would a check or cash deposit.

- Click the **Record Deposits** icon in the *Banking* section of the Home page.

- Select **Grandprey Cafe payment** for deposit. Click **OK**.

- 🖶 **Print** the deposit summary.

BAD DEBTS

At the time a credit sale occurs, it is recorded as an increase to sales and an increase to accounts receivable. Occasionally a company is unable to collect a customer payment and must write off the customer's account as a bad debt or uncollectible account. When an account is uncollectible, the account receivable is written off or removed from the accounting records.

There are two different methods that can be used to account for bad debts:

1. **Direct write-off method.** This method records bad debt expense when it becomes apparent that the customer is not going to pay the amount due. If the direct write-off method is used, the customer's uncollectible account receivable is removed and bad debt expense is recorded at the time a specific customer's account becomes uncollectible. The direct write-off method is used for tax purposes.

2. **Allowance method.** The allowance method *estimates* bad debt expense and establishes an allowance or reserve for uncollectible accounts. When using the allowance method, uncollectible accounts expense is estimated in advance of the write-off. The estimate can be calculated as a percentage of sales or as a percentage of accounts receivable. (For example, 2% of credit sales might be estimated to be uncollectible.) This method should be used if uncollectible accounts have a material effect on the company's financial statements used by investors and creditors and the company must comply with Generally Accepted Accounting Principles (GAAP).

Paint Palette will use the direct write-off method and record the uncollectible accounts expense when an account actually becomes uncollectible.

When Milton paid the bill for $750 for Grandprey Cafe, he tells you that his business has plummeted since a new restaurant opened next door. To your dismay, he tells you his cafe is closing and he will not be able to pay you the remainder that he owes. You decide to write off the Grandprey Cafe remaining $580 account balance as uncollectible.

First, create an account for tracking uncollectible accounts expense and then write off the customer's uncollectible account receivable.

To add a Bad Debt Expense account to the Chart of Accounts for Paint Palette, complete the following steps:

Step 1: Click the **Chart of Accounts** icon in the *Company* section of the Home page.

Step 2: Add the following account to the Chart of Accounts.

Account Type	Expense
Account No.	67000
Account Name	Bad Debt Expense
Description	Bad Debt Expense
Tax Line	Schedule C: Bad debts from sales/services

Next, record the write-off of the uncollectible account receivable. There are three different methods to record a bad debt using QuickBooks:

1. Make a journal entry to remove the customer's account receivable (credit Accounts Receivable) and debit either Bad Debt Expense (direct write-off method) or the Allowance for Uncollectible Accounts (allowance method).

2. Use the *Credit Memo* window to record uncollectible accounts.

3. Use the *Receive Payments* window (Discount Info button) to record the write-off of the customer's uncollectible account.

If you charged sales tax on the transaction written off, use this method.

To record the write-off of an uncollectible accounts receivable using the *Receive Payments* window, complete the following steps:

Step 1: Change the preference for automatically calculating payments as follows:

- Select **Edit** menu **> Preferences > Payments > Company Preferences**.

- **Uncheck** the **Automatically calculate payments** preference.

- Click **OK** to close the *Preferences* window.

Step 2:   Click the **Receive Payments** icon in the *Customers* section of the Home page.

Step 3:   When the *Receive Payments* window appears, select Received From: **Grandprey Cafe**.

Step 4:   Enter Date: **01/30/2015**.

Step 5:   Leave the Amount as **$0.00**.

Step 6:   Enter Memo: **Write off Uncollectible Account**.

Step 7:   Select the outstanding invoice dated: **01/12/2015**.

Step 8:   Because the Amount field is $0.00, the following warning may appear. Click **OK**.

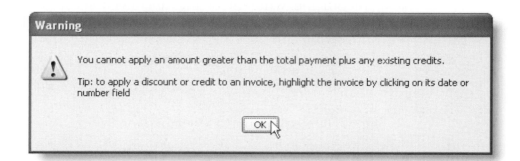

Step 9:   Highlight the invoice by clicking on its **Date** field.

Step 10:   Click the **Discount & Credits** button in the *Receive Payments* window.

Step 11: When the following *Discount and Credits* window appears:

- Enter Amount of Discount: **580.00**.

- Select Discount Account: **67000 Bad Debt Expense**.

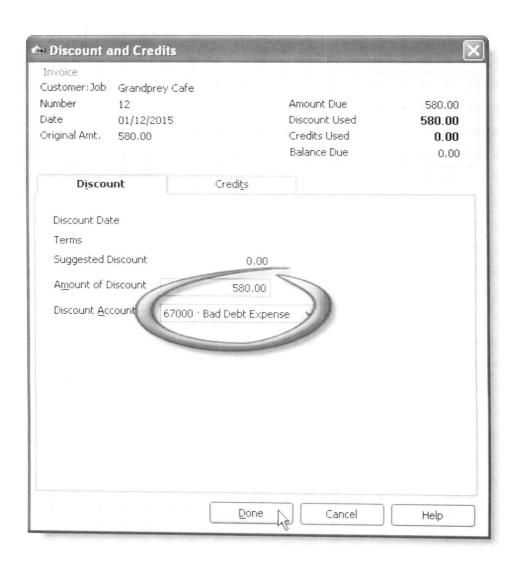

Step 12: Click **Done** to close the *Discount and Credits* window.

Step 13: Click **Save & Close** to close the *Receive Payments* window.

To view the Grandprey Cafe account:

Step 1: From the Report Center select **Customers & Receivables > Customer Balance Detail**.

Step 2: Select Dates: **All**. Click **Display report**.

Step 3: Customize the Customer Balance Detail report so the Memo field appears on the report:

- Click the **Modify Report** button to display the *Modify Report* window.

- Click the **Display** tab.

- Select Columns: **Memo**.

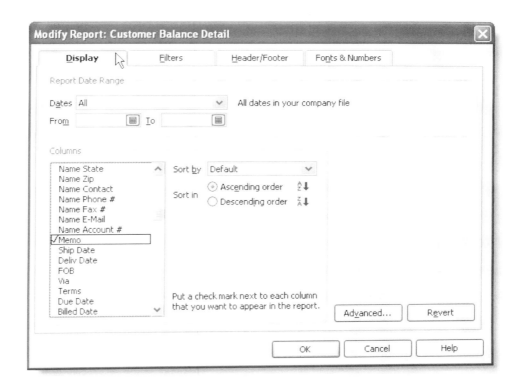

Step 4: Next, create a filter to display only Grandprey Cafe account information.

   - Click the **Filters** tab in the *Modify Report* window.
   - Select Filter: **Name**.
   - Select Name: **Grandprey Cafe**.
   - Click **OK** to close the *Modify Report* window.

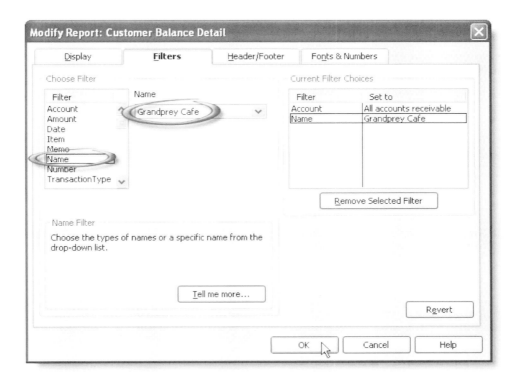

Step 5: The *Customer Balance Detail* window should now appear as follows. **Double-click** on the entry for 01/30/2015 to drill down to the *Receive Payments* window that displays the entry to write off $580 of the Grandprey Cafe account. **Close** the *Receive Payments* window.

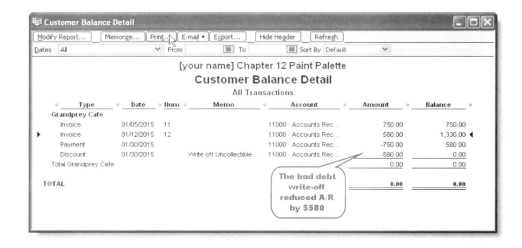

Step 6: 🖶 **Print** the *Customer Balance Detail* report for Grandprey Cafe From: **01/01/2015** To: **01/30/2015**.

The Accounts Receivable Aging Summary report (discussed in Chapter 4) provides information about the age of customers' accounts receivable which can be useful for tracking and managing collections. Also see Chapter 4 for information about how to use QuickBooks to generate collection letters to send to customers with past due accounts.

To reduce uncollectible customer accounts, some companies adopt a policy that requires customers to make a deposit or advance payment before beginning work on a project. In addition, companies often evaluate the creditworthiness of customers before extending credit.

MEMORIZED REPORTS

On March 1, 2015, a potential buyer contacts you, expressing an interest in purchasing your painting service business. The potential buyer offers to purchase your business for a price equal to five times the operating income of the business.

The buyer asks for a copy of the following prior year financial statements for his accountant to review.

- Profit & Loss (Income Statement)
- Balance Sheet
- Statement of Cash Flows

When you prepare the reports, you create memorized reports for future use. To memorize a report, first create the report and then use the memorize feature of QuickBooks.

To create a memorized Profit & Loss report for Paint Palette:

Step 1: From the Report Center select **Company & Financial > Profit & Loss Standard**.

Step 2: Select Dates: From: **01/01/2014** To: **12/31/2014**. Click **Display report**.

 Income for Paint Palette was $31,285. Therefore, the purchase price of the business would be $156,425 (five times income of $31,285).

Step 3: To memorize the report:

- Click the **Memorize** button at the top of the *Profit & Loss* window.

- When the following *Memorize Report* window appears, enter Memorized Report Name: **Paint Palette Profit & Loss**. Select **Save in Memorized Report Group: Accountant > OK**.

Step 4: **Close** the *Profit & Loss* window.

Step 5: To use a memorized report:

- Select **Reports** menu **> Memorized Reports > Memorized Report List**.

- When the following *Memorized Report List* window appears, double-click on **Paint Palette Profit & Loss** to display the Profit & Loss report.

For client convenience, accountants may create a list of memorized reports for their clients' most frequently used reports.

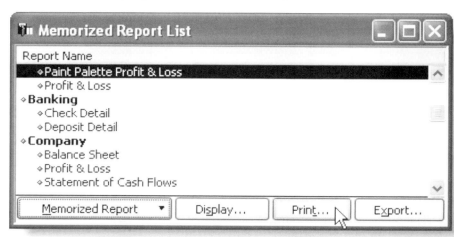

Step 6: 🖨 **Print** the Profit & Loss report.

EXPORT REPORTS

In Chapter 7, you learned how to export reports to Excel spreadsheet software. Now, you will export to Excel the Profit & Loss report you just created.

To export the Profit & Loss report to Excel:

Step 1: With the *Profit & Loss* report window still open, verify the dates are 01/01/2014 to 12/31/2014.

Step 2: Click the **Export** button at the top of the *Profit & Loss* report window.

Step 3: When the *Export Report* window appears, select Export QuickBooks report to: **a new Excel workbook**.

Step 4: Click **Export** to export the Profit & Loss report to an Excel spreadsheet.

Step 5: Save the Excel spreadsheet with the file name: **Profit & Loss 2014**.

Step 6: **Print** the Excel Profit & Loss spreadsheet.

Step 7: **Close** the Excel software by clicking the ⊠ in the upper right corner of the *Excel* window.

Step 8: **Close** the QuickBooks *Profit & Loss* report window.

You can also e-mail reports. Click the **E-mail** button at the top of the *Reports* window. For example, a client might e-mail reports to the accountant for review.

Next, **create** and **memorize** a Balance Sheet for Paint Palette as of December 31, 2014. With the *Balance Sheet* window still open, export the report to Excel as follows:

Step 1: Click the **Export** button at the top of the report window.

Step 2: Select **a new Excel workbook**, then click **Export** to export the report to Excel software.

Step 3: **Print** the Balance Sheet from Excel. **Close** the *Balance Sheet* window.

Create and **memorize** a Statement of Cash Flows for Paint Palette for the year 2014. With the *Statement of Cash Flows* window still open, export the report to Excel as follows:

Step 1:   Click the **Export** button at the top of the report window.

Step 2:   Select **a new Excel workbook**, then click **Export** to export the report to Excel software.

Step 3:   Print the *Statement of Cash Flows* from Excel. **Close** the Excel software, then **close** the *Statement of Cash Flows* window.

In addition to exporting reports to Excel from the *Reports* window, QuickBooks can save reports as electronic files. QuickBooks permits you to select from the following file formats:

- **ASCII text file**. After saving as a text file, the file can be used with word processing software.

- **Comma delimited file.** Comma delimited files can be used with word processing software or database software.

- **Tab delimited file.** Tab delimited files can be used with word processing or database software, such as Microsoft® Access®.

- **Adobe PDF files.** If you have the appropriate software, QuickBooks will save reports as pdf files that are easily e-mailed.

YOUR DECISION

Based on the financial statement results for Paint Palette, decide whether to sell the painting service business.

Sell painting service?	Yes	No
If you sell, the selling price you will accept:	$_____	
Reason(s) for decision:		

AUDIT TRAIL

The Audit Trail feature of QuickBooks permits you to track all changes (additions, modifications, and deletions) made to your QuickBooks records. This feature is especially important in tracking unauthorized changes to accounting records.

The Audit Trail report consists of two sections:

1. One section of the Audit Trail report shows all transactions that are currently active.

2. A second section of the report lists all deleted transactions.

To illustrate how an accounting clerk, Ima M. Bezler, might attempt to embezzle funds, assume Ima pockets a customer's cash payment and deletes any record of the customer's bill from QuickBooks.

To test the Audit Trail feature, first record a customer invoice to Katrina Beneficio for $80.

Ima might also try to write off the customer's account as uncollectible in order to ensure the customer does not receive another bill.

Step 1: Using the *Create Invoices* window, on **02/01/2015** record **2** hours of **mural painting** on the **Katrina Beneficio Kitchen job**. ⧉ **Print** the invoice.

Step 2: On 02/02/2015, Katrina Beneficio pays her bill in cash. If Ima decides to keep the cash and delete the invoice (so that Beneficio would not receive another bill), the Audit Trail feature maintains a record of the deleted invoice.

To delete the invoice on **02/02/2015**, open the Beneficio invoice for $80 and select **Edit** menu > **Delete Invoice**.

The Audit Trail report lists the original transaction and all changes made later. The Audit Trail report will list the above change that was made to delete the customer's invoice.

Access to the Audit Trail should be restricted to only the QuickBooks Administrator.

If you clean up a data file (**File > Utilities > Clean Up Company Data**), deleted transactions are removed from your Audit Trail report.

Use the Auto Filter to track all items recorded by a specific user.

🖨 **Print** an Audit Trail report:

Step 1: From the Report Center select **Accountant & Taxes > Audit Trail**.

Step 2: 🖨 **Print** the Audit Trail report.

Step 3: ✏️ **Circle** the record of the deleted invoice dated 02/01/2015.

The Audit Trail report is especially useful if you have more than one user for QuickBooks. This report permits you to determine which user made which changes.

The Audit Trail feature improves internal control by tracking unauthorized changes to accounting records. The owner (or manager) should periodically review the Audit Trail for discrepancies or unauthorized changes.

The Audit Trail feature requires more storage for larger files because both original transactions and changed transactions are saved. In addition, the Audit Trail feature may slow processing time.

To facilitate tracking of changes made by users, export the Audit Trail report to Excel using the Auto Filter feature:

Step 1: With the *Audit Trail* window open, click the **Export** button at the top of the report window.

Step 2: Select: **a new Excel workbook**.

Step 3: Click the **Advanced** tab on the *Export Report* window.

Step 4: ✓ Check **Auto Filtering**, then click **Export** to close the *Export Report* window and export the report to Excel.

Step 5: The Audit Trail report is exported to Excel with the Auto Filter feature. Each column heading is a drop-down list to use for filtering. Select a filter of your choice from one of the drop-down lists.

Step 6: **Close** Excel software without saving your changes.

Step 7: **Close** the *Audit Trail* window.

ACCOUNTANT'S COPY

If an accountant makes adjustments at year-end, QuickBooks can create a copy of the company data files for the accountant to use (Accountant's Copy). The accountant can make adjustments and changes to the Accountant's Copy. Then the Accountant's Copy is merged with the original company data. This permits the entrepreneur to continue using QuickBooks to record transactions at the same time the accountant reviews and makes changes to the records.

To create an Accountant's Copy of Paint Palette:

Step 1: Select **File** menu **> Accountant's Copy > Save File**.

The Accountant's Copy can be sent over the Internet to the accountant.

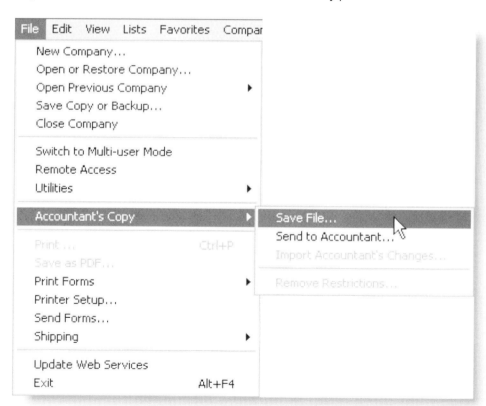

Step 2: Read the *Save Accountant's Copy* window. Select **Accountant's Copy > Next**.

Step 3: Select Dividing Date: **Custom 12/31/2008 > Next**.

Step 4: When the message appears that QuickBooks must close all windows to prepare an Accountant's Copy, click **OK**.

Step 5: When the *Save Accountant's Copy* window appears:

- Select *Save in* location.
- Enter File name: **[your name] Chapter 12**.
- Select Save as type**: Accountant's Copy Transfer File (*.QBX)**.
- Select **Save > OK**.

QuickBooks will create a copy of the QuickBooks company file for the accountant's temporary use. After the accountant has made necessary adjustments to the Accountant's Copy, the Accountant's Copy is then merged with the QuickBooks company data file, incorporating the accountant's changes into the company's records.

ASK MY ACCOUNTANT

In the Chart of Accounts is an account entitled Ask My Accountant. Entrepreneurs using QuickBooks can use this account to record items when they are uncertain how to record specific items properly. The items can be recorded in this account and the accountant can review these items and record them properly before financial statements are prepared.

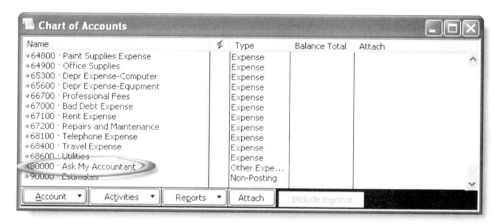

DOCUMENT MANAGEMENT

One of the challenges of any accounting system is managing the numerous and varied documents within the system. QuickBooks now offers a Document Management feature to organize your accounting and business documents within the QuickBooks software.

To view more information about this feature, click on the **Doc Center** icon in the Icon bar to display the following *QuickBooks Document Management* window.

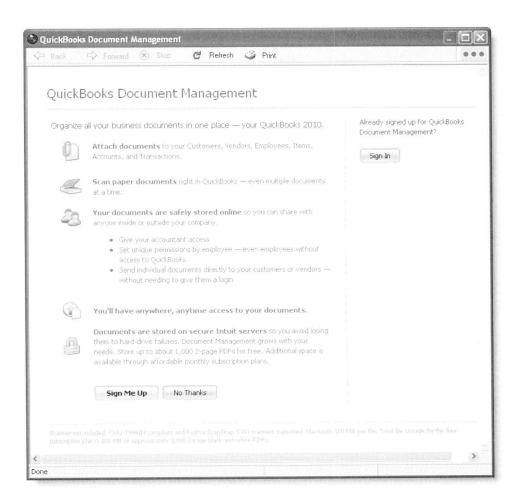

After signing up for QuickBooks Document Management, you can attach documents to QuickBooks forms. For example, when you are using the QuickBooks *Enter Bills* window, you could attach the bill you received electronically from a vendor as you enter the bill information into QuickBooks. If you received the vendor's bill in the mail, you can scan the bill and attach it when using the *Enter Bills* window.

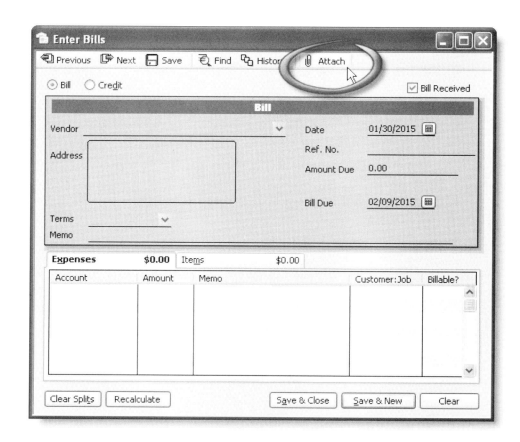

The documents are stored online on Intuit servers. QuickBooks Document Management feature is an example of how cloud computing can streamline accounting tasks.

SAVE CHAPTER 12

Save a backup of your Chapter 12 file using the file name: **[your name] Chapter 12 Backup.QBB**. See *Appendix B: Back Up & Restore QuickBooks Files* for instructions.

PODCASTS

Watch the Chapter 12 **Podcast** at www.QuickBooksBlog.info to view how to use advanced QuickBooks features.

MULTIPLE-CHOICE PRACTICE TEST

A **Multiple-Choice Practice Test** for Chapter 12 is on the *Computer Accounting for QuickBooks* Online Learning Center at www.mhhe.com/kay2010. Try the Practice Test and see how many questions you answer correctly.

EXTRAS!

Section 3: Quick Guide contains quick, easy step-by-step directions for frequently used QuickBooks tasks, including correcting errors. You can find *Quick Guide* at the back of your text or online at www.mhhe.com/kay2010. *Check it out!*

Deliverables Checklist is a list of the reports and documents that you are to deliver to your instructor for grading. You can find the Deliverables Checklist at the end of the chapter or online at www.mhhe.com/kay2010. Staying organized saves time. Use the checklist to organize your reports, checking off the reports as completed. Then include the checklist with your reports for grading.

Appendix D: Electronic Deliverables shows you how to save your QuickBooks reports electronically. Also, watch the Electronic Deliverables Podcast at www.QuickBooksBlog.info. Check with your instructor to see if you should deliver your reports electronically.

Join the QuickBooks Student Community to ask questions and share tips @ www.QuickBooksBlog.info.

LEARNING ACTIVITIES

Important: Ask your instructor whether you should complete the following assignments by printing requested reports or creating electronic deliverables (see Appendix D: Electronic Deliverables).

EXERCISE 12.1: QUICKBOOKS REMOTE ACCESS

QuickBooks Remote Access permits you to access your QuickBooks company data from remote locations.

Step 1:   Select **File** menu **> Remote Access**.

Step 2:   **Print** the information about Remote Access.

Step 3:   Summarize in a short e-mail that you can send to your accounting clients who want more information about using the QuickBooks remote access feature.

EXERCISE 12.2: QUICKBOOKS MULTIPLE CURRENCIES

New in QuickBooks 2010, multiple currencies are now supported. This feature permits you to use not only U.S. dollars, but a choice of other currencies.

To learn more about this new feature:

Step 1:   Select **Help** menu **> Learning Center Tutorials > Overview & Setup > Working with Multiple Currencies**. Watch the tutorial to learn more about the multiple currencies feature of QuickBooks.

Step 2:   Summarize your findings in a short e-mail that you can send to your accounting clients who want more information about using multiple currencies in QuickBooks.

 # EXERCISE 12.3: WEB QUEST ASSIGNMENT

Not ready to file your tax return by April 15? File an extension and postpone filing your tax return until mid October. File Form 4868 by April 15 and send a check for an estimate of the tax you owe to avoid interest and penalties.

To learn more about filing for a tax extension:

Step 1:   Go to the IRS website: www.irs.gov.

Step 2:   **Print** Form 4868 and instructions for filing a tax extension for a personal return (Form 1040 and Schedule C).

Step 3:   Prepare a short e-mail that you can use to send to your accounting clients who need more information about filing an extension.

DELIVERABLES CHECKLIST CHAPTER 12
NAME:

INSTRUCTIONS:
1. **CHECK OFF THE DELIVERABLES YOU HAVE COMPLETED.**
2. **TURN IN THIS PAGE WITH YOUR DELIVERABLES.**

CHAPTER 12
☐ Profit & Loss Budget Overview
☐ Estimate
☐ Invoice Nos. 11 and 12
☐ Deposit Summary
☐ Customer Balance Detail
☐ Profit & Loss Report
☐ Profit & Loss Excel Spreadsheet
☐ Balance Sheet Excel Spreadsheet
☐ Statement of Cash Flows Excel Spreadsheet
☐ Invoice No. 13
☐ Audit Trail Report

EXERCISE 12.1
☐ QuickBooks Remote Access

EXERCISE 12.2
☐ Multiple Currencies

EXERCISE 12.2
☐ IRS Form 4868 and Instructions

REFLECTION: A WISH AND A STAR ★

Reflection improves learning and retention. Reflect on what you have learned after completing Chapter 12 that you did not know before you started the chapter.

A Star:

What did you like best that you learned about QuickBooks in Chapter 12?

A Wish:

If you could pick one thing, what do you wish you knew more about when using QuickBooks?

QuickBooks Project 12.1
Tuscany Landscapes

Scenario

Project 12.1 is a continuation of Project 9.1.

Tuscany Landscapes needs to prepare a budget for 2015.

Task 1: Open Company File

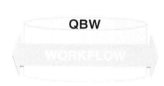

Workflow

Use the Workflow approach if you are using the same computer and the same .QBW file from Project 9.1.

Step 3: If your Project 9.1.QBW file is not already open, open it by selecting **File > Open Previous Company**. Select your **.QBW file.**

Step 4: Change the company name to **[your name] Project 12.1 Tuscany Landscapes** by selecting **Company** menu > **Company Information.**

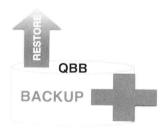

Restart & Restore

Use the Restart & Restore approach if you are restarting your work session on a different computer.

Step 3: Restore the .QBB file using the directions in *Appendix B: Back Up & Restore QuickBooks Files.*

You can restore your Project 9.1 Backup.QBB file or the Project 12.1.QBB data file that comes with the *Computer Accounting with QuickBooks* text (available on CD or download from the Online Learning Center).

Step 4: After restoring the file, change the company name to **[your name] Project 12.1 Tuscany Landscapes** by selecting **Company** menu > **Company Information**.

TASK 2: BUDGET, EXPORT TO EXCEL

Prepare a budget for Tuscany Landscapes for the year 2015.

Step 1: Prepare a Profit & Loss Budget Overview report for Tuscany Landscapes for the year 2015 using the following information:

- January service revenues are expected to be $800. Revenue is expected to increase by 2 percent each month.

- Gasoline and supplies for January are budgeted at $60. These costs are expected to increase by 1 percent each month.

Step 2: **Memorize** the P&L Budget Overview report for Tuscany Landscapes for the year 2015.

Step 3: **Export** the P&L Budget Overview to Excel software.

Step 4: ▤ **Print** the P&L Budget Overview report for Tuscany Landscapes for the year 2015 from Excel.

TASK 3: MEMORIZE REPORTS, EXPORT TO EXCEL

Prepare the following reports for Tuscany Landscapes for the year 2014.

- Profit & Loss, Standard
- Balance Sheet, Standard
- Statement of Cash Flows

Step 1: **Memorize** each report.

Step 2: 🖨 **Print** the reports.

Step 3: **Export** the reports to Excel software and **print**.

TASK 4: SAVE PROJECT 12.1

Save a backup of your Project 12.1 file using the file name: **[your name] Project 12.1 Backup.QBB**. See *Appendix B: Back Up & Restore QuickBooks Files* for instructions.

DELIVERABLES CHECKLIST PROJECT 12.1
NAME:

INSTRUCTIONS:
1. **CHECK OFF THE DELIVERABLES YOU HAVE COMPLETED.**
2. **TURN IN THIS PAGE WITH YOUR DELIVERABLES.**

PROJECT 12.1
- ☐ P&L Budget Overview Excel Printout
- ☐ Profit & Loss, Standard
- ☐ Balance Sheet, Standard
- ☐ Statement of Cash Flows
- ☐ Profit & Loss Excel Printout
- ☐ Balance Sheet Excel Printout
- ☐ Statement of Cash Flows Excel Printout

REFLECTION: A WISH AND A STAR ⭐

Reflection improves learning and retention. Reflect on what you have learned after completing Project 12.1 that you did not know before you started the chapter.

A Star:

What did you like best that you learned about QuickBooks in Project 12.1?

A Wish:

If you could pick one thing, what do you wish you knew more about when using QuickBooks?

CHAPTER 13
LIVE PROJECT:
QUICKBOOKS IN ACTION

SCENARIO

Chapter 13 provides an opportunity to apply the knowledge and skills you have acquired thus far to an authentic QuickBooks project. You will assume the role of a consultant providing QuickBooks consulting services to a client. This project provides an opportunity for realistic, valuable practical experience to better prepare you for professional employment as well as enhance your resume.

The chapter contains a project management framework to guide you through the development of an accounting system for entrepreneurs or not-for-profits using QuickBooks accounting software. The project management approach divides the project into milestones for system development that can be used with various types of organizations, allowing for flexibility to customize the system to meet the specific needs of the entrepreneur or not-for-profit.

The project management framework that you will be using to develop a real QuickBooks accounting system consists of the following seven milestones.

Milestone 1. Develop a proposal. In this milestone, you will identify a real-world client (either a small business or a nonprofit organization) that needs assistance in establishing an accounting system using QuickBooks. After identifying the client, gather information from the client and develop a plan for a QuickBooks accounting system that will meet the client's needs.

Milestone 2. Develop a prototype or sample QuickBooks accounting system for the client. Set up a company in QuickBooks with a sample chart of accounts for the client to review. After obtaining approval of the chart of accounts from the client and your instructor, enter beginning balances for the accounts.

Milestone 3. Develop sample QuickBooks lists for customers, vendors, items, and employees. Obtain client and instructor approval for the lists and enter the list information.

Milestone 4. Enter sample transactions to test the prototype.

Milestone 5. Identify the reports that the client needs and then create memorized reports using QuickBooks.

Milestone 6. Develop documentation for the project including instructions for future use.

Milestone 7. Present the final project first to your class and then to the client.

This project can be completed individually or in teams. Ask your instructor which approach you will be using.

CHAPTER 13
LEARNING OBJECTIVES

Chapter 13 contains a project management framework consisting of the following seven milestones to develop a live QuickBooks accounting system:

INTRODUCTION

This chapter will give you project management tools to develop a real QuickBooks accounting system. You will assume the role of a consultant providing consulting services to a client for developing an accounting system using QuickBooks software. This project provides an opportunity for realistic, valuable practical experience to better prepare you for professional employment and enhance your resume.

Consistent with a sound project management approach, developing a QuickBooks accounting system is divided into seven milestones. Each milestone should be reviewed by your instructor before you proceed to the next milestone. In addition, the QuickBooks in Action Project Approval form should be signed by the client as each step is completed and approved.

MILESTONE 1
PROPOSAL

For Milestone 1, you will create a project proposal. The purpose of the proposal is twofold. First, it forces you, the consultant, to plan the project from start to finish. Second, the proposal serves to improve communication between you and your client. When the client reads your proposal, there is an opportunity for the client to further clarify any misunderstandings. Furthermore, the client may think of additional information or user requirements that were not mentioned earlier.

Complete the following steps to create a project proposal:

Step 1: Identify a real QuickBooks project.

Step 2: Gather project information and user requirements.

Step 3: Write the project proposal.

IDENTIFY QUICKBOOKS PROJECT

It is important to inform the client that this is for a class project and all work should be reviewed by his or her own accountant to verify appropriateness.

The first step is to identify an actual client who needs a QuickBooks accounting system. The client can be an entrepreneur, small business, or not-for-profit organization. For example, the client can be a friend or relative who operates a small business and needs an updated accounting system. Some colleges have Service Learning Coordinators who assist in matching student volunteers with charitable organizations needing assistance.

GATHER QUICKBOOKS PROJECT INFORMATION AND USER REQUIREMENTS

All information the client shares with you is confidential and should not be shared with anyone else. If you need to share information of a confidential nature with your instructor, first ask the client's permission.

After identifying the client, the next step is to interview the client to determine specific accounting needs and user requirements. Communication is extremely important to the process of designing and developing a successful accounting system. Listening to the client's needs and then communicating to the client the possible solutions are part of the ongoing development process. If clients are not familiar with accounting or QuickBooks, they may not be able to communicate all of their needs. This requires you to gather enough information from the client to identify both the need and the solution.

To make the most effective use of your client's time during the interview, prepare in advance. Before the interview, review all seven milestones of the project to identify the types of information you need to collect. For example, when gathering information for the Customer List, what customer fields does the client need? Also review the QuickBooks New Company Setup (see Chapters 8 and 10) to make certain you ask your client the questions you will need to answer when setting up the new company QuickBooks file for your client.

When collecting information about the Chart of Accounts, first identify the tax return filed by the enterprise. This will help you determine the accounts that are needed for tax purposes. Then, collect information about the assets, liabilities, equity, revenue and expense accounts that the company currently uses. Also, collect information about the beginning balances for accounts with opening balances.

For new businesses, QuickBooks provides a New Business Checklist shown on the following page. To access this checklist select **Help** menu **> New Business Checklist**.

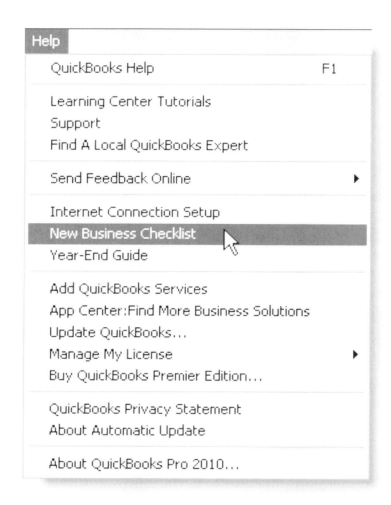

Prior to your interview, create your own User Requirements Checklist for gathering information from the client. A sample checklist follows.

QuickBooks New Business Checklist

Steps to Startup Success

Take some of the worry out of starting a business. From focusing your idea to seeking funding, this guide will walk you through the process. There are some activities, such as marketing and customer development, that are too specific to the kind of business you run to be covered here, so the guide isn't exhaustive, but it's a good place to start.

If you've already started your business, working through the checklist will ensure you haven't forgotten anything.

Note: You don't have to do the entire checklist at once. You can mark the steps you've completed then click Save Checkmarks. When you return to the checklist, you'll easily be able to see what you've already done.

1. Conceive your business   [Save Checkmarks] [Clear Checkmarks]

- ☐ A. Focus your idea
- ☐ B. Research your idea
- ☐ C. Choose a name
- ☐ D. Write a business plan

2. Structure your business

- ☐ A. Choose an organization type
- ☐ B. Consult professionals
- ☐ C. Set up your financial systems

3. Prepare all necessary forms, permits, and licenses

- ☐ A. Overview of federal, state, and local requirements
- ☐ B. File company papers with the Secretary of State's office
- ☐ C. Obtain a federal tax identification number
- ☐ D. Register your business name
- ☐ E. Obtain all necessary licenses and permits
- ☐ F. Fulfill all employer requirements
- ☐ G. Secure intellectual property
- ☐ H. Take care of local requirements

4. Fund your business

- ☐ A. Use your own assets
- ☐ B. Borrow from friends and family
- ☐ C. Borrow from a bank
- ☐ D. Check with minority or women's organizations
- ☐ E. Apply for a grant
- ☐ F. Other sources of equity funding

5. Taxes and insurance

- ☐ A. Fulfill all tax requirements
- ☐ B. Keep detailed records of all deductible expenditures
- ☐ C. Obtain insurance

Milestone 1 User Requirements Checklist	
☐ Organization name	
☐ Type of business (industry)	
☐ Chart of accounts information ☐ Tax return (Schedule C, Form 1120, Form 1120S) ☐ Beginning account balances	
☐ Customer List information	
☐ Vendor List information	
☐ Employee List information	
☐ Item List information	
☐ Types of transactions to be recorded	
☐ Types of reports needed	
☐ Users of the QuickBooks system and security access	
☐ Other user requirements	

WRITE QUICKBOOKS PROJECT PROPOSAL

After gathering information from the client, write a proposal that describes your plan for designing and developing your project. The proposal is a plan of what you intend to accomplish and how you will accomplish it.

Your proposal should have a professional appearance and tone that communicates to your client your competency and your enthusiasm for his or her project. Components of the proposal include:

1. **Cover Letter.** In the cover letter, you can thank the client for the opportunity to work together on this QuickBooks project, provide a brief introduction about yourself, summarize the main points in your proposal, and provide your contact information if the client has questions.

2. **Executive Summary.** Include the project name, your name, client name, and the date.

> **Paragraph 1.** Project objectives and initial feasibility assessment.
>
> **Paragraph 2.** Possible solutions that would meet project objectives.
>
> **Paragraph 3.** Your recommendation for the project and supporting rationale.

An Executive Summary Template appears on a following page.

3. **Proposal Report.** Include the following headings and sections:

   - **Overview and Objectives.** Briefly describe the client organization and operations. Identify the client's user requirements for an accounting system. For example, the client needs accounting records for tax purposes. Evaluate the feasibility of meeting the organization's needs with QuickBooks and the objectives of this project.

   - **Scope of Services.** Outline the services that you will provide for the client. What accounting features of QuickBooks will be implemented? Accounts receivable? Accounts payable?

Specify the services you will provide the client. Will you provide implementation and setup? Conversion assistance?

- **Client Responsibilities.** Clearly specify any responsibilities or information that the client will need to provide.

- **Cost/Benefit Analysis.** Provide a summary of the costs associated with the project that the client might expect to occur. Provide information about the benefits that might be expected, including financial and nonfinancial benefits. For example, estimated time that the client might save in maintaining accounting records.

- **Timeline.** Identify and list the major tasks involved in completing the project. Include a timeline with completion dates for each task. See the sample format below.

Task	Projected Completion Date
1._____	_____
2._____	_____
3._____	_____
4._____	_____
5._____	_____
Etc._____	_____

- **Recommendation.** State your recommendation and provide a short summary including any disclaimers or remaining challenges. End the proposal on a positive, upbeat note.

Submit the proposal to both the client and your instructor. Obtain approval from both the client and your instructor. Ask the client to sign off on the proposal using the approval form that appears at the end of Chapter 13.

Executive Summary [Template]		
Company Name	[your company name and logo]	
Contact Name	[your name]	
Date	[date of proposal]	
For	[client name]	
Project Name	[QuickBooks project name]	
Objectives	[Paragraph 1 contains a concise summary of the project objectives and the initial feasibility assessment.]	
Possible Solutions	[Paragraph 2 briefly summarizes possible solutions that satisfy the project objectives.]	
Recommendation	[Paragraph 3 contains your recommendation and supporting rationale.]	

MILESTONE 2
COMPANY SETUP AND CHART OF ACCOUNTS

When creating the Chart of Accounts, refer to the tax form the organization will use. Obtain copies of tax forms at www.irs.gov

In this milestone, you will set up a prototype or sample company for the client to review and revise.

Step 1: Based on the information collected from the client, set up a new company and customize the Chart of Accounts for the company.

Step 2: Submit the Chart of Accounts to your instructor for review and recommendations.

Step 3: Have the client review the Chart of Accounts and make recommendations. Ask the client to sign off on the Chart of Accounts using the approval form.

Step 4: After obtaining approval from both the client and instructor, enter beginning balances for the accounts.

Nonprofits use fund accounting. Use subaccounts or the class tracking preference for fund accounting.

MILESTONE 3
CUSTOMER, VENDOR, EMPLOYEE, AND ITEM LISTS

After the Chart of Accounts has been approved, proceed to developing lists (customer, vendor, employee, and item) for the client.

Step 1: After consulting with the client, list the customer information (fields) needed for each customer. If necessary, create user-defined fields in QuickBooks to accommodate the client's needs.

Step 2: List the information needed by the organization for each vendor. Create any user-defined fields that are needed for vendors.

Step 3: List the employee information needed by the organization for each employee. Determine any payroll items needed to accurately record payroll. If applicable, collect payroll year-to-date information.

Step 4:   Determine the items (inventory, non-inventory, and service items) required to meet the organization's needs. List the information needed for each item.

Step 5:   After obtaining approval for the lists from the client and your instructor, enter information for the following:

- Customer List
- Vendor List
- Item List
- Employee List
- Payroll year-to-date information

MILESTONE 4
TRANSACTIONS

Complete the following steps for Milestone 4.

Step 1:   Determine the types of transactions the client will enter in QuickBooks (for example: cash sales, credit card sales, purchase orders).

Step 2:   Enter test or sample transactions in QuickBooks. Obtain the client and instructor's approval of the results.

Step 3:   Modify forms as needed to meet the client's needs. For example, if the client needs a *Date* column on the invoice, customize the invoice by following the instructions in Project 9.1.

Step 4:   After obtaining the client's approval for transactions, create memorized transactions for the transactions that will be repeated periodically.

It is important that you and the client reach an agreement regarding what you will complete before you turn the project over to the client.

Discuss with the client whether you will be entering only a few sample transactions or entering all transactions for the year to date. For example, if entering all transactions is too time consuming, you may agree that you will enter only sample transactions and the client will enter the real transactions after you submit the final project.

MILESTONE 5
MEMORIZED REPORTS

Complete the following steps for Milestone 5:

Step 1: Determine which reports the client needs. Review Chapters 4, 5, 6, and 7 to obtain information about the different reports that QuickBooks can generate. You may need to make the client aware of the reports that are available in QuickBooks and then let the client select the reports that would be useful.

Step 2: Obtain client and instructor approval for the reports.

Step 3: After obtaining approval concerning the reports, create and memorize the reports using QuickBooks.

Provide the client with instructions for using QuickBooks Help feature.

MILESTONE 6
DOCUMENTATION AND CLIENT INSTRUCTIONS

Create documentation for the client. Include a history of the project development as well as instructions that the client will need. For example, instructions regarding how and when to back up and restore company files are essential. Providing instructions on how to use memorized transactions and memorized reports is also advisable.

An easy way to provide the client with adequate instructions is to recommend existing training materials to the client and then simply reference pages in the training materials. For example, if the client obtains a copy of this book, you may wish to reference pages of the text for each task the client will be performing.

Other documentation that the client might find useful is the Year-End Guide that appears on a following page. To view the Year-End Guide, select **Help** menu **> Year-End Guide**.

MILESTONE 7
PRESENTATION

There are three parts to this milestone:

Step 1:   Make any final changes to your project.

Step 2:   Make the project presentation to your class.

Step 3:   Make a project presentation to the client.

The presentation to your instructor and classmates is practice for the final presentation to the client. You may want to ask your classmates for suggestions you can incorporate into your final presentation for the client.

A suggested outline for the project presentation follows:

1. **History and Overview.** Provide background about the client and the client's needs as an introduction for your presentation.

2. **Demonstration.** If the room has projection equipment, demonstrate your QuickBooks project. Display memorized transactions, memorized reports, and lists for the class and/or client to view. *Remember to use test/sample data for the class presentation instead of actual client data that is confidential.*

3. **Examples.** Present examples of the documentation and client instructions you are providing the client (see Milestone 6).

4. **Cost/Benefit and Advantages/Disadvantages.** Briefly present advantages and disadvantages of using QuickBooks for this particular project as well as associated costs and benefits.

Be prepared for clients to ask if they may call if they need your assistance in the future. Adequate user instructions (Milestone 6) are essential in reducing the client's future dependence on you.

As you develop the accounting system, you may find that further customization of the Chart of Accounts is needed to meet specific business needs.
In your final project, highlight any new accounts added.

5. **Summary.** Present concluding remarks to summarize the major points of your presentation.

6. **Questions and Answers.** Provide classmates or the client an opportunity to ask questions about the project. In preparing for your presentation, you will want to anticipate possible questions and prepare appropriate answers.

QuickBooks Year-End Guide   Tech Support

✓ Year-End Guide Checklist

Reduce hassles with our Year-End Guide. We'll show you how to wrap up the business year, archive your QuickBooks files, and get ready for the next business year.

Tasks to prepare for filing taxes | Save Checkmarks | | Clear Checkmarks |

- ☐ A. Reconcile all bank and credit card accounts
- ☐ B. Verify petty cash entries for the tax year
- ☐ C. Make year-end accrual adjustments and corrections
- ☐ D. Close your books
- ☐ E. Adjust Retained Earnings
- ☐ F. Review details of all new equipment purchased during year
- ☐ G. Make all asset depreciation entries and adjustments
- ☐ H. Review fringe benefits that need to be reported on Form W-2
- ☐ I. Take a physical inventory and reconcile with book inventory
- ☐ J. Print financial reports
- ☐ K. Print income tax reports to verify tax tracking
- ☐ L. Import your tax-related data to TurboTax or ProSeries
- ☐ M. Print and mail Forms W-2, W-3, 1099, 940, 941 and 1096
- ☐ N. Archive and back up your data
- ☐ O. Order supplies and tax forms

Tasks to do if you use subcontractors

- ☐ A. Ensure that 1099 info is correct
- ☐ B. Print & mail 1099s

Tasks to do if you have employees

If you use the Assisted Payroll Service

- ☐ Click here for frequently asked questions about year-end tasks

  If you are enrolled in QuickBooks Assisted Payroll, the following items are handled by the payroll service for you:

  - Pay payroll taxes and other liabilities (Assisted Payroll automatically makes your federal and state payroll tax liability payments)
  - Print and distribute W-2s
  - Print and distribute W-3s
  - Process Form 940
  - Process Form 941

If you use QuickBooks Payroll or have no payroll service

- ☐ A. Confirm you have current payroll tax tables (QuickBooks Payroll only)
- ☑ B. Clear YTD payroll amounts - QuickBooks does this for you
- ☐ C. Pay payroll liabilities
- ☐ D. Review W-2 forms
- ☐ E. Print & distribute W-2s
- ☐ F. Print form W-3
- ☐ G. Process Form 940
- ☐ H. Process Form 941
- ☐ I. Verify W4 information

Tech Support   Access to the QuickBooks Knowledge Base

QuickBooks in Action Project Approval

Milestone	Comments	Approved	Date
1. Proposal		_____	_____
2. Company Setup & Chart of Accounts		_____	_____
3. Lists: Customer, Vendor, Item, & Employee		_____	_____
4. Transactions		_____	_____
5. Memorized Reports		_____	_____
6. Documentation		_____	_____
7. Final Presentation		_____	_____

SECTION 3
QUICK GUIDE

The Quick Guide contains step-by-step instructions for frequently used QuickBooks tasks, providing you with a convenient, easy-to-use resource that summarizes essential tasks.

The chapters in *Computer Accounting with QuickBooks* are designed as tutorials for you to initially learn the accounting software, providing numerous screen captures and detailed instructions. To improve long-term retention of your software skills, exercises and projects are designed with fewer instructions to test your understanding and, when needed, to develop your skill at quickly seeking out additional information to complete the task. JIT Learning, the ability to seek out information as needed, is an increasingly important skill in the rapidly changing business environment and the design of *Computer Accounting with QuickBooks* seamlessly facilitates your development of this crucial skill.

QUICKBOOKS SOFTWARE

COMPANY COMMANDS

CHART OF ACCOUNTS

CUSTOMER TRANSACTIONS

VENDOR TRANSACTIONS

EMPLOYEE TRANSACTIONS

BANKING TRANSACTIONS

ENTRIES

REPORTS

MICROSOFT OFFICE AND QUICKBOOKS

QUICKBOOKS HELP

QuickBooks Software

Install QuickBooks Software

 To install QuickBooks software, follow the step-by-step directions in *Appendix A: Install & Register QuickBooks Software*.

Register QuickBooks Software

 Register QuickBooks software online at the time you install the software, following the directions in *Appendix A: Install and Register QuickBooks Software*.

 Failure to register QuickBooks software within the first 30 days will result in the software no longer functioning. To avoid this, register the software at the time you install it. If you fail to register QuickBooks software within 30 days and you are locked out from using the software, select **Help** menu **> Register QuickBooks**. Another option is to uninstall and reinstall the QuickBooks software from your trial version CD that accompanies your text, registering the software when requested.

Update QuickBooks Software

1. Establish your Internet connection.

2. Select **Help** menu **> Update QuickBooks**.

3. Click the **Options** tab.

4. If you would like QuickBooks to automatically update each time you connect to the Internet, select **Yes** for Automatic Update.

5. To download an update, select **Update Now** tab **> Get Updates**. When asked if you want to update QuickBooks, click **Yes**.

SINGLE-USER AND MULTI-USER MODES

1. If you are in multi-user mode, to switch to single-user mode, select **File** menu **> Switch to Single-User Mode > Yes**.

2. If you are in single-user mode, to switch to multi-user mode, select **File** menu **> Switch to Multi-User Mode > Yes**.

COMPANY COMMANDS

START QUICKBOOKS SOFTWARE

1. Click the QuickBooks desktop icon or click **Start > Programs > QuickBooks Pro (or Premier) > QuickBooks 2010**.

2. If necessary, close the *QuickBooks Learning Center* window to begin using QuickBooks.

SET UP NEW COMPANY

1. Select **File** menu **> New Company**.

2. Follow the onscreen instructions to complete the EasyStep Interview to set up a new company. Also see *Chapter 8*.

CUSTOMIZE QUICKBOOKS

To customize QuickBooks to fit your accounting software needs, you can select preferences as follows:

1. Select **Edit** menu **> Preferences**.

2. From the left scroll bar *Preferences* window, select the appropriate preference category:

    - Accounting
    - Bills
    - Checking
    - Desktop View
    - Finance Charge

- General
- Integrated Applications
- Items & Inventory
- Jobs & Estimates
- Multiple Currencies
- Payments
- Payroll & Employees
- Reminders
- Reports & Graphs
- Sales & Customers
- Sales Tax
- Send Forms
- Service Connection
- Spelling
- Tax: 1099
- Time & Expenses

3. Select the **My Preferences** tab or the **Company Preferences** tab.

4. Enter the preference settings you desire to customize QuickBooks.

5. When finished selecting preferences, click **OK**.

OPEN COMPANY FILE (.QBW)

To open a QuickBooks company file (.QBW) that is on the hard drive (C:) or that has been restored to the C: drive:

1. After QuickBooks software is open, select **File** menu **> Open or Restore Company**.

2. Select **Open a company file (.QBW) > Next**.

3. Select the company file and location. Click **Open**.

CLOSE QUICKBOOKS COMPANY FILE (.QBW)

1. Select **File** menu.

2. Click **Close Company**.

BACK UP COMPANY FILE (.QBB)

Backup company files (.QBB) are compressed company files. Typically, you will want to back up your company at regular intervals. To save a QuickBooks backup company file:

1. Select **File** menu > **Save Copy or Backup**.
2. Select **Backup copy > Next**.
3. Select **Local backup > Next**.
4. If requested, select location of backup file. Click **OK**.
5. Select **Save it now > Next**.
6. Select location and backup file name (.QBB). Click **Save**.

 For more information, see *Appendix B: Back Up & Restore QuickBooks Files* and *Chapter 1*.

RESTORE COMPANY FILE (.QBB)

 Typically you restore a backup company file when the QuickBooks .QBW file fails. For purposes of this text, you will restore a backup file when you use the Restart and Restore approach. For more information, see *Appendix B: Back Up & Restore QuickBooks Files* and *Chapter 1*.

To restore a QuickBooks backup company file:

1. Select **File** menu > **Open or Restore Company**.
2. Select **Restore a backup copy > Next**.
3. Select **Local backup > Next**.
4. Select location of backup file and backup file name. Select **Open > Next**.
5. Select location and name of restored file. If saving to the hard drive, Intuit recommends storing company files in the following location:
   C:\Documents and Settings\All Users\(Shared) Documents\Intuit\QuickBooks\Company Files.
6. Click **Save**.
7. Click **OK**.

SAVE PORTABLE COMPANY FILE (.QBM)

Portable company files (.QBM) permit you to move your QuickBooks company file from one computer to another. To save a portable QuickBooks company file:

1. Select **File** menu > **Save Copy or Backup**.
2. Select **Portable company file > Next**.
3. Enter the location and file name.
4. Click **Save**.

OPEN PORTABLE COMPANY FILE (.QBM)

To open a QuickBooks portable company file:

1. Select **File** menu > **Open or Restore Company**.
2. Select **Restore a portable file > Next**.
3. Select the location and portable company file name (.QBM) to open. Select **Open > Next**.
4. Enter the QuickBooks working file name (.QBW) and location. If saving to the hard drive, Intuit recommends storing company files in the following location: C:\Documents and Settings\All Users\(Shared) Documents\Intuit\QuickBooks\Company Files.
5. Click **Save**.

CHANGE COMPANY NAME

1. Select **Company** menu > **Company Information**.
2. Enter the new company name.
3. Click **OK**.

UPDATE QUICKBOOKS COMPANY FILE

To update your company file created using a previous version of QuickBooks (for example, to update a QuickBooks company file created in QuickBooks 2009 to QuickBooks 2010):

1. Back up your company file.

2. Using QuickBooks 2010 software, select **File** menu > **Open or Restore Company**.

3. When asked if you want to update the file, enter **YES** and click **OK**.

EXIT QUICKBOOKS SOFTWARE

1. Click **File** menu.

2. Click **Exit**.

CHART OF ACCOUNTS

ENTER NEW ACCOUNTS

1. From the **Company** section of the Home page, click the **Chart of Accounts** icon.

2. **Right-click** to display the popup menu. Select **New**.

3. Enter **Type of Account, Account Number, Name, Description,** and **Tax Line**.

4. Click **Next** to enter another account.

5. Click **OK** to close the *New Account* window.

ENTER BEGINNING BALANCES

1. If the account has a beginning balance, when entering the new account, from the *New Account* (or *Edit Account*) window, select the **Enter Opening Balance** button.

2. Enter the opening balance and the As of Date for the beginning balance.

3. Click **OK**.

PRINT CHART OF ACCOUNTS

1. From the **Report Center**, select **Accountant & Taxes > Account Listing**.

2. Click **Print**.

CUSTOMER TRANSACTIONS

ENTER CUSTOMER INFORMATION

1. Click the **Customer Center** on the Icon bar.

2. Select **New Customer & Job > New Customer**.

3. Enter customer information.

4. Click **Next** to enter another customer or click **OK** to save and close the window.

INVOICE CUSTOMERS

1. From the **Customers** section of the Home page, click the **Create Invoices** icon.

2. Enter invoice information.

3. Click **Print** to print the invoice.

4. Click **Save & New** to enter another invoice or **Save & Close** to close the window.

RECEIVE CUSTOMER PAYMENTS

1. From the **Customers** section of the Home page, click the **Receive Payments** icon.

2. Enter receipt information.

3. Click **Save & New** to enter another receipt or **Save & Close** to close the window.

DEPOSIT CUSTOMER PAYMENTS

1. From the **Banking** section of the Home page, click the **Record Deposits** icon.

2. Enter deposit information.

3. Click **Save & New** to enter another deposit or **Save & Close** to close the window.

VENDOR TRANSACTIONS

ENTER VENDOR INFORMATION

1. From the **Vendor Center**, click the **New Vendor** button.

2. Enter vendor information.

3. Click **Next** to enter another vendor or click **OK** to save and close the window.

ENTER ITEMS

1. From the **Company** section of the Home page, click the **Items & Services** icon.

2. **Right-click** to display the popup menu. Select **New**.

3. Enter inventory item information.

4. To enter another item, click **Next**.

5. When finished, click **OK**.

CREATE PURCHASE ORDERS

1. After entering the inventory items, to record the purchase of inventory, from the **Vendors** section of the Home page, click **Purchase Orders**.

2. Enter purchase information.

3. To enter another purchase order, click **Save & New**.

4. When finished, click **Save & Close**.

RECEIVE ITEMS

1. From the **Vendors** section of the Home page, click **Receive Inventory**.

2. Select **Receive Inventory with Bill** or **Receive Inventory without Bill**.

3. Select the vendor. If asked if you want to match against outstanding purchase orders, click **Yes**.

4. Enter the remaining information.

5. To enter another item received, click **Save & New**.

6. When finished, click **Save & Close**.

ENTER BILLS AGAINST INVENTORY

1. From the **Vendors** section of the Home page, click **Enter Bills Against Inventory**.

2. Select the vendor and choose the Item Receipt that corresponds to the bill.

3. Enter the remaining information.

4. To enter another bill, click **Save & New**.

5. When finished, click **Save & Close.**

Pay Bills

1. From the **Vendors** section of the Home page, click **Pay Bills**.
2. Select **Show all bills**.
3. Select bills to pay.
4. Click **Pay Selected Bills**.

Print Checks

1. Select **File** menu > **Print Forms** > **Checks** (or click the **Print Checks** icon in the **Banking** section of the Home page).
2. Select **Bank Account**.
3. Enter **First Check Number**.
4. Select checks to print.
5. Click **OK**.
6. Select **Type of Check**.
7. Click **Print**.

Employee Transactions

Enter Employee Information

1. From the **Employee Center**, click the **New Employees** button.
2. Enter employee information.
3. Click **Next** to enter another employee or click **OK** to save and close the window.

TRACK TIME

1. From the **Employees** section of the Home page, select **Enter Time** icon > **Use Weekly Timesheet**.
2. Select **Employee Name**.
3. Select **Week**.
4. Enter time worked (if needed, select customer and service item).
5. To enter another timesheet, click **Save & New**.
6. Click **Print** to print the timesheets.
7. When finished, click **Save & Close.**

PAY EMPLOYEES

1. From the **Employees** section of the Home page, click **Pay Employees**.
2. In the Pay Employees screen, enter **Pay Period Ends** and **Check Date**.
3. Select **Employee**. Click on **Employee name**.
4. Enter withholding and deduction amounts.
5. Click **OK.**
6. Continue until all employee paychecks are completed. Then click **Continue**.
7. Click **Create Paychecks**.
8. Click **Print Paychecks** to print the paychecks.

BANKING TRANSACTIONS

WRITE CHECKS

1. From the **Banking** section of the Home page, click **Write Checks**.
2. Select **Bank Account**.
3. Enter **Check Date** and remaining check information.
4. Enter **Account** and **Amount**.

5. Select **To be printed**.

6. Click **Print** to print the checks.

MAKE DEPOSITS

1. From the **Banking** section of the Home page, click **Record Deposits**.

2. Select **Payments to Deposit**, then click **OK**.

3. Select **Bank Account**. Enter **Date** and deposit information.

4. Click **Print** to print the deposit summary.

5. Click **Save & Close**.

RECONCILE BANK STATEMENT

1. From the **Banking** section of the Home page, click **Reconcile**.

2. Select **Bank Account**.

3. Enter **Statement Date** and **Ending Balance**.

4. Enter **Service Charges** and **Interest Earned**.

5. Click **Continue**.

6. Check deposits and checks that appear on the bank statement.

7. Click **Reconcile Now**.

ENTRIES

JOURNAL ENTRIES

1. Select **Company** menu > **Make General Journal Entries**.

2. Enter **Date**, **Entry Number**, **Accounts**, and **Debit and Credit** amounts.

3. Click **Save & New** to enter another journal entry.

4. Click **Save & Close** to close the *Make General Journal Entries* window.

ADJUSTING ENTRIES

1. Select **Company** menu > **Make General Journal Entries**.

2. Enter **Date, Entry Number (ADJ #), Accounts,** and **Debit and Credit** amounts.

3. Click **Save & New** to enter another journal entry.

4. Click **Save & Close** to close the *Make General Journal Entries* window.

CORRECTING ENTRIES

To correct an error, make two correcting entries in the Journal:

1. Eliminate the effect of the incorrect entry by making the opposite journal entry.

   For example, assume the Cash account should have been debited for $200.00 and the Professional Fees Revenue account credited for $200.00. However, the following incorrect entry was made for $2,000.00 instead of $200.00.

Debit	Cash	2,000.00
Credit	Professional Fees Revenue	2,000.00

   To eliminate the effect of the incorrect entry, make the following entry:

Debit	Professional Fees Revenue	2,000.00
Credit	Cash	2,000.00

2. After eliminating the effect of the incorrect entry, make the following correct entry that should have been made initially:

Debit	Cash	200.00
Credit	Professional Fees Revenue	200.00

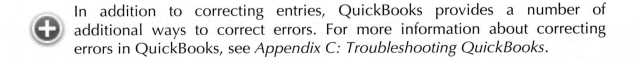 In addition to correcting entries, QuickBooks provides a number of additional ways to correct errors. For more information about correcting errors in QuickBooks, see *Appendix C: Troubleshooting QuickBooks*.

CLOSING

Before closing a fiscal period, prepare adjusting entries and print all reports needed. To close the fiscal period:

1. Select **Edit** menu **> Preferences > Accounting > Company Preferences.**

2. Under Closing Date, select **Set Date/Password.**

3. Enter the **Closing Date**. If desired, enter and confirm the **Closing Date Password**.

4. Click **OK**.

REPORTS

PRINT TRIAL BALANCE

1. From the **Report Center**, select **Accountant & Taxes > Trial Balance**.

2. Select **Dates**.

3. Click **Display reports** icon.

4. Click **Print**.

PRINT GENERAL JOURNAL

1. From the **Report Center**, select **Accountant & Taxes > Journal**.

2. Select **Dates**.

3. Click **Display reports** icon.

4. Click **Print**.

PRINT GENERAL LEDGER

1. From the **Report Center**, select **Accountant & Taxes > General Ledger**.

2. Select **Dates**.

3. Click **Display reports** icon.

4. Select **Modify Report > Advanced**. Choose to show only **Accounts in Use**.

5. Click **Print**.

PRINT INCOME STATEMENT

1. From the **Report Center**, select **Company & Financial**.

2. Under the **Profit & Loss (Income Statement)** section, select **Profit & Loss Standard**.

3. Select **Dates**.

4. Click **Display reports** icon.

5. Click **Print**.

PRINT BALANCE SHEET

1. From the **Report Center**, select **Company & Financial**.

2. Under the **Balance Sheet & Net Worth** section, select **Balance Sheet Standard**.

3. Select **Dates**.

4. Click **Display reports** icon.

5. Click **Print**.

MICROSOFT OFFICE AND QUICKBOOKS

PREPARE MICROSOFT WORD CUSTOMER LETTERS

1. From the **Customer Center**, click the **Word** icon.

2. From the drop-down list, select **Prepare Customer Letters**.

3. Complete the onscreen steps to prepare a customer letter.

PREPARE MICROSOFT WORD COLLECTION LETTERS

1. From the **Customer Center**, click the **Word** icon.

2. From the drop-down list, select **Prepare Collection Letters**.

3. Complete the onscreen steps to prepare a collection letter.

IMPORT DATA FROM MICROSOFT EXCEL

To import lists of customers, vendors, accounts, or items from Microsoft Excel into QuickBooks:

1. Back up the QuickBooks company file.

2. Select **File** menu > **Utilities** > **Import** > **Excel Files**.

3. From the *Add Your Excel Data to QuickBooks* window, click **Advanced Import** button.

4. Select the **Set up Import** tab > **Select the file** > **mappings**.

5. Click the **Preference** tab. Select how to handle duplicates and errors.

6. Click **Preview**. Make appropriate corrections.

7. Click **Import**.

Another way to import data from Excel is from the specific center. For example, to import the Customer List from Excel:

1. From the **Customer Center**, click the **Excel** button.

2. Select **Import from Excel**.

3. From the *Add Your Excel Data to QuickBooks* window, select **type of data you want to add to QuickBooks** button.

4. Follow the onscreen instructions.

5. Save the Excel file.

EXPORT DATA TO MICROSOFT EXCEL

You can export data to Microsoft Excel for customers, vendors, inventory items, transactions, payroll summary, and reports. For example, to export customer data to Excel:

1. Click the **Customer Center**.
2. Display the **Customer List**. If necessary, use the View drop-down menu to filter the Customer List.
3. Click the **Excel** button. Select **Export Customer List**.
4. Select **a new Excel workbook**. Click **Export**.
5. When the Excel file opens, save the Excel file.

EXPORT REPORTS TO MICROSOFT EXCEL

To export reports to Microsoft Excel:

1. Using the **Report Center**, display the desired report.
2. Click the **Export** button at the top of the report window.
3. Select **a new Excel workbook**. Click **Export**.
4. When the Excel file opens, save the Excel file.

QUICKBOOKS HELP

HELP FEATURE

1. Select **Help** menu > **QuickBooks Help** > **Search**.
2. Type your question.
3. Click the **Start Search** arrow.

LEARNING CENTER TUTORIALS

1. Select **Help** menu **> Learning Center Tutorials**.

2. Select the type of tutorial: Overview & Setup, Customers & Sales, Vendors & Expenses, Inventory, Payroll, Process Payments, or What's New.

3. Select the tutorial to view.

Section 4
QuickBooks Extras ✚

A

Install & Register QuickBooks Software

B

Back Up & Restore QuickBooks Files

C

Troubleshooting QuickBooks

D

Electronic Deliverables

E

QuickBooks for Mac

F

QuickBooks Blog

APPENDIX A
INSTALL & REGISTER QUICKBOOKS SOFTWARE

In Appendix A, you will learn about:

INSTALL QUICKBOOKS SOFTWARE

To install your QuickBooks trial version software that accompanies *Computer Accounting with QuickBooks*:

If you already have another version of QuickBooks software installed on your computer, you can select to replace it with the newer version or to install both versions.

Step 1: Close any open programs and disable your antivirus software.

Step 2: Insert the QuickBooks trial version CD in your CD drive.

Step 3: Follow the onscreen instructions that the QuickBooks Installer provides. Select **One User** and **Full QuickBooks with Database**.

Step 4: When requested, enter the License and Product number located on the back of the disk jacket for the QuickBooks software CD.

Step 5: You must register the QuickBooks trial version within 30 days. You will be able to use the trial version for 140 days. Therefore, you might want to wait to install the software until you need it for your QuickBooks course.

REGISTER QUICKBOOKS SOFTWARE

Register your QuickBooks software! Failure to register your QuickBooks trial version software will result in the software no longer functioning.

You can use the QuickBooks trial version for 30 days without registering. Three ways to register your QuickBooks trial version are:

1. Register the software when you install it.

2. Select **Help** menu **> Register QuickBooks**.

3. Register your QuickBooks software by phone at 888-246-8848 and select Customer Service.

If you fail to register QuickBooks software within 30 days and you are locked out from using the software, try uninstalling and reinstalling the QuickBooks software from your trial version CD that accompanies your text.

UPDATE QUICKBOOKS SOFTWARE

To update QuickBooks software automatically when the software updates become available:

Step 1: Establish your Internet connection.

Step 2: Select **Help** menu **> Update QuickBooks**.

Step 3: Click the **Options** tab.

Step 4: If you would like QuickBooks to automatically update each time you connect to the Internet, select **Yes** for Automatic Update.

Step 5: To download an update, select **Update Now** tab **> Get Updates**. When asked if you want to update QuickBooks, click **Yes**.

OPEN QUICKBOOKS DATA FILES

QuickBooks backup (.QBB) files are provided with *Computer Accounting with QuickBooks* for use as company data files. If you have an error in your QuickBooks company file that you cannot locate or correct, you can use the .QBB files provided with the text to restart with correct account balances.

The .QBB data files are provided on the data file CD packaged with your text and as a download on the *Computer Accounting with QuickBooks* Online Learning Center.

QuickBooks Data Files (CD accompanying text)

To use the data files (.QBB) on the CD that accompanies *Computer Accounting with QuickBooks*:

Step 1: Insert the data file CD into your CD drive.

Step 2: Follow the onscreen instructions.

Step 3: Copy the .QBB data files to your desktop or a USB drive.

Step 4: Follow the instructions in the text to open and use the .QBB data files.

QuickBooks Data Files (Online Learning Center)

To download and use the QuickBooks .QBB data files provided on the Online Learning Center:

Step 1: Go to www.mhhe.com/kay2010.

Step 2: From the Student Edition of the Online Learning Center, locate the Data Files.

Step 3: Follow the instructions to download and unzip the data files.

Step 4: Save the data files to your desktop or removable media.

Step 5: Restore the data files following the instructions in *Chapter 1* or *Appendix B: Back Up & Restore QuickBooks Files*.

APPENDIX B
BACK UP & RESTORE QUICKBOOKS FILES

In Appendix B, you will learn about:

QUICKBOOKS FILE VERSIONS

In addition to the QuickBooks software, QuickBooks uses a company file to store information about a specific enterprise. Thus, you can use the QuickBooks software installed on your computer with many different files. This is similar to using Microsoft Excel software, for example, with many different Excel data files.

The different versions of QuickBooks company files are summarized in the following table.

Extension	QuickBooks Company File
.QBW	**QuickBooks for Window**. You can think of this file as a QuickBooks working file. This is the file version that you use to enter transactions and data. It is usually saved to the hard drive of your computer.
.QBB	**QuickBooks Backup**. A QuickBooks Backup file should be created at regular intervals in case your .QBW file fails or is destroyed. The .QBB file version is a compressed file and cannot be opened directly. Furthermore, you cannot enter transactions directly into a .QBB file. Instead, you must unzip the file first by restoring the file into a .QBW file version.
.QBM	**QuickBooks Mobile**. A QuickBooks Mobile file, also called a QuickBooks Portable file, is used to move a QuickBooks file to another computer. Like the .QBB backup file version, the .QBM file version is compressed and must be unzipped and restored into a .QBW file version before it can be used to enter data.
.QBX	**QuickBooks Accountants**. A QuickBooks Accountants Copy is identified with a .QBX extension. This version of your company file is used to give to your accountant. The accountant can make changes, such as adjusting entries, to the .QBX version of your company file while you continue to use your .QBW company file version.

QUICKBOOKS FILE MANAGEMENT

QuickBooks file management involves managing your QuickBooks company files to ensure the security and integrity of your QuickBooks accounting system.

For a business, there are two aspects to QuickBooks file management:

1. Workflow
2. Restart and restore

WORKFLOW

In a typical business workflow, you use the same .QBW computer file on the same computer. Sound file management includes making backups as part of a disaster recovery plan. A good backup system is to have a different backup for each business day: Monday backup, Tuesday backup, Wednesday backup, and so on. Then if it is necessary to use the backup file and the Wednesday backup, for example, fails, the company has a Tuesday backup to use. Furthermore, it is recommended that a business store at least one backup at a remote location.

RESTART & RESTORE

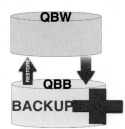

If a company's .QBW fails, then you must restart by restoring your most recent .QBB file version. The backup file (.QBB) is compressed and must be converted to a working file (.QBW) before you can use it to enter data or transactions.

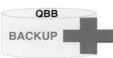

BACK UP QUICKBOOKS FILES

To save a backup (.QBB) file:

Step 1: With the QuickBooks working file (*.QBW) open, click **File > Save Copy or Backup**.

You can schedule a backup every time you close a QuickBooks company file or at regular intervals.

Step 2: Select **Backup copy** when the following window appears. Click **Next**.

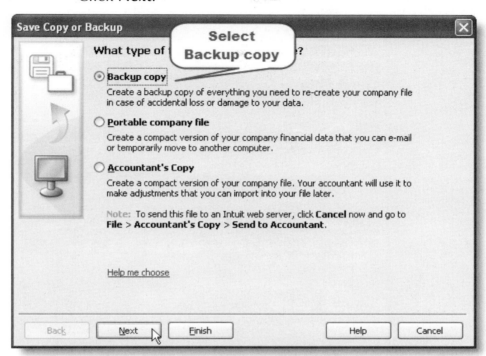

Step 3: When the following window appears, select **Local backup.**

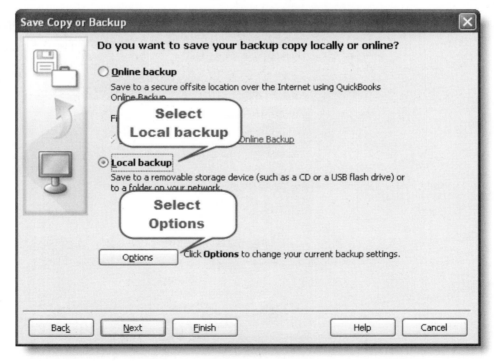

Step 4: Select **Options** to specify where you will be storing your backups.

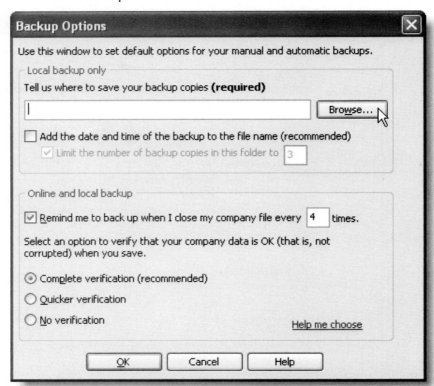

To make it easier to find your backup files, click the **Browse** button and select **Desktop**. Then click **OK**.

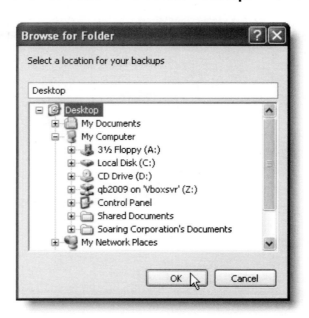

Click **OK** to close the **Backup Options** window. Select **Use this Location** if a *QuickBooks* warning window appears.

Click **Next** to finalize Local backup selection and move to the next window.

 Step 5: If you are saving the backup copy to a removable storage device such as a USB flash drive, insert the storage device now. Select **Save it now**. Click **Next**.

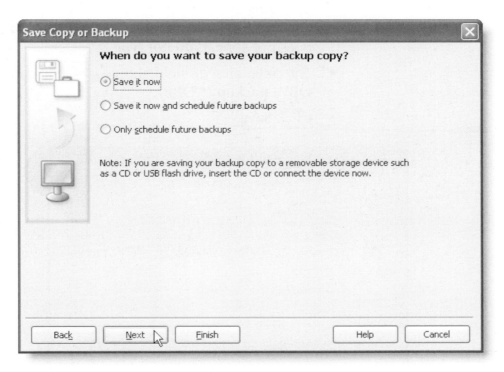

 Step 6: Designate where you would like your backup copies stored. You can save the backup to the desktop and then copy to a removable storage device later or you can save directly to the removable storage device.

Ask your instructor where you should save your backup files.

When the following *Save Backup Copy* window appears:

- Change the *Save in* field to the location your instructor specifies. For example, if saving to removable storage media, select the USB flash drive. If saving to the computer's hard disk, save to the Desktop to make it easier to locate the files later.

- Change the *File name* field to **[your name] [Chapter or Exercise No.] Backup** as shown. Depending on your operating system settings, the file extension .QBB may or may not appear automatically. If the .QBB extension does not appear, *do not type it.*

- The *Save as type* field should automatically appear as **QBW Backup (*.QBB).**

- Click **Save**.

Step 7: Click **OK** when the following message appears.

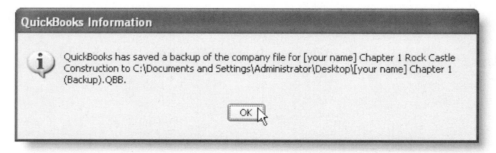

RESTART & RESTORE QUICKBOOKS FILES

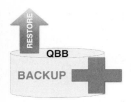

To restore a backup .QBB file:

Step 1: From the Menu bar, click **File > Open or Restore Company**.

Use your .QBB backup file, copy a .QBB backup file from the data file CD, or download a .QBB backup file from the Online Learning Center.

For your convenience, QuickBooks backup (*.QBB) data files accompany *Computer Accounting for QuickBooks Pro*. You will find the data files on the CD packaged with your text. Before using the data files on the CD, you must copy the files to your desktop or removable media.

Or you can download the backup data files from the Online Learning Center at www.mhhe.com/kay2010.

Step 2: Select **Restore a backup copy (.QBB)**. Click **Next**.

Step 3: When the following *Open or Restore Company* window appears, select **Local backup**. Click **Next**.

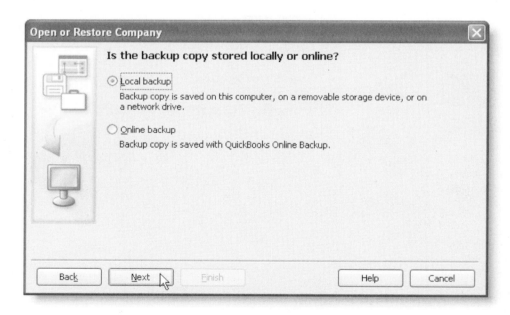

Step 4: Identify the location and file name of the backup company file.

In the following example, the data file was copied to a USB flash drive (E:), so first you would select Look in E:, the USB drive.

- Select the file.
- The *Files of type* field should automatically display: **QBW Backup (*.QBB)**.
- Click **Open**.

 Step 5: When the following window appears, click **Next**.

Step 6: Identify the file name and location of the new company file (.QBW) file.

- Select the location to save the .QBW file. If saving to the C: drive, select Save in: **C:\Documents and Settings \Users\(Shared) Documents\Intuit \QuickBooks\ Company Files**.

- File name: **[your name Chapter or Exercise No.]**. Insert your name in the file name so that you can identify your files.

- The *Save as type* field should automatically appear as **QuickBooks Files (*.QBW)**. The .QBW extension indicates that this is a QuickBooks working file.

- Click **Save** to save the QuickBooks working file.

QBW files can be saved to the Desktop or to your storage device if there is adequate storage space.

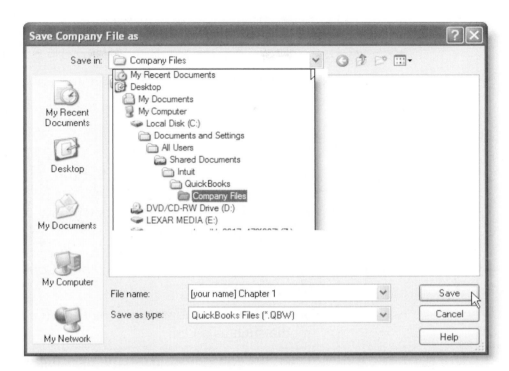

 Step 7: Click **OK** when the following window appears.

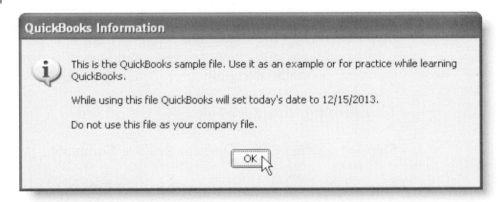

 Step 8: Click **OK**.

PORTABLE QUICKBOOKS FILES

QuickBooks portable files (.QBM) are used to move QuickBooks company files.

To save a portable .QBM file:

Step 1:   Select **File** menu **> Save Copy or Backup**.

Step 2:   When the *Save Copy or Backup* window appears, select **Portable company file > Next**.

Step 3:   When the following *Save Portable Company File as* window appears:

- Select the appropriate *Save in* field (C: or removable media such as a USB).
- Enter the file name: **[your name Chapter or Exercise No.] (Portable)**.
- Click **Save**.

Step 4:   When the *Close and reopen* window appears, click **OK** to close and reopen your company file before creating a portable company file.

To open a portable .QBM file:

Step 1:   Select **File > Open or Restore Company**.

Step 2:   Select **Restore a portable file (.QBM)**. Click **Next**.

Step 3:   Identify the location and file name of the portable company file.

- In the *Look in* field, identify the location of the portable company file on the hard drive or removable media.
- Select the file.
- The *Files of type* field should automatically appear as .QBM.
- Click **Open**.

Step 4: When the *Open or Restore Company* window appears, click **Next**.

Step 5: When the following *Save Company File as* window appears:

- In the *Save in* field, select the location to save the .QBW file on either the C: or removable media.

- Enter the file name.

- **QuickBooks Files (*.QBW)** should appear automatically in the *Save as type* field.

- Click **Save**.

APPENDIX C
TROUBLESHOOTING QUICKBOOKS

In Appendix C, you will learn about the following frequently asked questions (FAQs) and troubleshooting tips:

Special thanks to Sandy Roman for her assistance in preparing Appendix C with helpful troubleshooting tips and frequently asked questions.

QuickBooks Installation FAQs

How Do I Install My QuickBooks 140-Day Trial Version?

For step-by-step instructions to install your QuickBooks 140-day trial version software, see *Appendix A: Install & Register QuickBooks Software.*

My Text Does Not Have the 140-Day Trial Software

Only new copies of the textbook, purchased from bookstores or online vendors, come with the 140-day trial version. This is a trial version of the software that will allow you to complete the text assignments.

QuickBooks Registration FAQs

Register your QuickBooks software! Failure to register your QuickBooks trial version software will result in the software no longer functioning.

QuickBooks Keeps Prompting Me to Register

If QuickBooks prompts you to register your version of QuickBooks, please do so. Follow the prompts using the information on your CD jacket.

Why Am I Asked for a Validation Code?

A validation code is necessary only when registering the full version of QuickBooks. Please register the trial version when prompted at installation or when reminded using the codes on the CD jacket. If you decide to purchase the full version later, you will need the validation code at that time.

QUICKBOOKS EXPIRED BEFORE 140 DAYS

If QuickBooks tells you that your trial version has run out before the 140 days have passed, it may be due to one of the following:

1. The trial version was not registered when prompted.

2. The date on the operating computer has been set forward and is now past 140 days since installation.

3. The trial version came with a used textbook and has already been registered and used for its allotted time.

SOFTWARE FAQS

QUICKBOOKS GIVES ME A "FAILED" MESSAGE

When trying to open a QuickBooks file, if an *Error: Failed* window appears, try one of the following solutions:

1. Make sure that you are opening the file correctly: select **Open or Restore an existing company > Restore a backup file**. QuickBooks (.QBB) data files are compressed and cannot be opened simply by double-clicking on the file.

2. The files might have been corrupted at download and you might need to restart with a new downloaded file. Delete the files you downloaded onto your computer. Go to the Online Learning Center and download the files again. Instructions for accessing the Online Learning Center are provided in *Appendix A: Install & Register QuickBooks Software*.

3. If the previous solutions do not work, you may need to repair QuickBooks. To repair QuickBooks, insert the QuickBooks software CD in the CD drive of your computer. In the Windows operating system, select **Start > Settings > Control Panel > Add/Remove Program > QuickBooks > Repair**.

QUICKBOOKS HAS LOCKED ME OUT

If you did not register your trial version of QuickBooks at installation or when prompted, you will eventually be locked out of the software. If this happens, go to **Help** menu > **Register QuickBooks**. Complete the registration process. If this solution is not successful, try uninstalling QuickBooks software, reinstalling the software, and then registering QuickBooks.

QUICKBOOKS HAS LOCKED UP OR FROZEN

If this happens, try one of the following solutions:

1. Shutdown QuickBooks software using the Task Manager. Press the CTRL+ALT+DELETE keys at the same time. Select **Start Task Manager > Applications** tab > **QuickBooks > End Task**.

2. Reboot your computer. QuickBooks uses a large amount of memory when operating. If your system does not have adequate memory, this can cause your computer to freeze. Rebooting may take care of this problem.

DATA FILE FAQS

HOW DO I USE THE DATA FILES?

For step-by-step instructions to use the .QBB backup data files that accompany *Computer Accounting with QuickBooks*, see *Appendix B: Back Up & Restore QuickBooks Files*.

The data files are available on a CD that accompanies the text or can be downloaded from the text Online Learning Center at www.mhhe.com/kay2010.

The data files can be restored and used when your data file is corrupted or contains an irresolvable error.

WHEN MY DATA FILES OPEN THE HOME PAGE DOESN'T APPEAR

Occasionally when opening a data file, an additional window will appear on the screen based on what you last had open when you were using QuickBooks. Simply close the window and click the Home icon to go back to the Home page.

THE DATA FILES TAKE A LONG TIME TO DOWNLOAD

If the data files are slow to download directly from the Data CD, try the following:

1. Copy the files to your desktop first. If you are downloading to a removable drive that is almost full, it may take a long time to download the files.

2. Make sure you are restoring the data file as directed in *Appendix B: Back Up & Restore QuickBooks Files*. You cannot open the data files by double-clicking on the file. Instead, you must restore the file using QuickBooks software.

3. Close other programs running on your computer that might be slowing your computer down.

4. Reboot your computer.

WHAT DO I DO IF THE DATA FILES ARE ZIPPED?

Unzip compressed backup data files from the Online Learning Center at www.mhhe.com/kay2010 as follows:

1. Double-click the file link on the Online Learning Center.

2. From the File Download menu, select **Save**.

3. Choose the folder to save the file, and click **Save**.

4. From the File Download menu, choose **Open Folder**.

5. **Right-click** on the zipped file and choose **Extract here**.

6. The files within the zipped file will then appear within that folder. Choose which file to unzip and double click.

Some versions of Windows will open up an Extraction Wizard. If so, simply follow the defaults and choose **Show extracted files** to view and open files.

BACK UP & RESTORE FAQS

HOW DO I BACK UP OR RESTORE?

Detailed backup and restore instructions are provided in *Appendix B: Back Up & Restore QuickBooks Files*.

Depending on your classroom situation, there are two different approaches to completing the assignments: Workflow or Restart & Restore. The Workflow approach is similar to the workflow that most businesses use. In a typical business environment, you would continue to use the same .QBW file, backing up periodically. This is a good option if you will be using the same computer throughout your entire course.

If you will be switching between campus and home computers, then you may want to use the Restart & Restore approach, where you will make a backup data file each time you complete a chapter. Then when you change computers, you will restore the backup file to restart your work in QuickBooks. You can use your own backup data file or use the data files that are provided on the data file CD or the Online Learning Center.

Additional information about the Workflow and Restart & Restore approaches are contained in *Appendix B*.

MY QUICKBOOKS FILE WON'T OPEN

If you are trying to open a backup file from the student CD or after downloading the file from the Online Learning Center, you cannot simply double click on the backup file to open it. In order to open a backup file you must restore the backup using QuickBooks software.

See *Appendix B: Back Up & Restore QuickBooks* Files for step-by-step directions on opening and using your backup files.

Text Instruction FAQs

The Text Instructions Do Not Match My Screen

If your screen does not match the text instructions, it may be due to software updates. To see the latest updates and changes, go to the QuickBooks Blog at www.QuickBooksBlog.info or the Online Learning Center (select Text Updates).

The Text Screen Captures Do Not Match My Screen

If your screen or printed report does not match those in the text, it may be due to differences in software systems. The text is created using Windows XP operating system and QuickBooks Pro 2010. If your QuickBooks software is a different version or your operating system is different, this may explain the discrepancy.

I Think I Found an Error in the Text

Every effort is made to eliminate all errors in the text; however, if you think you found an error, it might have already been discovered. Go to www.QuickBooksBlog.info, the QuickBooks Blog, for the latest updates. Or go to the Text Updates section of the Online Learning Center to see the latest updates and changes. If the discrepancy is not listed in the text updates, please speak with your instructor for assistance.

CORRECTING ERRORS

QuickBooks provides a number of ways to correct errors. When you discover an error often determines how you correct the error. For example, if you make an error when you are entering information into an onscreen check form, you can correct the error using the Backspace key. However, if you do not discover the error until after the check is saved, you should void the check and prepare a new check.

CORRECTING ERRORS BEFORE DOCUMENT IS SAVED

In general, errors detected before the document is saved can be corrected in one of the following ways:

1. **Backspace key:** Deletes characters to the left of the cursor in the current field you are entering.

2. **Delete key:** Deletes characters to the right of the cursor.

3. **Undo command:** Before you press the *Enter* key, you can undo typing on the current line.

4. **Clear button:** On some onscreen forms, a Clear button appears in the lower right corner of the window. Clicking this button clears all fields on the screen.

5. **Revert command** (Edit menu): Reverts the entire screen back to its original appearance.

BACKSPACE

The Backspace key is used to correct errors that occur when you are entering data. For example, if you mistype a company name on a check, you can use the Backspace key to delete the incorrect letters. Then enter the correct spelling.

Assume you need to write a check to Davis Business Associates for professional services performed for your company.

To use the Backspace key to correct an error on a check:

1. With the Rock Castle Construction Company file open, click **Write Checks** in the **Banking** section of the Home page to display the *Write Checks* window.

2. When the *Write Checks* window appears:
   - Select **To be printed**.
   - Select from the *Pay to the Order of* drop-down list: **Davis Business Associates**.
   - Type the street address: **1234 Brentwodo**.

3. The correct address is 1234 Brentwood. Press the **Backspace** key **twice** to erase "**do**."

4. Type "**od**" to finish entering Brentwood.

UNDO

The Undo command can be used to undo typing before you press the Enter key.

To use the Undo command:

1. With the same *Write Checks* window still open and the check for Davis Business Associates displayed, type the city and state for the Davis address: **Bayshore, CA**. Do not press Enter.

The Backspace key erases the character to the *left* of the cursor. The Delete key erases the letter to the *right* of the cursor.

Use the data file for any of the Chapters 1 through 7 company files.

Davis Business Associates should automatically appear in the *Address* field.

2. After you type the address, Mr. Castle tells you the address is San Diego, CA, not Bayshore. To use the undo command, click **Edit** on the Menu bar. Then click **Undo Typing**. Bayshore, CA, will be deleted.

3. Next, enter the correct city and state: **San Diego, CA**.

The Undo command is useful if you want to delete an entire line of typing.

CLEAR

A Clear button is usually located in the lower right corner of an unsaved onscreen form. If you start entering data and want to clear all the fields in the onscreen form, click the **Clear** button.

After an onscreen form has been saved, the Clear button changes to a Revert button.

The Clear command also appears on the Edit menu. This command can be used before a document, such as a check, has been saved.

To illustrate, assume that you decide to wait to pay Davis Business Associates until they complete all the work they are performing for you. Therefore, you want to erase everything that you have entered on the check.

To use the Clear function:

1. With the *Write Checks* window still open and the check for Davis Business Associates displayed, click **Edit** on the Menu bar.

2. Click **Clear**. The *Write Checks* window returns to its original appearance with blank fields. The information you entered about Davis Business Associates has been erased.

The Clear command on the Edit menu and the Clear button on the onscreen form perform the same function: both clear the contents of an onscreen form that has not yet been saved.

CORRECTING ERRORS ON SAVED DOCUMENTS

Once a document has been saved, you can use one of three approaches to correct the error:

If the correction involves a check (Write Checks, Pay Bills, or Create Paychecks), display the check in the *Write Checks* window by clicking **Previous** or select **Edit** menu > **Find**.

1. **Display** the document, correct the error, then save the document again.

2. **Void** the erroneous document, then create a new document.

3. **Delete** the erroneous document, then create a new document.

ENTER CORRECTIONS IN SAVED ONSCREEN FORM

To enter corrections in a saved onscreen form, complete three steps:

You cannot correct deposits using this approach. If you attempt to make changes to a saved deposit, you will receive a warning that you must delete the deposit and then reenter the appropriate information.

1. Display the erroneous onscreen form. For example, display an incorrect invoice in the *Create Invoices* window.

2. Correct the error by entering changes directly in the onscreen form.

3. Save the onscreen form.

VOID

The Void command will void a document and remove its effect from your accounting records. For example, if you void a check, the check amount is no longer deducted from your checking account. The check will still appear in your QuickBooks records, but it is labeled Void.

To void a document in QuickBooks, first display the document on your screen. Then select **Edit** from the Menu bar. The Edit menu will change depending upon the document that has been opened. For example, if you open a check, the Edit menu will display "Void Check." If you open an invoice, then the Edit menu will display "Void Invoice."

INTRODUCTION

Consistent with the growing number of QuickBooks online courses and increased global awareness of economic and environmental sustainability, *Computer Accounting with QuickBooks* offers colleges and students options for using electronic deliverables instead of paper printouts.

Ask your instructor if you are to provide electronic deliverables. If so, find out which one of the following three options you should use.

Option	QuickBooks Electronic Deliverables
Excel	**Microsoft Excel Spreadsheets**. Use Excel spreadsheets to send your instructor your assignments electronically.
PDF	**Adobe® PDF Files**. Print your assignments to PDF files and then send the PDF files to your instructor via e-mail or courseware dropbox.
.QBB	**QuickBooks Backup .QBB Files**. Using the memorized reports feature in QuickBooks software, save your reports electronically in QuickBooks. Then send your .QBB backup file to your instructor electronically.

EXCEL ELECTRONIC DELIVERABLES

For this option of electronic deliverables, save your QuickBooks reports to Excel templates provided on the text's QuickBooks Blog (www.QuickBooksBlog.info). Just follow the steps below to use this easy option.

Step 1: Go to the QuickBooks Student Blog at www.QuickBooksBlog.info.

Step 2: Select the **Electronic Deliverables** link.

Step 3: Download the Electronic Deliverables Excel template for the chapter you are completing.

Step 4: Open the spreadsheet. Select **File > Save As**. **Add your name** to the Excel workbook file name and save.

Step 5: Follow the text chapter and exercise instructions until you are instructed to print a report. Using the Report Center, display the report on your screen.

Step 6: With the report displayed onscreen, select **Export > Basic tab > an existing Excel workbook**.

Step 7: Browse for the Excel template you downloaded.

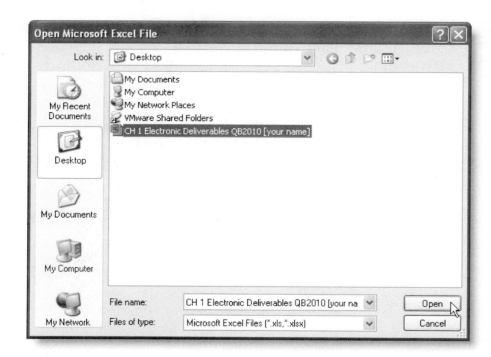

Step 8: Select **create a new sheet in the workbook > Export**.

Step 9: Excel software should open on your screen with your QuickBooks report inserted into a new sheet.

Next, rename the sheet as follows:

- **Double-click** the sheet tab at the bottom of the Excel window.

- **Enter the sheet name using the EXACT SAME sheet name listed in the Deliverables Checklist.**

Step 10:   Format your Excel report as follows:

- Display report headings by selecting **View** tab **> Page Layout** icon. If a message regarding freeze panes appears, click **OK**.

- Adjust the top margin as necessary by clicking and dragging the blue bar in the upper left corner of the window. Double-click on or drag blue freeze frame lines as needed for viewing the report.

Step 11:   If there is no Excel export for the document, such as checks, ***ask your instructor*** if you are to omit those deliverables OR create a ***screen capture*** and paste it into Excel. Deliverables without an Excel report are identified with the letters SC on the Deliverables Checklist Excel Template. Create screen captures as follows:

- Prepare the onscreen form, such as a check, by entering the appropriate data into the form.

- Make a screen capture. (On a PC, press the **Print Screen** key. Although it looks like nothing has happened, your computer has pasted a screen capture on the clipboard.)

- Insert a blank sheet into the Excel spreadsheet (**Right-click** a sheet tab, select **Insert**.)

- Click on the blank sheet to select it. Then **Right-click > Paste**. The screen capture should now appear on the Excel sheet.

- Rename the Excel sheet as described in Step 9 above.

Step 12:   **On the Checklist sheet, check off the deliverables that you have completed and are delivering in your Excel workbook.**

Step 13:   **Save your Excel workbook. To identify your electronic deliverables, make certain your name is included in the Excel workbook file name.**

Ask your instructor if you should e-mail the Excel spreadsheet or use a courseware dropbox.

To make a screen capture on a Mac, press **Shift-Command-4**. Select the area to capture. The screen capture will appear on your desktop. Open the file, then select **Edit** menu > **Copy**.

PDF ELECTRONIC DELIVERABLES

To create PDF electronic deliverables, you will print your reports to an electronic Portable Document Format (PDF) file. If you have PDF software available on your computer, when printing reports, instead of selecting a printer, you will select the PDF software option from the drop-down printer list.

Follow the steps below to use this option.

Some documents can be printed as PDF files by selecting **File** menu > **Save as PDF**.

Step 1: When instructed to print a report in the text, from the Report Center, display the report you wish to create.

Step 2: Select **Print > Printer**.

Step 3: Select the drop-down list to view the installed printers. Select the PDF software option.

Before using this option, open a report, select **Print**. Verify that your printer drop-down list has an option to print to PDF.

If a PDF option is not included, see the QuickBooks Blog for information about downloading PDF software.

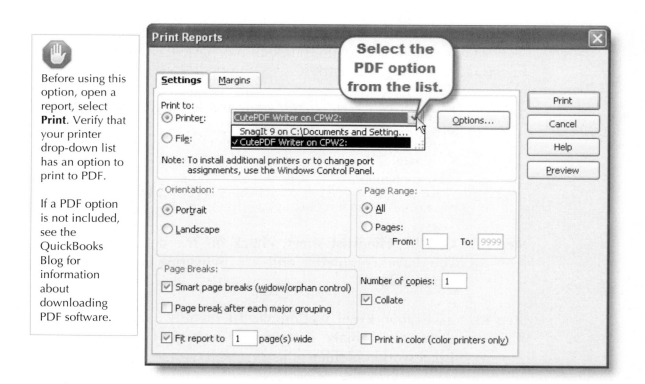

Step 4: Select **Print**.

Step 5: Enter a file name using your initials and Chapter, Exercise, or Project number. For example, if it is the first report in Chapter 1, name the file: **[your name] CH 1.1**. If it is the second report in Chapter 3, name the file: **[your name] CH 3.2**. If it is task 3 of exercise 4.2, name the file: **EX 4.2 T3**.

Step 6: Select **Save**.

Ask your instructor if you should e-mail the PDF files as attachments or use a courseware dropbox.

.QBB ELECTRONIC DELIVERABLES

For this electronic deliverables option, you will use the memorized reports feature of QuickBooks to save your reports. Then send your .QBB company file electronically to your instructor. To use the .QBB electronic deliverables option, follow the steps below.

First, create a new Memorized Report Group. You will create one report group for each chapter. Thus, you will have a Deliverables Report Group for Chapter 1, another one for Chapter 2, and so on.

Step 1: Select **Reports** menu > **Memorized Reports** > **Memorized Report List**.

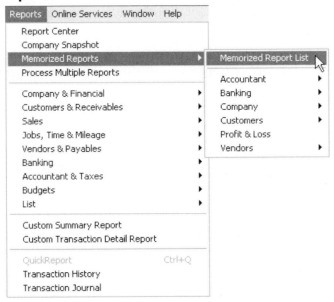

Step 2: From the following *Memorized Report List* window, select **Memorized Report > New Group**.

Step 3: Enter Memorized Report Group name: **Deliverables Chapter** and the chapter number. Click **OK**. You will complete Steps 1 through 3 each time you begin a new chapter.

Next, for each chapter, add memorized reports to the Report Group:

Step 1:　　When instructed to print a report in the text, from the Report Center, display the report you wish to create.

Step 2:　　Select **Memorize**.

Step 3:　　Enter Name as follows, specifying chapter or exercise, number, and name of report.

Step 4:　　Select **Save in Memorized Report Group**.

Step 5:　　Select the deliverables report group for the appropriate chapter. Click **OK**.

Step 6:　　The memorized report should now appear in the chapter deliverables report group.

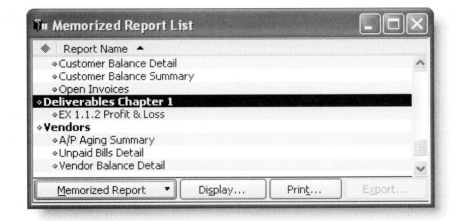

Step 7:   Memorize each of the reports requested in the chapter, exercise, or project.

Step 8:   After memorizing all the report assignments for a chapter, back up your QuickBooks file. See *Appendix B: Back Up & Restore QuickBooks Files* for step-by-step directions for backing up QuickBooks files.

Ask your instructor if you should deliver your .QBB file using e-mail or a courseware dropbox.

APPENDIX E
QUICKBOOKS FOR MAC

Would you like to use QuickBooks on an Apple computer? Now you can.

Two general approaches to running QuickBooks on a Mac are:

1. **QuickBooks for Mac software.** QuickBooks 2010 for Mac software runs on Apple computers. However, the features of QuickBooks for Mac software differ from QuickBooks for Windows. See the QuickBooks Blog at www.QuickBooksBlog.info for highlights of differences between QuickBooks for Windows and QuickBooks for Mac.

2. **QuickBooks for Windows software running on a Mac.** You have several options for installing QuickBooks for Windows on a Mac. You can use the Bootcamp feature on Apple's Leopard and Snow Leopard operating systems. Another option is to use virtualization to operate QuickBooks for Windows on a Mac. To learn more about these options, visit www.QuickBooksBlog.info.

APPENDIX F
QUICKBOOKS BLOG
WWW.QUICKBOOKSBLOG.INFO

Go to www.QuickBooksBlog.info to view the QuickBooks Student Blog that accompanies *Computer Accounting with QuickBooks*.

The QuickBooks Blog includes:

- **Go Green with Electronic Deliverables Excel Templates.** Use these Excel templates to create electronic deliverables instead of paper printouts for your assignments.

- **QuickBooks Student Community.** Connect to other QuickBooks students in this online community.

- **QuickBooks Podcasts.** View podcasts on QuickBooks topics such as back up, restore, and much more.

- ***Computer Accounting with QuickBooks* Updates**. Check out the latest updates section of the blog to stay current with the latest updates for QuickBooks software and this text.

- **QuickBooks for Mac.** Explore different approaches and ideas for using QuickBooks for Mac.

- **And Much More….**

INDEX

-D-